U.S. Official Propaganda During the Vietnam War, 1965–1973

The Limits of Persuasion

CAROLINE PAGE

Leicester University Press
London and New York

LEICESTER UNIVERSITY PRESS
A Cassell Imprint
Wellington House, 125 Strand, London WC2R 0BB
215 Park Avenue South, New York, New York 10003

First published in Great Britain 1996

British Library Cataloguing in Publication Data
A CIP catalogue record for this book is available from The British Library.

ISBN 0-7185-1376-2 (hpk)
0-7185-1999-X (pbk)

Library of Congress Cataloging-in-Publication Data
Page, Caroline, 1953–
U.S. Official propaganda during the Vietnam War, 1965–1973; the limits of persuasion / Caroline Page.
p. cm.
Includes bibliographical references and index.
ISBN 0-7185-1376-2 (cloth) – ISBN 0-7185-1999-X (paperback)
1. Vietnamese Conflict, 1961–1975 – Propaganda. 2. Propaganda, American. 3. Public opinion – Great Britain. 4. Public opinion – Germany (West) 5. Public opinion – France. I. Title.
DS559.8.P65P34 1996
959.704'38–dc20 95–41263
CIP

Typeset by Falcon Oast Graphic Art
Printed and bound in Great Britain by Biddles Ltd, Guildford and King's Lynn

Royalties from the sale of this book are being donated to cancer charities.

Contents

Acknowledgements

In researching and writing this book a number of people have given me advice and help. As always, Mr Martin Manning, head of USIA's Historical Archives in Washington, DC, has been generous and tireless with his assistance in providing quantities of pertinent records. Thanks are due to Dr Humphrey and Mrs Hanson of the Lyndon Baines Johnson Library in Texas, and to the staff of the National Archives and Records Administration handling the Nixon Presidential Materials. And Dr R.J. McKeever of the Department of Politics at Reading University has offered valuable support over the years for this project.

I am especially indebted to Mr Hans Pokorny of Gallup GmbH in Wiesbaden, Germany and to Ms Linda Williamson, U.S. Studies Librarian at Rhodes House Library, University of Oxford, without whose help in locating and obtaining poll data on German and French public opinion on the Vietnam War this book could not have been completed. Gallup Poll in London were also very helpful, and I would like to thank Mr Peter Duffin and Mr Graham Williams for their assistance. The Institut für Demoskopie Allensbach in Germany kindly searched their files and at short notice sent material on German opinion from their polls.

Research for this book was completed using funds awarded by the Nuffield Foundation in 1991.

I would also like to thank a number of personal friends who so generously offered me hospitality and good company on my research trips to America: Mr and Mrs John James; Ms Lotte Bexhoeft; and Mr and Mrs Michael Snell.

Finally, Nicola Viinikka of Pinter Publishers – now Cassell – has been unfailingly patient and encouraging, despite the time taken to complete this book.

To the memory of my father, Dennis Robinson,
with love and admiration for his qualities both as
a father and as a very special person.

Introduction

America's involvement in the Vietnam War was one of the most important events in the post-Second World War period. This war was the leitmotiv of the 1960s, when its impact was felt in every corner of the globe, and in many aspects of many nations' national and international lives. The political, social and military consequences of American involvement and defeat in Vietnam have been keenly felt in America and the international community, and the 'lessons' learned have continued to exert an influence up to the present day.[1]

America's position as leader and guarantor of the Western Alliance ensured that America's rhetoric, actions and their consequences, past and present, reflected on America's allies and formed the major point of reference for opponents. One of the reasons that the war became so important was that America chose to make Vietnam the battleground for a 'decisive' confrontation, on behalf of its free democratic bloc, with the 'unfree' communist bloc. Without American intervention it seems unlikely that the outcome of a conflict in a remote (from Europe) part of the world would have been the focus of such widespread attention. American perceptions of the importance of the Vietnam conflict also tended to alter the initial perceptions of other nations, whether friendly or hostile, just as America's actions raised the stakes of success or defeat for both sides.

American involvement in the Vietnam War required explanation and justification, as is usually the case with most conflicts, and though commentators vary in their estimates of the degree of importance that propaganda can attain generally in the modern world,[2] it still appears that the presentation of a government's position in the best possible light, to both its home audience and foreign observers, is an important feature of policy. The information[3] that both Lyndon Johnson's and Richard Nixon's administrations felt compelled to issue – despite their shared preference for secrecy concerning the war – is illustrative of this contemporary feature.

During the Vietnam War 'presentation' was of particular importance due to a number of factors, which can be divided into those concerning South Vietnam and the war itself and those centring on advances in communication. The first group of factors concerned Vietnam's remoteness from the American continent, which made it difficult to uphold the U.S. Administration's claim that it was an area vital to America's national security.

The second factor was that the length and nature of the conflict was bound to strain the propaganda apparatus to the utmost, given that America itself was not directly under attack: this poses the question, for how long can a democratic government keep the supportive interest of its people and allies when that nation is not directly threatened?

Third, the type of regime that America was supporting in South Vietnam (mostly ever-changing military juntas lacking legitimacy and popular suppport) contradicted all the political and human ideals that the American Administration professed to be preserving and pursuing in South Vietnam and was also seen as making a mockery of America's own allegiance to these ideals.

Fourth, because of the secrecy and low-key approach which characterized American involvement in this area in the beginning, most observers of the conflict became aware of the extent of the American commitment only when the war was escalating. At this time the Administration had decided that America's prestige and credibility were at stake, not to mention South Vietnam's physical existence. So, against a background of allied ignorance, publics in both America and Europe awoke to find their governments already involved in this war – though obviously involved in different degrees and with different roles. The American Administration was caught in a trap of its own making and governments supporting America shared in some of the consequences.

Concerning the second group of factors, the spread of modern-day communication networks while enlarging the scope of the Administration's communications also enlarged the potential number of rival viewpoints that the Administration might have to counter, and limited the possibilities for the successful promotion of distinctive propaganda campaigns in different parts of the world. Additionally, the speed of communications ensured that it would be difficult to contain the damage caused when propaganda errors committed in one area were transmitted to other arenas.

The primary concern of this book is the interaction of U.S. official propaganda with European opinion, both governmental and public. However, as 'Europe' comprises so many countries it is necessary to reduce the number under study in order to narrow the topic to manageable – and sensible – proportions (bearing in mind also the number of words and amount of paper generated during this war). This reduction will be achieved by concentrating on three countries: Britain, France and Germany.

The reason for choosing these three countries lies in the degree of their importance to the U.S. as European allies and in the nature of their relations with America, specifically in the differences in these relationships, which initially ran the gamut from public support to public condemnation. Thus in the category of supporter came Britain, America's closest non-combatant ally and also Co-Chairman with the Soviet Union of the Geneva Conference in 1954. It was this conference which had 'settled' the First Indo-China War, but which, due to the unsatisfactory nature of the settlement and an inability to enforce it, had also helped prepare the ground for the Vietnam War involving the United States. So, Britain and the Soviet Union were left with a continuing diplomatic responsibility towards South and North Vietnam and could therefore be expected to involve themselves in initiatives to end the war. However, for a variety of reasons (to be explored later) this joint British–Soviet responsibility very often seemed to be purely and simply a technicality, endowing neither country with any real chance of reconvening the Geneva Conference in order to resove the conflict.

Germany's role during the war is of interest due to its awkward position as an ally of the United States who was required to offer some sort of support, but who was also an ally with an historical background that required that it eschew the appearance of supporting such a military venture. Consequently the German Government's rhetoric and actions were subject to both domestic and foreign scrutiny as it tried to tread the fine line of keeping the U.S. satisified whilst not abandoning its post-war non-militaristic approach to international affairs.

In contrast to the British and German Governments, the French Government disapproved of U.S. involvement in Vietnam and was vocal in its condemnation of the venture from the very beginning. Furthermore, this attitude was heartily endorsed by the rest of the French nation, thereby uniting all shades of opinion across the political spectrum.

Although these three countries will form the nucleus of this study, obviously the reactions of other European countries will be considered as and when they were important enough to make an impact on the political scene, thus focusing yet more attention on the U.S. involvement in Vietnam – for example, Sweden's hosting in 1967 of the 'Tribunal' that 'tried' the U.S. Administration.

The study will examine U.S. official information about the war from the time when the conflict began to escalate in February 1965 up to the peace settlement in January 1973, a timespan which encompasses varying climates of opinion about the war. The aim is to trace the two Administrations' patterns of response to different events in relation to their efforts to influence opinion on the war. This should also reveal whether opinion on certain events in turn influenced the Administrations' handling of information.

The three main lines of enquiry embrace the theoretical and empirical problems which must be addressed. Firstly opinion on the war in the three countries must be examined during this period and any shifts analysed to determine the roots of such change, using sources of information which will include media reports and opinion polls. The second objective is to assess the nature and effectiveness of the Administrations' propaganda campaigns, by focusing on the basic justifications used in U.S. official statements and on the information available in the media (principally the press) in these three countries about certain events and themes and the way in which these were handled by the Administrations. The third objective is to attempt to draw conclusions from the above studies concerning opinion change and the successes or failures of the U.S. propaganda campaign. The role of television is not specifically examined in this study, partly because access to television archives is expensive and would also result in only commercial coverage being used as far as Britain was concerned, as the BBC archives are available only to BBC staff unless exorbitant expense is undertaken. In addition, early radio and television news bulletins were then much shorter than today's bulletins and although television had its news programmes, by comparison, on a daily basis newspapers carried far more 'news' and analysis than the other two media branches. In any case, at this time public reactions to television programmes of note were manifested in letters to the press. Also, in this early period much of the information on the war that was disseminated in the media tended to come from sources in Washington, and television equipment and technology was then far more cumbersome and resulted in fewer programmes coming from South Vietnam itself. Of course, in the later stages of the war there were greater numbers of television journalists stationed in South Vietnam, and thus, as such coverage grew, USIA's Media Reaction Reports began to include comment from radio and television journalists, and this reaction is then incorporated in the study.

Within the broad framework outlined, special attention will be focused on the following questions and issues: first, when did alternative points of view emerge to challenge the Administration's view of the war, and why? Second, when did the propaganda audience begin to disbelieve the Administration? Third, what role did the Administration assign to propaganda during the war and what degree of effort at what level went into coordinating the information and presenting it? Fourth, how suitable were American propaganda themes and techniques for their purposes. Fifth, were there any American information errors of particular magnitude which helped to turn the tide of opinion and/or constituted a turning point? Sixth, what were the effects of the military situation on the audiences' reaction to Administration propaganda and how was the military situation reported? Seventh and finally, how important were extraneous factors such as general anti-Americanism in forming and fuelling opposition to the war?

Notes

1. For example, see the discussion concerning media and military relations in Valerie Adams, *The Media and the Falklands Campaign* (The Macmillan Press Ltd, Basingstoke/London 1986: 36–9).
2. See, for instance, Leo Bogart, *Premises for Propaganda* (New York, Free Press, 1976).
3. The use of the word 'information' here does not connote any degree of accuracy and is thus not used as a means of distinguishing it from propaganda, just as the use of 'propaganda' does not necessarily connote inaccuracy or lying – for on closer examination the two terms can be used interchangeably: see Chapter 2 for further explanation.

1

The beginning and escalation of the war, 1965–1968

The United States' involvement in South Vietnam was a political and military problem that U.S. President Lyndon Johnson undoubtedly 'inherited', but thereafter increased far beyond the original legacy. The complexity of this 'problem' in 1965 encompassed several dimensions. Firstly, whilst the political situation in South Vietnam had come to U.S. and international public attention, if only via appalling television coverage in 1963 of the self-immolation of several Buddhist monks (prior to the overthrow of South Vietnamese President Ngo Dinh Diem's repressive regime), the military situation had remained a relatively unknown quantity. Thus U.S. involvement in South Vietnamese military operations and particularly U.S. reconnaissance flights over Laos were secret military measures about which the public knew nothing – until U.S. planes were shot down over Laos in January 1965 (Gravel, 1971, vol. 3: 251). Already therefore the framework was in place that characterized certain military aspects of the war and would continue to condition U.S. information policies: the Administration was quietly fighting an undeclared and remote war in peacetime.

Secondly, though the North Vietnamese and Vietcong were to wage 'total' war, the effort made by the South Vietnamese varied, and the Americans certainly did not wage 'total' war. For though the military draft eventually bit deeper into the fabric of American society, the

Reserves were never mobilized. So, except for those either fighting the war, administering it, or providing war *matériel*, the majority of Americans were not directly involved in the war. The tempo of their lives continued undisturbed, unless they had relatives fighting, or chose to concern themselves with the morality of the conflict. The economy of the country was not put on a war footing – guns *and* butter could be provided, so said the Administration – and politics revolved around a great many other problems in addition to that of the war, one of the most important for Lyndon Johnson being the establishment of the 'Great Society'.

Thirdly, Lyndon Johnson's electoral platform in 1964 was concerned with creating and nurturing the impression that Johnson was the 'peace' candidate who would keep America out of an Asian war, as opposed to his opponent Barry Goldwater who was portrayed as, and perceived by the electorate as a warmonger. This aspect, together with the secrecy of previous U.S. involvement (despite the Tonkin Gulf incidents in mid-1964), meant that Johnson had a particularly difficult task initially when the war began, and then escalated. This difficulty related both to the military requirements of the war – initiating bombing raids and subsequently deploying troops – and to the propaganda requirements of publicly explaining and justifying these actions.

The following overview of the war during Lyndon Johnson's Administration is not a comprehensive account of wartime events and military engagements, but instead concentrates on those events and themes that were important for propaganda purposes, that is, events and themes which received public attention and required public explanation and justification. Within this framework, therefore, the year 1965 is crucial, as the year in which the Administration visibly and vastly increased its commitment to South Vietnam, progressing rapidly towards a full-scale war.

In this study of the first four years of the war extensive use has been made of the three versions of the Defense Department's history of decision-making during the war, known as *The Pentagon Papers*. Originally collated and written secretly from the Defense Department's standpoint, these documents and analysis do not constitute a complete record of all wartime planning and decisions – for there were several other departments and decision-making centres involved including, of course, the White House and State Department – but they do reveal in remarkable detail the Defense Department's dealings with other figures and departments on planning and implementing most aspects of policy on Vietnam.

1965: setting the pattern

Despite the problems that it faced, the Administration judged South Vietnam to be of sufficient importance to undertake policy reviews in late 1964 and early 1965 (Gravel, 1971, vol. 3: 221–55, 266–71) which, coupled with and fuelled by the deteriorating situation in South Vietnam (Porter, 1979, vol. 2: 353–4), culminated in the decision in February 1965 to bomb North Vietnam in retaliation for South Vietnamese communist guerrilla (termed Vietcong) attacks on the U.S. installations at Pleiku and Camp Holloway. By mid-February Johnson had authorized sustained and non-retaliatory bombing of North Vietnam, under a programme code-named Rolling Thunder, which, together with airstrikes on Vietcong positions in South Vietnam, effectively inaugurated the Vietnam War on 2 March 1965.

The next step was the rapid introduction of two U.S. Marine Corps battalions to guard the U.S. airfield at Danang. Requested by the U.S. military commander in Vietnam, General Westmoreland, on 22 February, and authorized by Johnson on 25 February (see chronology in Smith, 1985, vol. 2: 377), the Marines landed in South Vietnam on 8 March in a defensive capacity.

Following these initial actions, the Administration moved quickly, having, by the third week of March, examined the efficacy of the bombing programme, extended its purpose from being primarily a political and psychological weapon into one 'aimed at destroying the capabilities of North Vietnam to support a war in the South' (Gravel, 1971, vol. 3: 279), and expanded its targets. At the same time General Westmoreland requested reinforcements to bring U.S. troop strength up to approximately 70,000. Westmoreland wanted the troops by June and 'indicated that more troops might be required thereafter if the bombing failed to achieve results' (Sheehan et al., 1971: 398–9).

From now on events moved inexorably towards escalation of the war, both in terms of the expansion of the U.S. war effort on the ground and in the air, the corresponding increase in activity by the Vietcong and help from North Vietnam, and in the intensity of the conflict. Another White House policy review on 1–2 April, undertaken for the same reason as previous policy reviews – namely because U.S. objectives in South Vietnam had not been achieved by earlier military measures and thus past policy had already been rendered redundant by events – now shifted the focus in the war from using air power to try to affect North Vietnam's will, to using ground troops to force a conclusion in South Vietnam. This was the beginning of America's ground war in Asia.

The White House policy review decisions were embodied in National Security Action Memorandum (NSAM) 328, which was signed on 6 April. Most important was the decision to change the role of the troops deployed to South Vietnam from a defensive to an offensive role. An additional 18,000–20,000 military support personnel were to be dispatched to Vietnam and two more Marine battalions and a Marine air squadron were to be deployed. Rolling Thunder operations were to continue slowly, aiming at North Vietnamese lines of communication and a study was to be undertaken on blockading or aerial mining North Vietnamese ports for possible future actions. However, most important of all was the decision not to publicize these changes and to represent these actions as a continuation of the same policy, not as a new one (Sheehan et al., 1971: 442).

After the initial troop commitments, recommendations for further reinforcements quickly followed. By 20 April U.S. troop strength was recommended to be increased to 82,000 and by 7 June another 44 battalions had been requested to deal with increased Vietcong activity in their summer offensive which had resulted in high South Vietnamese Army (ARVN) casualties in already under-strength battalions (Sheehan et al., 1971: 407–10). Westmoreland also indicated that more troops could be required in 1966, but in fact before the end of July he had requested another 100,000 troops. Johnson approved the deployment of 34 battalions on 17 July and by 30 July the entire request had been approved, bringing U.S. troop strength in South Vietnam at the end of 1965 to 184,314. To put this figure into perspective, U.S. troop strength in South Vietnam at the end of December 1964 was approximately 23,300, so the five-month period from March to July 1965 witnessed an almost eightfold increase in the numbers of troops. And, of course, to cope with this expanding commitment of forces the conscription draft now also had to increase.

At the same time that the Administration was secretly deepening its military commitment in Vietnam, attention was also paid to the issues of 'negotiations' and 'peace', for these were issues upon which both the U.S. and international press were already focusing. In brief (for this subject – including what the Administration meant by 'negotiations' –

will be analysed at greater length in Chapter 2), immediately after NSAM 328 was issued, Johnson made a major speech on peace at Johns Hopkins University in Baltimore on 7 April, offering 'unconditional discussions' to North Vietnam on the conflict. According to *The Pentagon Papers* the timing of this speech was linked to public pressure about the Administration's attitude to negotiations and peace, which had formerly consisted of blaming Hanoi for the war and demanding an end to communist aggression. Now Johnson sought 'a more spectacular way of dramatizing his peaceful intent' (Gravel, 1971, vol. 3: 355). On the same theme Johnson ordered a supposedly 'secret' week-long halt in the bombing of North Vietnam in mid-May. On the genesis of this move *The Negotiating Volumes of The Pentagon Papers* state:

> But while the public clamor persisted and became more and more difficult to ignore, the President was receiving intelligence assessments from Saigon and Washington that tended to confirm his reading of Hanoi's disinterest in negotiations, but that provided him with a quite different argument for a bombing pause at this time: if the conflict was going to have to be expanded and bombing intensified before Hanoi would "come to reason," it would be easier and politically more palatable to do so *after* a pause, which would afford an opportunity for the enemy's intentions to be more clearly revealed. (Herring, 1983: 50)

It had also become apparent by now that Russia was beginning to provide 'considerably increased quantities' of military equipment and was therefore becoming more committed to aiding North Vietnam; for instance, photographs had been obtained of the first SAM missile site being constructed near Hanoi. Thus, a *Pentagon Papers* analyst suggests that because a 'decision involving a major Soviet "flashpoint," therefore, would soon have to be faced' the President 'may well have wished to provide a prior opportunity for a quiet Hanoi backdown, before proceeding with more forceful military activity' (Herring, 1983: 53). President Johnson privately informed the U.S. Ambassador to South Vietnam of the proposed bombing halt beforehand on 10 May, stating:

> This fact [completion of the week's bombing operations] and the days of Buddha's birthday seem to me to provide an excellent opportunity for a pause in air attacks which might go into next week and which I could use to good effect with world opinion.
>
> You should understand that my purpose in this plan is to begin to clear a path either toward restoration of peace or toward increased military action,

depending upon the reaction of the communists. We have amply demonstrated our determination and commitment in the last two months, and now I wish to gain some flexibility. (Herring, 1983: 53–4; square brackets added)

However, despite the reference to restoring peace and waiting for communist reactions, the private message in which the Administration tried to inform North Vietnam of the temporary bombing halt laid the blame for the conflict on North Vietnam; in effect required the immediate cessation of enemy activity in South Vietnam; stated that if the pause was taken for weakness the U.S. would demonstrate its determination to withstand aggression 'more clearly than ever'; and emphasized that the pause could be reversed at any time if there was enemy action. North Vietnam refused to officially accept the message, despite several attempts through different channels including the British Consul in Hanoi, but later denounced the bombing pause (Herring, 1983: 59–65). More than anything this episode demonstrated the Administration's clear determination at this stage of the war to negotiate only on its own terms. On 18 May U.S. bombing of North Vietnam was resumed.

As noted above, the mission of the U.S. forces changed rapidly, from the initial defensive – later enclave – strategy in March to a combat role, for in June Westmoreland requested and received permission to commit U.S. troops in battle in support of the ARVN when necessary. By mid-July his other request had been authorized: to engage in search-and-destroy operations aimed at defeating the enemy in the South. The latter decision altered the entire U.S. strategy, which had formerly been aimed at denying victory to the other side. *The Pentagon Papers* state:

"Final acceptance of the desirability of inflicting defeat on the enemy rather than merely denying him victory opened the door to an indeterminate amount of additional forces."

Precisely what President Johnson and Secretary McNamara expected their decisions of July to bring within the near term "is not clear," the study says, "but there are manifold indications that they were prepared for a long war." (Sheehan et al., 1971: 417)

In fact, the Administration's July announcement, via a press conference given by Johnson, publicly signalled the beginning of the open-ended war in Vietnam. Now the Administration could concentrate on its main objective of fighting and winning the war, pouring in more money and troops and exploring various methods of intensifying the pressure on North Vietnam and the Vietcong. In monetary terms the war's financial costs were climbing rapidly, for in mid-August the Senate approved Johnson's *second* request for additional defence funds, of $1.7 billion: yet the U.S. commitment in the war had started in earnest only six months previously.

Concerning the troop levels, already the war's increasing costs in manpower were becoming apparent to the Administration because before considering Westmoreland's July request for a further 100,000 men, U.S. Defense Secretary McNamara had asked for assurance from the chairman of the U.S. Joint Chiefs of Staff, General Earle Wheeler, that the U.S. *could* win the conflict in South Vietnam. Following a Defense Department study, Wheeler duly assured McNamara that 'there appears no reason we cannot win if such is our will – and if that will is manifested in strategy and tactical operations' (Sheehan et al., 1971: 464). Interestingly, in view of the later debate over what, precisely, *winning* the war meant, the definition of 'winning' that had been provided for Wheeler by U.S. Assistant Secretary of Defense McNaughton harked back to the old idea of 'demonstrating to the VC [Vietcong] that they cannot win' (Sheehan et al., 1971: 464). This passive concept of 'winning' both implied an open-ended commitment to fighting the war – for as long as the Vietcong continued fighting – and also appeared to envisage victory as a stalemate, both of which were unusual and vague goals to pursue using such large numbers of troops and amounts of money.

There were also propaganda problems with this version of 'winning', for there was confusion over what 'winning' meant and communicating this to the public. In addition, this concept appeared to contradict the definition of 'winning' that was implied in Westmoreland's search-and-destroy strategy for fighting the war, which, though equally open-ended, had the concrete goal of attacking, destroying and defeating the enemy in South Vietnam. And it was this method of fighting the war that determined Westmoreland's disposition of resources and partly fuelled the troop requests to which the Administration responded.

In pursuit of these tactics and impelled by the enemy's response, Westmoreland soon requested more troops, despite the huge increases authorized during July. Endeavouring to explain Westmoreland's new request for another 154,000 men in November, *The Pentagon Papers* surmises that either the U.S. military reckoned from the beginning that winning the war would require approximately one million troops which would be politically easier to acquire in instalments, or that the U.S. military command thought little about U.S. troop requirements and also underestimated the enemy's rate of build-up (Sheehan et al., 1971: 467). Of the two explanations the *Pentagon Papers* analyst opts for the latter, which merely gives the impression of U.S. military short-sightedness, rather than deliberate deception (Sheehan et al., 1971: 467). As *The Pentagon Papers* study also points out, the U.S. military apparently underestimated the rate of enemy build-up despite the numerous public Administration statements about the early 1965 rate of North Vietnamese infiltration into South Vietnam. Yet this rate of infiltration had been cited as the precise reason for U.S. bombing of North Vietnam and increased involvement in, and escalation of, the war in South Vietnam. The study makes no attempt to reconcile this contradiction, but if the earlier rate of infiltration had been exaggerated for Administration propaganda purposes, then this would provide an obvious reason for the U.S. military's later miscalculations.

In addition, the conclusion was drawn from U.S. military documents that Westmoreland's overall military plan of action stemmed from the manpower that would be available, rather than Westmoreland requesting the troops necessary for a particular plan (Sheehan et al., 1971: 467). However, while this may point to a grievous lack of thought about the needs of a rapidly escalating war, and indeed the nature of this particular war, it nevertheless remains the case that Westmoreland's aggressive search-and-destroy military tactics would always have required huge force levels. For not only was this a much more active method of fighting the war, but these tactics were being applied to jungle warfare among a population that at best was not prepared to aid the South Vietnamese and U.S. forces, and at worst actively aided the Vietcong and North Vietnamese against the South Vietnamese and Americans.

Thus, against a background of rapid North Vietnamese and Vietcong build-up and increased combat, Westmoreland's requests for more troops continued to flow into Washington. When McNamara was considering the November request for another 154,000 men, the projected troop deployment to the end of 1966 was then close to 400,000. On 16 December Westmoreland requested more troops, which would bring the total for 1966 up to 443,000, and then at the end of January 1966 he requested another 16,000 men (Sheehan et al., 1971: 466–7). And, of course, as the troop levels soared so did the Administration's casualty projections. In mid-July McNamara had estimated that at the end of the year U.S. killed-in-action could be approximately 500 per month, but by the end of November McNamara's estimate for the coming year was 1000 killed-in-action per month. McNamara also accompanied this estimate with an evaluation of the results that this policy might achieve: '". . . and the odds are even that we will be faced in early 1967 with a 'no decision' at an even higher level"' (Sheehan et al., 1971: 464–6). So, despite the ever-increasing numbers of troops McNamara's evaluation of the Administration's chances of success with its current war policy was essentially gloomy.

The increased troop commitment was also accompanied by an expansion in the Rolling Thunder bombing programme. At this stage of the war the publicly declared purpose of the bombing raids on North Vietnam was to interdict North Vietnam's lines of communication and to reduce its war-making capacity. To achieve this and to 'emphasize American airpower', the Administration envisaged a '"slow, steady, deliberate"' bombing campaign, '"beginning with a few infiltration-associated targets in southern NVN and gradually moving northward with progressively more severe attacks on a wider variety of targets"' (Sheehan et al., 1971: 468). In the period from July to December, according to figures provided in *The Pentagon Papers*, the bombing attacks were stepped up greatly, from 900 sorties per week to 1500 per week (Sheehan et al., 1971: 468).

As when the sustained bombing began in March, the Administration continued to be acutely aware of the sensitive nature of the bombing programme and still exercised tight control over the selection and authorization of the bombing targets, which were approved on a weekly basis by senior officials in the Defense Secretary's Office, the State Department and the White House. The only latitude in picking targets that Washington allowed to pilots was in 'armed reconnaissance' attacks against certain 'broad' target categories, 'such as vehicles, locomotives and barges', which were obviously seen as militarily useful, but politically harmless targets. And even these 'broad' target categories were decided by Washington (Sheehan et al., 1971: 468). There was thus little chance of sensitive targets being bombed without high-level Administration approval.

As to the effectiveness of Rolling Thunder, at the end of July Defense Secretary McNamara evaluated the results of the bombing programme in a Memorandum for President Johnson. McNamara cited the two broad 'major purposes' of the bombing programme as: 'to promote a settlement' and 'to interdict infiltration'. In promoting a settlement the bombing was expected to influence North Vietnam to negotiate and to give the U.S. a 'bargaining counter within negotiations' (Porter, 1979, vol. 2: document 209: 393). On these two overall purposes McNamara concluded that the programme had not achieved its objectives, for there was no settlement and 'substantially uninterrupted supply' was continuing 'to meet major North Vietnamese military, industrial and civilian needs' (Porter, 1979, vol. 2: 394). Only as a bargaining counter did McNamara view the programme as a success, reckoning that it 'has become an important counter in the current tacit and explicit bargaining process and will be an important counter in any future bargaining' (Porter, 1979, vol. 2: 393). But what the Administration appeared to have disregarded was that without negotiations the bombing was useless as a bargaining counter, and the North Vietnamese had already made it plain that they would not negotiate under the threat of bombs (Herring, 1983: 59–65). In addition, McNamara concluded that the bombing had had no effect on Vietcong activities in the south (Porter, 1979, vol. 2: 394).

However, despite this negative evaluation McNamara still recommended continuing the bombing programme, but with the main emphasis on the threat of 'future destruction which can be avoided by agreeing to negotiate or agreeing to some settlement in negotiations' (Porter, 1979, vol. 2: 395). In other words, the Administration was using Rolling Thunder, among other purposes, to bomb North Vietnam to the negotiating table – an objective which the Administration had always denied publicly.

By November the bombing campaign had again been assessed as ineffective. The Defense Intelligence Agency reported to McNamara that although North Vietnam's industry was ' "reduced" ' by the bombing, ' "the primarily rural nature of the area permits continued functioning of the subsistence economy" ' (Sheehan et al., 1971: 469). This report also stated: ' "The airstrikes do not appear to have altered Hanoi's determination to continue supporting the war in South Vietnam" ' (Sheehan et al., 1971: 469). For as a *Pentagon Papers* analyst points out:

"NVN was an extremely poor target for air attack. The theory of either strategic or interdiction bombing assumed highly developed industrial nations producing large quantities of military goods to sustain mass armies engaged in intensive warfare. NVN, as U.S. intelligence knew, was an agricultural country with a rudimentary transportation system and little industry of any kind.

"What intelligence agencies liked to call 'the modern industrial sector' of the economy was tiny even by Asian standards . . . There were only a handful of 'major industrial facilities.' When NVN was targeted, the JCS found only eight industrial installations worth listing." (Sheehan et al., 1971: 469)

In addition, the gradual build-up in U.S. bombing – which was so necessary politically to avoid alarming the public, the media, and U.S. enemies and allies alike – had allowed North Vietnam's industry to be dispersed into the countryside. These were the concrete reasons why the bombing campaign could not greatly hurt North Vietnam, partly explaining why neither the threat of destruction, nor actual destruction, had so far influenced North Vietnam's policies in favour of negotiations. Added to this was the North Vietnamese will to resist the bombing and to continue fighting the war.

However, despite the demonstrable ineffectiveness of the bombing, the Administration's view of Rolling Thunder as both a form of pressure and a bargaining counter meant that the Administration continued to use the bombing as a large part of both its military and its diplomatic effort. Thus, militarily the Administration calculated that if North Vietnam could not be bombed to the negotiating table, then it could be lured there with the suggestion of a bombing halt in return for North Vietnamese concessions. And obviously this meant that the bombing had both to continue and to become heavier, inflicting enough of a degree of 'pain' on North Vietnam for a bombing halt to constitute a sufficiently attractive negotiating proposition to the North Vietnamese.

In diplomatic terms, at this stage of the war the Administration's war objectives and bargaining-counter concept of the bombing ruled out a *permanent* halt to the bombing unless, in effect, the North Vietnamese surrendered and negotiated on U.S. terms. However, in late 1965 a *temporary* bombing pause was viewed as a useful device to probe North Vietnam's willingness to negotiate on U.S. terms, and as a demonstration of the Administration's peaceful intentions in the face of growing public pressure, prior to escalation. In fact, this was to be a repeat performance of the 'secret' and unofficial May bombing pause, but with the vital difference that this bombing pause was 'official' and was to be conducted with maximum publicity.

Apparently the impetus for this bombing pause came from Defense Secretary McNamara, who had proposed the idea to President Johnson as early as mid-July:

"After the 44 U.S.–third country battalions have been deployed and after some strong action has been taken in the program of bombing in the North, we could, as part of a diplomatic initiative, consider introducing a 6–8 week pause in the program of bombing the North." (Sheehan et al., 1971: 470)

The Pentagon Papers study states that McNamara's rationale for a longer pause was due to his belief that the May pause 'had been too short and too hastily arranged to be effective' and the analyst also commented on the lack of time allowed for Hanoi to reply to the pause in May (Sheehan et al., 1971: 470). McNamara's purpose in proposing a bombing pause followed that of the May pause: negotiations favourable to the U.S., or escalation of the war effort. Overall, McNamara's concept of the bombing pause was pressure by another means:

As he [McNamara] and Assistant Secretary of Defense McNaughton envisioned it, the pause would be used a kind of "ratchet," – which the analyst likens to "the device which raises the net on a tennis court, backing off tension between each phase of increasing it." (Sheehan et al., 1971: 470)

In addition, it seems that Administration officials were certain that this pause would be temporary, because the terms that were set for a permanent cessation of the bombing were acknowledged to be unacceptable to Hanoi, as McNaughton pointed out to McNamara:

After noting these conditions [for permanent cessation of the bombing], Mr. McNaughton wrote that they amounted to "capitulation by a communist force that is far from beaten." (Sheehan et al., 1971: 471; square brackets added)

However, even a temporary bombing pause was opposed by Secretary of State Dean Rusk and the Joint Chiefs of Staff, indicating the differences that existed between Johnson's principal advisers concerning the conduct of the war and diplomatic/negotiating initiatives – whether or not the latter were 'real' attempts or more in the nature of public relations exercises. Replying to McNamara's reasons for a pause, Secretary of State Rusk calculated in early November that at this stage a pause would merely be using a 'very important card without receiving anything substantial in return' (Sheehan et al., 1971: 487).

Despite this opposition, according to President Johnson's memoirs, by early December the Vietnam 'principals' (senior National Security

Council [NSC] officials), including Rusk, had decided that a bombing pause might be useful and only the U.S. military and the U.S. Embassy in Saigon – yet another factor in the decision-making and information process – still opposed a pause (Johnson, 1971: 235). Johnson wrote that he had been doubtful of the value of a pause when it was first mooted, citing Rusk's objections, but eventually in mid-December, despite his fear that resuming the bombing would be difficult after a pause, Johnson decided to accept advice proposing a bombing halt and 'risk' a pause before escalating the war:

> If there was a chance, however remote, that stopping the bombing might open a road to peace, I was prepared to take a few risks. I knew too that I faced a serious decision regarding sending more men to Vietnam. I wanted to explore every possible avenue of settlement before we undertook additional military measures. (Johnson, 1971: 234–7)

But Assistant Secretary of State for Far Eastern Affairs William Bundy's account of the agreement to a bombing pause differs considerably. He stated that it was only on the night of 27 December that Johnson decided, after previous refusals, on a '"real full pause"', after extending the Christmas bombing truce 'for another twenty-four or thirty-six hours' (Bundy, Oral History Interview, 1969, Tape 3: 17). This last-minute decision resulted in hasty diplomatic cables to both the South Vietnamese and Russian Governments, informing them both of the pause and enlisting the former's agreement to it. After that the Administration 'went into wholesale full gear' (Bundy, Oral History Interview, 1969, Tape 3: 17). Bundy's version of events thus endows the decision on a pause with a much more makeshift character than does Johnson's version of deliberate discussions with a decision in mid-December. And Bundy states clearly that the style of the diplomatic 'offensive' that accompanied this bombing pause was 'very much the President's idea', that is, the diplomatic moves did not follow the scenarios that had previously been discussed in the Administration (Bundy, Oral History Interview, 1969, Tape 3: 18).

This official bombing pause lasted until 31 January 1966, allowing plenty of time for the Administration to try to achieve its diplomatic and propaganda goals. As for the results of the pause, previous Administration judgements that Hanoi would not settle the war on the terms offered proved to be correct. As a propaganda move William Bundy considered the pause to have been of great value:

To me the pause was essential in terms of domestic things alone, but also had an immensely useful impact abroad, particularly in Britain . . .

I think it made an immense difference. It immensely lengthened our lease on an adequate level of world-wide support, again speaking in terms of key quarters. It lengthened our support in this country; it didn't seriously damage the situation in South Vietnam that I could detect. I think it was a net plus, myself . . .

But the President never believed that. He thought he had been talked into doing something that was essentially a sucker's move. (Bundy, Oral History Interview, 1969, Tape 3: 24)

Johnson himself makes it clear in his memoirs that he viewed the pause as a failure, reckoning that his main worry had been vindicated, for he wrote: '. . . we received little credit for stopping the bombing and heavy criticism for renewing it' (Johnson, 1971: 235). As a result Johnson's attitude on peace efforts, and the war alike, hardened, and Bundy viewed this as something of a 'break point in policy, as well as in the relationships of the senior people to each other and all the rest' (Bundy, Oral History Interview, 1969, Tape 3: 29–30).

So, the Administration's public attempts to open discussions – even on its own, uncompromising terms – through a bombing halt, came to an end. The war continued to escalate, the public clamour about the bombing increased, and the North Vietnamese public position hardened with the requirement for the bombing of North Vietnam to be halted permanently and unconditionally before discussions could begin – which were terms the U.S. could not then accept.

The first ten months of war had thus inaugurated an upwardly spiralling U.S. commitment in a conflict in which the initiative was primarily held by the Vietcong and North Vietnamese, which meant that U.S. escalation could be matched at each turn of the screw, thus denying the U.S. the military advantage and instead tying it to an ever-intensifying military stalemate.

1966–1967: increasing the pressure

Despite some military successes by U.S. and ARVN forces during 1965, most notably in August in the Mekong Delta and Vantuong near the U.S. base at Chulai, and in the Ia Drang valley in November, as 1966 began the U.S. and South Vietnamese Governments were still no nearer to winning the war – however winning was defined. Indeed the deterioration in South Vietnam had forced the U.S. to 'take over' fighting the war by August 1965, and thus it was now the primary combatant in the conflict, with ARVN forces playing a supporting role. And by the end of 1965, the Administration had been left in no doubt by the Central Intelligence Agency (CIA) that North Vietnam intended to continue the struggle, come what may:

"Present Communist policy is to continue to prosecute the war vigorously in the south. . .

"The Communists recognize that the U.S. reinforcements of 1965 signify a determination to avoid defeat. They expect more U.S. troops and probably anticipate that targets in the Hanoi–Haiphong area will come under air attack. Nevertheless, they remain unwilling to damp down the conflict or move toward negotiation. They expect a long war, but they continue to believe that time is their ally and that their own staying power is superior." (Sheehan et al., 1971: 477)

But, as in the previous year, notwithstanding this and other depressing estimates in early 1966, the Administration's response was to escalate the war once the bombing pause had ended. For while the Administration's envoys toured the world, discussing the possibility of negotiations in various capitals, the efficacy of the bombing programme was once more under consideration by the President's advisers. Thus, in mid-January Assistant Secretary of Defense McNaughton drafted and redrafted a memorandum which again highlighted the failure of the bombing programme to achieve its objectives of interdicting North Vietnam's supply routes and reducing North Vietnam's aid to the South, and noted that North Vietnam could still sustain the struggle (Sheehan et al., 1971: 472). This memorandum is an interesting document – by an important adviser to the Defense Secretary – covering as it does most aspects of the war, and it is therefore worth quoting at some length. In his redrafted version McNaughton analysed current developments in South Vietnam and outlined possible results:

We . . . have in Vietnam the ingredients of an enormous miscalculation . . . The ARVN is tired, passive and accommodation-prone . . . The PAVN/VC [Peoples Army of Vietnam/Viet Cong] are effectively matching our deployments . . . The bombing of the North . . . may or may not be able effectively to interdict infiltration (partly because the PAVN/VC can simply refuse to do battle if supplies are short) . . . Pacification is stalled despite efforts and hopes. The

GVN [Government of (South) Vietnam] political infrastructure is moribund and weaker than the VC infrastructure among most of the rural population . . . South Vietnam is near the edge of serious inflation and economic chaos. (Sheehan et al., 1971: 491; square brackets added)

From this grim opening McNaughton moved on to consider why the U.S. was still involved in Vietnam, summarizing the main arguments advanced both privately and publicly by the President and his advisers – and demolishing most of them!

C. The present U.S. objective in Vietnam is to avoid humiliation. The reasons why we *went into* Vietnam to the present depth are varied; but they are now largely academic. Why we have *not withdrawn* from Vietnam is, by all odds, *one* reason: (1) to preserve our reputation as a guarantor, and thus to preserve our effectiveness in the rest of the world. We have not hung on (2) to save a friend, or (3) to deny the Communists the added acres and heads (because the dominoes don't fall for that reason in this case), or even (4) to prove that 'wars of national liberation' won't work (except as our reputation is involved). At each decision point we have gambled; at each point, to avoid the damage to our effectiveness of defaulting on our commitment, we have upped the ante. We have not defaulted, and the ante (and commitment) is now very high. It is important that we behave so as to protect our reputation. At the same time, since it is our *reputation* that is at stake, it is important that we do not construe our obligation to be more than do the countries whose opinions of us *are* our reputation. (Sheehan et al., 1971: 491–2)

So, McNaughton dismissed most of the Administration's propaganda on the reasons for the U.S. commitment in Vietnam, focusing on one intangible, but to the U.S., vital, factor: the way in which other nations perceived the U.S., its world image. It should be noted, however, that other advisers did not share McNaughton's views, for his colleague in the State Department, Assistant Secretary for Far Eastern Affairs William Bundy, still clung to a version of the domino theory as the underlying rationale for the U.S. commitment (Gravel, 1971, vol. 4: 89).

McNaughton then considered the military situation, and though he noted that there was 'an honest difference of judgement as to the success of the present military efforts in the South' and that 'There is no question that the U.S. deployments thwarted the VC hope to achieve a quick victory in 1965', his own analysis of this part of the problem concluded on a much more sombre note:

But there is a serious question whether we are now defeating the VC/PAVN main forces and whether planned U.S. deployments will more than hold our position in the country. Population and area control has not changed significantly in the past year; and the best judgement is that, even with the Phase IIA deployments, we will be faced in early 1967 with a continued stalemate at a higher level of forces and casualties. (Sheehan et al., 1971: 492)

Positing a revised commitment – or as McNaughton termed it '"the softest credible formulation of the U.S. commitment"' – to South Vietnam that precluded only a North Vietnamese forcible seizure of power, McNaughton outlined some results that would be less than a U.S. military victory, but which could still be acceptable:

b. A coalition government including Communists.
c. A free decision by the South to succumb to the VC or to the North.
d. A neutral (or even anti-U.S.) government in SVN.
e. A live-and-let-live "reversion to 1959."

Furthermore, we must recognize that even if we fail to [sic] in achieving this "soft" formulation, we could over time come out with minimum damage:

f. If the reason was GVN gross wrongheadedness or apathy.
g. If victorious North Vietnam "went Titoist."
h. If the Communist take-over was fuzzy and very slow. (Sheehan et al., 1971: 492)

Despite this pessimistic analysis, the apparent willingness to withdraw and let South Vietnam 'go communist', and the all-important conclusion that damage to the U.S. image (see Chapter 2 for analysis of U.S. image) could be minimized even if North Vietnam achieved victory, McNaughton's final recommendations followed the previous pattern: increases in troops, in bombing, stronger support for the South Vietnamese Government and a greater pacification effort in the countryside. These surprising recommendations – given the prior analysis – followed from McNaughton's fear that if the U.S. was known to have lowered its '"sights from victory to compromise"' then South Vietnam would come apart and North Vietnam would '"smell blood"'. And McNaughton further concluded that the U.S. would have to be prepared to escalate the war if North Vietnam should '"miscalculate"' and interpret U.S. '"willingness to compromise"' as a sign of '"being on the run"' (Sheehan et al., 1971: 493). However, McNaughton's recommendations, far from facilitating a compromise solution, were a recipe for continuing precisely the situation he feared and had termed in his memorandum an '"escalating military stalemate"' (Sheehan et al., 1971: 492).

McNaughton's recommendations roughly agreed with those of the Saigon Embassy and the U.S. military. This was an interesting convergence because the U.S. Ambassador to Saigon, Henry Cabot Lodge, held views on Vietnam that were diametrically opposed to McNaughton's: Lodge believed that the U.S. had a 'strong interest' in Vietnam and that in order to avoid a Third World War the U.S. might 'have to decide how much it is worth to us to deny Viet-Nam to Hanoi and Peking – regardless of what the Vietnamese think' (Gravel, vol. 4, 1971: 100). Thus these two advisers arrived at the same recommendations by totally different routes, and forwarded the same proposals on the war to the decision-makers. McNaughton was not alone in his view of the war, for Defense Secretary McNamara's revised version of his November memorandum on the bombing 'echoed much of his Assistant Secretary's pessimism', but nevertheless advocated the same policies to the President (Sheehan et al., 1971: 473).

The Joint Chiefs of Staff were also concerned with the failure of the bombing campaign to achieve its objectives and they used this failure as an argument to bolster their case for bombing North Vietnam's petroleum, oil and lubricants – termed P.O.L. – stores in Hanoi and Haiphong. As they well knew, this would be a highly visible escalation and extension of the bombing campaign which would attract public scrutiny, and it was not a new idea, for since the autumn of 1965 the Joint Chiefs of Staff had urged that the scope of the bombing be widened and changed into '"a program of strategic bombing aimed at all industrial and economic resources as well as at interdiction targets"' (Sheehan et al., 1971: 475).

The Joint Chiefs had maintained in a November 1965 memorandum to McNamara that while there were '"constraints"' on the bombing '"only limited success in air operations in D.R.V./Laos"' could be achieved, and therefore what was needed '"is an immediate and sharply accelerated program which will leave no room for doubt that the U.S. intends to win and achieve a level of destruction which they will not be able to overcome"' (Sheehan et al., 1971: 475–6). The effects of attacking North Vietnam's P.O.L., the Joint Chiefs stated, '"would be more damaging to the D.R.V. capability to move war-supporting resources within the country and along the infiltration routes to SVN than any attack against any other target system . . . The flow of supplies would be greatly impeded ... recuperability of the D.R.V. P.O.L. system from the effects of an attack is very poor"' (Sheehan et al., 1971: 476). And in January the U.S. Commander-in-Chief Pacific (CINCPAC), Admiral U. S. Grant Sharp, sent the Joint Chiefs an even more persuasive assessment of the effects of P.O.L. attacks, stating that they would '"bring the enemy to the conference table or cause the insurgency to wither from lack of support"' (Sheehan et al., 1971: 476).

Clearly the U.S. military expected great results from P.O.L. attacks, results which had so far eluded the U.S. despite huge increases in troops, weapons and bombing. However, not only was the Joint Chiefs' assessment of P.O.L. attacks not shared by the CIA, but according to *The Pentagon Papers* the CIA had also discounted the effects of virtually any type of bombing, including strategic bombing:

> "The Chiefs did so [pressed for a strategic bombing programme], it may be added, despite the steady stream of memoranda from the intelligence community consistently expressing skepticism that bombing of any conceivable sort (that is, any except bombing aimed primarily at the destruction of North Vietnam's population) could either persuade Hanoi to negotiate a settlement on U.S./GVN terms or effectively limit Hanoi's ability to infiltrate men and supplies into the South." (Sheehan et al., 1971: 475; square brackets added)

On the effects of bombing P.O.L., CIA sources had estimated: '"It is unlikely that this loss would cripple the Communist military operations in the South, though it would certainly embarrass them"' (Sheehan et al., 1971: 476–7). However, the dissension that characterized the President's principal advisers over war strategy also pertained among the intelligence community, and the Joint Chiefs subsequently fielded a more favourable CIA memorandum on P.O.L. attacks to McNamara (U.S. Department of Defense, 1971, Book 6, vol. I: 85) who eventually accepted the recommendations to bomb P.O.L. targets and submitted this proposal to Johnson in March 1966. Johnson delayed agreeing to this escalation, 'in spite of the near consensus among his top advisers on its desirability', until late May (Gravel, 1971, vol. 4: 100), probably because of a severe political crisis in South Vietnam lasting from early March until mid-June; and a variety of international leaders' attempts at peace-making, beginning in February, continuing until June and encompassing some fifteen proposals for negotiations.

In late May President Johnson also informed British Prime Minister Harold Wilson of the proposed P.O.L. strikes and arranged a special, but ultimately unsuccessful, briefing on the strikes for Wilson, following the latter's protest, in order to enlist his support. Wilson thanked Johnson and then explained why he would be forced, for the first time, to dissociate from this U.S. action; the main, interlinked, reasons being that the 'political disadavantages' would outweigh the 'possible military benefits'; that this was an undeclared war, which, by implication, rendered these strikes inappropriate; and that the strikes were incompatible with the declared U.S. aim of a negotiated settlement, as opposed to 'total military victory in the field' (U.S. Department of Defense, 1971, Book 6, vol. I: 121).

Though the Administration did not want to lose British support – for Britain was their staunchest non-combatant ally – nevertheless the persuasive military estimates of the effects of the P.O.L. bombings – that is, that the bombings would cripple the North Vietnamese war effort – were more important still to the Administration. And so, despite the knowledge that the British Government would dissociate, the P.O.L. air-strikes were carried out.

The original date for the P.O.L. strikes was also delayed at Secretary of State Dean Rusk's request to the President, in order to avoid prejudicing a peace probe that the Canadians were then undertaking with U.S. concurrence (U.S. Department of Defense, 1971, Book 6, vol. I: 123–4). The terms of Rusk's subsequent explanation to McNamara reveal both his concern about the damage that could be caused to the U.S. image, and his desire not to interrupt the flow of events too greatly with his request:

"... I am deeply disturbed by general international revulsion, and perhaps a great deal at home, if it becomes known that we took an action which sabotaged the Ronning [Canadian diplomat] mission to which we had given our agreement. I recognize the agony of this problem for all concerned. We could make arrangements to get an immediate report from Ronning. If he has a negative report, as we expect, that provides a firmer base for the action we contemplate and would make a difference to people like Wilson and Pearson [Canadian Prime Minister]. If, on the other hand, he learns that there is any serious breakthrough towards peace, the President would surely want to know of that before an action which would knock such a possibility off the tracks. I strongly recommend, therefore, against ninth or tenth [June]. I regret this because of my maximum desire to support you and your colleagues in your tough job." (U.S. Department of Defense, 1971, Book 6, vol. I: 124; square brackets added)

The P.O.L. strikes eventually took place on 29 June, authorized by a 'remarkable document, attesting in detail to the political sensitivity of the strikes' (Gravel, 1971, vol. 4: 105) and under strict operational guidelines aimed at minimizing civilian casualties – which the Joint Chiefs and CINCPAC had estimated would be 'under 500', as opposed to the CIA estimate of '200–300' – and avoiding damage to merchant shipping in the port of Haiphong (Gravel, 1971, vol. 4: 105).

The Administration intially judged the strikes to be successful, and assessed international reaction as 'relatively mild' (Gravel, 1971, vol. 4: 107). But this appears to have been a misjudgement, in view of the subsequent flood of international comment and criticism by governments and press and in view of the fact that in Britain's case there was violence for the first time at an anti-war demonstration after the P.O.L. strikes. In addition, by the end of the summer it had become clear that the strikes had failed to achieve their objectives: the P.O.L. attacks had eliminated 76 per cent of North Vietnam's bulk storage capacity, but sufficient P.O.L. was contained in dispersed sites, supplemented by imports, to meet North Vietnam's requirements; infiltration continued and North Vietnam kept up the fight (Gravel, 1971, vol. 4: 137).

There were other important events in this period in addition to the P.O.L. strikes. On 31 January, after the large-scale and well-publicized Administration peace 'offensive', the bombing of North Vietnam resumed. As justification the Administration claimed that there had been no response to this peace initiative, passing over a North Vietnamese statement on 4 January that might have been a faint indication of interest, also brushing aside signs of a drop in North Vietnam's military effort, and focusing instead on North Vietnam's South-bound supply efforts during the period of the bombing pause (Herring, 1983: 117). Almost immediately after the bombing resumed the North Vietnamese representative in Rangoon contacted the U.S. Ambassador there to arrange a meeting. The U.S. Ambassador had previously delivered a message secretly to the North Vietnamese representative during the bombing pause. No new proposals came from this meeting, and although North Vietnam initially appeared to want the contact to continue, it ended the contact abruptly soon after (Herring, 1983: 121–58).

On 4 February, the same day that the U.S. Senate Foreign Relations Committee was due to hold its second Open Hearings session on U.S. policy in Vietnam, President Johnson anounced that a summit meeting between the U.S. and South Vietnam was to be held in Honolulu from 6 to 8 February. The arrangements were made hurriedly and the meeting concentrated on the non-military side of the U.S. effort:

pacification, economic and social reform, and elections. The Joint Declaration and Final Communiqué strongly emphasized these aspects.

The strong U.S. support for the Saigon government manifested at Honolulu had the unfortunate consequence of helping to spark off the next round of political turmoil in South Vietnam – the worst for some time. For the conference had been so hastily arranged that the Saigon government appeared to be there at the U.S. Administration's command, and this, coupled with President Johnson and South Vietnamese Prime Minister Ky's embrace – which to the South Vietnamese public underlined the client state relationship between the two governments – damaged Ky's prestige in South Vietnam. Briefly, the Saigon government, bolstered by this recent public U.S. commitment, attempted to remove what it saw as a political rival by dismissing a powerful and popular South Vietnamese Buddhist army commander, General Nguyen Chanh Thi, whose area of command, I Corps, included Danang and Hue. U.S. Ambassador Lodge concurred in this move, and he and Westmoreland played a role in the subsequent events, advising and supporting the Saigon government.

General Thi's dismissal led to popular protests in Danang, Hue and Saigon, which the Buddhist Struggle Movement then politicized, demanding elections and a civilian government to replace the military junta. Although Thi was returned to his command area, the unrest continued, and Ky's later revocation of promises on accelerated elections and a civilian government sparked off demonstrations in Hue and Saigon which had a distinct anti-American theme. At Lodge's prompting on 5 April the Saigon government prepared to try and crush the opposition in Danang, mustering 1900 troops and various equipment at the U.S. air base, but Ky was out-manoeuvred by the new I Corps Commander and was forced to withdraw. The Hue commander had also stated that he would fight if government troops arrived in Hue. There followed some weeks of political manoeuvring, with more Saigon government pledges on elections, eliciting Buddhist action to quieten the unrest, followed again by Ky reneging on these promises. On 21 May a second Saigon government assault was undertaken against Danang, with U.S. support, and after bitter fighting Ky's troops regained the city. At this point the Buddhists retaliated by sacking and burning the U.S. Information Service (USIS) Library and U.S. consulate in Hue on 26 and 31 May respectively. Hue then came under attack by Ky's troops and was regained by mid-June. Finally, Buddhist opposition in Saigon was completely crushed, the leaders arrested and imprisoned. (This account drawn from Kahin, 1987: 417–31.) Thus, for four months the Saigon government was busily engaged, with U.S. help, in fighting for its existence against the opposition of its own people.

During 1966 Westmoreland continued to request more troops. On 28 January he asked for an increase that would bring the total for 1966 to 459,000. In June McNamara approved a schedule for deployment of 391,000 U.S. soldiers for 1966, with a projected total of 431,000 for 1967. However, McNamara had no sooner approved this schedule than Westmoreland petitioned for another 111,588 troops which would bring the total he needed for 1967 up to 542,588 (Sheehan et al., 1971: 481–2). The new request reached McNamara on 5 August, but for the first time the Defense Secretary requested a 'detailed, line-by-line analysis' proving that these new requirements were 'truly essential to the carrying out of our war plan', and he further commented: 'Excessive deployments weaken our ability to win by undermining the economic structure of the RVN [South Vietnam] and by raising doubts concerning the soundness of our planning' (Sheehan et al., 1971: 500–1). Although further troop requests were authorized later, McNamara refused this request in October: the period of virtually automatic troop increases authorized by McNamara and the President had come to an end (Sheehan et al., 1971: 482).

The basis of the growing dissension between McNamara and the Joint Chiefs, encapsulated in this episode, centred on their respective assessments of progress in the war, for where the former saw little improvement, the latter maintained that the 'military situation . . . had "improved substantially over the past year"' and thus they wanted to apply more pressure (Sheehan et al., 1971: 519). However, McNamara focused on not only the military side of the war – on which he reckoned the U.S. efforts '"had blunted the Communist military initiative"' – but also the political, economic and social aspects of the conflict. In a memorandum to President Johnson in mid-October, after noting the failure of the Saigon government to win over its own people, McNamara examined the record on pacification, a vital aspect of the battle throughout the South Vietnamese countryside:

"Pacification has if anything gone backward. As compared with two, or four, years ago, enemy full-time regional forces with part-time guerilla forces are larger; attacks, terrorism and sabotage have increased in scope and intensity; more railroads are closed and highways cut; the rice crop expected to come to market is smaller; we control little, if any, more of the population . . . In essence, we find ourselves . . . no better, and if anything worse off." (Sheehan et al., 1971: 517)

Thus the eighteen-month infusion of troops, money and attempts to exert a moderating influence on the Saigon government had achieved nothing permanent, for it was plain to see that it was U.S. military efforts that kept the Vietcong and North Vietnamese at bay, and the underlying malaise in South Vietnamese government and society, which fuelled the political and social discontent in the beginning, was still present. Furthermore, military efforts alone could not change these underlying problems and McNamara recognized this fact.

This pessimistic analysis – and prognosis – increased McNamara's desire for a change in tack, which in turn led to increasing disagreement between McNamara and his civilian advisers on the one side, the Joint Chiefs on the other, and with the White House caught in the middle of this battle. The essence of the disagreement was expressed in differences over war strategy and tactics, particularly Westmoreland's war of attrition using search-and-destroy tactics, and the effectiveness of the bombing to the war effort; and McNamara's suggestion that efforts be made to '"try to split the VC off from Hanoi"' and '"develop a realistic plan providing a role for the VC in negotiations, postwar life and government of the nation"' (Sheehan et al., 1971: 518). While McNamara favoured '"girding, openly, for a longer war"', stabilizing both troop levels in 1967 to 470,000 men (100,000 less than the military wanted) and the bombing, building an electronic barrier to infiltration across South Vietnam, and pursuing pacification more vigorously, the Joint Chiefs wanted 493,969 troops by the end of 1967 with a planned increase to 555,741, more extensive bombing, and permission to engage in operations that had so far been regarded as too politically sensitive: '"such as mining ports, naval quarantine, spoiling attacks and raids against the enemy in Cambodia and Laos, and certain special operations"' (Sheehan et al., 1971: 518–20). Faced with these two sets of recommendations, President Johnson opted for the Chiefs' proposals on extending the bombing, 'though only step-by-step', thus continuing his previous strategy of effectively steering a middle course in prosecuting the war, endeavouring to placate both doves and hawks within his Administration, as well as outside it (Sheehan et al., 1971: 520).

The Manila Conference on Vietnam from 24 to 25 October, attended by allied leaders, was an ideal opportunity for the President to stress the U.S. desire for peace, for the Final Communiqué stated that allied forces would withdraw '"not later than six months"' after the other side had withdrawn, ceased infiltration and '"as the level of violence thus subsides"' (Sheehan et al., 1971: 521). Johnson thus reassured doves at home, Congressmen – for this was a Congressional election year – and anxious world leaders about U.S. intentions, as well as neatly reinforcing the primary U.S. propaganda line that Hanoi was responsible for all the ills afflicting South Vietnam that were manifested through the violent conflict.

Unfortunately any good that accrued to the Administration had evaporated by the end of the year when bombing raids that were closer in to Hanoi were witnessed and reported by the *New York Times'* assistant managing editor, Harrison Salisbury, who disagreed with the Administration's public version of civilian casualties and damage. And worse still, these same raids also sank an apparent peace probe from Hanoi, involving Polish diplomats, which resulted in further criticism of the Administration (Herring, 1983: 213, 274–309). So these raids and Salisbury's eyewitness dispatches focused yet more attention on the destructive capabilities of U.S. weaponry and the likelihood and numbers of civilian casualties, factors which had for some time been an issue of world-wide public concern, and which again became the subject of public debate.

Despite the abrupt end to the previous mediation attempt, 1967 began with yet more efforts to open talks on the conflict, including apparently encouraging statements by North Vietnamese Premier Pham Van Dong and Foreign Minister Nguyen Duy Trinh via interviews with American journalist Harrison Salisbury and Australian journalist Wilfred Burchett respectively; by North Vietnam's diplomat in Paris, Mai Van Bo; and finally via an extension of the Tet truce in February. The latter episode comprised talks in London between British Prime Minister Wilson and visiting Soviet Premier Alexei Kosygin, acting as intermediaries on behalf of their respective ally, with the aim of achieving a bombing halt in return for talks. This attempt, the most important British peace initiative of the war, also foundered, amid embarrassment and bitter recriminations on the British side over what was perceived as U.S. changes of terms during the diplomatic process, while U.S. officials maintained that the British had misrepresented the U.S. position. However, as *The Secret Diplomacy of the Vietnam War* makes clear, British Prime Minister Wilson heavily over-estimated the chances of success of this initiative, for the Administration did not trust Wilson; the Russians were cautious on Hanoi's behalf; and in any case the negotiating positions of both sides had already hardened prior to this attempt. So Wilson's over-eagerness and Johnson's distrust combined to sour relations (Herring, 1983: 373–476). According to William Bundy, Johnson's distrust appeared to have stemmed in part from Wilson's earlier dissociation from the P.O.L. bombings in summer 1966, which Bundy saw as a '. . . break point in the President's relationship with Wilson . . .' (Bundy, Oral History Interview, 1969, Tape 3: 36), resulting in Johnson's later treatment of Wilson's peace-making efforts:

> So we had, in effect, to have Wilson give the same message to Kosygin that the President had sent in a letter to Ho [Chi Minh – North Vietnamese leader], but without telling Wilson or Kosygin, but Wilson particularly, about the letter because the President just didn't trust Wilson, particularly since the Haiphong POL disassociation. He thought he was trying to make time politically, and I have no doubt that was as far as it went a correct judgement. (Bundy, Oral History Interview, 1969, Tape 4: 25)

Following the failure of this crop of peace attempts, both the bombing and the debate over the war within the Administration resumed. Notwithstanding President Johnson's preference for a middle course, when faced with pressure from the military to widen the bombing, accompanied by favourable judgements of its value which were supported by some of his White House staff, Johnson put his faith in the military and intensified the bombing, contrary to the advice and judgements of his civilian advisers in the Pentagon and CIA.

Nor was the disagreement among the President's advisers confined to the bombing, for there was even more conflict over the ground war, sparked off, as it often was, by the latest Westmoreland troop request in mid-March 1967 for another 200,000 to bring the total by mid-1968 up to 671,616 men. In forwarding Westmoreland's request the Joint Chiefs again pressed for mobilization of the Reserves in order to provide these troops, a suggestion which, if implemented, would pose Johnson with the very dilemma he had always sought to avoid: a Congressional – and very public – debate on the war. And although, obviously, there was public debate through the media and rival Senate Committee Hearings, it was not yet of the proportions, or official standing, that it would immediately assume if the Reserves were called up. The Chiefs also responded to Westmoreland's worries about North Vietnam's use of sanctuaries in Laos and Cambodia, and its troops above the Demilitarized Zone (DMZ), with the suggestion that the war be effectively widened by conducting military operations in these areas – and Westmoreland already had contingency plans for such operations. Most of Johnson's civilian advisers, however, advocated increasing troop strength without recourse to a Reserve call-up, favoured curtailing the bombing, and opposed military ground operations against North Vietnam, Laos and Cambodia (Sheehan et al., 1971: 524–31).

Again Johnson was caught between these two camps, whose views expressed not only differing strategies for fighting the war, but also ultimately differences on the results to be achieved, that is, what 'winning' meant: the Joint Chiefs wanted a classic 'military victory' over their military enemy, whereas some civilian advisers were more concerned about the underlying political complexities and thus more prepared to settle for a compromise solution, which did not necessarily entail a military victory. In addition these two camps tended to express quite different views on progress in the war, with the military, the Saigon embassy, and some White House advisers tending to be more optimistic about progress than McNamara and his close advisers. Perhaps naturally, Johnson preferred to listen to good reports about the war, rather than bad ones – a characteristic of which all his advisers were aware.

These arguments also revealed a fundamental disagreement about the genesis of the war, and hence the most effective – for morality was not an issue under discussion – method of tackling its root cause and continuing stimulus. For if the war was primarily a product of North Vietnamese military aggression, then the Joint Chiefs' military methods to repel an invader could be considered an appropriate way to achieve the desired result of victory through the enemy's defeat, thus removing the stimulus to further conflict. If, however, the origins of the war lay more in South Vietnam's own political and social problems – as some of Johnson's civilian advisers surmised – which North Vietnam had then exploited but not actually created, then even defeating the North Vietnamese would not remove the underlying causes of the conflict. And these two views were important not only in estimating the type and potential numbers of opponent the U.S. faced, whether this was primarily North Vietnamese Regular Army or whether Southern guerrillas constituted a significant pool of recruits, but they also had implications for the eventual length and depth of U.S. involvement in the conflict.

One of the crucial strands in the above arguments lay in an assessment of the South Vietnamese Government's instability and inability to govern its own people and the reasons for this failure; specifically, whether this failure was due more to North Vietnamese intervention, or whether the Vietcong, even with North Vietnamese aid, had merely exploited political and social grievances that had already existed in the country. Although official U.S. propaganda laid the blame for South Vietnam's instability on the destabilizing efforts of the Vietcong and North Vietnam, in pressing the Saigon government to undertake political and social reform – particularly land reform – the Administration showed that it was well aware that these issues were important wellsprings of popular discontent. South Vietnam's leaders had invariably shown that they were equally well aware of the Administration's worries on these issues and obligingly paid lip-service to these concerns in order to create the more favourable impression, in the absence of any more concrete manifestations, that Washington so clearly desired. As to the conflict, the practical manifestations of Saigon's failings came in the form of central government coups, ineffective and corrupt government of the country as a whole, and a South Vietnamese Army with a high rate of desertion and an erratic fighting record.

This particular policy battle in the Administration ended in the summer with the usual messy compromise, for although the options presented to Johnson represented alternatives, he avoided a clear-cut decision on whether to escalate the war fairly dramatically as the Chiefs wanted, or to cut back as McNamara desired. Instead the troop increase was kept to 55,000, which was modest by comparison with the Chiefs' proposals and thus accorded more with McNamara's original figure of 30,000, but the air war was stepped up in line with the Chiefs' recommendations. By taking this route Johnson again kept his Congressional hawks at bay – spearheaded by the Senate Preparedness Subcommittee of the Armed Services Committee, which backed the Chiefs – while not alarming too much the Senate doves, led by the Senate Foreign Relations Committee (Sheehan et al., 1971: 538–40).

While Johnson was treading his political tightrope in Washington, South Vietnam went to the polls to try and elect a new government democratically, under the watchful gaze of a group of American observers. Although the elections left something to be desired by Western standards of democracy, with a restricted candidature, some voting constraints, and military interference resulting in former Premier Ky becoming former Chief of State Thieu's running mate rather than his challenger, nevertheless this was a step in the direction that U.S. propaganda had always insisted South Vietnam was going. Thus, although President Thieu and Vice-President Ky had merely exchanged one ruling title for another, they had at least now been installed as a result of an election rather than the more usual military coup.

In line with past practice, following the decision to widen the bombing and in a climate of military optimism over 'progress' in the war, the President once more offered Hanoi the chance to negotiate, stating in a speech in late September in San Antonio, Texas, that the U.S. would halt the bombing '. . . when this will lead promptly to productive discussions' and assuming that 'while discussions proceed, Hanoi would not take advantage of the bombing cessation or limitation' (Williams et al., 1989: 264). Interpreting the latter phrase as a form of condition Hanoi rejected this initiative, again demanding an unconditional halt to the bombing. The contacts that were undertaken at this time continued for some months even after this rejection, but, as in the past, ultimately led nowhere.

In an effort to generate more support for the war from an increasingly disenchanted public and to try and overcome the twin public impressions of an Administration divided on war policy in a stalemated conflict, a public relations campaign was now mounted to try and spread the news about the progress in the war that the military could detect, that is, the nearness of the 'crossover point' at which enemy forces would be killed faster than they could be replaced. Compared with the dire situation in South Vietnam when the U.S. had entered the war in early 1965 it was possible to see some signs of progress, but now Johnson was being warned that the public's patience was running out at a time when the 1968 Presidential election was coming up, meaning that Johnson's war options and time available were also contracting – a development that Hanoi had long factored into its war strategy. In November 1967, not long before leaving the Administration, McNamara warned the President that all military measures implemented so far had not affected Hanoi's will to continue the fight:

"Nothing can be expected to break this will other than the conviction that they cannot succeed. This conviction will not be created unless and until they come to the conclusion that the U.S. is prepared to remain in Vietnam for whatever period of time is necessary to assure the independent choice of the South Vietnamese people. The enemy cannot be expected to arrive at that conclusion in advance of the American public. And the American public, frustrated by the slow rate of progress, fearing continued escalation, and doubting that all approaches to peace have been sincerely probed, does not give the appearance of having the will to persist." (Berman, 1989: 94)

On the basis of this analysis and his previously held belief that the war was a stand-off, McNamara again advised stabilizing the war effort and negotiating, predicting that otherwise Johnson would face public pressure either to escalate the war or to withdraw (Berman, 1989: 95). However, neither McNamara's analysis nor his recommendations were supported by Johnson's other main advisers, including the incoming defense secretary Clark Clifford, for the belief was still held by principal advisers such as Rusk, Rostow and the Joint Chiefs that the U.S. *would* prevail over the enemy, given time – although how much time was a moot point. Thus, working on the premise that the U.S. public should and could be persuaded to offer more backing for the war for a lengthy period, the Administration quite deliberately broadcast reports of progress in the war in order to counteract the public's impression of a stalemate and to keep them 'on board' and supporting the President.

1968: the credibility trap

Unfortunately for the Administration its calculations about both the war and public support were rendered redundant almost as soon as the new year began, when it faced two of its most important crises since entering the war: the siege of Khe Sanh beginning 20 January and lasting until mid-April, and the Tet Offensive which started on 30–31 January and continued in Hue until 26 February. Initially it was the attack on the U.S. base at Khe Sanh which appeared to be of vital import, for it carried strong overtones of the 1954 battle at Dien Bien Phu, when the French were decisively defeated by Ho Chi Minh's forces. Well aware of this frightening precedent, and acting on Westmoreland's advice that this was a 'critical area' both militarily and psychologically, the Administration was determined to win this battle and instructed the military to hold the base using whatever resources were required. Until the end of January the war, and war reporting, revolved around this siege, which was a ferocious battle that could well have fitted in with the prior intelligence that the U.S. military command had had about North Vietnamese and Vietcong plans for a forthcoming major attack (Berman, 1989: 139–44).

So, when the Vietcong and North Vietnamese then launched assaults on virtually every major city and provincial capital in South Vietnam during the Vietnamese New Year on 30–31 January, and even attacked the U.S.embassy compound in Saigon, the degree of surprise and shock was considerable, due not only to the timing, but also the scale, coordination and ferocity of the attacks. For it was not until 10 February that most of the towns and cities (including Saigon) that had been overrun were retaken – while the old Imperial capital of Hue was held by the Vietcong for almost a month. Furthermore, the offensive was undertaken mainly by the Vietcong with the assistance of only '20 to 35 per cent' of the North Vietnamese forces 'employed as gap fillers' (Sheehan et al., 1971: 593), thus undercutting the theory that the war was primarily one of 'Northern aggression' and as such was mainly fought by the North Vietnamese Army.

In view of the rebuttal to previous estimates and predictions provided by the Tet Offensive, it was hardly surprising that one of the outcomes was another U.S. policy review, because although the offensive proved to be a military, and to some extent a political reversal for the Vietcong – who had not only sustained fairly heavy casualties in the fighting, but had also committed appalling atrocities against the population on a wide scale during this period – psychologically it was a success for them and a disaster for the Administration. And it was a disaster that the latter had helped to fashion, for the fact that both Khe Sanh and the Tet Offensive assumed an importance far beyond their military significance can be attributed in part to the Administration's public relations campaign, stressing progress in the war only a month before these attacks were launched.

The catalyst for the last major policy review of President Johnson's administration was yet again a request from Westmoreland for more troops to cope with the consequences of the Tet Offensive. Under prodding from General Wheeler and the other Chiefs of Staff, Westmoreland asked for another 206,756 men, which would take the total number of troops to 731,756 by the year's end. As the Joint Chiefs well knew, these additional troops could not be safely provided and kept in the field without a Reserve call-up, so in effect Westmoreland's request was being used to pressure the President again into acceding to the Joint Chiefs' desire for such a call-up (U.S. Department of Defense, 1971, Book 6, vol. II: 148–9). However, the attempt eventually backfired, for after sending an emergency force of 10,500 men the Administration then engaged in a protracted, bitter and temporarily far-reaching debate on U.S. policy (until Richard Nixon was elected as President) in Vietnam which finally culminated in President Johnson's decision, transmitted in his 31 March speech, to de-escalate the war by cutting back the bombing to the 20th parallel, seeking peace negotiations, and bowing out of the presidential election race.

Given the previous history of official decision-making, which had so far led almost inexorably towards escalation, the crucial question is: why did the President and his advisers finally start to de-escalate? The record of the discussions and memoranda leading to this outcome are revealing, for despite the manifest failure of U.S. policy to date, after the earliest policy review in the first week of March, presided over by the incoming Defense Secretary Clark Clifford, the Joint Chiefs actually appeared to have prevailed over the civilian 'doves' in the Pentagon and the President was advised to deploy 22,000 more troops, reserve the decision on deploying the other 185,000, approve a Reserve call-up of 262,000, increase the draft and extend service, and not to engage in a peace initiative (Sheehan et al., 1971: 603–4)! However, between this review and the last major – and critical – review involving the 'Wise men' (the Senior Informal Advisory Group) there was a considerable deterioration in the domestic political standing of the President, with the narrowly unsuccessful challenge from Senator Eugene McCarthy in the New Hampshire Democratic primary, followed by Senator Robert Kennedy's decision to challenge Johnson for the Democratic nomination. Added to this was an increase in public pressure over the war after the press publication of both Westmoreland's 206,000 troop request and the later decision to send more troops, and televised Senate Foreign Relations Hearings on foreign aid with Secretary of State Dean Rusk being questioned for two days solely on the war. And to complete this picture of Presidential woes a Resolution was sponsored in the House of Representatives pressing for a total review of Administration policy on Vietnam.

Thus, when Johnson requested the views of the Wise men, as he had done at previous stages of the war, it was not only in the aftermath of the Tet Offensive but against this background of continuing domestic disarray. In the past the majority of these senior advisers, comprising former Administration, army and civilian life luminaries, had always advised Johnson to continue the war, not to de-escalate, and only to negotiate on U.S. terms. So the advice they now tendered on de-escalating, after briefings by Administration officials, was in fact a complete volte-face, representing a victory of the group of disenchanted civilian Administration officials over the military and their Administration sympathizers. As a *Pentagon Papers* analyst points out, the bleak prognosis now presented to Johnson himself finally forced him to abandon his incremental, consensual approach to the war:

> "In March 1968, the choice had become clear cut. The price for military victory had increased vastly, and there was no assurance that it would not grow again in the future. There were also strong indications that large and growing elements of the American public had begun to believe the cost had already reached unacceptable levels and would strongly protest a large increase in that cost.
>
> "The political reality which faced President Johnson was that 'more of the same' in South Vietnam, with an increased commitment of American lives and money and its consequent impact on the country, accompanied by no guarantee of victory in the near future, had become unacceptable to these elements of the American public. The optimistic military reports of progress in the war no longer rang true after the shock of the Tet offensive." (Sheehan et al., 1971: 611–12)

Thus there is no doubt that the Tet Offensive was a vitally important factor in this major change in Administration policy, and there is a particular irony in that after three years of using the bombing as a blue chip bargaining counter, it was now to be curtailed with no expectation of any quid pro quo from Hanoi in the shape of a negotiation offer! Not surprisingly therefore both supporters and critics of the war see the Tet Offensive as a turning point, but opinions differ on the reasons for its impact: for some observers (see Braestrup, 1978) it was the media misinterpreting the carnage as victory for the Vietcong/North Vietnamese which turned Tet into a public relations disaster for the Administration; whereas others viewed the Vietcong/North Vietnamese ability to actually mount the offensive as the crucial factor, proving their will and capability were more or less unaffected by three years of bombing and ground operations and that Tet, as well as being a propaganda disaster, also proved that the war was indeed stalemated. Whatever the interpretation, the mere fact of the offensive added to the Administration's famed credibility gap, while the cheerful tone of Administration propaganda beforehand heightened the contrast between its own rhetoric and harsh reality.

Amidst this confusion and gloom however, and confounding the pessimism of the Administration, President Johnson's offer to negotiate was taken up by the North Vietnamese on 3 April. And even the subsequent public disagreements about where peace talks would take place (Paris, ultimately), who and with what title would be included in the delegations, and, of course, the shape of the table, could not obscure what appeared to be happening, if erratically: that both sides were now working towards a peaceful settlement and that the spectre of a seemingly endless war was receding.

Unfortunately the reality, as always with Vietnam, was even more complicated than the confusing public image, for the peace negotiations had resulted not only from battlefield calculations but also from domestic political calculations, and the latter bedevilled the arrangements. In short, South Vietnamese President Thieu was encouraged by the election team of Republican Presidential candidate Richard Nixon to obstruct the peace process, thereby prejudicing Democratic Vice-President Hubert Humphrey's chance in the Presidential election. Thus on 31 October, when President Johnson announced both a complete bombing halt and 6 November as the date for the opening session of the Paris peace talks, Thieu firstly declared his disapproval and then the following day publicly refused to participate in the talks. Not surprisingly this severely embarrassed the Johnson Administration, undermined U.S. public confidence in the peace talks, and thus aided Richard Nixon's election campaign (see Hung and Schecter, 1986: 23–9).

Despite the uncertainty now surrounding the talks, Nixon had still been elected to take the U.S. out of the Vietnam War, for this had been the clear message from his campaign, though he had refused to provide details of how he would achieve his '"honorable" bargain' (Ambrose, 1989: 142–4). In the event there was to be a further four years of war before any sort of 'bargain' was achieved, honourable or otherwise.

2

Propaganda I: theory, strategy and history

Propaganda is a phenomenon that has spawned many definitions, for it is a form of communication and activity that is difficult to define from other forms of communication and this alone generates considerable argument, whilst the pejorative connotations that attach to the term 'propaganda' serve to ensure continued efforts to develop just such a definition so that other types of 'information' activities such as education or persuasion are not tarred with the same brush. However, there are also definitions of 'neutral' terms such as 'information' and 'communication' which have within them an element of suppression and manipulation and influence, thereby blurring the distinctions between propaganda and information (see essays by Anatol Rapoport and Warren Weaver in Smith, 1966: 43, 15–16). Adding to these difficulties there are also some scholars who believe that propaganda in modern society is so complex and ubiquitous that it cannot be defined accurately – or necessarily distinguished from other types of communication – and thus such attempts at definition are fruitless (see Ellul, 1965: Preface).

However, whilst acknowledging these problems this study will not add to the definitional arguments, if only because the context of this study – war – predetermines the use of propaganda. But, because there is a need for some guide to the most common elements of 'propaganda', the amoral definition of propaganda formulated by Jowett and O'Donnell will be used: 'Propaganda is the deliberate and systematic attempt to shape perceptions, manipulate cognitions, and direct behavior to achieve a response that furthers the desired intent of the propagandist' (Jowett and O'Donnell, 1992: 4).

Although this definition covers all types of propaganda and all propaganda techniques – from positive to negative propaganda and from accurate information to lies – and is thus satisfactory for analytical purposes, the derogatory meaning that is popularly attached to 'propaganda' means that governments in Western democracies prefer to refer to their 'information programmes' rather than their propaganda output. And whilst this is obviously a matter of substituting more popularly acceptable terminology – for Western democratic governments most certainly use propaganda, in which information plays a part – nevertheless the underlying moral and political principles on which Western democratic societies are based restrain, or are supposed to restrain the information/propaganda *techniques* that these governments may routinely use (total war is the exception to this precept).

This view has been supported by propaganda theorists such as T.H. Qualter who, whilst formulating an early neutral definition of propaganda and the modern-day propagandist's task, excluding as irrelevant 'considerations of the moral or political nature of those ends [of the propagandist] or of the means he adopts' (Qualter, 1962: 29), nevertheless arrived at a totally different conclusion when considering the role of a propagandist in democratic society. For Qualter, the 'basic ideals' of the democrat limited the propaganda techniques that could be used:

> Although he may colour his material to give it more popular appeal and to make it stand out in a competitive background . . . he cannot adopt practices that would make a mockery of his professed belief in the worth of human dignity. He must eschew tactics which would go beyond mere recognition of human weaknesses, which would tend to to the further debasement of political morality. The moral limitation on the propaganda techniques available to the democrat is of fundamental importance in separating a democratic from a non-democratic approach to the use of propaganda. (Qualter, 1962: 152)

Considering these two approaches to 'propaganda', the latter does seem to sum up popular feeling in Western society about the use of propaganda/information, even externally. And the consciousness of the dividing line between democrat and non-democrat does seem to extend to some propagandists too. Even when 'information' techniques have been within the accepted boundaries, an extension of their role has been seen by some propagandists themselves as contravening the democratic ethic. Robert Elder's study of the United States Information Agency (USIA) pinpointed the problems:

> In January 1967, Agency officials just back from Vietnam or about to visit there considered the level of USIA operations in Vietnam annd Thailand fascinating, but were ambivalent in their feelings as to whether USIA should be carrying out what would normally be the domestic information activities of foreign governments. In fact USIA was drawn into its contemporary role because the job was not being done locally; and while the Agency is not really qualified to conduct such activist policies, it is in a better position than any other agency to do the required job, which supports the military effort, though directed at civilians. (Elder, 1968: 21)

Internally, the spectre of Hitler and Goebbels and the loud condemnation of the techniques that were used by communist regimes has ensured that Western democratic governments usually preserve a relatively low-key approach when 'educating' their publics. And of course the ideas and information that these governments disseminate are by no means the only viewpoints and facts to be aired publicly. As well as political opposition and interest groups of every variety, the media themselves, which carry the government's message to people, also offer comment and criticism. Obviously there is a difference between these information centres (government and groups) in the ease with which the government and its agencies can command attention and make their views known simply by being the national focal point. Only the media can make their views known with this ease – other groups must compete for attention and coverage. However, on the whole modern Western democracies do foster and disseminate a plurality of opinions. This is one of the most fundamental attributes of a democracy – the obvious expression of freedom and the initial safeguard against political repression, which fact is recognized by those who seize power undemocratically, for their first actions are to establish and subsequently maintain an absolute monopoly of the instruments of communication and suppress any expression of opposition.

However, the free expression of differences (articulated politically through the ballot box), so necessary to democratic life, is not the best mode of social and politial organization when fighting a war. For this is a time when unity and conformity are needed to project a national image of strength; an image which is of great practical and political value to leaders in this situation. The knowledge of a united nation in the background frees a leader to face an enemy and concentrate purely on victory (however defined) rather than facing two fronts at once – home critics as well as foreign opponents. In addition, an image of national unity offers little in the way of obvious targets to an enemy propagandist.

On the other hand, if national divisions and differences of opinion do emerge, as happens in a democracy, even in wartime, then this is an obvious weapon and weakness which may be exploited by opponents. Much of a professional propagandist's task is concerned with identifying, prior to exploiting, such divisions in the ranks of the enemy. If differences emerge quite naturally as a result of the political system, then not only is the propagandist's job made easier, but also the propaganda targets (in this case the divisions in society) are obviously authentic, whereas the professional propagandist's speculations about possible differences in another society may be incorrect.

During the Vietnam War, the U.S. anti-war groups and the arguments used to criticize U.S. involvement in the conflict were of value to the North Vietnamese and Vietcong. Here were ready-made divisions to exploit and arguments to use in addition to their own propaganda lines. This was probably doubly welcome in view of the vast differences in culture and society between America and Vietnam, which would pose the first problem for a propagandist: understanding the enemy environment in order to attack it most effectively. The corollary of this, though, is that a wrong assumption on the part of a propagandist and the resulting dissemination of a 'wrong' propaganda line to another society (and sometimes within the propagandist's own society) can have the effect of strengthening an opposing united front (or hardening internal opposition) where such unity might previously have been fragile. The other result is to diminish the effectiveness of future propaganda, according to the gravity of the original error (for a discussion of psychological warfare, see Qualter, 1962: 102–37).

In a state of war a liberal democracy is thus at a practical disadvantage compared with more tightly controlled regimes, which practise state censorship as a matter of course and suppress opposition, and can therefore create an impression of national unity whether or not it actually exists. When liberal democracies do introduce government censorship it is an obvious departure from the norm, requires justification, and may be regarded with suspicion. Nevertheless, it has been tolerated in wartime: justified on the grounds of denying the enemy information which might be useful in any way – a definition which can be interpreted very widely. And censorship can aid a propagandist considerably, allowing him (or her) to create the optimum picture of his own state and supress the dissemination of disturbing features – for example, low morale or any difficulties experienced in maintaining the war effort, or containing the spread of enemy propaganda (total censorship being practically impossible to achieve in any society).

Given that liberal democracies have practised state censorship in war, even though this strikes at the foundations of democracy, the question must be asked as to whether there are different 'types' of war which make it more, or less, easy to justify – and to be accepted as justifying – censorship and the loss of certain democratic rights. (For a portrayal of censorship in Britain during the Second World War, see Balfour, 1979: 57–63, 78–9.)

The sort of wars that have been waged twice in this century – the total wars of the First and Second World Wars – were seen by the democracies as justifying the sacrifice of all activity except that directed to pursuing and winning the war. The loss of virtually complete freedom of expression, or the monopoly of information output by the government, were accepted as part of the war effort. In the Second World War particularly, the danger to the nation was felt to be sufficiently acute (bombs do speak louder than words) to warrant the suspension of some democratic rights in order that the battle might be fought more effectively and thus allow the nation a better chance of survival.

This was the crux of the Second World War and the mark of its distinction; it was a matter of survival in the face of a direct threat – physical destruction – and the longer-term threat contained in the thought of defeat: the destruction by this enemy, possibly once and for all, of the life and values accepted as of right. Both World Wars, however, had an element in common with many other conflicts: they began, nominally, because of treaty obligations. But in the case of Britain and France, especially in the Second World War, the initial threat to an ally (Poland) was perceived as the beginning of a threat to their own *physical* existence (see the general comments on the nature of the Nazi threat in Walzer, 1980: 245–53, 259). Whereas in other conflicts the correlation has not always been so direct and immediate between treaty obligations, requiring assistance to a beleaguered ally, and the threat to home territory. In other conflicts therefore, principles, without the threat of physical destruction, must be the basis for justifying the fight. This could have a number of consequences. Firstly, the reasons for fighting and the consequences of either victory or defeat may not be so clear-cut, and therefore the case for entering the conflict – that is, the precise nature of, and reasons for obligations to an ally – must be all the more clearly explained. This applies even if the conflict involves only a professional volunteer army and not conscripts. If conscripts are concerned then the need for clear explanation becomes even more acute, for the war then touches more than just those who choose the possibility of fighting and death as a job – the ordinary citizen becomes involved (for comment on consent for a war, see Walzer, 1980: 25–32).

Secondly, the very distancing of the conflict from home territory might tend to sharpen the focus on troop casualty rates and the reasons for the conflict. And thus, at a time when the political leadership may be emphasizing the need for a united stand, using the media to convey its message, the media might also engage in a debate on the conflict. For though the media may well support the leadership's position – and are quite likely to initially if only because the first interpretation of events is likely to be the government's – the capacity obviously exists from the beginning for government and media to pull in opposite directions. The initial factors likely to prevent this happening are the practical and emotional ones of backing the political leadership, particularly once it has set a course, and then backing the fighting troops. The urge to close ranks and not to undermine the war effort takes precedence and generates the endeavour to maintain morale at home and at the front. However, the length of a conflict, its nature and extent, and its remoteness (in terms of both distance and its isolation from domestic life) can make inroads on these emotional responses. This is a time when a more concrete/rational justification is most needed, in order to sustain emotion and morale. In particular the length of a conflict and troop casualties seem to be factors which can most affect public morale (see the report on the effect of casualties on U.S. public opinion in the Rand Corporation Report by Lorell and Kelley, 1985: vii, 16, 78; and Mueller, 1985: 155–67).

In some cases, for example the Korean War, high troop losses may act as a stimulant to continuing the conflict (assuming negotiation/withdrawal is an option), for once troops are killed it becomes that much more difficult to withdraw, because to do so would appear to invalidate their deaths. The common reaction is to plough grimly on in order to justify the losses and gain something from the investment in lives. But in some other cases, even though heavy losses have been incurred, the length and nature of the conflict and its effects on society have eventually resulted in a serious split between those wishing to continue ploughing on, and those prepared by this time to cut the losses. The Vietnam War was apparently the cause of such a split in American society, generating a considerable amount of public opposition, and helping to terminate Lyndon Johnson's presidency.

From even such a cursory analysis as this it is apparent that a number of factors may affect continuing support for, or hostility towards, such a war. It is the handling of these factors, their interrelationship and their effect on public morale that a propagandist seeks to control. Assessing the factors that a successful propagandist needed to take into account when planning a campaign Qualter listed the following: the size and broad intellectual level of the audience; the existing attitudes of the audience to both the situation envisaged by the propagandist, and their attitude to the latter himself; the extent to which the audience has access to the various media of communication; the presence of competing propaganda and other non-propaganda influences (Qualter, 1962: 75). These form the immediate factors with which, and the parameters within which, a propagandist must work. To a large extent, whether or not they are accurately assessed, they shape the propaganda message. And this is, or should be, a continuous process, taking account of the constant flow of information, about public opinion (at home and abroad, and including the media itself here) and about other governments' views. Only by checking reactions constantly can a propagandist assess whether his message is having the desired effect; whether changes need to be made and in which direction; and which rival influences at any particular time it will be necessary to counteract (see Jowett and O'Donnell, 1992: 68–70).

Within this broad framework both long-term/strategic aims and short-term/tactical manoeuvres are planned and executed. The long-term optimum aim for a propagandist must be to have his interpretation of reality/events believed by his audience – no easy task in a democracy with varied sources of information. However, even if his interpretation of certain incidents is queried, it is still vital (and still possible) to aim for, and maintain, the general long-term goal of credibility. Without this attribute, even if rival propaganda does not hold sway or begin to gain ground (though this is unlikely), no propagandist's message will be fully believed, or possibly, be believed at all (for discussions of credibility during the Second World War and the Cold

War, see respectively Balfour, 1979: 426–9; and Bogart, 1976: 128–41).

Assuming that an operational level of credibility exists (although, of course, the ideal is to control completely the picture that an audience receives) then according to the pressure of events, and, probably, other viewpoints – both fluctuating variables – the emphases in a propaganda message can be altered to explain or counter particular points. These are tactical manoeuvres, and they may or may not be incorporated into the long-term propaganda message. In an ideal propaganda world, whether or not they endure would be under a propagandist's control, but as the democratic environment is far from ideal – as should inherently be the case – it can happen that what was envisaged as a short-term propaganda palliative must become a long-term policy aim because the point is remembered and reiterated by influential members of the audience, for instance the media, or other governments. And if this happens it may considerably increase both the propagandist's difficulty in maintaining credibility, and the penalties of failure to do so. This certainly happened during the Vietnam War over the issue of negotiation. The U.S. Administration made a statement on this issue for a variety of reasons, partly tactical, partly as a response to public/media pressure, and thereafter had to relate its actions to its propaganda and keep interpreting many of its subsequent moves in the light of its publicly expressed attitude to negotiations. Ultimately the gulf between the Administration's views on negotiations and its ways of trying to achieve such talks – primarily through escalation – and its refusal of various opportunities for talks (for a variety of reasons which were not always entirely comprehensible to observers) proved impossible for the Administration to reconcile, or the public to accept.

The above forms the immediate working environment of a propagandist, but Qualter's fourth point contained a very important factor in addition to competing propaganda: 'other non-propaganda influences'. Into this category come a whole series of of inter-connecting factors, the most important of which is the international environment that a propagandist must work in. Interwoven are historical, political and economic factors which affect the way other nations view another nation's foreign policy or war. And the view held by others of a particular nation's policy can go some way to helping or hindering that nation in the achievement of its aims. To ensure that his nation's foreign policy is viewed as favourably as possible by other nations, these other factors must be taken into account by a propagandist. Not to do so – unless the opinion of allies is of no interest (a relatively rare phenomenon) – is to court disaster.

Organization of U.S. propaganda

The principal agency for disseminating U.S. propaganda abroad is USIA, with a headquarters in Washington, DC, and posts in U.S. embassies overseas. This is the agency which is effectively intended to support the U.S. Administration's foreign policy objectives, and more generally aims to 'sell' America to the rest of the world (Elder, 1968: 2–4). To aid USIA in its task of supporting U.S. foreign policy, USIA is represented in a number of committees and groups with a foreign-policy-making function and thus there should be a USIA contribution to the decision-making process about propaganda issues (see Black, 1969: 114–15). In theory this should provide an adequate framework for using USIA's expertise both on the likely reception of U.S. foreign policy decisions by foreign governments and publics and in planning and disseminating propaganda to foreign audiences, and for this expertise to have some influence on U.S. policy and its implementation. However, for a number of reasons it appears that during this period USIA's role in the foreign policy process was more that of a supporter of policies already determined by Johnson and his top advisers. The main reasons were that Johnson used the the formal foreign-policy-making machinery – in which USIA was represented – less than his predecessor, preferring a more informal style of decision-making, and he had little interest in USIA and its abilities (see Black, 1969: 115–18). Unfortunately this lack of presidential support impacted greatly on USIA's role and status, affecting its ability to carry out its duties adequately and coherently:

> The nature of the U.S. system of government places the focus of attention regarding the 'executive branch' on one man – the President. For USIA, relations with the President are particularly vital since the Agency's status and place in the execution of foreign policy largely depends on the Chief Executive's view of its role and the support he provides. The USIA has no domestic constituency or pressure group to fight for it and hence the need for Presidential support and interest becomes greater. (Black, 1969: 118)

Thus under Johnson USIA 'appeared to lose some of the "self-confidence" it had begun to show only very recently before' (Black, 1969: 118–19). Thomas Sorensen, a former deputy director of USIA during Johnson's Administration, put the case more bluntly, noting that Johnson viewed USIA as: 'an oversized mimeograph machine spewing out information, rather than as a source of expert counsel in Washington and a means of persuasion abroad' (Sorensen, 1968: 250; see also Rowan, 1991: 262–77). Endeavouring to arrive at an overall assessment of USIA's role in foreign-policy-making, after a reorganization aimed at strengthening the Secretary of State's role in March 1966, Black offered the following estimate:

> Apart from the knowledge that the USIA was a full member of these various groups, it is as yet difficult to assess the role it played in their proceedings. It is probable, however, that Agency participation did not have any great impact on the particular policies under consideration, but at least it provided an opportunity to bring foreign opinion factors directly into the discussions. (Black, 1969: 117)

Thus it appears that USIA, the Administration's formal propaganda apparatus, played a secondary, rather mechanical role during this period, with the President and his advisers maintaining firm control of policy. This estimate is corroborated in *The Pentagon Papers*, where there is considerable evidence of Johnson's top advisers considering the propaganda implications of decisions and planning the public relations/propaganda campaign accordingly. Also, as Black observed, the U.S. government structure concentrates attention on the President and therefore what the President, or his top advisers said, constituted the highest-level expression of U.S. propaganda – USIA spread the word. Thus President Johnson and his top advisers' speeches and activities, and their press briefings and those of the departmental spokesmen, informal talks with journalists, meetings with politicians, both domestic and foreign, all formed the fabric of the U.S. official propaganda campaign during the Vietnam War. Ultimately the primary burden of justifying U.S. involvement in Vietnam devolved on Johnson as Chief Executive. Thus domestic and foreign opinion focused on these speeches and press briefings and the press reporting and analysis of them. Although USIA did eventually assume a greater propaganda role in South Vietnam, elsewhere in the field the Agency often appeared ill-equipped to support U.S. policy if events in South Vietnam moved at a faster pace than Washington's policy-making – as frequently happened (for instance, the gas warfare episode mentioned below). In this situation not only was the Agency bereft of policy advice, but the policy-makers themselves were left floundering, and the U.S. propaganda effort suffered as a result.

However, there was one other role which USIA played in addition to trying to support U.S. foreign policy directly, and that was to act as a research service, commissioning public opinion surveys and analysing world media treatment of major issues from press, radio, television, wire service and Agency sources. Thus the Administration was supplied with analysis of foreign media and public reaction (for example, there were three relevant surveys of public opinion in 1965: U.S. standing in European and worldwide opinion [R-145-65 and R-176-65, in October and December] and on West European views on Atlantic Alliance problems [R-201-65, December]) to its policies and actions concerning Vietnam (USIA Archives, World Media Treatment of Major Issues, series beginning 1966).

The image of America

One of the major factors affecting the planning of a propaganda campaign is the way in which the propagandist's country is perceived by other countries, that is, its image. This is important because in general terms images can facilitate or hinder the implementation of a state's policies, for example by forming one of the factors influencing a state's behaviour towards another state. In forming an image of another state decision-makers take into account both the rhetoric and the current and past actions of a state (on images and perception see Jervis, 1970, 1976).

In the case of America, one of the most potent images aiding U.S. propagandists was that of American 'invincibility'. This image was created primarily by U.S. participation in the two World Wars, America being reckoned in each war to have made the decisive contribution that brought victory to its allies. Despite the post-Second World War complexities of relations with the communist countries and occasional diplomatic 'defeats', at the time that U.S. involvement in Vietnam deepened into combat in 1965 America was popularly credited with never having 'lost' a war. In addition to this, the other enduring image associated with America, resulting from its history and strengthened by its participation in the Second World War against Hitler, was that of a state which pursued 'just' causes. Thus American involvement in Vietnam could be seen in the framework of past American actions, aimed, it was believed, at promoting 'justice' and ultimately 'peace' (an assessment reflected in USIA's October 1965 survey of U.S. standing in worldwide opinion, R-176-65).

The foundation of American invincibility lay in America's wealth and economic power, expressed in the form of world-wide commercial concerns, level of technology and possession of nuclear weapons. By virtue of the latter America was a superpower, a determining force in international relations along with the U.S.S.R. However, the image created by U.S. wealth and technology was a double-edged weapon for U.S. propagandists. On the one hand this wealth bespoke huge resources to pursue such policies as the U.S. chose to espouse – including the Vietnam War – thereby adding to the image of will and capability. And on the other hand America's huge wealth could be seen as conferring a disproportionate advantage in a *regional* conflict, that is, America could be viewed as a rich 'bully' when facing smaller, poorer nations. Also, America's far-flung commercial ventures, while being a natural part of a trading nation's concerns, could easily be portrayed as global exploitation and neo-colonialism by America's opponents. Overall, American wealth could be seen to be supporting an increasingly interventionist role in world affairs against the background of America's post-Second World War foreign policy of 'containing' communism. It was primarily this image of American wealth allied to an active foreign policy that frequently activated the latent anti-Americanism in other countries, an emotion that U.S. propagandists had to try and counteract.

Another important factor in the American image in the 1960s was the battle over civil rights. The civil rights disturbances forcibly highlighted the inequality and discrimination that existed in American society and focused attention on a particularly unsavoury aspect of it. Much of the propaganda explaining U.S. support for South Vietnam, for example the claims about fighting for democracy and freedom, contrasted very strongly with events in America itself where a section of society was still fighting for basic democratic rights.

Propaganda strategy

The manner in which the Administration entered this undeclared and remote war during peacetime and the fact that the U.S. did not wage total war, together with the type of war fought, had a great impact on the information campaign that the Administration pursued at home and abroad. Of course, propaganda policy was meant to complement the Administration's war policy. The results frequently backfired, but the initial aim, as with any such campaign, was to control public opinion and to create a climate enabling the Administration to prosecute the war to its desired pattern. However, as the war dragged on the Administration's aim, rather than controlling public opinion, became increasingly that of placating public opinion.

Continuing the low-key approach that had characterized past American involvement in South Vietnam, Johnson's Administration initiated an information campaign that laid great stress on information about the enemy – their culpability, tactics and ultimate aims – but which said far less about the Administration's aims and tactics. The former stress would be expected, in order to explain the reasons for the Administration's overall policy, but the lack of detail about the Administration's own policy was intended to conceal its plans for escalation and also to avoid any possibility of public pressure (Sheehan et al., 1971: 338, 382). The aims that the Administration laid claim to in the early stages of the conflict in 1965 appeared to be quite modest: honouring its commitments (and previous U.S. Administrations' commitments) to South Vietnam in the latter's fight to remain independent and free (see the President's 'State of the Union' message to Congress, 4 January 1965; cited in Stebbins, 1966: 4); standing firm against communist North Vietnam's aggression, although seeking 'no wider war' (see William Bundy address before Washington Chamber of Commerce, 23 January 1965; in Stebbins, 1966: 128); and generally ensuring America's own security in repelling aggression in Asia. In Johnson's simple language, the U.S. goal was 'peace in Southeast Asia' which would 'come only when aggressors leave their neighbors in peace' ('State of the Union' message, 4 January 1965; Stebbins, 1966: 4).

These aims, as well as forming the Administration's early 'goals', also contained its initial public articulation of the Administration's perception of the conflict and will be discussed in greater detail later, when the accuracy and utility of these perceptions will be assessed. The point here is that though the Administration gave some indication of its aims and reasons for involvement in South Vietnam, nothing was said publicly about how these vague phrases were to be backed up. In this way the Administration laid the foundation for building up a picture of enemy aggression and infiltration into South Vietnam for its audience which would justify any future action of the Administration. At the same time care was taken to avoid either alerting or alarming the audience into thinking that a major war was in the offing. However, in case events should escalate, the blame for any escalation was shifted in advance on to the enemy, thus absolving the Administration of any war-like intent – hence the oft-repeated slogan of the Johnson Administration about seeking no wider war. Thus early U.S. official propaganda concentrated on establishing a pattern of enemy *action* and U.S./South Vietnamese *reaction*. This approach initially minimized the U.S. role in the war, both as an initiator of events and policies and also as a fighting partner in the conflict (see the President's message to Congress on 'The National Defense', 18 January 1965; and statement by Secretary Rusk, 25 February 1965; both in Stebbins, 1966: 19, 131–4, respectively).

This pattern of concentrating attention on the enemy was mirrored in the Administration's early method of presenting information during 1965. Announcements about enemy actions or broad statements on U.S. policy regarding commitments to allies or, later, on negotiations, were almost always the province of the top echelons of the Administration – usually the President or the Secretaries of State or Defense. Statements by these figures were of course guaranteed wide coverage by the media: the information – or lack of information – in their statements would be dissected carefully. By contrast, after the first reprisal bombing raids on North Vietnam in February 1965, which were announced by the White House and the President, information on the details of U.S. policy and actions on a daily basis, including the Rolling Thunder bombing strikes, was frequently relayed by relatively minor officials to the public. This would have been a normal enough arrangement in a conflict, except for the fact that some major U.S. policy decisions were introduced as mere changes in the details of current policy by these minor officials. This 'low-key' method of announcing major decisions frequently caused a furore in the press (and the domestic media uproar was often the subject of international media comment), thereby affording the Administration even more unwelcome publicity than would have been engendered by a top-level announcement.

For instance, it was via a routine press conference in June 1965 that the State Department *Press Officer* announced a vital change in the role of U.S. troops in South Vietnam, from static defence of U.S. installations, to combat. Although initially the new role of the U.S. troops was to support the South Vietnamese Army, when and where they were needed, this was recognized by the press to be the thin end of the wedge and to signal a major policy change. Not unnaturally the press, particularly in America, was uniformly astounded, and in most cases angry, to learn of this decision in this manner. This 'quiet' approach to public information by the Administration was also the subject of comment in British newspapers, though not in such caustic terms as the U.S. press, as befitted the press of a country which was not directly involved in the conflict – although for a variety of reasons Her Majesty's Government backed the Administration. However, even the *Daily Telegraph*, a stalwart supporter of the Administration's Vietnam policy, suggested in an editorial that President Johnson would have to be more 'communicative', especially now that casualties would start to mount, unless he wished to find himself in serious trouble ('Committed to Combat', 10 June 1965).

Occasionally this pattern of public relations varied (for example, the President's news conference on 28 July 1965, 'We Will Stand in Vietnam', on increased troop deployments to Vietnam, was one of the few times when a major Administration announcement did not provoke an equally major press explosion; cited in Stebbins, 1966: 178–83), but by and large the Administration's preferred strategy was to fight the war with as little publicity as possible, though of course negotiation offers from the Administration were usually well advertised. Unless a particular action was likely to be so dramatic that it could not be played down or disguised (and some of these types of action were not recognized early enough by the Administration), or unless the government had a particular reason for desiring widespread publicity, then camouflage was the usual practice.

The results of this policy were certainly criticized by the interested press in America and Europe at an early stage. However, this criticism, in most cases, was not initially levelled at the Administration in order to demonstrate opposition to it and the war, but to convey the feeling of confusion and uncertainty that the Administration was engendering in its audience, and to warn of possible adverse general public reaction if the Administration was not more communicative. Later in the war there was more general criticism, centring on the war itself and U.S. methods of fighting the war, for the European press did not have the emotional pressures to support the Administration and the war – come what may – that the American press obviously had (Britain was America's closest non-combatant ally, but by mid-1966 some British newspapers were turning against the war and British support for it). Though there was a feeling on occasions that the Administration was being less than forthcoming and telling less than the whole truth, it was not until the publication of *The Pentagon Papers* in 1971 that the extent of the Administration's efforts to control the public's perceptions of the conflict became apparent, and of course the meticulous planning accompanying most stages of the war.

So, for some considerable length of time the Johnson Administation was able to count on the goodwill of most of the press in at least America and Europe, resulting in a favourable interpretation being put on most Administration statements and actions. Any propaganda errors during this period therefore were purely the result of official ineptitude and miscalculation, not due to an intense and hostile public scrutiny seeking to stir up trouble for, or resentment against, the Administration and the war. Indeed, the feedback that the U.S. Government received through the media should have been of great practical value in alerting it to aspects of information policy which required modification. Yet in comparatively few instances did official statements appear at the right moment in relation to public comment. Undoubtedly this is a difficult exercise to accomplish without falling into the trap of being accused of making statements purely for press and public consumption, intended only to allay public fears and not intended to serve as a true indication of policy. But somehow the Administration, even though few of its statements were of such a timely nature, fell into this trap with consummate ease. By the end of 1966 the historian Arthur M. Schlesinger could write: 'Expansive rhetoric is the occupational disease of national leaders. But serious leaders preserve a relationship, however tenuous, between rhetoric and reality. One cannot remember a more complete disassociation between words and responsibility than in the United States Government today: Official speeches are always manipulative in part, but now they are almost nothing else' (Schlesinger, 1966: 87).

Fortunately the domestic press in America still generally supported the Administration's stated aims in South Vietnam and were therefore more inclined to give the Administration the benefit of any doubt – unlike Schlesinger – although their faith and patience were tried hard.

In brief the aims of U.S. official propaganda were: first, to persuade its audience to perceive the conflict as the Administration wished it to be perceived, whether or not this view coincided with the actual perceptions of the policy-making members of the Administration. Officially the war was a case of North Vietnamese aggression – backed by China – against South Vietnam. In setting the conflict within this framework the Administration required that its interpretation of a number of related facts be accepted: that the 17th Parallel marked the boundary between two separate countries, and that the North Vietnamese were therefore violating South Vietnamese sovereignty, that is, that the conflict was *not* a civil war. This view in return required a reinterpretation of the 1954 Geneva Agreements which had stated that the 17th Parallel was a temporary demarcation line, until reunification could be achieved. The assumption that the problem was caused by North Vietnamese aggression necessitated a new look at South Vietnamese history and politics, in order to minimize the political unrest in the south that had existed almost as long as the state itself, and to further deny the possibility that the conflict had an affinity with, and the roots of, a civil war. Additionally, the Administration obviously felt that it had to produce evidence for its audience of North Vietnamese aggression and infiltration (for instance, the Administration produced a booklet in February 1965 entitled *Aggression from the North*). This was expected to serve the purpose of absolving the Administration of responsibility for escalating the war: the blame for this was laid squarely on the North Vietnamese, while the Administration insisted that it simply reacted each time to a new, higher level of enemy activity. According to this view of events, it was assumed that enemy aggression conferred on the South Vietnamese the right to seek assistance from its ally America and thus translated their actions into self-defence (Administration speeches and announcements on the war invariably made this point, for example the President's 'State of the Union' message in January 1965 mentioned earlier, or his speech at Johns Hopkins University in Baltimore, 7 April 1965, cited in Stebbins, 1966: 140–7).

The second requirement of U.S. official propaganda was to convince its audience of the necessity for, and importance of, this war and the increasing U.S. commitment to it. All wars must be justified to those who fight them, even those wars in which the population is under physical attack and in which immediate catastrophe would follow defeat. A war fought as far away as Vietnam was from America, in a land to which America had not had a long-standing commitment, and during which the American population would never be attacked, required careful handling from the start. Thus the Administration emphasized the importance of the Vietnam War in an international context. The war was portrayed as a test case for all wars of national liberation rather than just a localized conflict, and was also effectively presented as being subject to the domino theory: to lose the Vietnam War, so the Administration's argument ran, would automatically expose the surrounding countries to communist subversion and subsequent conquest – regardless of individual conditions in those countries. The primary threat to U.S. and world stability was perceived to emanate from China, and according to the Administration what was threatened by Chinese ambitions in Southeast Asia was not only South Vietnam's independence but also U.S. national security and peace in general, and it was these high stakes that necessitated the commitment to Vietnam (see the President's Baltimore speech, or his request to Congress for more money for the war on 4 May 1965: 'Supplemental Appropriation for Vietnam', in Stebbins, 1966: 158–63).

President Johnson gave the impression of believing in this thesis, for in his memoirs the UN Secretary General U Thant observed after meeting Johnson: 'I do not remember having met any head of government so informal and warm toward me, and at the same time so juvenile in his concept of international developments. He once told me that if South Vietnam were to fall to the communists, then the next target would be Hawaii!' (U Thant, 1978: 59–60). The projection of a regional and then a global framework on to the conflict increased its importance beyond the immediate boundaries of the war. Those countries in the vicinity such as South Korea, the Philippines and two further away, Australia and New Zealand, felt themselves justified in actually joining in on the South Vietnamese side, on the assumption that if South Vietnam fell then they would be next in line. If, on occasion, a more concrete element was needed to provide justification, then the SEATO (Southeast Asia Treaty Organization) Treaty was cited as a legal basis for intervention, requiring that allies render what assistance they could to South Vietnam (for example, this Treaty was cited by Johnson in his 'Supplemental Appropriation for Vietnam' message to Congress mentioned above).

America's European allies, while far enough away to avoid being engulfed in the first wave of falling dominoes, nevertheless took a keen interest in the outcome and rendered all the verbal assistance that they felt America's efforts on their behalf demanded, apart from

France's President de Gaulle, who publicly deplored the U.S. commitment. Occasionally the Administration made it known that it considered its European allies and audience – especially the British – to be taking insufficient action towards securing their own future in the face of the communist menace: diplomatic solidarity was the least the Europeans could provide, but troops would have been a more convincing indicator that they appreciated the importance of the war (for instance, in December 1964 President Johnson asked for the assistance of a token British force, but Prime Minister Wilson refused; see Wilson, 1971: 48).

One of the problems in pursuing this propaganda line, though, was that while the Administration wished to raise its audience's consciousness of the war's importance in order to secure support, it did not want the audience too concerned about the possibility of a general conflagration resulting from America's involvement in Vietnam. Not, that is, if this resulted in public discussion of a possible Third World War and so generated pressure on America to negotiate, rather than the Administration's desired outcome of generalized pressure on the communists. This was a classic case for a test of a propagandist's skills: the need to be able to arouse a sufficient degree of fear/concern in the audience and then to be able to control and channel this concern in the way desired by the propagandist, that is, to support the propagandist's policies.

The other strands in the Administration's arguments on the value of the war centred on its commitments to its South Vietnamese ally and, by extension, its commitments to its other allies. The Johnson Administration justified its actions partly by referring to three previous Presidents' pledges to South Vietnam, stating that this present Administration had inherited the problem of Vietnam, not made it. The corollary to this view was that while the current policies for solving the Vietnam problem might differ in degree from previous policies, nevertheless they were essentially of the same kind. This line of defence was used by the Administration against any observers who questioned in any way the commitment to South Vietnam (the substance of such questioning is discussed later) and for a while this explanation was generally accepted by its audience (see Presidential Press Conference, 13 March 1965, cited in Kearns Goodwin, 1978: 275–6). Elaborating on this theme U.S. official propaganda also wove in the idea that if the former commitment to South Vietnam were to be reneged on, then other allies around the world would immediately begin to doubt the American will to honour other treaty obligations.

Defeat in Vietnam might then cause these same nations to doubt the American capability to help others (see Johnson's Baltimore speech, 7 April 1965, in Stebbins, 1966: 140–7).

Thirdly, the last broad goal of the Administration's propaganda effort was to try and convey the lasting impression – despite any actions pointing to a different conclusion – that its intentions were peaceful and that the use of force was a justified last resort. In this way the escalation of the conflict was blamed on the communists: if the Administration desired peace, then war was obviously not its fault. Subsequent escalatory steps were similarly explained away, with the added justification that each step was in search of peace (see '"Appraisal of Current Trends": Statement by the President at LBJ Ranch, Johnson City, Texas, April 17, 1965', in Stebbins, 1966: 149–52). And the Administration certainly hoped that each new escalatory step *would* bring 'peace' – on its terms (as *The Pentagon Papers*, noted in Chapter 1, make clear). The danger was that observers would finally realize that the Administration's actions could only be perceived as straightforward escalation rather than 'peace' steps or reaction to communist-originated escalation. This in turn would pose a problem for the Administration on the issue of negotiations, for if U.S. policy was perceived to be offensive rather than defensive then observers might also perceive U.S. policy itself as an obstacle to negotiations, and public pressure could then build up for the Administration to modify its policy in order to achieve such negotiations.

The lack of negotiations was publicly said to be the result of communist intransigence. The explanation for the communist attitude tied in neatly with the Administration's views on escalation. It was agreed that as long as the communists felt they could win the war outright (the monsoon season was said to be their best period) then they would not negotiate. So the logical outcome for U.S. policy of such a projection of the communists' strategic thinking was to demonstrate to them that they could not achieve a military victory. Hence the numbers of American troops poured in and the progressive tightening of the screw through air-strikes: it was argued that once the North Vietnamese realized the error of their aggression and ceased fighting, then the Administration would stop the bombing that the communists had necessitated in the first place (see Stebbins, 1966: 158–64; also Kearns Goodwin, 1978: 300–1, 302–6). Prior to the 1968 Tet Offensive there were four bombing pauses during Johnson's Administration, in the course of which the Administration said that it was waiting for a sign from the North Vietnamese that they were willing to bargain, but for one reason or another privately, and one reason publicly – the communist refusal to negotiate – these opportunities, if such they were, came to nothing (see Chapter 1).

To further complicate the issue of negotiations – and this issue did appear murky despite the Administration's repeated attempts to simplify it for public consumption – the attitude of China was initially assumed, by both the Administration and observers, to be crucial in determining the success or failure of negotiation bids (see '" Four Steps to Peace", Address by Secretary Rusk Before the American Foreign Service Association, June 23, 1965'; cited in Stebbins, 1966: 167–76). In addition, as Soviet aid to the North Vietnamese increased, the Administration had to ponder the Kremlin's ideas of what was in Hanoi's, and its own, best interests. The practical effect of apparently having to deal with at least two, and sometimes three countries' ideas on negotiations should have been a propaganda bonus for the Administration. For some considerable time it was, because the confusion and disagreement concerning the issue of negotiations that surfaced publicly from time to time between the communist countries involved – particularly in the context of the ideological rivalry between Russia and China – was perceived to constitute an obstacle that would have to be overcome before negotiations could start. And while Hanoi was seen to be heavily influenced in its policy by Peking, which flatly rejected talks, then the Administration hardly needed to say much more to be able to put the onus on the communists for the lack of progress towards negotiations. While this was happening communist statements were invaluable for U.S. official propagandists.

The historical themes and devices that were used in U.S. official propaganda to help build up the desired image of the war will now be discussed in detail, together with some of the problems that U.S. official propagandists faced in using these analogies. There were of course other problems that the propagandists had to tackle – some were simply a part of the war, while others were created by the propagandists – but those problems will be discussed in the next chapter.

Historical aspects and analogies

The Geneva Agreements of 1954

The most striking feature of both the American and the North Vietnamese public negotiating positions was that they agreed that the Geneva Agreements of 1954 formed an acceptable basis for peace. Both countries argued that if the other side had honoured these Agreements then there would have been no conflict, and hence a return to the Agreements now would remove the cause of hostilities. However, this was as far as their mutual understanding extended: their interpretations of the provisions of the 1954 Agreements differed radically, as might be expected of opponents claiming the same source of authority for their actions.

The U.S. interpretation initially laid its greatest emphasis on the independence of South Vietnam – as a political entity. Thus the provisional demarcation line of the 1954 Agreements became an international boundary for the South Vietnamese and Americans, and South Vietnam, rather than being a part of a temporarily divided country, became a sovereign state. Elections to reunite North and South Vietnam should have been held in 1956, but were not. The then head of South Vietnam, Ngo Dinh Diem, refused, with American support, to hold them, claiming that the conditions for free and fair elections did not pertain; that is, that North Vietnam would rig the elections. However, several times after Diem's repeated refusal to cooperate in the matter of elections, the North Vietnamese contacted the Geneva Conference Co-Chairman to complain about the deadlock and pressed for country-wide elections (Kahin and Lewis, 1967: 80–7). Whether or not the South Vietnamese and American claim about probable election-rigging could be supported by reference to the Geneva Agreements, the fact is that for future propaganda purposes the South's refusal to participate in any election arrangements was a decision that might be hard to justify in anything but a favourable climate of opinion. It was also a major potential, if not at the time actual, propaganda weapon for the North Vietnamese. While the American and South Vietnamese version of events was trusted, then factors such as these might remain hidden, or if known might be overlooked in favour of the overall American interpretation. However, these actions and interpretations could be difficult to defend when set against the provisions of the 1954 Agreements (for instance, French officials, as one of the original combatants signing the Treaty, were well aware of the provisions; and in the UK in April 1965, leaders in *The Guardian* contained early criticism of the Administration's interpretation of the Geneva Agreements).

Additionally, the Administration's method of handling infringements of the Geneva Agreement provisions was to highlight North Vietnamese violations while omitting any mention of its own and South Vietnam's transgressions. Again, while the Administration was trusted as a source of information on the conflict, then its version of this aspect prevailed; but there was easily available documentary evidence of the infringements committed by *both* sides in the dispute. This fact alone should have been enough to make the Administration take a more accurate approach to such allegations. However, not content with simply living with documents which could, if quoted in full, cause doubts to be registered which might influence attitudes to future official explanations, the Administration actually used one such report to buttress its own case. Through the simple expedient of quoting only selections of the International Control Commission's report dealing with North Vietnam, the sole blame for violating the Treaty and the origins of the war were traced back to the North Vietnamese decision to intervene in South Vietnam's affairs and to support the Vietcong (Kahin and Lewis, 1967: 130; see also Secretary Rusk's 'Statement on "The Bases of American Policy, February 25, 1965"', in Stebbins, 1966: 131–4).

This method used by the Administration to justify its course of action is a difficult one to handle even in the best of conditions. The 'best' of conditions would consist in the type of information control exercised by totalitarian or authoritarian regimes, where the *full* report would never be available to any section of the public, with the latter being fed merely selected quotations. For the Administration to try and use this method in an environment in which censorship could never be imposed on the relevant document, either at home or abroad, was short-sighted at the very least. Nevertheless, due to a general early presumption in favour of the American and South Vietnamese cause, this ploy worked with most observers, for a while. However, as with the earlier examples of American interpretation, this approach was quite obviously potentially damaging to the Administration – even more so, because this was deliberate distortion and, therefore, not even dependable as one government's perception/interpretation against another government's version. Again, this particular element was used as an important part of the Administration's arguments in proving North

Vietnamese culpability. However, once it was pointed out that that *both* sides had infringed the Geneva Agreements, then this alone could damage the Administration's credibility in the eyes of the public (for example see the *Observer*, 13 June 1965: 'Mr. Wilson and The President').

The lessons of Munich and Korea

The theme of aggression was a major component of the Administration's propaganda campaign. Obviously North Vietnamese aggression was the foremost element to be stressed, and its effects, if it was to continue unchecked, explained to the public. China's – and subsequently the Soviet Union's – support for the Vietcong/North Vietnamese immediately widened the scope of the aggression and the propaganda framework was correspondingly widened. The conflict was thus pictured as a vital episode in the fight to preserve freedom and democracy and to stem the advance of world communism. In this way the Administration linked and likened the onslaught of the communist 'bloc' to that of the Axis powers before and during the Second World War: 'Munich' was used as a propaganda device that operated on several levels (for a short, interesting, though arguable analysis of historical analogies used by the Administration, see May, 1973: 87–121).

Firstly, it was intended to recall explicitly the dishonour associated with that event, particularly since the Second World War: the betrayal of a country which led inexorably – the general feeling is now – to the later miseries of the war. By the same token it also summed up the short-sightedness of the policy of appeasement – not only was it dishonourable but it also failed to check the appetite of the aggressor; indeed, it merely increased Hitler's desire for, and expectation of, further triumphs. Thus the emotions of Munich – shame, failure and stupidity – were transferred and translated by the Administration into a *refusal* to commit the *same* mistake in the Vietnam War.

Secondly, the linkage of Munich and South Vietnam, in attributing to North Vietnam and China (and world communism) the expansionist and unlimited desires of Hitler's regime, was intended to legitimize American actions, not only on behalf of South Vietnam but also on behalf of other American allies throughout the world. The struggle in Indochina was invested with the same historical significance as the

Second World War, with the difference that the aim now was the prevention of another war on that scale, by, if necessary, fighting a smaller war first.

Thirdly, 'Munich' at the time meant the destruction and denial of freedom in one country and the later fight to retain freedom and democracy in others. Used in connection with South Vietnam, 'Munich' symbolized the will of, and necessity for, the Americans and South Vietnamese to fight for the same freedom and democracy, but without the initial betrayal that 'Munich' also represented. This particular analogy was much used in Administration rhetoric, whether the primary purpose of a statement was to stress peaceful intentions or a determination to pour men and money into the conflict: most Administration statements on the war included both of these elements. Two important occasions when Lyndon Johhnson used the 'Munich' analogy occurred during 1965. The first speech, in April at Johns Hopkins University in Baltimore, contained the Administration's offer of 'unconditional' discussions, but also included the following words:

> We are also there because there are great stakes in the balance. Let no-one think for a moment that retreat from Viet-Nam would bring an end to the conflict. The battle would be renewed in one country and then another. The central lesson of our time is that the appetite of aggression is never satisfied. To withdraw from one battle field means only to prepare for the next. We must say in Southeast Asia – as we did in Europe – in the words of the Bible: "Hitherto shalt thou come, but no further." (Stebbins, 1966: 140–7)

Approximately four months later at the end of July, in a news conference statement announcing an increase in the number of combat troops destined for South Vietnam, the necessity for additional troops later and, therefore, an increase in the draft over a period of time, Johnson again used the 'Munich' analogy as a justification and an emotional rallying call:

> We did not choose to be the guardians at the gate, but there is no one else.
>
> Nor would surrender in Viet-Nam bring peace, because we learned from Hitler that success only feeds the appetite of aggression. The battle would be renewed in one country and then another country, bringing with it perhaps even larger and crueler conflict, as we have learned from the lessons of history. (Ibid.: 178–83)

The use of such emotive events is intended to short-circuit thought among the audience – to produce feeling from hearing, not analysis. For along with the analogy – if it is at all apt or relevant – comes a set of emotions and values that are shared among the audience, if the correct calculations have been made by the propagandist. The danger of course when using this technique is that it is open to attack on the grounds that the sets of circumstances are totally different and have no bearing on one another – even if events bear a sufficient resemblance to make an analogy reasonably apt. The analogy is useful for only so long as it stirs up the required sympathy and identification with a cause. But if sympathy begins to wane in an audience generally and/or there are observers (who need not necessarily be critics) capable of analysing official rhetoric and of making their views known more widely, then this particular propaganda device constitutes probably the weakest link in the chain of arguments and the easiest to attack.

Korea – and also, sometimes, Greece, Iran, Turkey, the Philippines, Indonesia, the Formosa Strait, Cuba and Lebanon – which was at least in the same part of the world as Vietnam, was referred to as a successful example of curtailing aggression through firmness. Again, the use of this war analogy simply assumed that the two events, Korea and Vietnam, were similar. The picture was blurred by concentrating mainly on the aspects of aggression and freedom:

> In the Philippines, Korea, Indonesia and elsewhere we were on the side of national independence. For this was also consistent with our belief in the right of all people to shape their own destinies.
>
> That principle soon received another test in the fire of war. And we fought in Korea, so that South Korea might remain free.
>
> Now, in Vietnam, we pursue the same principle which has infused American action in the Far East for a quarter of a century. (Johnson to Congress, May 1965, in Stebbins, 1966: 158–63)

This statement was a masterly piece of obfuscation. South Vietnamese political wrangling was ignored, and the roots of the conflict were assumed to lie in aggression by another state – not a part of a temporarily divided country. By the same implication the principle at stake was the right of the South Vietnamese to their national independence. Finally, the differing nature of the two wars was ignored. The Korean War began through a straightforward invasion of South Korea and a series of conventional engagements, as opposed to the origins of the Vietnam War, which the Administration, despite its later propaganda, had earlier acknowledged to be an insurgency (see Sheehan et al., 1971: 433, 437; and Gravel, 1971, vol. 3: 304), but which it was now claimed was overwhelmingly a product of North Vietnamese and Chinese territorial ambition.

In addition the Korean experience was used when the subject of negotiations was raised by the Administration or discussed by the press. This example was cited both by observers who were general supporters of the U.S. involvement in the war, and those less enthusiastic about some aspects of the venture (see, for instance, Joseph Alsop's articles in the *New York Herald Tribune* on 19 and 20–21 November 1965; Alsop supported U.S. involvement but, from his hawkish standpoint and exasperated with the Administration's ambiguous public statements, he frequently exposed the 'contradictions' underlying the Administration's propaganda). The lesson learned then, and reiterated during the Vietnam War, centred on the negotiations in Panmunjom. These negotiations dragged on for two years during which time, it was felt, the communists took unfair advantage of the supposed lull and continued to wage war by way of numerous local engagements along the front line. Whenever negotiations were mentioned in the context of Vietnam, Panmunjom and the loss of American and allied lives was cited, or implied, to justify the Administration's pre-negotiation stance: cessation of North Vietnamese/Vietcong infiltration into, and activity in, South Vietnam before American bombing would stop and negotiations could begin on how to achieve a durable peace with an independent South Vietnam able to determine its own future. Notwithstanding these terms, the Administration publicly insisted that it was always ready for 'unconditional discussions'. But the Administration's stance was later undermined on two grounds: firstly that it was setting conditions for talks with the North Vietnamese; and secondly that while conducting 'unconditional discussions' the Administration would continue to bomb North Vietnam (see coverage of Johnson's Baltimore speech, supposedly containing an offer of unconditional discussions, in *The Guardian*, 9 April and the *New York Herald Tribune*, 10 and 11 April 1965).

The French connection

America entered into its commitments to South Vietnam by way of aiding the French in their effort to defeat Ho Chi Minh's communist regime, between the years 1946 and 1954. After the French defeat at Dien Bien Phu in May 1954 and the subsequent temporary partition of Vietnam, the Americans then became the principal supporters of South Vietnam. The French quietly faded from that scene to engage in the Algerian Civil War, which lasted until 1962. After the end of that war France became much more active in international diplomacy, re-emerging vigorously at about the time that the Administration's commitment to South Vietnam hardened into the aerial bombing of North Vietnam and subsequent actions.

The effects of the links between France, South Vietnam and America were important in propaganda terms. For the Americans could be seen as following in the footsteps of the French, who had fought a war against the Vietminh (Ho Chi Minh's supporters and guerrilla army) – after signing a Treaty in 1946 recognizing the Democratic Republic of Vietnam as a free state within the French Union. During the Second World War numbers of former colonies assumed that they would gain national independence once the war was over. Under Ho Chi Minh, the Vietminh had given some aid to the Americans against the Japanese, on the assumption that Vietnam would afterwards gain some form of autonomy. In addition, during that war America certainly championed the cause of national independence, which meant the disintegration of the colonial empires, primarily of France and Britain (Kahin and Lewis, 1967: 14–18). Yet from 1950 onwards America poured vast sums of money (paying for 80 per cent of the French war effort in Vietnam according to some estimates) into helping the French regain a foothold in part of its empire (Kahin and Lewis, 1967: 32). Of course America could claim that it was still supporting decolonization, for the French had been forced to take note of some nationalist demands and had set up a Vietnamese government in 1949. This, as Bernard Fall remarks in *Vietnam Witness*, transformed 'what had essentially been a colonial war into a *civil war*' (Fall, 1966: 13; emphasis in original). However, considering that the new Vietnamese chief of state installed by the French was the former Emperor Bao-Dai – who had even been retained in that capacity when the Japanese granted 'nominal' independence to Vietnam almost at the end of the Second World War (Kahin and Lewis, 1967: 18) – the new state and its head seemed both artificial and a creature of the French.

While the Cold War existed and various moves by the communist bloc added to the atmosphere of tension between East and West, then the American emphasis on the containment of communism as being the most important goal to pursue could be seen to be aimed at keeping other regions free – that is, non-communist. However, in pursuing this goal America would always be open to the basic criticism – and a criticism hard to counteract – that America's very foundations and ideals were being compromised in the types of regimes that the U.S. Administration was supporting in its anti-communist 'crusade' and in the effects on the countries in which the battles were fought. And where its commitment to Vietnam was concerned, the Administration was aware that America itself might appear to the Vietnamese people in the guise of the old colonial power of France (a concern expressed by U.S. Ambassador Taylor in a telegram to Secretary Rusk, cited in Porter, 1979, vol. 2: 364).

In addition to being labelled as France's successor in Indochina, the Americans had another spectre haunting them which gained public mention. This concerned the general chaos which constituted the First Indochina War, leading to the defeat of the French (for instance, see *The Guardian*, 26 April 1965: 'Sceptical Americans'). However, once the American war machine swung into action and despite the periodic gloomy media assessments of the war, it was expected that American military might would eventually prevail over the North Vietnamese and Vietcong. But, as the war ground on, seemingly ever more confusing and frustrating, doubts began to grow on this score and were publicly aired in the press (see, for instance, *The Times*, 6 January 1966: 'Pentagon Threat to Resume Bombing'; or Paris *Figaro*, or *Le Monde*, cited in USIA's World Media Treatment of Major Issues, weeks ending 15 August and 9 December 1966 respectively).

Thus there was a considerable historical legacy that U.S. official propagandists deliberately evoked for their own ends, but they also had to contend with the more unfavourable aspects of this history, in addition to a number of contemporary political problems which will now be discussed.

3

Propaganda II: political and military themes and problems

Political aspects

The Administration's view of China, national wars of liberation and the domino theory

Early in the war the most frequent method used by the Administration to connect the North Vietnamese with China was to lay the emphasis on North Vietnamese aggression backed by China. In this way China featured in most statements containing references to North Vietnam; to a large extent the two countries were treated as inseparable, as in Johnson's announcement on 28 July 1965:

> But we must not let this mask the central fact that this is really war. It is guided by North Viet-Nam, and it is spurred by Communist China. Its goal is to conquer the South, to defeat American power, and to extend the Asiatic dominion of communism . . .
>
> Our power, therefore, is a very vital shield. If we are driven from the field in Viet-Nam, then no nation can ever again have the same confidence in American promise or in American protection. (Cited in Stebbins, 1966: 178–83)

This version of events was sometimes reflected in the press and occasionally made its appearance in a stronger form in the U.S. press. In

November 1965, for example, the *New York Times*, after a brief reference to the growth of the war, stated in an editorial: 'All the time there are the Communist Chinese, sitting back calmly withouut losing a man; yet Communist China is the real opponent in Asia' (*New York Times*, 19 November 1965: 'The Disasters of War').

The corollary of the view of China as the real enemy or driving force behind North Vietnam was that when the question of negotiations was discussed, the attitude of China was assumed to be crucial. Given that Chinese rhetoric could only be described as abusive where America was concerned, the response of the Chinese to any American moves – whether these moves concentrated on war or peace – was generally predictable. This was of great value to the Administration, for after American bombing pauses or speeches about possible discussions, the Chinese could invariably be relied upon to heap scorn on these gestures, thereby exonerating the Administration's policy in the eyes of the West. The depiction of North Vietnam's refusals of U.S. negotiating terms, or peace moves, varied: sometimes Hanoi was depicted as following its own course in such refusals; sometimes the heavy hand of Peking was detected (for example, see press coverage of the communist response to Johnson's Baltimore speech in April 1965 in the *Observer* and *Sunday Telegraph*, 11 April; and *The Times*, 13 April). Whichever view was taken, the Administration's protestations that it was genuinely searching for a negotiated solution were believed for some considerable length of time (although the French were doubtful; see Sullivan, 1978: 75–80). This was no mean feat for a government which, to mention but a few incidents: initially *ruled out* negotiations in the early part of 1965; turned down a peace proposal in March of that year by the U.N. Secretary General; was publicly stated to be 'cool' towards its principal ally's (Britain's) peace efforts; and quoted conditions and stipulated an end result of negotiations – that is, South Vietnam's independence – terms which were largely characterized in the press, following the Administration's viewpoint, as 'unconditional' (see *The Times*, *Daily Telegraph* and *The Guardian* for February, March and April 1965).

From the view of China as the main driving force of North Vietnamese actions it was only a short step to the idea that the principle motivation behind American actions was the containment of perceived Chinese expansionism. This was a view that made its appearance in this form in the media (for example, see the *Observer*, 29 May 1966; also Sullivan, 1978: 76). However, any fears that the U.S. intention of frustrating China's aims might lead to war with China were countered by the Administration's insistence that it sought no wider war, and in practical terms by its careful control of the bombing of North Vietnam – away from the Chinese border. For, as stated previously, the U.S. Administration needed its audience to have sufficient knowledge of, and interest in, the war in order for it to support the Administration's viewpoint and actions. But what the U.S. Administration did not require, or want, was the level of interest and alarm that could be generated through the impression that America and China might be teetering on the brink of a shooting war.

As the war progressed, some members of the Administration developed a more subtle approach to China's role in the war and hence its regional and global role. But although the new approach loosened the virtually automatic link that had previously been made between North Vietnamese actions/aggression and Chinese influence, nevertheless it still tied the war neatly to national wars of liberation and via this to China's influence regionally and globally (the President's National Security Advisor W.W. Rostow publicly articulated this view when delivering the Sir Montague Burton Lecture at the University of Leeds on 23 February 1967, entitled: 'The Great Transition: Tasks of the First and the Second Post-War Generation'; White House press release, 23 February 1967).

This change in approach may have been helped by the great increase in Soviet aid to Hanoi from mid-1966 (see Sheehan et al., 1971, Document No. 117: 503) – although according to Kahin and Lewis, Russia had 'always been the North's principal supplier' (Kahin and Lewis, 1967: 190) – and also by the increasing acrimony between Russia and China (see Rupen and Farrell, 1967: 106–9). Bearing these factors in mind it could be argued that the earlier American view of China would have to have been modified to correspond more to this new reality. It could also be the case, however, that tying China so closely to the origins and progress of the conflict was counterproductive; that approach certainly helped to concentrate attention on the conflict and its wider implications, and this was not always useful to the Administration.

Thus the new propaganda line was an improvement on earlier versions. It was rather vague on China's exact role and was therefore more difficult for Administration opponents to challenge. Also it was probably a more accurate reflection of the then current situation, yet still incorporated one of the Administration's main propaganda lines on national wars of liberation.

The other main component of the Administration's view of the dynamics of Southeast Asian relations was the domino theory, and linked to national wars of liberation it was a mainstay of American official propaganda during the Vietnam War (see address by William P. Bundy, 23 January 1965: 'American Policy in South Vietnam and Southeast Asia', in Stebbins, 1966: 128; also Kahin and Lewis, 1967: 316–18). The concept of Southeast Asian nations being a row of dominoes that would automatically fall if South Vietnam was lost to communism was a rigid, mechanistic theory that took little account of each nation's individual circumstances, and it was therefore easily attacked on these grounds by critics. Nevertheless, the Administration still clung to this theory and it was used in various attenuated forms to explain and legitimize the U.S. commitment to the war, and also to recruit support for the U.S. involvement (for instance, the domino theory figured in the deliberations of the SEATO Council, see 'The Southeast Asia Treaty Organization: Communiqué of the Tenth Meeting of the SEATO Council, London, May 3–5, 1965', in Stebbins, 1966: 152–7; see also 'The ANZUS Treaty: Communiqué on the Fourteenth Meeting of the ANZUS Council, Washington, June 28, 1965', ibid.: 176–8).

The image of the South Vietnamese government and 'democracy' and 'freedom'

The major problem facing American propagandists concerning South Vietnam centred on the relationship between America and South Vietnam. American aid to its ally was on a vast scale; American force levels rose dramatically in 1965 and continued to rise until after the Tet Offensive in March 1968, as did the amount of weaponry that these troops wielded; and South Vietnam's economy was receiving huge amounts of U.S. aid (for an account of the impact of U.S. policies and aid on South Vietnam's economy, see Kolko, 1986: 199–207, 223–30). The only sphere of life which appeared to be free of American control was the political arena, and though nominally the most important sphere in national life, the result here was a mainly South Vietnamese shambles with American assistance.

In theory the relationship between the two states was that of sovereign equals and thus, at least publicly, American actions and rhetoric were limited by the attributes of South Vietnamese sovereignty. Additionally, because North Vietnamese and Vietcong propaganda always referred to South Vietnam as America's puppet state, it was necessary to counter this by stressing South Vietnam's independence of America. So the question of American influence in South Vietnamese affairs via America's aid and war effort was a delicate one for propagandists to tackle. Their task was to portray a *newly independent* nation, ready and willing to fight an enemy which was being heavily reinforced and armed by another *nation* – North Vietnam – and also equipped by outsiders, that is China and Russia; and all these circumstances thus laid the burden on America of helping its gallant ally in a hitherto unequal struggle. Impressions that America was the prime war-maker, even if these were a more accurate reflection of reality, were unwelcome. Yet even in the information field, leaving aside the battlefield, the Americans assumed the greater role, even in South Vietnam itself:

> In conducting massive psychological efforts to counter insurgency against the existing regime in South Vietnam, the Agency [United States Information Agency] is performing a role which would normally be carried out by a government with its own people. Although attempts are being made by USIA personnel to train local government officials to take over this responsibility, they are not as yet very successful, for the population of Vietnam is not too nationally oriented and lacks motivation to learn to do what USIA is now doing for it. (Elder, 1968: 20)

The assumption by the Americans of the major role in the information field simply on the basis of their greater experience would have constituted enough of a drawback, when they were trying to portray South Vietnam's independence and willingness to fight all aspects of the war. Still, had the Americans been acting primarily as tutor to a willing pupil then their lopsided relationship would have held some future hope of the South Vietnamese Government network running perhaps one aspect of the war on its own. However, judging from the above assessment by USIA officials, the South Vietnamese were both unwilling pupils and to a large extent lacked a sense of identity with their republic, proclaimed twelve years earlier. There is, of course, the possibility that these government officials were lukewarm about *South* Vietnam because they were more oriented to the concept of a wider nation which included the North. There is also the likelihood that the leadership in Saigon inspired neither confidence nor loyalty, being drawn mainly from the top echelons of society with a high proportion originally hailing from the North and adhering to the Catholic religion. (The original basis for the strong position of Catholic refugees lay in the use that Diem made of them to secure his own power base after he became head of state in 1955; see Kahin and Lewis, 1967: 72–5; also President Thieu and Prime Minister Ky were Northerners, see Kahin and Lewis, 1967: 166, 241; and a quarter of the officers in the South Vietnamese Army were from the North with Catholics comprising 'double South Vietnam's average' percentage, see Kolko, 1986: 209.) This all suggests that in addition to the gulf between the Saigon leadership and the mass of South Vietnamese peasants, there was also a divide between the South Vietnamese leadership and its own lower-ranking government officials.

Whatever the reason for this lack of South Vietnamese national feeling, American propaganda consistently emphasized those very qualities which USIA officials privately believed were virtually non-existent. And the U.S. Administration devoted much rhetoric to trying to convince its various audiences that South Vietnam was a *nation*. Here the Administration was, of course, caught in the usual cleft stick: to admit that the South Vietnamese were unenthusiastic about their nationhood destroyed one of the major pillars of American propaganda – that this was a case of a nation fighting for survival against an outside aggressor. The only way out of the dilemma was to stress the newness of the South Vietnamese nation and the difficulties caused by North Vietnamese aggression. A more sophisticated official explanation of American intervention in the war centred on the thesis that South Vietnam needed time to sort out its problems and American troops were helping to buy that time by staving off the North Vietnamese and Vietcong (for example, see *New York Herald Tribune*, 5 and 6 June 1965: 'Humphrey: Saigon Can Win If Given Enough Time'). Obviously this still left open the question of South Vietnamese 'motivation', or the lack of it, but as an explanation at least it avoided some of the pitfalls that previous statements were subject to and thus did not actively erode what credibility the Administration retained.

Logically the central part of American government propaganda should have been concerned with South Vietnam itself, for America claimed to be fighting to preserve South Vietnam's independence. Much of the Administration's propaganda campaign *did* revolve around South Vietnam, but rather than lauding the achievements of

South Vietnam, it was mostly aimed at counteracting the published details of the more unfortunate aspects of its ally's behaviour. Naturally the Administration would have preferred to say nothing about the darker side of its commitment, but in the absence of systematic censorship of information leaving South Vietnam the Administration was frequently forced into commenting on the latest press allegations about the South Vietnamese leadership or Army, and thereby added to the publicity and controversy.

One of the most prominent features of South Vietnamese political life, which could scarcely be ignored, was the tendency for unsatisfactory governments to be replaced through the machinery of the coup. In the last analysis the South Vietnamese Armed Forces were the judges of which particular faction should be in power at any given moment, while other political forces such as the Buddhists and students could, on occasions, create sufficient chaos to make yet another change of government inevitable or, alternatively, force their set of demands on the government.

During the first half of 1965 there were approximately eight severe political crises in Saigon, involving three changes of government. While 1966 began promisingly, with Prime Minister Air Vice-Marshal Nguyen Cao Ky offering a referendum which would lead to a new constitution and elections in 1967 for a civilian government, it then deteriorated with a political crisis beginning around 10 March that lasted until the middle of June. In order to regain control of Danang and Hue and quell the South Vietnamese dissident factions, the Saigon leadership had to use the South Vietnamese Army, and thus the world witnessed the elevating spectacle of Saigon's military junta attacking its own people with weapons provided by the U.S. to fight the war. While Hue was still under Buddhist control the United States Information Service (USIS) library and cultural centre and the U.S. consulate and Residence were attacked and burned in what were quite clearly anti-American actions, both disturbing and embarrassing. Previous U.S. official propaganda, portraying South Vietnam as a nation striving for democracy and endeavouring to create a new and better society, thus had a hollow ring to it by comparison with events in South Vietnam, and the Administration had the task of reconciling what was fundamentally irreconcilable: its words, and the South Vietnamese Government's actions. The answer was to stress the 'fledgeling' condition of the South Vietnamese nation, still struggling to achieve democracy in difficult times (Kearns Goodwin, 1978, vol. 1, 22 April 1966:

455). However, commentators tended to recall the long line of past crises, pointing out that this, and other crises, demonstrated just how little the Americans could influence events in general. In short, the image that South Vietnam presented to the world in the crucial early years of the conflict was one of chronic instability, with the war against the Vietcong and North Vietnamese taking second place to domestic political in-fighting.

This one aspect alone was enough to cause observers to question Administration statements that American troops were fighting to preserve freedom and democracy in South Vietnam. Also, Johnson's tactic, when under pressure to invoke the pledges that earlier administrations had made to the then South Vietnamese Government, was inclined to boomerang when commentators enumerated the changes of government that had taken place in Saigon and suggested that the original pledges to a specific government were rapidly becoming an open-ended commitment to *any* Saigon 'government'. When the Administration broadened the American commitment so that it embraced the South Vietnamese people, as opposed to just the South Vietnamese Government, this proved a scarcely more satisfactory way of either explaining American policies or deflecting criticism. For as observers pointed out, the wishes of the South Vietnamese people were hard to deduce from the political chaos in South Vietnam – unless the chaos itself was taken as an indication of their wishes – for South Vietnam was not a democracy and in addition the Vietcong and North Vietnamese controlled large portions of the countryside, so the chances of the people being able to express their true wishes were indeed remote.

The very fact that the Administration could state that to win this war it was necessary to win the battle for the 'hearts and minds' of the people suggested that at best the latter were uncertain as to where their sympathies lay. However, amidst this uncertainty, the Administration apparently detected signs that, but for the Vietcong use of assassination and terror, the South Vietnamese peasants would support Saigon and the Americans. Thus American propaganda emphasized repeatedly, for the benefit of its audience, lists of Vietcong assassinations of South Vietnamese Government employees and supporters and issued descriptions of Vietcong atrocities in order, amongst other aims, to help justify the Administration's assumptions about the sympathies of the South Vietnamese people (for example see William P. Bundy, address on 23 January 1965; 'American Policy in South Vietnam and Southeast

Asia', cited in Stebbins, 1966: 128).

As with so much American official propaganda these two potentially conflicting views of the South Vietnamese people's sympathies ran side by side: on the one hand it was necessary to win over the South Vietnamese, and on the other hand it was apparently obvious that only Vietcong coercion was preventing the South Vietnamese from declaring their allegiance to Saigon. Such unexplained contradictions in Administration propaganda invited dissection and ridicule by the Administration's opponents, or by those observers who found the Administration's approach to the 'truth' and 'information' too idiosyncratic. And when even such a stalwart supporter of the U.S. venture in Vietnam (as part of the fight against communist expansionism) as the *Daily Telegraph* felt obliged to express its disappointment over the political instability in South Vietnam in 1966, then it was obvious that the Administration had tied itself to a never-ending source of propaganda problems (as well as political, military and social problems): 'Each successive Government in South Vietnam has embarrassed its American allies either by being too authoritarian or by being too weak to rule. Marshal KY, it seems, has contrived to indict himself on both counts' (*Daily Telegraph* editorial, 17 May 1966: 'Marshal Ky's gamble').

Overall, the broad image of the U.S.–South Vietnamese relationship that was created by the South Vietnamese leadership's concentration on internal politicking was of America ensnared by a corrupt and unstable ally, whose people sometimes demonstrated a violent anti-Americanism. Unfortunately, even when this disquieting public impression was occasionally contradicted, and the Americans appeared to be influencing their unruly ally in a more acceptable direction, the improvement in image of either the South Vietnamese Government or the American Administration was rarely great and usually short-lived.

For example, in February 1966, approximately one week after the resumption of U.S. bombing raids and two days after the U.S. Senate Foreign Relations Committee began another round of open hearings on the Administration's policy in Vietnam, Johnson and his top officials held a conference in Honolulu with the participation of South Vietnam. The main theme of this meeting concerned economic and social reforms and the issue of pacification – that is, specifically non-military issues. Chester Cooper, who was the Assistant for Asian Affairs in the White House and was involved in the meeting, summed up its effects:

> The Conference was a success both in terms of reaching significant decisions and of establishing closer working relations between the top levels of the two governments. The Saigon Government, Ky especially, improved its image in the United States. But there was, nevertheless, a persistent feeling in Washington that the Administration had hastily contrived the whole affair to direct public attention from the bombing resumption. In addition many felt the Honolulu meeting had been a gimmick to steal the spotlight from Senator Fulbright, whose Foreign Relations Committee was just about to start a new round of Hearings on the Administration's Vietnam policy. The latter suspicion was given added credibility by the President's sudden decision on the last day of the Honolulu Conference to send Vice-President Humphrey on a trip to Asia to 'explain' the development at Honolulu. This applied particularly to our 'third country' allies in Vietnam who were annoyed at not having been invited. (Cooper, 1970: 300)

That there was suspicion about the timing and motives for this conference indicated again both the existence and the extent of the famed 'credibility gap' concerning the Administration, and of course added to it, while the clumsiness of Administration public relations was amply demonstrated in the abruptness with which the conference was called. As Kahin and Lewis wrote:

> Considerations of domestic U.S. politics evidently outweighed those of diplomatic courtesy and respect for South Vietnamese sensibilities, as Ky and General Thieu, Saigon's Chief of State, were summoned to this meeting with the President – on U.S. soil – a scant two days before the opening of the conference. (Kahin and Lewis, 1967: 243)

This manoeuvre was, as usual, only partially successful even in its most immediate objective of spotlighting the conference instead of the Congressional Hearings, for there was both domestic and foreign press comment later on the timing of the conference (see, for example, *The Times*, 10 February 1966: 'Cool Reception in U.S. For Honolulu Declaration'). The attempt to create an impression of two countries united in their fight against communism and in their desire for reform in South Vietnam, expressed in the Declaration and Joint Communiqué of the Honolulu Conference, was shattered the following month in March when a four-month-long political crisis erupted in South Vietnam. The use of South Vietnamese troops to recapture major South Vietnamese cities from rioting anti-government demonstrators, coupled with Johnson's public disapproval, contrasted strongly with the optimism and amity expressed in the Honolulu Conference (see

President Johnson's press conference on 21 May 1966, in Kearns Goodwin, 1978, vol. 1: 460). The irony was that the Administration had, by its own efforts and with great success in one sense, focused attention on South Vietnamese affairs and thereby highlighted the contrast.

By this time, after a number of years of collaboration with such a volatile and unstable ally, it should have been obvious to the Administration that predictions about future social and economic progress in South Vietnam were a hazardous form of propaganda. However, in this instance it seems likely that the Administration perpetrated an even greater blunder than it appears at first sight. For, according to Kahin and Lewis, the political crisis in March in Saigon was a direct result of the Honolulu Conference:

> The Honolulu Conference had serious and largely unanticipated consequences in Saigon. On the one hand, the prestige of the Ky government plummeted within South Vietnam as the story of the Premier's summons to Honolulu and his embrace by the American President circulated freely in Saigon. On the other hand, the conference encouraged Ky to believe that the United States was now so committed to him that he could act more freely against his rivals in the military junta. Ky obviously concluded that so soon after the Honolulu Conference Washington could not afford to withhold its backing from him. (Kahin and Lewis, 1967: 244)

But there was yet another facet to this particular crisis which also surfaced publicly – that this time the U.S. embassy in Saigon had been heavily involved in the political turmoil, having supported the Saigon government in its desire to remove Ky's popular military rival, General Thi. Thus the Administration was charged both with being inherently unable to prevent these outbursts, but also with having interfered, thereby helping to spark off this specific crisis. And effectively the U.S. Embassy in Saigon had helped to make a mockery of its own Government's propaganda on South Vietnam, revealing also the differences that existed on occasions between the U.S. Embassy's approach to South Vietnam's political affairs and the Washington Administration's approach. Such a syndrome was not without precedent. In broader terms the same political calculations had been made by Diem and the Nhus when they were in power; that is, that America was so committed to the fight against communism and had sunk so much money and prestige in South Vietnam and Diem that it could not afford to abandon them. Until Diem and Nhu's assassination in November 1963 these assumptions were fairly accurate and gave them a vast amount of leverage with Washington. Ultimately Washington did abandon this particular ruling clique, but only after years of increasingly desperate support (see Gravel, 1971, vol. 2: 201–7). And of course the U.S. embassy had also played a part in the events leading to the successful coup against Diem and Nhu.

Many of the Administration's problems with the South Vietnamese Government's image can be traced back to Washington's manifest inability to influence its ally's behaviour, to any lasting degree, in acceptable directions, concerning both the conduct of the war and internal progress in the country. Naturally preferring a government publicly committed to fighting the communists, even if privately engaged more in political manoeuvering, whether representative of the people or not, Washington helped to fashion a cleft stick for itself. For the Administration could not risk 'rocking the boat' through taking too tough a stance, such as for instance on internal progress. This was not only because of public commitments such as Ky received, but also because if the war was to be fought by any South Vietnamese units at all, then the additional political instability that a tough Administration stance might have provoked had to be avoided at almost any cost. So in order to counteract and explain its unpredictable conduct, South Vietnam was portrayed as a 'young nation' which needed time to 'mature politically', but which, under constant attack from the communists, was being denied the opportunity to develop as rapidly as it might otherwise.

However, though the political ruthlessness and inefficiency of the various South Vietnamese governments could be 'explained' in this way, defending their conduct of the war, when many of the same characteristics were exhibited, was an entirely different matter. The South Vietnamese tendency to subordinate fighting the war to domestic politics was clearly an immense handicap to the Americans. When the latter were bearing the brunt of the fighting, having key South Vietnamese units shifted around according to political moves in Saigon rather than those of the Vietcong was obviously a propaganda disaster, even if not a military one. In addition, promotion in the South Vietnamese Army depended on political loyalty to the current Saigon rulers rather than military efficiency (for an analysis of the South Vietnamese Army and its relationship to U.S. policies, see Kolko, 1986: 209–16, 231–5).

These aspects of the South Vietnamese conduct of the war were difficult enough to deal with, but an even worse aspect was the treatment meted out to prisoners. Observers found this to be one of the most repugnant features of the regime. At the same time that American and South Vietnamese propaganda highlighted the brutality of the Vietcong and life as it would be under communist rule, America's ally committed similar barbarities with both political prisoners and prisoners of war (see Howard S. Levie, 'Maltreatment of Prisoners of War in Vietnam', in Falk, 1969, vol. 2: 361–97). Here, the relationship between the American and South Vietnamese forces appeared in a particularly unfavourable light. This relationship was bound to be a complex one, as is the case where any two sovereign armies are concerned in a joint venture. For this was the crux of the matter: that these were sovereign armies, because the last image that Washington wanted to convey to the world was that of South Vietnam as a puppet state and army, subordinate to American aims – as Hanoi's propaganda so claimed. Nevertheless, though it was recognized that the South Vietnamese Army was autonomous and not simply under American command, it was American money that was keeping the entire operation afloat and equipping the South Vietnamese Army. As a result, publication of South Vietnamese cruelty damaged not only South Vietnam's standing in the eyes of the world, but also, by association, tarnished America's reputation. The constant barrage of American propaganda stressing that both armies were fighting for freedom and democracy merely added to the outrage (press analysis of the Honolulu Conference was linked in some instances to discussion of the South Vietnamese use, or 'alleged' use, of torture; see *The Times* and *Observer*, 10 and 13 February 1966 respectively).

The general impact of the American intervention on the social and economic structure of South Vietnam was little discussed publicly – fortunately for the American war effort. Obviously a foreign army, the size of which amounted to a friendly occupation force, was bound to cause a considerable degree of disruption; this was only to be expected. But, for instance, the level of corruption, or the disintegration of the moral and social fabric of Vietnamese life, were only occasionally commented on by journalists. The explanation for this apparent stroke of luck benefiting the Americans, at least as far as the Western nations were concerned, seems to be that firstly there were other aspects of the war which were more highly visible – for instance, the physical destruction and refugee problem – and secondly other aspects were more compelling to reporters (either determining and/or satisfying audience tastes), such as combat descriptions and film footage. Philip

Knightley suggests a further reason for the paucity of information on corruption:

> Neither the British nor Amerian correspondents did very well in writing about the unimaginable scale of corruption in Vietnam, perhaps because few correspondents could claim to be completely untainted themselves. Most of them changed dollars and pounds on the black market, and many bought stolen army goods ... In fact, as Murray Sayle, in 1967 the correspondent for the *Sunday Times* of London wrote: "Economic activity in the South has practically ceased, except for the war; Saigon is a vast brothel; between the Americans who are trying more or less sincerely to promote a copy of their society on Vietnamese soil, and the mass of the population who are to be 'reconstructed', stand the fat cats of Saigon." (Knightley, 1975: 384)

Knightley goes on to say: 'Most correspondents considered corruption stories peripheral to the war itself. It seemed to many of them more important to devote their time to the army or Marine Corps, to attach themselves to a unit going into action and to write about it, usually in simple Second World War terms' (Knightley, 1975: 385).

Thus the Administration came off lightly in the press with regard to, in some ways, the more long-lasting effects of their friendly occupation, Of course official propaganda focused on the amounts of aid donated by America; on appeals for aid from other countries; and on efforts to improve life for the South Vietnamese people (see Johnson's Message to Congress on 1 June 1965; in Stebbins, 1966: 388–91; also Johnson's press conference on 5 July 1966, cited in Kearns Goodwin, 1978: 488–9). Nevertheless, the overall impression gained of the South Vietnamese state was not one to inspire the majority of observers with a sense of progress achieved in any field.

Domestic politics, influences and American foreign policy

On a general level the intertwining of domestic politics with foreign policy is a feature which is well known to observers of the American political system (for a lengthy discusssion of 'societal' input into U.S. foreign policy, see Kegley and Wittkopf, 1987: 247–329). During the Vietnam War this feature was manifested in the way in which the Johnson Administration, when presenting its policies, took into consideration their possible impact on a number of broad opinion groups, which were not necessarily pressure groups, and was concerned that

America presented as united a front as possible to the rest of the world – hence the Administration's annoyance with later public expressions of opposition. These overlapping groups can be divided as follows: firstly there was the largest, most amorphous group which is traditionally 'uninformed' about, and uninterested in foreign policy, comprising the American 'public', who are also voters; and secondly there were the groups which, though part of the overall 'public' are generally 'informed' and interested in foreign policy, including politicians, both past and present; the communications industry; university faculties and students; and anti-war groups and groupings. (This is only a very broad categorization, for the Administration also took other groups into consideration as noted below; for a brief discussion of special interest groups, see Kegley and Wittkopf, 1987: 276–85; before the escalation of the war the Administration considered how to handle world and public opinion, see Sheehan et al., 1971: 363–4; and of course U.S. domestic opinion on the war was also of interest to the world's media – which often used the U.S. domestic press as a guide – and via this channel, and others such as anti-war groups, the state of U.S. opinion was disseminated round the world, a fact of which the Administration was well aware.)

The amount of attention paid to these groups by the Administration varied, for instance where the 'interested' groups were concerned the Administration often put its case in special briefings for Congressmen and Senators, and sometimes journalists, and sent emissaries to teach-ins. But general domestic opinion also mattered because the Administration did require some degree of public support for its policies. The 'bottom line' was that the public would have to accept the deaths of Americans – their own flesh and blood – as Assistant Secretary of Defense McNaughton noted in a memorandum about U.S. policy and 'image' for Secretary of Defense McNamara in March 1965: 'In this connection the relevant audiences are . . . [Communists, South Vietnamese and allies] and the U.S. public (which must support our risk-taking with U.S. lives and prestige)' (Sheehan et al., 1971: 438; square brackets added). There were also electoral considerations for Johnson to take into account, with Congressional elections due in 1966, and the rather more distant Presidential election due in 1968.

When considering the effect on the public of its war policies the Administration apparently bore in mind a number of traditional public preoccupations, which included the fear of communist expansion, the 'loss' of China, and the various evils associated with the Korean war. Commenting in September/October 1966, in an article entitled 'The President, the Polls, and Vietnam', Seymour Martin Lipset offered the following view of the interaction between Presidential policies and the public's traditional anti-communism:

> The findings of the surveys clearly indicate that the President, while having a relatively free hand in the actual decision-making to escalate or to de-escalate the war, is more restricted when considering the generic issues of action or inaction. He must give the appearance of a man *engagé*, of being certain of what he is doing, i.e., that the anticipated consequences do in fact come about.
>
> The President seems to present his program along two parameters:
>
> as part of a plan to secure peace, particularly if the action involved is actually escalation; pacific actions are presented as ways to contain communism, or even to weaken it.
>
> The President knows that in order to get the support of the American people for a war they wish were never in, he must continually put his 'best peace foot' forward – he continually talks and offers peace, so that he may have public endorsement for war.
>
> And conversely, any effort to make peace, to reach agreement with any communist state, would best be presented as a way to 'contain' communism, to weaken it by facilitating splits among the various communist states, or to help change it internally so that it will be less totalitarian, more humane and less expansionist. (Rosenbaum (ed.), 1970: 72–3)

As well as illustrating the President's concern with particular public attitudes, Lipset's short analysis gives some idea of the confusion which must have beset observers of the Administration's actions and rhetoric. For its part, Hanoi frequently complained that every time the Administration talked of peace it then escalated the war (as happened after the 'unofficial' May bombing pause; after the visibly official December/January pause in 1965; and the joint Soviet/British efforts in January/February 1967).

In 1965, a year before Lipset's article appeared, the well-known commentator James Reston, writing in *The New York Times*, had pointed to the popular foundations of Administration thinking, while deploring the resulting policies. In an article entitled 'Washington: Where Did We Go Wrong?', Reston wrote:

President Johnson's only consolation about Vietnam is that the public opinion polls seem to support his conduct of the war. He keeps them close in his pocket, as a reassurance to himself and a rebuke to his critics, but they really do not prove him right or wrong.

All they prove is that the American people rally round the flag in trouble. The more the nation has become involved in the leadership of dangerous and complicated events all over the world, the more the people have tended to back the President's judgement. (*The New York Times*, 21 November 1965)

Reston then related a series of events concerning which the public had supported previous presidents' decisions, however contradictory, returning to the theme of Vietnam by way of reference to the 'not unpopular' landing of Marines in Santo Domingo in the recent Dominican Republic crisis:

And the popular assumptions about Vietnam have led us into even more serious troubles.

It is popular in this country to oppose communist aggression or expansion wherever it appears. It is popular to assume that whenever Uncle Sam appears on the battlefield the opposition will knuckle under. It is popular here to believe that even if the French lost 187,000 casualties and a war to the North Vietnamese regulars and guerillas, we are different and not subject to the same disasters. But these assumptions, though popular, are not necessarily true. (*The New York Times*, 21 November 1965)

Moving on to the question of forthcoming decisions on the war, namely the pressure to extend the bombing to 'industrial installations' near Hanoi and Haiphong, Reston commented that as regards this decision:

Maybe this should be done and maybe it shouldn't, but the popularity polls are a poor basis for judgement. Nothing irritates President Johnson and his principal advisers more than the suggestion that they allow popular feelings at home to influence their foreign policy decisions abroad. They both defend their support of popular attitudes and deny that they act on these attitudes, but it is perfectly clear from the record that in both Vietnam and the Dominican Republic they have been influenced profoundly by popular assumptions and have confused popularity with effective policy. (*The New York Times*, 21 November 1965)

However, the public's attitude to Vietnam had not always been so easy to 'determine'. For in the 1964 Presidential contest, faced with a choice between the hardline candidate Goldwater and the more moderate Johnson, the public had chosen the latter, which appeared to indicate that the public wished to stay out of a land war with Asian communists. And though Kegley and Wittkopf point out that subsequent studies showed that both 'hawks' and 'doves' had voted for Johnson and that he could therefore interpret the election result as he wished (Kegley and Wittkopf, 1987: 313), nevertheless, whether or not the public had voted to stay out of an Asian land war, the fact is that during the 1964 election the Administration's rhetoric on Vietnam had been pacific, concerned with allaying fears that U.S. troops would be sent to fight in the conflict. Thus this rhetoric contrasted strongly with the Administration's subsequent escalatory actions in early 1965.

Regardless of any possible earlier public ambiguity, as Reston states, once in the war – having been presented with a *fait accompli* – the public rallied to the flag, dutifully if unethusiastically. This early lack of enthusiasm would make the official propagandists' task of maintaining public support more difficult, and yet this lack of public emotion was precisely what the Administration wanted in its desire to fight the war 'quietly' with as little public knowledge – and thus pressure – as possible. The public received only such information as the Administration judged absolutely necessary to maintain some semblance of dialogue with, and support from, its electorate, and frequently such information when disseminated had already been superseded in the Administration's plans, as when Johnson announced the dispatch of 50,000 more troops on 28 July 1965 (bringing the total to 125,000), but neglected to mention that 60,000 more had already been requested and were about to be authorized, and that Westmoreland had since asked for another 100,000.

Though both Lipset and Reston espouse circular arguments in their respective articles concerning the cause and effect of Presidential policies – both point to the public backing for the President's policies and then state that the President's policies derived in part from popular attitudes – what does emerge clearly is that once Johnson decided on a course in Vietnam he paid attention to public opinion. And on occasions there were attempts to 'prepare' the public in advance of certain actions, and efforts to keep a check on public reactions. This happened, for instance, with the 28 July announcement mentioned above: beforehand there were widely publicized Administration policy review meetings and press conferences by Johnson suggesting, among other measures, the possibility of a Reserve call-up, which naturally fuelled press speculation about a great increase in the war effort to such an extent that the subsequent announcement of a 50,000-man increase was received with relief! (For a detailed account of the meetings leading to this decision and public statement, and the aftermath, see Kahin, 1987: 366–99.)

Concerning other opinion groups, Johnson also devoted time to explaining and seeking support for his policies. For example, he expended much effort in ensuring that the majority of Congressmen supported, and continued to support, his Vietnam policies – at least publicly. Congressional opinion was important both in its own right, as a source of support and funds for the war, and as an opinion group with views that were widely disseminated and which could exert some influence on the American electorate and on world opinion. The obvious way to have secured Congressional support would have been to obtain a majority Congressional vote specifically authorizing the war. However, Johnson preferred to enlist support without resorting to a public declaration of war, and he also used the Gulf of Tonkin Resolution as evidence of Congressional authorization for his policies. Thus he sought support and understanding on a private and frequently individual basis, as Alastair Cooke noted in *The Guardian*:

> The truth . . . is that since last spring he [Johnson] has canvassed the ideas of 58 Heads of Government, innumerable professors, liberals, Democrats, Republicans, Tories, and Labour men, Negroes, trade union leaders, churchmen and soldiers; he has talked with every Senator and Congressman; had frequent bouts with the leaders of both parties; and had flown in the fifty governors en masse. (*The Guardian*, 17 October 1965)

Again, in addition to being important in their own right, these were groups and individuals whose views on the war, when disseminated, might be of interest to, and exert influence on, the general public. The amount of attention paid to the various opinion groups by the Administration tended to vary according to how widely their views might be broadcast – that is, how much attention the media was giving, or might give, to a group or individual – how prestigious and well-known the group or individual was to the public, and what views were held. Although the Administration did spend time preaching to the converted, great efforts were made to convert doubters. Failing conversion, there was the secondary goal of muting criticism through the devices of stressing the sheer complexity of the war, the necessity of honouring commitments, the Administration's overwhelming desire for peace, and, if all else failed, emphasizing how unpatriotic criticism was and what aid and comfort the enemy must be drawing from any domestic criticism. And personal and professional eminence was no safeguard against the latter type of smear as Senator Fulbright discovered as soon as he began to question the Administration's war policies and methods and thus became a prime target for Administration gibes, some of which were delivered by Johnson himself.

In the short term, in the early stages of the war's escalation, these tactics worked fairly well: few opponents were able to resist a personal appeal from so prestigious a figure as the President, or one of his top aides (even Walter Lippmann, the respected and influential *New York Herald Tribune* observer, was temporarily sidetracked from his criticism of the Administration's Vietnam policy when Johnson appealed to him for advice; see Steel, 1980: 556–65). In addition, to begin with, the President and his advisers were able to profit from the idea that in this confusing war only they possessed sufficient and extensive enough information to form a true picture of the situation – particularly where the issue of negotiations was concerned. Over a longer period, however, what was initially flattering and unusual in the personal approach inevitably began to pall as it was seen to be the customary method of dealing with critics – if they were judged to be of any importance – and as Johnson and his Administration's prestige and credibility began to wane. And as casualties increased the media demanded more information – and more accurate information – from the Adminstration.

In its statements on the war the Administration endeavoured to keep what it defined as its majority audience – leaving aside both doves and hawks – happy, while to a large extent pursuing the war separately. For instance, the knowledge that the American public might be uneasy about involvement in another land war in Asia (after the experience of Korea which, though successful, was unpopular) was a factor which led the Administration to disclaim repeatedly any desire for a wider war, contributed to the Administration's failure to declare war in the first place, and influenced its wish to pursue the war with minimum publicity.

In the very short term, that is, approximately five to six months, the lack of a declaration of war did not hamper the Administration's freedom of action or rhetoric. The first bombing raids in February 1965 on

North Vietnam were publicly stated to be retaliatory and not the beginning of a long-term campaign. The long-term bombing campaign that began soon after in March 1965 was also justified as retaliation for North Vietnamese aggression against its neighbour, South Vietnam. The increased commitment of troops was initially passed off as an increased commitment to static defence of South Vietnam, and when their offensive role was later revealed this was still stated to be part of the same defensive policy, rather than the prelude to an American offensive against North Vietnam and the Vietcong which would continue, regardless of cost, until the Administration had achieved its aims. With official statements such as these, and an as yet limited number of ground troops, it was still possible for the Administration's audience, both domestic and foreign, to be uncertain about the Administration's intentions and where these actions were leading to. But the revelation in June 1965 of an offensive role for the U.S. military, and the July announcement of the dispatch of yet more troops to South Vietnam and other measures, began to alter audience perceptions.

However, over a longer period the absence of Congressional ratification of the war through a specific Congressional declaration of war was to prove a costly error. Had the conflict been of a short duration and/or had it shown signs of being concluded successfully, then the fact that this was an undeclared war might have been tolerated. But as the war dragged on and as casualties rose and it became more obvious that this was both an undeclared and a major war, the Administration discovered that it had provided its opponents with a useful propaganda weapon, for in failing to obtain a Congressional declaration of war the Administration left itself open to the charge that it was fighting a war without the people's consent, as expressed through the will of Congress. In defence Johnson cited the Tonkin Gulf Resolution as sufficient authority for his war policy (for example, see Johnson's replies to correspondents at press conferences on 17 June 1965 and 26 February 1966 in Kearns Goodwin, 1978: vol. 1: 327–9, 417–18 respectively). However, despite Johnson's belief in the legitimacy of his authority to conduct such a major war without a further Congressional Resolution, when the Nixon Administration finally curtailed American involvement in the war in 1972, steps were taken – as a direct result of this war – to ensure that in future no President could introduce troops into a long war without Congressional consent and hence the War Powers Resolution was enacted in 1973.

Propaganda problems posed by the war

The nature of the war

One of the most difficult problems that the American propaganda organs faced during the Vietnam War concerned the nature of the conflict. The Administration most often portrayed the conflict politically as a straightforward contest between communists and non-communists and hence America's role in it was part of a moral crusade against communist expansion. This, though a gross over-simplification, was comprehensible to audiences.

However, explaining the war militarily to the public was an entirely different matter. For instance, it was no easy task to give a clear picture of the Southern enemy facing American troops. The Vietcong adopted no special uniform to denote their combat status, but like traditional guerrilla forces elsewhere merged into the local population. In addition, guerrillas who came from North Vietnam to aid the Vietcong had frequently originated in the South and so they too spoke the local dialect, were familiar with local customs, and could blend into the background. Visually, the black pyjamas which the guerrillas wore, in common with the local peasants, did not present a military aspect, particularly when contrasted with the uniformed American and South Vietnamese troops (for a description of the Vietcong and North Vietnamese Army, see Kolko, 1986: 252–60).

Another problem facing the Administration was how to measure, and thus be able to publicize, progress in the field. There appeared to be no pattern to this war, as there had been in previous wars. Instead of a series of engagements yielding territory, or key points, that were then held as part of a general objective of advancing on other enemy positions or headquarters, this war seemed to be a random conglomeration of terrorist incidents in villages and cities and seemingly isolated engagements between American and South Vietnamese troops and the Vietcong and North Vietnamese. The enemy forces seemed to come and go as they pleased, sometimes staying to fight in force and sometimes fading away – an elusive and frustrating war, epitomized by the battles for numbered 'Hills', which the enemy would occupy and defend until it suited them to vanish, leaving the Americans temporarily in possession, with the enemy perhaps appearing and reoccupying the since-vacated Hill at a later date. The only gain from such engagements was a growth in the body count – for both sides.

However, though there were no front lines to focus on and by which to judge the 'progress' of one or the other side in the war, the fact that the war continued, and continued to expand, in itself constituted a negative comment on U.S. 'progress' – as media commentators noted.

For a certain period of time though, the confusion engendered by this type of war was of use to the Administration. While its credibility still held in the eyes of the public, then the Administration's overall assessment of the tangled and chaotic events was likely to prevail, even with the existence of other interpretations, given the initial advantage that any government possesses – or is thought by its public to possess – in the range of information available to it. Obviously as the war lengthened and as observers and journalists became more familiar, through more exposure, with the events they were dealing with, then the Administration's view of events was open to challenge. But it was not only the passage of time that fostered different interpretations: the Administration, by lying on some issues and then being publicly shown to have lied, helped to undermine its own credibility. For instance, the public revelations in November 1965 about the Administration's rejection of a possible North Vietnamese peace initiative in Rangoon in 1964 dealt a serious blow to the Administration's posture on peace talks, which had hitherto rested on the simple statement that the Administration was willing to talk but the communists were not. Not surprisingly the media savaged the Administration and later pronouncements on peace encountered a much more sceptical reception from the media, which were now inclined to doubt whether such statements and offers were made in good faith as opposed to being purely public relations exercises.

As progress, or otherwise, could not be determined by the usual criteria, the American military turned to such methods as the body count of enemy dead in order both to measure and demonstrate their success. In fact the numbers game, as it was called, was used in this way in most facets of the American war effort. For example, pacification was measured in terms of the numbers of hamlets controlled by each side, the Hamlet Evaluation System. But as Kolko points out, not only were the monthly statistics inaccurate, but they could not measure the South Vietnamese villagers' allegiance, and he states: 'The war was a monumental human, political and social event whose complex effects required nuanced analysis' (Kolko, 1986: 211; see also 236–44 for a description of the pacification and Revolutionary Development programmes). Furthermore, this reliance on statistics to evaluate progress in this aspect of the war had already been criticized by U.S. officials involved in earlier pacification schemes, as noted by the Director of Provincial Operations for the Agency of International Development, in his study of the pacification effort up to 1965:

> Finally, there has been a tendency to haste in Vietnam and to insist on statistics even though they do not really reveal the true nature of progress or lack of it in political, social, and economic development. It is important to realize that the basic problems being dealt with cannot be solved quickly. People's loyalties and beliefs and actions do not change quickly, nor do their customs and social institutions. Thus, evaluations of certain programs cannot be made on a weekly or monthly basis. (Tanham, 1966: 130–1)

Where military planning for the war and evaluation of progress were concerned, the body count system was equally suspect, for the figures themselves could easily be inaccurate, either by accident or design. For instance, South Vietnamese males killed in battle zones, unless positively identified as 'friendly', tended to be classified as enemy dead – and others slipped into the statistics too – thus inflating the figures for enemy losses. However, it was from these body count figures that the American military planners calculated their assessment of how badly the enemy 'was hurting' and at what rate they were recruiting to fill the gaps, indeed at what rate the enemy would *have* to recruit to keep going (for an analysis of the body count system, see Lewy, 1978: 78–84). And President Johnson himself sometimes used the figures to illustrate progress in the war (see Johnson's replies to correspondents during his press conferences on 9 July 1965 and 31 March 1966, cited in Kearns Goodwin, 1978, vol. 1: 334 and 453 respectively).

Eventually the flaws inherent in this system became apparent; indeed the U.S. military produced its own critical survey of the figures in late 1968, and earlier the Systems Analysis Office in the Pentagon had not only reported the inaccuracy of the figures but had also produced pessimistic evaluations of the war (Lewy, 1978: 79–81). For the drawbacks to these particular figures are obvious: firstly, they said nothing about the morale, will and capability of the enemy, which were supposedly the prime target of American ground and air attacks. Secondly, no inference could be drawn as to the state of the war itself: whether headway was being made with peasants in enlisting their support for the South Vietnamese Government's cause, or whether support for the Vietcong and North Vietnamese was strengthening.

The body count figures said nothing about territorial control, or whether the war was being won or lost. As indicators to judge the war's progress they were useless, but there were few other ways in which the war could be measured and this statistical method of analysis suited the Pentagon: the figures could be used as evidence of success; only as the war lengthened could it be seen that the figures proved nothing (see Kolko, 1986: 196). Gelb and Betts summed up the dilemma thus in *The Irony of Vietnam: The System Worked*:

> Much of the most important information about Vietnam was essentially unquantifiable, and even when it could be quantified the dangers of misinterpretation and overinterpretation were ever present . . . Many of those who derived genuine hope from these indicators suffered from either a lack of knowledge about Vietnam or a lack of sensitivity toward politics, or both. On balance, data generally made Americans unduly optimistic. (Gelb and Betts, 1979: 303)

The American troop build-up

At the end of December 1964 U.S. military strength in South Vietnam had reached 23,300 troops, stationed there in the advisory role that America was still playing. By July 1965 U.S. troop strength was 75,000 and on 28 July President Johnson announced that a further 50,000 U.S. troops would be dispatched to Vietnam, bringing American troop strength up to 125,000. Thus in seven months American troop levels escalated by over 100,000 men and their role also changed officially from advisers to combatants. The problems that American propaganda had to resolve concerning the troop build-up were contained in the dramatic leap in force levels and the change in role. Though these were events that are to be expected in a war and which may be more or less difficult to explain depending on the 'popularity' of the war, the way in which the Administration chose to fight this war – without a declaration of war – and the way in which it decided to present information to the public, constituted a more than usually difficult problem for U.S. propagandists.

The arrival of two Marine battalions in Danang on 8 March 1965, in effect the beginning of the U.S. troop build-up, was presented publicly as a defensive move to protect Danang airfield following the start of the bombing campaign against North Vietnam in February. Any offensive role was pointedly ruled out in the Administration's announcement of the troop dispatch. However, this static security mission was short-lived, for on 1 April Johnson approved a change in the Marines' role from defence to offence and authorized a further dispatch of two more Marine battalions and an increase in support forces in South Vietnam. Thus, less than one month after denying any change in the Marines' mission in South Vietnam, the Administration had reversed its position and decided to go over to the offensive. But this part of the 1 April decision was not to be made public, by specific order of President Johnson, and officials were to present these moves as part of the existing policy, based on past Presidents' policies. So at the beginning of the troop build-up U.S. officials were under orders to conceal a major policy change from the media and the public. Effectively Johnson was already laying the foundations of the 'credibility gap' which came to characterize his Administration's conduct of the war.

Even without the President's wish for minimal publicity about the troop dispatches to South Vietnam, and his desire for secrecy over their changed mission, official propagandists could well have encountered problems over this increased commitment due to Johnson's earlier apparently pacific statements on the conflict during the 1964 Presidential election. For Johnson had specifically told American voters that U.S. troops would not be sent to Vietnam to do the fighting for the South Vietnamese, and nor would North Vietnam be bombed (Johnson, 1971: 68). Yet only three months after the elections American planes were bombing North Vietnam, and the following month Marines were disembarking in South Vietnam, in direct contradiction of Johnson's public statements.

After the realization by the press and public in mid-1965 that America was at war in South Vietnam, the initial propaganda problems created by the desire for secrecy over the change in the size of military force and role were superseded by a different set of problems centring on the length of the war and the ever-increasing numbers of troops needed to fight it. For as the war continued, so the numbers of casualties increased and the Administration came under pressure to show some progress in the war – either towards winning it or negotiating a settlement – from both hawks and doves among its audiences. These were problems that U.S. propaganda had to tackle if public support was to be maintained for this war and the Administration's war policies.

The growing size of the military operation soon posed another problem for propagandists, a problem which grew with each increase in troop levels. For this war, which seemed to appear so suddenly and to escalate so rapidly, was being fought in what was supposed to be peacetime. Although the American economy was not on a war footing and the battle was 'limited' to South Vietnam and selected bombing targets in North Vietnam, yet this was no minor conflict, and nor could it be passed off as such. As U.S. troops poured into South Vietnam, the scale of the destruction and the casualties mounted, and the media spotlight stayed firmly on events in Vietnam and the war which America had never declared.

The portrayal of the bombing

America used air power in the Vietnam War in two ways. Firstly, it was used to attempt to cripple North Vietnam's war-making capacity and to interdict its supply lines to the South. Secondly, air power was part of the war effort in the South, used to clear areas before troops moved in, and in supporting military operations.

Taking the first of these two roles, it was the bombing of North Vietnam in February 1965 which, in effect, began America's involvement in the Vietnam War. Initially the bombing raids were portrayed by the Administration as reprisals for Vietcong attacks in South Vietnam. Specifically, the first raids on 7–8 and 11 February were announced as retaliation for the attacks on the U.S. installations at Pleiku and Quinhon. In bombing North Vietnam in response to Vietcong actions in South Vietnam, the Administration sought to emphasize the idea that North Vietnam was the motivating force behind the continuing unrest and violence in South Vietnam. This rationale was used by the Administration as justification not only for the early retaliatory raids, but also for the policy of sustained bombing of North Vietnam, code-named Operation Rolling Thunder, which was authorized by Johnson on 13 February.

The propaganda problems posed by the early bombing raids differed in degree from those created by the sustained bombing programme. Initially the Administration required public and allied acceptance that the U.S response was 'appropriate and fitting', which was no small requirement given the geography of the Vietcong attacks and the American response. In addition the Administration needed to overcome the notion that the bombing was an over-reaction, particularly as there had been previous attacks on U.S. installations which had not occasioned bombing raids on the North. Thus it was also necessary for Johnson and his advisers to differentiate between earlier Vietcong attacks and Pleiku and Quinhon. The next step on the way to Rolling Thunder was to loosen the connection between specific Vietcong attacks and bombing the North: to use the bombing not just as a reprisal but as a method of fighting the war.

Once the sustained bombing programme was under way then the problems of maintaining audience support multiplied. Firstly, there were the effects of the bombing: the destruction that it caused. Although North Vietnam's major cities were not attacked there were plenty of other targets for the U.S. Air Force. In Britain and and Europe in particular (and other nations), the spectacle of this persistent bombardment brought back memories of the Second World War blitzes – not the sort of image to aid U.S. propagandists.

Secondly, there were doubts about the efficacy of such bombing, expressed both as a measure of the current campaign and with reference to studies of the Second World War blitzes. For as the war lengthened it became obvious that the North Vietnamese were not going to be bombed to the negotiating table by this programme, and nor were they going to cease aiding and fighting the war in the South. This perception was reinforced by the American studies of the bombing campaigns in the Second World War, which had concluded that strategic bombing aimed at breaking a population's will to resist had not succeeded. Interdiction bombing was similarly assessed as unable to achieve its goals. Yet the Administration continued with the bombing programme, despite the lack of results, which rendered the public justification for the bombing increasingly invalid, whilst at the same time increasing the likelihood that it would be viewed purely as a punitive measure, or as a means to bomb the North Vietnamese into negotiating – both accusations that the Administration wished to avoid.

America's use of air power gave the war its overwhelmingly technological character, with the massive bombardments seemingly requiring a lesser degree of manpower to achieve a greater degree of devastation while risking fewer American lives. Although the results of the air-strikes against North Vietnam could only occasionally be assessed at first hand by observers, the consequences of using air power to fight the war in South Vietnam were only too visible: great destruction and vast numbers of refugees. This was the other role for the U.S. Air Force: carpeting an area with bombs prior to U.S. military operations; bombing specific villages thought to be 'unfriendly'; and reinforcing military operations with air-strikes on enemy positions. The problem was that the enormous devastation caused by the bombing laid waste the territory of America's *ally*. Even if a village was correctly identified as 'unfriendly' – which obviously required reliable and accurate intelligence – and was then bombed, it was still the dwellings and livelihood of the South Vietnamese peasants which disappeared in the bomb craters along with the Vietcong. Of course mistakes were made, and then 'friendly' villages were obliterated – this could happen if a pilot overshot his target, or if the coordinates for an air-strike were incorrect, or if U.S. intelligence was defective. The net result was that ever greater areas of South Vietnam were turned into a wasteland and, far from seeming 'limited', the U.S. war effort appeared to be wreaking unlimited destruction on the very people it was trying to save. And this was the irony, that while officially no populated areas in North Vietnam were targeted for bombing raids in an endeavour not to kill civilians, the methods used to fight the war in the South and the desire to avoid troop casualties guaranteed a high proportion of civilian casualties. And so, with this indiscriminate method of warfare the Americans compared badly with the Vietcong and North Vietnamese, who, though ruthless, were far more selective in the people they killed (see Lewy, 1978: 95–105).

The other great by-product of the war was the refugees, the greater proportion of whom were created when their villages were destroyed, or when they were forced to move in order to avoid air-strikes. From 1965 onwards the numbers of refugees grew steadily, straining the already slender organizational resources of the South Vietnamese and the funds available to cope with them. As Lewy writes:

> No reliable statistics on the number of refugees are available until 1968, but it was estimated that between December 1965 and June 1968 there were 1.2 million officially recorded refugees and a far larger number who blended in with the general population as best they could and received no government assistance whatever. During the first eight months of 1966 alone the number of refugees officially processed was half a million. Between 1964 and 1969, as many as 3.5 million South Vietnamese, over 20 percent of the population, had been refugees at one time or another. (Lewy, 1978: 107–8)

The effects of the bombing in South Vietnam were easily ascertainable, even without the aid of statistics, in terms of ravaged countryside and displaced people.

War casualties

In any conflict casualties are a prime concern for propagandists because troops and civilians killed and wounded are one of the most obvious and emotional results of war. Thus a reason is required to justify these deaths and injuries to the audience in the homeland and, on occasions, to outside observers. It would seem logical to suppose that the more casualties there are, then the greater the need for a satisfactory – to the audience – explanation and justification for the carnage. The latter also applies to the length of a conflict, and where the factors coincide, of a lengthy and bloody war, then the requirement for propagandists to justify casualties is vital. In addition, either of these two factors might lead an audience to scrutinize a conflict more carefully, reviewing the official reasons given for participation, and seeking indications of progress towards officially stated goals.

America's participation in the Vietnam conflict would always have required careful explanation and justification, for in addition to being a bloody and long conflict it was fought 8000 miles away from the American homeland in an area with which few Americans were familiar until the war began and American troops were killed. Once U.S. military involvement began in earnest inevitably the casualty figures started to rise, fairly slowly at first, but then more quickly as the war continued to escalate. In 1965 the number of troops killed in action was 1363, a monthly average of roughly 113 (Kahin and Lewis, 1967: 188). However, according to Lewy, during 1966 the monthly average of American troops killed in action was 477, while in only the first half of 1967 the monthly average jumped to 816 killed in action (Lewy, 1978: 73). Overall, the number of U.S. military casualties during Lyndon Johnson's term in office from 1964 to 1968, including both wounded and dead, totalled 222,351 (Lewy, 1978: 146). What American official propaganda had to do was to make these casualties seem worthwhile to the American public in order to retain their support.

In addition to the U.S. military casualties there were the civilian casualties in the war (South Vietnamese Army casualties appeared to be of less importance except as indicators of the war's intensity and savagery). Again the effects of the conflict were obvious in South

Vietnam: increasing numbers of civilians were killed and wounded. The type of war waged and the weapons used by the U.S., such as napalm, ensured a high casualty rate among civilians, accepting that such casualties were unintentional. As Lewy points out, in general arriving at accurate figures for civilian war casualties is difficult. However, using the figures and calculations Lewy provides, in the period of Lyndon Johnson's Presidency overall from 1965 to 1968 the approximate number of civilians admitted to hospital due to military action was 215,193; the approximate number of civilians killed was 81,204; and the approximate number of civilians who died after admission to hospital was 32,279 (Lewy, 1978: 443–4; note that due to an error in calculation Professor Lewy recalculated the figure for total number of civilian deaths on p.444, as follows: civilians who died after hospital admission 85,590; total number of civilian deaths in South Vietnam 300,910). Considering both U.S. military and civilian casualty figures, whereas American casualties would concern mainly the American public, civilian casualties could be expected to be of concern to outside observers. And irrespective of approval or support for the U.S. war effort, observers were concerned about the carnage in South Vietnam. Civilian casualties were perceived as a particularly unjustifiable outcome of the conflict, and thus likely to generate considerable opposition to the war on humanitarian grounds alone.

Lastly, there were the North Vietnamese and Vietcong casualties. North Vietnam sustained both military and civilian casualties, the former while fighting the war in the South and the latter due to American bombing in the North. Whilst the U.S. military could assess to a certain extent what North Vietnam's battle casualties were, there was no reliable means of assessing the number of civilian casualties caused by American bombing, although on the rare occasions when correspondents visited North Vietnam an effort was usually made to evaluate the effects of the bombing on civilians. Such efforts by correspondents could produce a startling impact, as *The Pentagon Papers* notes in connection with civilian casualties from the bombing:

> During the prolonged internal debate [in the Administration from late 1966 to early 1967], the Pentagon account discloses, such issues as stalemate in the ground war and civilian casualties of the air war were of much more concern to some policy makers than the Administration publicly acknowledged.
>
> Press dispatches from Hanoi in late 1966 stimulated what the analysts call an 'explosive debate' in public about civilian casualties. Privately, the analysts add, the Central Intelligence Agency produced a summary of the bombing in

1965 and 1966 that estimated that there had been nearly 29,000 civilian casualties in North Vietnam – a figure far higher than Hanoi itself had ever used. (Sheehan et al., 1971: 515; the dispatches referred to were those of Harrison Salisbury, Assistant Managing Editor of the *New York Times*)

Vietcong casualties too were not easy to estimate, due to the difficulty of distinguishing between guerrillas and peasants in South Vietnam, and the concomitant tendency, as already discussed, for the U.S. military to inflate the figures for guerrilla deaths. However, in 1965 there were reported to be 35,436 enemy, but in 1967 that figure had more than doubled to 88,104 enemy dead, making a total figure for enemy deaths from 1965 to the end of 1967 of 179,064 (figures from Lewy, 1978: 83). Nevertheless, even if these figures were debatable, again the carnage was easily visible in South Vietnam and the supply of guerrillas seemed inexhaustible, whatever the casualty rate. As the war lengthened and casualties on all sides rose, increasingly the willingness and ability of the North Vietnamese and Vietcong to both sustain losses and replace them, and ultimately their sheer tenacity, caused some observers to ponder the reasons underlying the depth of commitment displayed by America's enemies. This too was a phenomenon that U.S. propaganda had to address.

Conduct of the war/negotiations

One of the most striking features of the war in Vietnam was the way in which the Administration increased both troops and bombing in graduated steps. This was a deliberate policy designed to prevent a North Vietnamese and Vietcong victory and hence avoid an American defeat, and also to try to limit any domestic outcry over America's commitment. In addition this gradual approach enabled Lyndon Johnson to pursue his preferred strategy of consensus politics, which sudden huge increases in troop and bombing levels would not have permitted.

The Administration initially presented bombing raids on North Vietnam as a means of pressuring the North Vietnamese leaders to cease the war in the South and to negotiate. Each increment in the bombing level was publicly justified as a step on the road to negotiations and ultimately peace. In this way the Administration blamed the North Vietnamese for the continuation of the war and also

endeavoured to avoid the impression of punitive bombing raids aiming at reducing the whole of North Vietnam to ruins.

The time factor posed a major problem with this justification for the U.S. propaganda effort, for as the war lengthened and the bombing was stepped up it became increasingly apparent that North Vietnam was not going to negotiate. Indeed the North Vietnamese were quite explicit about their refusal to negotiate under the threat of bombs. Thus in the summer of 1965 the purpose of the bombing programme privately shifted from endeavouring to break Hanoi's will to interdicting North Vietnam's supply lines (Sheehan et al., 1971: 468–9).

As a corollary to the bombing raids the Administration conceived of bombing pauses, used both as a diplomatic device and as a means of conducting the war. In diplomatic terms the bombing pauses were presented as an inducement to North Vietnam to negotiate and thus provided the Administration with an opportunity to ascertain whether or not Hanoi was prepared to talk. These pauses were also used to demonstrate to America's allies and public opinion in general that U.S. policy was not based solely on force. As a device for conducting the war, the pauses were used to legitimize further escalation of the bombing after Hanoi predictably turned down an Administration offer of talks, or negotiations, on U.S. terms. To the Administration the bombing programme was a means to negotiating from strength – through intensifying the 'pain level' before a bombing pause – and also constituted a vital bargaining counter, to be reduced or halted completely only in return for important concesssions. Hanoi recognized and responded to the functions of the bombing pauses: for instance, by delaying reaction to the pauses Hanoi bypassed the bargaining counter strategy, and by stating publicly that U.S. bombing pauses and talk of peace were always followed by escalation Hanoi drew attention to the 'legitimizing' function of the pauses. Not surprisingly the U.S. military opposed the bombing pauses, which in their estimate merely allowed the enemy to reinforce and resupply freely. Thus the Administration encountered both resistance from the U.S. military whenever a pause was under consideration, and then pressure to resume the bombing programme as soon as possible (for instance, concerning the December 1965 pause, see Johnson, 1971: 234 and Cooper, 1970: 294).

Clearly the questions that U.S. propaganda had to address on the bombing pauses centred on the credibility of the initiatives: firstly, were these pauses genuine attempts to initiate a dialogue, or were they primarily for public consumption; secondly, if Hanoi did not respond to these bombing pauses could this alone justify the U.S. resuming and escalating the bombing; thirdly, would Hanoi's lack of response prompt a critical examination of its reasons for rejecting the talks and hence probably a closer examination of the U.S. terms for talks; fourthly, could Hanoi justify its lack of response to U.S. overtures, and if so how would this affect audience perception of the U.S. bombing pauses and escalation of the bombing programme?

On the issue of negotiations the Administration first endeavoured to create the impression through its rhetoric that it was always ready for unconditional discussions, as for example in Johnson's major speech on the war at Johns Hopkins University on 7 April 1965. By emphasizing its desire for peace in Vietnam and willingness to enter into 'unconditional' talks, not only did the Administration endeavour to highlight its own 'peaceful' intentions but it also tried to throw the blame for the lack of negotiations – and hence the continuation of the war – solely on the North Vietnamese. Though the Administration did soften its terms over time, as for instance in Johnson's San Antonio speech on 29 September 1967, nevertheless its offer was still not 'unconditional' as claimed: the quid pro quo for a bombing halt was to be the prompt initiation of 'productive discussions'. Whilst for Hanoi, the attachment of any sort of condition to an offer of a bombing halt – which was how the demand for prompt and 'productive discussions' was perceived – was unacceptable (see Cooper, 1970: 380–1). Thus the central arguments on the Administration's position on negotiations hinged on whether the Administration genuinely desired peace; whether it was actively seeking a peaceful solution; and whether the offers of 'unconditional' discussions that the Administration always claimed it was ready to conduct would be so perceived by its audiences (the communists apart).

For U.S. official propaganda, one of the pitfalls over negotiations lay in part in the eagerness with which observers seized on any hint of peace talks or approaches: a speech by a top official containing references to either peace or talks usually received wide media coverage and close scrutiny. Concomitantly a phase of the war which was unaccompanied by any Administration remarks on peace also tended to provoke media reaction, as Joseph Alsop, writing in the *New York Herald Tribune* on Johnson's Johns Hopkins speech, noted: 'For many weary weeks on end, the President has been beseeched, urged, even bullyragged to announce his war aims, to explain his decisions, to declare his willingness to negotiate. Under this incessant barrage of advice he kept obstinately silent . . .' (*New York Herald Tribune*, 10–11 April 1965: 'A Great Speech').

Alsop's article itself illustrated the Administration's dilemma, for in addition to the above comments it also contained an interesting analysis of Johnson's speech, focusing on elements that were not favourable to the Administration (drawing the conclusion that Johnson was absolutely determined to avoid defeat in Vietnam) and lauding its 'craftiness and toughness'. But the particular irony of this article was that Alsop's criticism of the Administration stemmed from his hard-line, hawkish position on the war, and thus he exposed the contradictions in the Administration's rhetoric and war policy that followed from Johnson's efforts to pursue a middle course between hawks and doves in his Administration as well as among the public.

The progress of time also compounded other problems concerning the rhetoric of negotiations for the Administration. For instance, the Administration always claimed publicly that it would welcome serious efforts by other nations to help the peace process. So as the war continued and negotiations still did not begin, other nations took the Administration at its word and either offered to mediate or endeavoured to begin the mediation process on their own initiative. Thus the Administration was faced with various peace proposals and initiatives which, in general terms, it had previously stated would be welcome, but which might have arrived at an inauspicious stage of the war, or be unwelcome for other reasons. When these peace moves were undertaken by individual nations, then usually the Administration made a reasonable case for dismissing the initiatives. However, in addition to individual peacemakers the United Nations and the Nonaligned Movement attempted to initiate peace moves and though these efforts were also dismissed the Administration ran more risk. For naturally the media devoted considerable attention to any peace moves by these two organizations, and the failure of their initiatives evoked comment and analysis. Thus it behoved the Administration to treat these peace moves with more respect than it accorded to others – if only to avoid adverse press comment – but this rarely happened. For instance, in 1965 the Administration faced a heavy barrage of press criticism when it became known that the Administration had rejected a peace initiative for talks with North Vietnam undertaken by the U.N. Secretary General U Thant with U.S. concurrence. And the fact that Hanoi now denied the legitimacy of U.N. efforts at mediation in no way moderated criticism of

Washington for its dismissal of this U.N. initiative. The onus was on the U.S. Administration to act according to its own rhetoric, for in the main the Western media could sensibly examine and document only the rhetoric and actions of the United States.

4

European perspectives

,Just as the U.S. Administration viewed the Vietnam War through its own national and international political and security perspectives and concerns, so too did the governments of the European nations (despite the desire of the U.S. Administration that European nations perceive the war through U.S. eyes rather than their own). Thus their approach to the war reflected their own contemporary political and security interests, but their attitudes were also influenced by their relationship as European nations with the U.S., by their individual national relationships with America, and thus by the needs and demands imposed by these relationships. In order for U.S. propaganda to be successful in the context of its European allies it was necessary for propagandists to be aware of the intricacies of these relationships, and in particular to be aware of the sources of European support for the war (both governmental and public), and possible limitations, in order to be able to continue to tap that support and when necessary to contain dissent within acceptable public relations boundaries, that is, without publication of major dissension among its allies.

In general terms European governments were well aware that West European security and the political and military status quo in Europe was underwritten by NATO and the American military presence in Europe. Furthermore, with the exception of France, most European governments considered that Europe was the natural and proper focus for American attention and therefore the increasing U.S. absorption in the Vietnam War was perceived as a threat to Europe, involving as it did a diminution in U.S. interest in the European arena and concentration on Southeast Asia. For though the period of the coldest relations between East and West was over by 1965 and there had been a degree of thawing since the Cuban missile crisis in 1963, nevertheless the relationship between the two 'blocs' still involved tensions, and Europe was still the seat of seemingly intractable and continuing political problems with international implications, such as the division of Germany, the post-war borders, and the political position of Berlin; and of course for these reasons and others the world's two opposing major military alliances were focused on Europe.

Thus the attitude of European governments to the U.S. involvement in Vietnam, viewing it as peripheral to the 'real' political concerns, is understandable. But by the same token, because the world was still divided into East and West and two opposing ideological blocs it was also possible to perceive, and more importantly to portray, the Vietnam War as an episode in the continuing fight against communist expansionism – an episode that was taking place in a different geographical arena, but that was still a part of the same general problem that faced Europe. There was, therefore, an inherent tension in European government perceptions of the U.S. involvement in South Vietnam, which was only containable so long as the war was perceived (or said to be perceived) as the U.S. portrayed it – in this international framework of Sino-Soviet communist expansion, which, if not halted in Vietnam, would eventually threaten the Western world. This, then, was the link in U.S. propaganda between Southeast Asia and Europe. So, despite the concern about this refocusing of U.S. attention, America's principal European partners (the U.K., France and West Germany) – with the notable and vocal exception of France – supported U.S. involvement and once escalation began helped to justify it. And it is this difference in reaction between the U.K., West Germany and France which raises the first and most obvious question of why the British and West German Governments supported the Americans on the war, but not the French; and this leads on to the further question of whether there were differences between the British and West German Governments in their support for America. In order to answer these questions it is necessary to determine the factors, domestic and international, that influenced the perspectives of these individual governments, which will now be examined in turn.

The United Kingdom

Turning first to the more positive aspects of U.K.–U.S. relations, and thus elements that would aid U.S. propagandists, one of the most important factors influencing the British Government during this era was the 'special relationship' between Britain and America. Although the warmth of this relationship has varied considerably in different periods, nevertheless in the 1960s British policy-makers acted on the assumption that a 'special relationship' did exist, indeed, Prime Minister Harold Wilson took special pains to nurture the relationship, as Paul Foot notes:

> . . . the December [1964] confrontation [with the U.S. President; see below] did not shake Wilson from his main scheme: that an economic military and diplomatic special relationship with the United States should form the basis of British foreign policy.
>
> That had been the basis of Ernest Bevin's foreign policy from 1945 to 1950 and it had, as Wilson remembered it, worked very well indeed. It had also carried distinct advantages for Britain in the world's council chambers. (Foot, 1968: 213)

Thus, because of this orientation towards America (and regardless of later attempts to join the Common Market), U.S. propagandists could expect to encounter a more sympathetic climate in British official circles than they might in other countries. In addition, the close economic relationship that Prime Minister Wilson desired certainly did materialize: the British economy was heavily dependent on American support, primarily to avoid any devaluation of sterling. Paul Foot sums up the results of this dependency:

> On 6 December, six weeks after he had assumed office, Wilson set off for Washington with one of the biggest retinues ever to accompany a Prime Minister on a trip abroad. He clearly regarded the confrontation with the American President as crucial to the whole of Labour's foreign policy – a foundation for the rebuilding of a 'special relationship' in a constructive and radical form. To his surprise, however, Johnson was abrupt, almost rude. He harped again and again on the sterling crisis and the dangers to the international monetary system in a British devaluation. He reminded Wilson that

> while in crisis Britain depended almost entirely on American support to keep sterling strong, and urged the British Prime Minister to construct a foreign policy in keeping with Britain's economic situation. Wilson gave assurances that Britain's 'commitments' in the Far East, the 'defence' of Singapore and other expensive idiosyncracies of Empire, would scrupulously be maintained. Above all, he promised support for the American cause in Vietnam. (Ibid.: 212)

Notwithstanding Foot's obvious distaste for the continuing remnants of Empire, this was an accurate summary of Britain's position *vis-à-vis* America.The fact that Britain's economy was underwritten to such a large extent by America underlined the latter's role of senior partner in the relationship, with America obviously wielding the greater amount of influence and leverage. Wilson, however, had hopes that British support for America in Vietnam would confer the ability to exercise some influence over U.S. policy in Vietnam. Despite being made aware at the earliest stages of escalation of the war that the U.S. had no intention of being swayed by its British ally, Wilson nonetheless persevered for some considerable time on these lines, until the Administration bombed oil installations near Hanoi and Haiphong in July 1966 which led to a British Government dissociation, and then helped to wreck a British peace initiative in February 1967. The sequence of events leading to the failure of this intiative further soured relations, to some extent, between the two countries. However, overall from 1965 to mid-1966 Britain's economic dependence on the U.S., coupled with Wilson's views on the 'special relationship' and on supporting his U.S. ally in the hope of political influence, meant that the official U.S. version of the war was generally supported by the British Government. (In an interview with Sir Harold Wilson by the author on 26 June 1981 in London, Sir Harold claimed that his support was 'negative support', but he also held the view that 'the moment we had dissociated ... we'd have had no influence whatsoever'.) And even after the 1966 dissociation official British support continued, though with qualifications.

Despite Britain's shedding of imperial commitments another link in the relationship between Britain and America during the Vietnam War in fact arose from Britain's imperial past, specifically Britain's former activities in Malaya. For the British experience fighting the communist insurgency in Malaya proved to be useful for U.S. propagandists. Firstly, along with the Philippines insurgency, it was thought to demonstrate that the West could defeat a communist insurgency and thus boosted confidence that the U.S. could do the same in Vietnam –

leaving aside the question of whether these sets of events were similar. Secondly, on the basis of the success in Malaya the Americans specifically sought to use counter-insurgency techniques in South Vietnam that had been developed by the British in Malaya. In addition, President Kennedy and President Diem both used British advice and expertise in the form of the British Advisory Mission in Saigon. This Mission existed from 1962 to 1965, advising the South Vietnamese Government on pacification, and the Mission's head, R.G.K. Thompson, also advised President Kennedy and later President Nixon. When the Mission was disbanded in 1965 Britain continued to help train the South Vietnamese police through the British Embassy in Saigon. So from 1961 to 1965 there was a tangible British commitment to South Vietnam and this continued in a small way even after the war escalated in 1965. This small amount of aid that Britain granted to the South Vietnamese was still useful to U.S. propagandists in that it could be used to identify Britain with the South Vietnamese–U.S. cause, despite Britain's position as Co-Chairman of the Geneva Conference (for further analysis of Britain as Co-Chairman see below).

The accession to power in 1964 of the Labour Party with Harold Wilson as Prime Minister was also a particular boon to the Americans, in that the Labour government could support the U.S. without being instantly labelled war-mongering or neo-colonialist. Had the Conservatives been in power it would have been more difficult for them – being identified with the Right – to support the Americans in Vietnam, had they been so inclined. As it was, the Labour government, securely identified with peaceful international traditions, rendered what assistance it wished to the Americans. In addition, Wilson was initially aided in his policy of supporting the U.S. by the fact that the first Labour government had a majority of only five in the House of Commons. This slender majority tended to define the limit of Labour MPs' – even left-wing Labour MPs' – opposition in the House to the government's policies, since rebellion could have led to an unnecessarily early general election.

There were, however, more negative perceptions and experiences in the U.K.–U.S. relationship, factors which posed difficulties for the British Government and U.S. propagandists alike. These factors can be divided into perceptions about the U.S., perceptions about U.S. war methods in Vietnam and about Vietnam in general, and about Britain's diplomatic role during the Vietnam War.

Prior to America's involvement in the Vietnam War, a major source of British perceptions – particularly public perceptions – about the U.S. lay in American involvement in the two world wars, especially the Second World War. At a time when American soldiers were stationed in Britain and were fighting alongside the Allies, the ordinary British people gained more acquaintance with 'Americans' than they would otherwise have been able to do. The relationship between the British population and the American troops and officials was complicated by the higher standard of living generally enjoyed by American troops in Britain, for while the local population might benefit, British troops were said to resent the disparity. Although the conclusion reached by the British authorities was that public reaction was favourable, nevertheless there had been some anti-Americanism initially: 'The complaints and accusations levelled at the American troops were many. They were said to drink too heavily, to be boastful and contemptuous of the British Armed Forces . . . to be too highly paid, to corrupt young women, and to practise discrimination against their black comrades' (McLaine, 1979: 267). It is possible that the anti-Americanism that existed for some time during the Second World War could have grown again afterwards, with America's further growth in wealth and power. Thus British opinion polls on U.S. involvement in Vietnam could have tapped a latent anti-Americanism rather than simple straightforward opposition to the Vietnam War. The U.S. administration was aware of this feeling in other nations when it followed opinion on the war through the channels at its disposal: contacts with foreign governments; embassies; foreign media, both print and broadcast; and USIA surveys of foreign opinion on the war. Again, anti-Americanism, as well as attitudes to authority among the youth of the 1960s, helped to fuel the anti-Vietnam War riots of this period (see the USIA surveys mentioned in Chapter 2).

Resentment of American wealth did not end with the Second World War. On the contrary, America's rise in the world wealth and power structure coincided with, and was fuelled by, Britain's and the rest of Europe's decline (Europe's subsequent recovery was in the future). America's economic strength and development of nuclear weapons put it into the superpower category that Europe now seemed unable to attain (and still cannot, operating as individual nations) after the devastation wrought by two world wars. Thus both economically and politically Britain and the rest of Europe could not play the international roles that they had done formerly: it was America which was now a principal international actor. America's role in the world was conditioned by and expressed through two major concerns: firstly, her widespread trading ventures, called neo-imperialism by some observers; and, secondly, its anti-communism, expressed as it was in the Truman Doctrine. Taken together these two concerns virtually guaranteed a 'high profile' American presence in world affairs. So in the 1960s American wealth and power could provoke the same resentment in some sections of the British population that it had during the Second World War, while its new world role, so different now from Britain's, could provoke accusations of interference in other nations' affairs (see USIA Survey, October 1965: 'The Standing of the U.S. in West European Opinion': 6; USIA Archives Research Section, R-145-65).

If the British public's attitude to America was sometimes equivocal, exhibiting both support and hostility, there was far less ambivalence about the attitude of some sections of the Labour Party to America. Their political convictions were directly opposed to everything that America epitomized, and the Vietnam War was another issue to confront. So the Labour government was likely to come under pressure from these sections because of its support for the U.S. on Vietnam.

Concerning U.S. war methods, the British experience of bombing during the Second World War did pose some difficulties for U.S. propagandists. For, according to National Opinion Polls (NOP) in July 1966, although the British public thought the bombing of military targets in North Vietnam was justified, the public emphatically disapproved of any bombing of civilian targets. And this view was expressed when military targets around Hanoi and Haiphong – near the civilian population – had been bombed for the very first time (NOP, July 1966 and Gallup Poll, July 1966). Interestingly, during the early period of the war (1965–66), apart from general questions on support for American policy or 'American armed action' in Vietnam, neither of the major polling organizations (NOP and Gallup) in Britain investigated public reaction to U.S. bombing in South Vietnam, where civilian casualties in 1966 were already much higher. One possible reason for this apparent lacuna could be that it was assumed that what America did in South Vietnam it did with its ally's help and approval and was thus not a matter necessitating an opinion poll.

Officially the British Government viewed the U.S. bombing campaign as a legitimate method of fighting the war, and having assured the U.S. Administration of support for the conflict it seemed unlikely that U.S. official propagandists would need to be unduly concerned about the reaction of this particular audience on this issue. However, there were clearly stated limits to the British Government's support for U.S. bombing: just as the British public disapproved of North Vietnamese civilian casualties, so too did the Government. This meant that any change in U.S. bombing targets which might involve the civilian population – and any other target changes which might also make a political settlement harder to reach (such as the mid-1966 Hanoi/Haiphong bombings) – could be expected to displease the British Government – a potential problem which the U.S. Administration had been made aware of from the beginning of escalation by the British Government itself. Thus, although this stance of the British Government could pose difficulties for U.S. propaganda – Britain being considered America's staunchest non-combatant supporter – there was advantage in the fact that U.S. officials would have known for some time beforehand of any forthcoming problem concerning the bombing and would therefore not have been taken by surprise. The following telegram, classified Secret and sent on 3 June 1965, from U.S. Ambassador Bruce in London to U.S. Secretary of State Rusk in Washington shows the close understanding between the two governments of their respective difficulties and requirements in this relationship, and is thus quoted at length:

> Michael Stewart's [British Foreign Secretary] statement to the Commons on June 3 (on the preparation of which he personally spent much a great deal of time and thought) indicates how much the British remain preoccupied with Vietnam.
>
> While the Wilson government will continue to give us solid support we must recognize that uneasiness persists and that the domestic political problem for the Labor government is correspondingly difficult. The pressure on Wilson comes not just from the Left but from Labor moderates and from the general public as well . . .
>
> With all of this, it is understandable the British are sensitive to the probelm [*sic*] of Southeast Asia . . . They are very much aware of the increased US troop commitment and our expanded combat mission, of the dangers of the air war in North Vietnam and of the Russians SAM involvement. As you know, also, the Dominican Republic experience has sharpened worries here about Vietnam. Under the circumstances the temptation might be to buy some easy political credit at the expense of the US on the Vietnam issue. Wilson has not done so and I do not think he will. If nothing else, self interest dictates that he must risk no serious split with the Americans.
>
> In order to manage their own party and public, however, the Labor government are depending very much on our undertaking to consult with them about

any major changes in our policy or in conduct of the war in Vietnam. If we fail to do so when there are things they think we should talk to them about, it greatly complicates Wilson's political problems and our mutual relations. Your conversations when you were last here were helpful on this score and I hope we can keep the British fully and currently informed of our thinking and our plans in Vietnam. This applies especially to any escalation that might involve bombing Hanoi or even Haiphong, with attendant possibility of civilian casualties.

I discussed this last Sunday with Bob McNamara [U.S. Secretary of Defense], who may already have spoken to you about it. Later, Denis Healey [U.K. Minister of Defence] brought up same topic with him. (Embtel 5835 [London] Bruce to Rusk, 3 June 1965, Box 206–207, volume IV, Cables 5/65–6/65, UK Country File [305], NSF, LBJ Library; square brackets in text added)

The importance of this particular telegram lies not only in its clear indication of the efforts made by the U.S. to help Wilson continue his policy of support on Vietnam, but it also provides evidence of the Administration informing a foreign ally of major war developments in advance of its own public: for it was only on 8 June, via a routine State Department press announcement, that the U.S. public inadvertently learned of the 'expanded combat mission' that the British Government already knew about before 3 June. Not surprisingly the announcement that the U.S. was now engaged in an offensive role in Vietnam, and the way in which it was announced, caused a very public uproar in America (see *The New York Times*, 9 June 1965, editorial: 'Ground War in Asia'), which was further compounded when the White House issued a statement on 9 June which flatly denied a change in the U.S. troop role, claiming that a combat role had already been authorized back in March – both of which claims were untrue.

In Britain the press immediately questioned whether the government had been informed of the new U.S. troop role, a question which Whitehall refused to comment upon directly, leaving the matter still open to public speculation. This episode illustrates the problems caused by the U.S. propaganda campaign – specifically the policy of saying as little as possible about its war policy – for the British Government in supporting the Administration. For though the British Government did not share in making either U.S. policy on Vietnam or propaganda on the war, due to its support for the U.S. it did share in the consequences of both, especially in the frequently disastrous propaganda techniques which the Administration employed, and which could rebound in unexpected and therefore unanticipated ways, making an adequate public defence all the more difficult.

Concerning this particular incident, the Administration was eventually let off relatively lightly by the press, with a common view prevailing that the Administration was in arrears with its policy announcements, rather than deliberately withholding information, although this was accompanied by a recommendation that the Administration should be 'more communicative' and a warning of more domestic dissent unless the President took his own nation into his confidence (see *Daily Telegraph*, 10 June 1965, editorial: 'Committed to Combat'; also article 'Washington Fog on Viet-Nam policy'). Obviously, the press associated 'communication' with 'information', but where the Administration was concerned the two were not necessarily linked. For the President had on occasions been most 'communicative' on certain issues, about his desire for peace, for instance, but this merely obscured the Administration's real intentions. And the amount and type of 'information' he actually gave on the Administration's real intentions was minimal compared to the amount and type he could have given, as *The Pentagon Papers* clearly demonstrates. And on the issue of peace the Administration was often less than candid with its allies, as well as its own public, as the British Government was later to discover to its cost (see Chapter 6). In addition, much of the more accurate information in press reports on future actions or policy on Vietnam 'emerged' through 'private sources' or the 'private' reflections of unnamed Administration officials, thus showing the gap between official U.S. announcements and private views on the war. This may have been a way of quietly preparing the U.S. public for greater commitments, but it was not the best way to run a propaganda campaign with the prospect of a full-scale war looming rapidly.

The bombing campaign was the most striking feature of U.S. warfare in Vietnam, but there were also other aspects which tended to focus attention more generally on the U.S. effort in Vietnam. Firstly, there was the sophisticated technology used, which was constantly developed throughout the war. Although North Vietnam itself came to possess a sophisticated air defence system which could pose problems for U.S. bombers, overall, U.S. technology was ranged against an enemy using much more basic equipment in the field, and the image thus created was of the U.S. 'Goliath' facing a North Vietnamese 'David'.

Secondly, there was the way in which the U.S. military used this weaponry; in general their major concern was to maximize the weaponry's destructive capabilities, with apparently scant regard for the consequences of such a policy. And even when an attempt was made to control the amount of destruction that the war involved, it resulted instead in considerable damage to the U.S. propaganda effort due to the substitute weapon used: non-lethal gas. For the 'gas warfare' incident in March 1965 was reported to have been inspired partly by the desire of a U.S. troop commander to minimize civilian casualties by declining to order a preparatory air-strike on a suspect village. But to Britain and the rest of the world the substitution of CS gas appeared scarcely more humane. The logic which the Americans applied to fighting the war seemed to leave little room for humanity, an approach which on occasions disturbed foreign observers, as in the case of this incident – which was ironic in view of the stated reason for using the gas. The use of this gas in South Vietnam, militarily worthless in itself, produced a world-wide barrage of criticism directed at the U.S. and was a major propaganda disaster for the Administration. This episode is worth discussing in a little more detail to illustrate the damage done to the U.S. propaganda effort by an entirely unanticipated incident; the inept methods used to counter criticism, which were by no means unusual for the Administration; and the problems that were thus caused for the British Government.

Briefly, on 23 March an Associated Press (AP) correspondent reported that the U.S. was 'experimenting' with gas warfare in South Vietnam (*New York Herald Tribune*, 23 March 1965). There were comical elements in the story about a gas-laying operation which an AP photographer had attended after a military spokesman had confirmed the experiments.

The U.S. Defense Department issued a statement to the press in Washington and Saigon defending U.S. actions. This defence was incorporated in a USIS bulletin on the issue, which also included other departments' views (USIS bulletin, 23 March 1965). The justifications were:

1 The non-lethal, temporarily disabling gas was only used in situations where the Vietcong mingled with or took refuge amongst non-combatants.
2 The gas was supplied by the U.S., but was dispensed by South Vietnamese personnel, and it was the same gas used by the British in Cyprus.
3 The use of tear gas in riots or tactical situations was not contrary to

international law and practice, and, as the State Department Press Officer pointed out, America had never ratified the 1925 Protocol on gas warfare.
4 Other U.S. officials felt that it was more humane to use tear gas than to subject innocent citizens to fire power.

The world-wide press furore that began on 24 March did not finally subside until August. The day after the news broke, James Reston outlined the main effects of the disclosure, in an article headlined 'Just a Little Old Benevolent Incapacitator':

> One unfortunate aspect of the incident was that it occurred precisely at the moment when the U.S. was beginning to gain a little more understanding in the world for its policy in Vietnam . . . Accordingly the propaganda war over Vietnam was beginning to turn a little to the American side, when the gas incident was disclosed, incapacitating our own propagandists, and not very benevolently either. (*The New York Times*, 24 March 1965)

The Times of London pointed out that American military spokesmen could only blame themselves for the outcry, which they had generated themselves 'by releasing driblets of information in imprecise language . . .' (*The Times*, 24 March 1965: 'U.S. Seeks to Justify Use of Gas') Articles in other newpapers pointed out that the incident and controversy were a propaganda gift to the communists (see *The Guardian*, 24 March 1965; *New York Herald Tribune*, 25 and 26 March 1965; and *The New York Times*, 25 March 1965). The North Vietnamese and the Chinese then issued statements about the use of 'poison' gas through their press agencies and radio broadcasts. These reports were then relayed to the West through dispatches from Tokyo and Hong Kong which expressed the anxiety felt by many Asians about the use of special weapons by white men against Asians. In their anxiety these dispatches tended to blur the distinction between poisonous and non-poisonous gases.

The Russians put out a measured condemnation of U.S. actions, which they said flouted international law and common humanity. Then they delivered a note to the U.S. Ambassador in Moscow which deplored the use of 'toxic' gases in Vietnam. The American Ambassador refused to accept the note and the press reported that too (*The New York Times*, 25 March 1965, 'Moscow Dispatch'; *New York Herald Tribune*, 27 and 28 March 1965)

In Britain, a Commons motion was tabled by seven Labour MPs deploring the use of gas and a telegram of protest was sent to Foreign Secretary Michael Stewart in Washington. According to an *Observer* report, Stewart was caught unprepared, but responded to the telegram:

> After a tolerably successful, most cautiously conducted 90 minute talk at the White House on Tuesday, Stewart made his gas gaffe at the National Press Club, calling for the U.S. to show 'a decent respect for the opinion of mankind' in a quote from the Declaration of Independence. It was like blowing one's nose on the American flag. President Johnson and other officials were peeved and said so. (*Observer*, 28 March 1965: 'British Gas Clouds Over Vietnam Fighting')

There was a march by sixteen Labour MPs to the U.S. embassy in Grosvenor Square, to protest against the use of gas and napalm in Vietnam. The MPs were reported to have shown appreciation of the embassy's lack of concrete information and policy direction and only one MP made unhelpful comments (*The Guardian*, 25 March 1965).

The Times summed up the incident in more sedate language than did some newspapers (for example, see the *Daily Express*, 25 March 1965: 'Crocodile Tears: How Could *Anything* be so Mismanaged?'), but with an equally damning conclusion:

> The whole incident, which naturally hinges on one's faith in authoritative sources, seems to indicate incompetence and insensitive handling rather than dark deeds. The original news agency dispatch came openly from South Vietnamese sources, and the American military spokesmen, apparently at a loss, were sufficiently ill-advised to talk about such an emotive subject before referring to the experts, from whom precise information was said today to be freely available. (*The Times*, 24 March 1965: 'U.S. Seeks to Justify Use of Gas')

In addition to criticism about the Administration's handling of the gas issue, later reports focused on why the gas was used in villages, concluding that there was something wrong with the handling of the conflict if the alternative to gas was bombs or napalm. The main effect of the controversy was pinpointed in an *Observer* analysis (which also noted the above points), stating that the political impact was 'symptomatic of spreading fears about U.S. policy' (28 March 1965: 'British Gas Clouds Over Vietnam Fighting').

This incident highlighted a number of basic propaganda errors committed by the Administration, while the speed of modern-day communications demonstrated the difficulty of containing, or even limiting the propaganda damage.

Firstly, since one of the basic requirements for a propagandist is to know the audiences receiving communications and the intermediaries transmitting the message – in this case the press, which also constituted an audience – American propagandists should have known that the very word 'gas' had been anathema to Europeans since the First World War and the use at that time of mustard gas. It should also have been known that this weapon could be portrayed in the context of the Vietnam War as something being used only on Asians, even if administered by South Vietnamese Asians, thus setting it in a racial context. Other Asians might therefore be expected to be anxious, over and above the type of weapon used.

Secondly, the U.S. propaganda defence also embroiled its main ally, Britain, in the row, forcing the British Government to explain the use of gas in Cyprus. Thirdly, pointing out that the U.S. had not ratified an International Protocol on gas warfare merely drew attention to a general deficiency in U.S. international conduct. Fourthly, the justification that it was better to use gas than to bomb villages highlighted what many observers already thought was wrong in the U.S. conduct of the war and further concentrated attention on the nature of the war. Fifthly, although Britain had been implicated in the incident, U.S. representatives in Britain were shown to be ill-informed about their own government's policy. In addition, this incident took place just before the Administration planned to escalate the war in April, when the U.S. would need its allies' support, and when its main ally, Britain, would again have to face opposition in its own ranks, heightened now by this propaganda blunder.

In general, where perceptions of Vietnam were concerned, most of the British public's information came from media sources and was only as comprehensive as the source itself. Few people in Britain, apart from journalists, had first-hand knowledge of Vietnam, either North or South. There were, however, a few Labour MPs who did possess such knowledge, having visited the country in 1957. These MPs thus had a different basis from which to view the U.S. involvement and escalation – a different yardstick by which to measure U.S. information, especially the origins of the present conflict (for example, a Parliamentary Labour Party delegation visited North and South Vietnam in May 1957. The delegation was composed of William Warbey, Lena Jeger, who also wrote a column for *The Guardian*, and Harold Davies, who became Parliamentary Private Secretary to Prime Minister Harold Wilson in 1967).

Lastly, one of the factors that U.S. propagandists had to deal with and which should have tempered British support for U.S. policies in Vietnam, particularly military policy, was Britain's Co-Chairmanship, with the Soviet Union, of the Geneva Conference of 1954. This was the reason put forward to justify Britain's refusal to accede to the U.S. request to send troops to Vietnam (see Wilson, 1971: 48). Despite this refusal, the British Government supported the U.S. goals in the conflict, that is, an independent South Vietnam, and agreed with the U.S. interpretation of the origins of the conflict: that it was a case of North Vietnamese aggression against another sovereign state, and that the U.S. was not therefore interfering in a civil war. Thus, even while the Co-Chairmanship committed both the Soviet Union and Britain to finding a diplomatic solution to the war although they supported opposing sides (though the degrees of support differed greatly), this interpretation of the origins of the conflict alone and the clear insistence on South Vietnam's sovereignty and independence effectively nullified the original Geneva Agreements' provisions, and rendered pointless a diplomatic search for peace using the device of the Co-Chairmanship. Nevertheless, in Britain the government was frequently urged to negotiate an end to the war, on the assumptions that the Co-Chairmanship still retained the validity and credibility necessary to undertake such a task, and that as a close ally of the U.S. peace moves must surely be welcomed by the latter (if not by the North Vietnamese). But as events subsequently demonstrated, neither assumption was correct. Yet because of the Administration's propaganda about peace, and partly because of the British Government's willingness to believe the Administration and desire to act as peacemaker, the British Government continued to try and effect a settlement, and when these peace efforts failed the Wilson government's credibility as a possible intermediary suffered considerable damage, as did the suppposed 'special relationship'.

France

The French attitude – governmental, press and public – to U.S. involvement in Vietnam, expressed most forcefully and unambiguously in President de Gaulle's pronouncements, was diametrically opposed to that of the British Government's and early press and public's attitude. From 1965 to 1968, until President Johnson's announcement on a bombing cut-back, French President de Gaulle and the French press criticized U.S. involvement in Vietnam. Thus analysis of the French perspective on the war and their reception of U.S. propaganda is comparatively straightforward (unlike the U.K. and West Germany).

De Gaulle's position was based mainly on his assessment of the origins and likely outcome of the conflict (a civil war which would end in defeat for the U.S.); on past French experience in the First Indochina War fighting, and being defeated by, the Vietminh (Vietnamese communists led by Ho Chi Minh, now leader of North Vietnam); on the current war's possible role as a catalyst for a larger conflict in Asia; on his belief that all of Southeast Asia should be neutralized; on his general desire to exert France's independence from U.S. leadership of the Western bloc; and on his wish for a degree of independence from the lingering exigencies of the Cold War – which required better relations with the Eastern bloc (see Sullivan, 1978: 71–5; and Lacouture, 1992: 400–3). There was thus a mixture of domestic and international factors, both historical and current, built into de Gaulle's assessment of the war and U.S. involvement.

Perceiving the conflict as a civil war, provoked by South Vietnam's repressive government and lack of political freedom, de Gaulle discounted the military methods used first to try and quell the unrest in South Vietnam and then subsequently to settle the conflict, on the grounds that political problems could not be solved militarily. And he held the U.S. responsible for escalating the war, propping up the South Vietnamese Government (and so averting its collapse), prolonging the conflict, and thereby preventing a political settlement between North and South Vietnam. For the perceptual framework in which de Gaulle viewed Vietnam was the Algerian Civil War, not the Munich and Second World War of U.S. official propaganda. Thus, President de Gaulle's views on the war – apart from the possibility of a wider conflagration, for which he held the U.S. primarily responsible – were totally at odds with the U.S. Administration's assessments of the conflict and its chances of success (see Sullivan, 1978: 71–4, 90).

These views, and de Gaulle's habit of airing them privately, but more importantly publicly, were profoundly unwelcome to an Administration which portrayed the war as a crusade for freedom against future communist tyranny, and also perceived the pursuit of the war as a vital manifestation of America's general reliability as an ally. So the Administration was hardly likely to see itself (as others saw it) as merely France's successor in a now quasi-colonial venture. Not unnaturally, Administration officials perceived the current French official and public attitudes to be primarily a product of their previous defeat in Indochina and their resentment over being replaced by the U.S. (see Airgram A-2829 [Paris Embassy] Counselor Funkhauser to State Department, 12 June 1965; France, Cables 2/65–6/65, Volume VI, France Country File, NSF, Box 171, LBJ Library; see also Sullivan, 1978: 92–3).

Although the press sometimes opined that de Gaulle's criticisms of the U.S. in Vietnam were a little too one-sided – as for instance on the occasion of his Phnom Penh speech on the war in September 1966 when he stated that the U.S. should unilaterally withdraw its troops and stop the bombing – in the main his general foreign policy stance and views on the Vietnam War and the U.S. role were supported by both press and public in France. Thus there was no real danger for de Gaulle of political or public dissension or embarrassment over the official attitude to either U.S. policies or propaganda, as there was in Britain where the potential already existed for the government, its Official Parliamentary opposition, its own Parliamentary Party, and the public to pull in different directions over governmental support for America in Vietnam. For though the British Government might voice careful disapproval of particular U.S. policies – and be embarrassed by them – as it had already done over the gas warfare episode, it nevertheless couched such disapproval within a general framework of support for U.S. objectives in Vietnam. De Gaulle, however, could condemn U.S. policies and actions such as the use of gas and blame the U.S. entirely for escalating the war, and know that he spoke not only for himself but also for other political parties, the French public, and with the approval of the press – which disapproved strongly of U.S. methods of fighting the war (see *Le Monde*, 24 March 1965, on the use of gas and escalation of the war).

The diplomatic consequence of de Gaulle's (and other officials') statements on Vietnam, particularly after his Phnom Penh speech, was that both the U.S. Administration and the South Vietnamese Government regarded the French position as too biased to be of assistance to them – indeed, diplomatic relations between the French and South Vietnamese governments had ceased in June 1965 on the initiative of the latter due to the French attitude to Saigon and the war. However, while rendering France unacceptable to one side in the conflict, de Gaulle's stance was progressively more appreciated by the North Vietnamese, and thus French officials were well-placed to participate in the continuing saga of peace moves and counter-moves that lasted throughout the war (see, for instance, the highly sensitive Hanoi 'signal' in May 1965 passed through North Vietnam's Paris representative, Mai Van Bo, referred to in a series of U.S. Paris Embassy telegrams [sanitized]: 6711, 6701, 6691, 6690, 6612, in May 1965 contained in France Cables, Volume VI, 2/65–6/65, France Country File, NSF, Box 171, LBJ Library). For though the U.S. Administration was displeased by the French attitude and high-level contact was frequently strained, nevertheless a significant degree of contact was maintained between the two governments at lower levels, particularly between the various departments of the Quai and the U.S. embassy.

On occasions these contacts – leaving aside the thorny issue of the peace moves – were of considerable use to the Americans, yielding information from a number of sources, such as the French contact with the North Vietnamese representative in Paris, Mai Van Bo, or the French Ambassadors to China and the Soviet Union. This information added to the general picture of the North Vietnamese and their allies, but sometimes French officials also attempted to help the Americans through their access to the North Vietnamese, as in the case of the latter's threat in December 1965 to put U.S. prisoners of war on trial and execute them. The Quai d'Orsay (French Foreign Office) official in charge of Asian Affairs, Etienne Manac'h, protested to Mai Van Bo on humanitarian grounds, pointing out that 'world public opinion would consider it inadmissible to execute prisoners of war under such circumstances', a message that Bo agreed to transmit to Hanoi 'immediately' (Embtel 3486 [Paris] McBride to Secretary of State, 18 December 1965, France Cables, Volume VIII, 9/65–1/66, France Country File, NSF, Box 172, LBJ Library). The threatened trials never took place, and whilst the precise effect of the French intervention cannot be ascertained, the fact is that the North Vietnamese valued the increasingly friendly contact with the French Government (Sullivan, 1978: 99–102), and at the very least the French protest would have added to the weight of condemnation of the proposed trials.

Thus, though the French Government was impervious to U.S. official propaganda on the war's origins and the dangers of monolithic Sino-Soviet communist expansionism, though it consistently opposed U.S. policies in Vietnam and the means used to try and attain its objectives, specifically the bombing raids whether used as a carrot or a stick, still French officials played a useful role. In addition, de Gaulle's assessment of the will and capability of the North Vietnamese, as opposed to the inherent and fatal political and social weakness of the South Vietnamese regime(s), proved to be far more accurate than the analyses of the U.S. and its other European supporters. Unfortunately the demands of U.S. global and regional policy, and the predilections of some of Johnson's advisers, determined that French expertise and advice on this issue would be ignored in favour of more optimistic assessments of the war's outcome and support from more compliant European allies, until the shock of the Tet Offensive in 1968, when the Administration was finally forced to confront the spectre of a never-ending and continuously escalating war of attrition, which three years of continual bombing and ground combat had failed to stave off.

West Germany

The attitude of the West German (FRG) Government on the U.S. role in Vietnam, as was the case with the UK, sprang primarily from its domestic political concerns, but also contained elements peculiar to the FRG's position – historical, political and geographical – within post-war Europe and the then prevailing international system. Even more than the U.K., West Germany at this time had a particular interest in maintaining good relations with the U.S. Administration. For West Germany not only required the good economic relations with the U.S. that Britain too needed, but since the end of the Second World War the FRG had also been especially indebted to the U.S. for its defence, guaranteed through NATO and by the very visible presence of U.S. troops in Germany. Because it was the FRG which was the Western 'front-line' state in the Cold War, and which, in its partitioned form, was the literal manifestation of the continuing divide between East and West, ideologically, politically, and geographically – with West Berlin as another political and geographical reminder of the problems still remaining from the Second World War, and the Berlin Wall as a physical 'Iron Curtain'. Thus for West German Governments the Cold War was more of a reality than it was for other European nations and that fact alone helped mould their attitude to America and American policies in general. Nevertheless, despite Chancellor Erhard's and Kiesinger's public declarations of gratitude for U.S. efforts in defence of world-wide freedom, peace and security via the Vietnam War, as with other European nations, the linkage between fighting communism in Asia and European security was apparently regarded by some German ministers (see Brandt below) as rather less obvious than it was to the U.S. Administration (for Erhard and Kiesinger statements, see Germany, Erhard Visit 12/65, Press Release Toasts, 20 December 1965, Germany Country File, NSF, Box 192; and Germany, Visit of Chancellor Kiesinger, 8/67 III, Cable, Bonn Embassy to State Department, 23 August 1967, Germany Country File, NSF, Box 193, LBJ Library).

However, politically it was U.S. policies towards the Soviet Union and Eastern Europe that were of particular importance to the FRG Government, and which constituted an additional reason why the FRG required good relations with America, because these policies impinged on the ultimate goal of German reunification, for which U.S. support was especially needed to oppose Soviet bloc intentions of a permanently divided Germany.

Thus it was in the FRG's own interests to support America publicly on the issue of Vietnam, whatever the private sentiments of ministers (see below). And though the U.S. Administration periodically pressed the West German Government to provide higher levels of material and humanitarian assistance as well as verbal support, FRG Chancellor Erhard never faced repeated U.S. requests for troops – unlike the British Prime Minister – for obvious reasons, which made support rather easier. The following exchange between the State Department and the Bonn embassy, concerning briefing papers for Erhard's December 1965 visit to Washington, shows the prevailing historical and political sensitivities and the implicit recognition by the U.S. Administration that even requesting German troops for Vietnam would harm the U.S. image:

> B. We would suggest that the last sentence of the first paragraph be amended to read: "Out of concern over Germany's militarist image and fear of damage to its reunification policy, however, the FRG avoids any kind of military assistance to all areas of tension or conflict, including Viet-Nam" and that a final sentence be added to read as follows, "Recognizing this, we have not asked the FRG for a military contribution." This would avoid any impression that German reluctance to give military aid is directed exclusively toward Viet-Nam or that we have requested such aid. (Embtel 1438 [Bonn] McGhee to Secretary of State, 18 November 1965, Germany Cables, Volume IX, 7/65–1/66, Germany Country File, National Security File, Boxes 186 and 187, LBJ Library)

These practical policy considerations were also apparently reinforced by a feeling on the part of German policy-makers that criticism of U.S. policy on Vietnam would be unwise, as well as unwarranted because of Germany's past, as Willy Brandt, Foreign Minister in Chancellor Kiesinger's government and Chancellor himself from 1969, writes:

> I have never believed in the domino theory – that if Saigon falls today, all Asia will fall tomorrow and Europe the day after. Nor did I believe that Berlin was being defended in Vietnam. But I was not indifferent to seeing the United States described as a 'paper tiger', as Mao put it. I thought that it was certainly not for us Germans to put ourselves forward as lecturers in international politics and certainly not as moral judges; nor did I feel it advisable to interfere with the American Government in an area it said was vital. Consequently I swallowed my grave doubts and held my tongue where it might have been better to make my opposition explicit on the one hand, and on the other make open display of my suppressed sympathies. (Brandt, 1992: 364)

The suppressed sympathies to which Brandt refers were those he felt for the anti-Vietnam War protesters, although his sympathy stopped short of support for their methods of protest – as did the general public's in most of Europe, as David Caute notes in his analysis of youth politics during this era and the differences between New and Old Left: 'It is by the street scenes and campus occupations of 1967–1969 that the New Left is remembered – and rejected – by the population at large' (Caute, 1988: 27). Nevertheless, despite Brandt's suppressed sympathies and his (and his ambassadors') inability to 'identify' with the Vietnam War by spring 1967 (Brandt, 1992: 364), the fact is that the West German Government continued to express appreciation of U.S. efforts in Vietnam and to 'respect American efforts in this regard' (Germany, Visit of Chancellor Kiesinger, 8/67 III, Cable, Bonn Embassy to State Department, 23 August 1967, Germany Country File, NSF, Box 193, LBJ Library).

The early government attitude to U.S. involvement in Vietnam was, for the most part, endorsed by the press and public, and though by November 1967 Gallup International reported that a majority (58 per cent) of West German opinion polled thought that the U.S. 'should begin to withdraw its troops', this sentiment still did not lead to public approval of violent anti-war demonstrations, inescapably associated with students. Such demonstrations were, if anything, counterproductive, engendering a public backlash against students being allowed to stage political demonstrations (Caute, 1988: 77–85). Nor, of course, did the knowledge in 1967 that the general public no longer supported U.S. involvement in Vietnam (a change from their position in 1965 and 1966, according to Gallup International) lead the West German Government to reconsider its own policy of supporting the U.S. Administration, any more than it did the British Government, which from mid-1966 faced the same gap between its policies and the public's disapproval.

So, of America's three most important European allies, only the French Government was in the happy position of pursuing an official policy, *vis-à-vis* the Vietnam War, with which its media and public were in accord. By contrast, both the British and West German governments pursued official policies (that may have differed from private views) which, while in their own interests for domestic political and economic reasons, and though initially supported by their general publics, very soon became publicly unpopular. Thus the next three chapters examine the balance sheet for this period of the war, looking at the successes and failures of U.S. propaganda in the European context, and thereby outlining the propaganda legacy that Richard Nixon inherited as President in 1969.

5

The balance sheet for LBJ (I): European media by 1968

As stated earlier, the U.S. Administration's propaganda campaign was waged with three broad goals in mind: to persuade its audiences to perceive the war as the Administration wished it to be perceived; to convince its audiences of the necessity and importance of the war; and to persuade its audiences that the Administration's intentions were peaceful, with force used only as a last resort.

Within this broad framework there are several issues to consider when examining and judging the success or failure of the Administration's propaganda campaign. This campaign can be judged both as a whole and as a series of propaganda operations, or as a response to a particular incident during the war and the subsequent publicity that was usually generated. The issues to consider are: Administration planning and knowledge at different stages of the war, a considerable amount of which is contained in *The Pentagon Papers*; what newspapers (the main source of information in this early period of the war) reported at these same stages; how this reporting fitted in with the Administration's plans; how European allied governments acted and what their publics thought, according to opinion polls; and the effects of Administration propaganda policies and moves as reflected in the media, and as they affected allied governments and public opinion.

For a number of reasons Administration planning and knowledge is especially important in relation to the early stages and subsequent escalation of the war.

Firstly, from the Administration's point of view this was a crucial stage in the conflict itself. In only three months the Administration had switched from the previous policy of limited involvement with American advisers, to air raids, and then to the dispatch of ground troops, even though in a defensive role. In the short term the tactics that the Administration used to handle publicity at this early stage – before greater involvement and growing casualties, and while the possibility of withdrawal was still thought to be an alternative – could affect more seriously the way that the next set of policy decisions on conducting the expanded conflict would be received and perceived by both press and publics (national and international).

Secondly, in view of the Administration's previously expressed reluctance to 'go North', during the early stage of increased activity it was necessary to fix in the press and publics' perceptions the necessity for the Administration's decision to bomb North Vietnam and then to convince them of the Administration's basically peaceful intentions, reluctance to escalate, and desire for negotiations. In propaganda terms this could then be used to justify the Administration's future conduct of the conflict.

Thirdly, from the point of view of assessing the Administration's propaganda campaign, recapping briefly on the Administration's knowledge and planning in the early stages of the war will show the extent to which the Administration privately realized what lay ahead, that is, the massive growth of the conflict with its attendant casualties. And having recalled the Administration's private perceptions of the future course of the war it then becomes possible to compare these perceptions with the Administration's view of the conflict contained in official statements and speeches disseminated through the media, and to determine the accuracy and veracity of Administration statements.

As *The Pentagon Papers* demonstrate, Administration planning in the initial stages of the war was detailed, moved rapidly from a defensive to an offensive strategy based on General Westmoreland's search-and-destroy tactics, and focused on the kill ratio as a means to winning this war of attrition (see Chapter 1). The Administration's troop and casualty projections also rose rapidly and as early as November 1965 Defense Secretary McNamara was recommending that by the end of 1966 there should be almost 400,000 troops in South Vietnam, but at the same time he warned the President that this level of deployment 'will not guarantee success' and that there was an even chance that the war would be stalemated at 'an even higher level' (Sheehan et al., 1971: 466). And as the troop figures rocketed, so naturally did those for casualties: by November 1965 McNamara estimated that 'U.S. killed-in-action can be expected to reach 1,000 a month' – compared with his recommendation to the President a mere three months earlier in July that 'U.S. killed-in-action might be in the vicinity of 500 a month by the end of the year' (Sheehan et al., 1971: 464–6).

The results of the Administration's propaganda policy will now be examined, concentrating on media coverage (primarily press coverage in the first three years of the conflict) of some particularly important incidents and issues following escalation of the war. Chapter 6 will examine the state of public opinion by 1968, and the impact of violent opposition to the war.

Media coverage

Not surprisingly, the planning of the Administration often bore little resemblance to press coverage of these issues, for in Washington the press was dependent on official briefings, on private contacts in the Administration and other officials' views, and on what it could piece together from any other relevant sources (in South Vietnam, however, there were not only official sources, but there was also the possibility of eye-witness accounts of the war and events in Saigon – which might contradict the official version).

Thus, when McNamara and Johnson were contemplating sending 400,000 troops to Vietnam, the press was wondering whether the figure might reach 200,000, at a time when there were still 'only' 184,000 troops there (Sheehan et al., 1971: 466). And this discrepancy was due to the Administration's desire to keep publicity about its war policies to a minimum, and thereby to avoid public disquiet about U.S. involvement in a conflict which had already assumed vastly greater proportions and intensity than only a few months previously. And of course this publicity embargo also covered the unwelcome discovery that the enemy was matching U.S. troop deployments, which meant that the U.S. commitment – given the opposing views of the U.S. and the Vietcong/North Vietnam, and South Vietnam's weakness – was open-ended in a war in which 'winning' would be hard to determine, as the Administration knew.

This, however, was not a conclusion which the Administration wanted publicized, for it had rejected from the beginning the other course open to it, that of openly declaring war, seeking a Congressional Declaration, and publicly rallying the nation in support of its objectives. So instead the Administration tried to fight what quickly became a major war with minimal information, hoping that as the conflict dragged on the public would support an ill-understood and vicious war for which it had not been prepared. And when the media speculated about the war more than the Administration wished, or provided estimates closer to the truth than the latter wished – thereby enabling the general public to gain a more accurate (usually less optimistic) view of the war – then the Administration promptly rounded on the U.S. press, accusing it of hostile and inaccurate news coverage, as did the British and West German Governments with their media.

On the other hand, eager press speculation about vague Administration hints about peace moves (however unlikely) *was* encouraged at particular junctures – and discouraged at others: what top Administration officials wanted from the press was the dissemination of the official line on the war – whatever it was and however contradictory the statements – and the portrayal of the war in the type of black and white terms in which the Second World War could be perceived and portrayed. The irony was that even those journalists who agreed wholeheartedly with the U.S. involvement in Vietnam still criticized the Administration's public relations campaign for its ineptitude and paucity of information (*Daily Telegraph*, 10 June 1965), and for its 'misleading' public stance on peace talks (Alsop in the *New York Herald Tribune*, 20–21 November 1965).

Considering the number of times that the Administration was caught out by its own information policy – that is, when its war policies or current events directly contradicted official statements, or when the past intruded into the present and demonstrated how economical with 'details' the Administration had been – the Administration was given the benefit of the doubt for a considerable length of time. For most press criticism in the U.S., U.K. and West Germany was initially directed at the results of U.S. war methods and the difficulties engendered by U.S. official propaganda. *The Guardian*'s leader writer in Britain questioned U.S. involvement from early 1965 on legal, political and moral grounds, while the *Observer* fretted about the war's deleterious impact on international relations, considering it to be an obstacle to the growing *détente* between East and West. But most other main stream newspapers in the U.K., and those in West Germany (France was obviously the exception from the beginning), supported the U.S. with much the same justifications that U.S. official propaganda put forward, with the added elements that the U.S. had never lost a war (so victory was expected) and was still associated with 'just' causes.

Nevertheless journalists still reported what they saw in the field in South Vietnam, and Washington correspondents reported official Administration statements and private views, and often these reports alone were enough to cast doubts on the Administration's credibility, despite the overall agreement with the Administration's objectives. Because the root cause of the Administration's 'credibility gap' lay in its own information policies: the 'gap' was merely exposed by the press, often inadvertently, not created by them.

This issue of credibility affected the Administration in several ways. Firstly there was the straightforward issue of 'truth'-telling or – to remove the element of subjective perception contained in the word 'truth' – whether and to what degree the Administration's version of events, current and past, accorded with the actual events being reported, by participants or eye-witnesses. Such an issue could be determined on a reasonably factual basis, even though interpretations of the events in question could still differ.

For instance, the Administration's stance on peace talks was that the U.S. was willing to discuss this issue at any time and any place with the communists, but the latter unfortunately refused to contemplate such discussion. The President's speeches on peace were invariably welcomed enthusiastically by the press and public and were believed for quite some time; thus the onus for the lack of talks was placed entirely on the intransigence of the communists. However, in November 1965 it became known through the press (in fact U Thant had hinted of this even earlier in the year, but the issue was not taken up then) that the U.S. had turned down an opportunity to discuss the war with Hanoi in late 1964. And in view of the Administration's previous trumpeting of the communist unwillingness to talk, this revelation caused a storm of press protest. In a stinging editorial *The New York Times* commented:

> The details, and just what each person did or said at the period a year ago when Hanoi sought a discussion with the United States on ending hostilities in Vietnam, must and will be sifted by history. The outstanding – and many will think devastating – fact is that Hanoi offered to talk and Washington

refused. This may well prove a heavy burden for the Johnson Administration to rectify. (*The New York Times*, 17 November 1965: 'A Chance that was Missed')

Pouring scorn on State Department Spokesman Robert McCloskey's previous reference to Secretary of State Dean Rusk's sensitivity to 'serious peace moves', and also revealing considerable anxiety, the editorial stated:

Secretary Rusk, according to Mr. McCloskey has a 'sensitive antenna' and he would have known – or sensed – when North Vietnam was really prepared for peace talks. This comment reminds one of the ancient Roman practice of drawing auspices from the flight or entrails of birds. It would be a shuddering thought that the fate of nations and of thousands of young Americans depended on Dean Rusk's antenna. Yet this is what Mr. McCloskey indicated. (Ibid.)

In Britain *The Guardian* suggested that the Administration 'has done itself serious damage by thus sowing the seeds of distrust among the public, less ready than most to accept unquestioningly the statements of its leaders' (18 November 1965: 'Rising Criticism in U.S. over Rejected Peace Feeler'). The *Daily Express* went one step further than *The Guardian* in its interpretation of this rejection, with a dispatch from its Washington correspondent which began with the dramatic question:

Is the United States now bent only on bludgeoning North Vietnam to sue for peace after inflicting a crushing, humiliating military defeat?

This is emerging from the fog of Washington's half-truths this week about the history of repeated peace overtures from Hanoi over 13 months. (19 November 1965: 'The Hottest Topic in the White House')

These opening paragraphs shaped and disseminated to the audience the precise impression of its policies that the Administration had taken such pains to avoid creating. The dispatch then dwelt on the diplomatic results of Washington's 'half-truths':

I find sincere doubt in the embassies of many allied and neutral nations that the U.S. will agree to cease fire talks short of complete surrender by North Vietnam, the Vietcong, and the National Liberation Front of all their interests and claims south of the 17th parallel.

> Over the next six weeks a torrent of reinforcements will build American forces on the ground to over 200,000.
>
> Early in 1966 the U.S. will have amassed 250,000 troops in Vietnam. (Ibid.)

Interestingly this report also mentioned the ambiguous peace feeler by North Vietnam in May following the unofficial U.S. bombing pause, explaining that Washington rejected this offer because it was 'woolly'. Summing up the climate of opinion on peace moves, the *Daily Express* report stated: 'Usually well-informed sources say that the White House and the State Department will eventually have to acknowledge that Washington had rejected several similar Hanoi feelers while claiming there were none.'

Not all press criticism of the Administration treated this episode as a lost opportunity for peace. In the *New York Herald Tribune* (European edition), Joseph Alsop, commenting from his hawkish standpoint, took the Administration to task for its public attitude to negotiations. Alsop brushed aside North Vietnam's 'exceedingly vague' negotiation offer, made at a time when South Vietnam's resistance 'was very nearly on its last legs' and would have completely collapsed if the U.S. had negotiated 'behind' South Vietnam's back. Stating that this was why Rusk had rejected the offer, Alsop then attacked the Administration's propaganda on peace talks:

> But these facts [about rejecting the peace offer] do not exonerate the administration from all blame. The administration is to blame, not for rejecting the Hanoi offer, but simply for creating the public climate in which so much nonsense is talked.
>
> Unless very high authorities are also very good liars, the whole prevailing notion of the official American attitude to negotiation is almost completely false and misleading. The truth is that the president made his original offer of 'unconditional' negotiations [the Johns Hopkins University speech], and has since repeated that offer, for the main purpose of disarming the domestic and foreign critics of his Vietnamese policy. (*New York Herald Tribune*, 20–21 November 1965: 'The Flurry over Hanoi's "Peace Offer"'; square brackets added)

After a brief discussion about the meaning of 'unconditional' talks – the U.S. would continue to bomb North Vietnam while negotiating – the columnist returned to the theme of the Administration's 'misleading' public stance on peace talks. Quoting a recent speech by Army Chief of Staff Harold K. Johnson about the 'mistake' of the Korean War negotiations, Alsop concluded: 'The fact remains that Gen. Johnson's speech is almost the only forthright word that has been officially said. All sorts of wrong interpretations of the American attitude have been accepted without rebuttal, and have even, on occasion, been sedulously fostered. This, it must be said, is a dangerous thing to have done' (ibid.).

Alsop's illuminating analysis, revealing the gulf between the Administration's private and public views on peace offers, could not have been helpful to a government which was intent on fostering the false impressions that Alsop both exposed and fulminated against. As noted before, the irony of Alsop's criticism was that it stemmed from his belief in the importance of the U.S. involvement in Vietnam: he saw the Administration's protestations of a desire for peace as not only 'misleading' but also harmful to the U.S. goal of victory in the war.

Thus this particular episode dealt a blow not only to the credibility of the Administration's stance on peace talks – having not only rejected an offer, but also according to Alsop having made its offer(s) purely for public consumption, that is, purely for propaganda purposes in popular terms – but also undermined its general credibility, having been firstly 'economical' with its facts about the communists refusing to talk and then having to admit to the original allegation that an offer was turned down. This was a syndrome that had already happened in the past on an equally important issue: the tardy public admission in June 1965 of a change in troop role (secretly authorized in April) from defensive to offensive, that is, the admission of a ground war in Asia. And the difficulty for the Administration lay in the fact that whether or not its original peace offer(s) were just 'propaganda', it was now more than ever imperative that it continue to make such offers in order to avoid being labelled more widely as 'mere propagandists' and so further eroding its support among the public. And this was a trap that the Administration had created for itself in originally whetting its audiences' appetite for peace, whilst having – according to *The Pentagon Papers* – no intention of negotiating on terms that were less than a North Vietnamese surrender, which the Administration also knew was highly unlikely.

Similarly, when the U.S. bombed the Hanoi area in December 1966, Administration spokesmen categorically denied that there were civilian casualties. However, due to the presence of the Managing Director of the *New York Times* (Harrison Salisbury) in Hanoi at the same time as the bombing raids, these official U.S. statements were themselves comprehensively and damningly contradicted – on a matter of fact, not interpretation. Again the Administration's credibility was damaged, and the damage was compounded in the way in which spokesmen first denied the charge and then were forced to admit it. The U.S. Information Agency's (USIA) analysis of media coverage summarized 'free world' countries' reactions to the bombings on 19 December as follows:

> The sustained Communist propaganda campaign denouncing the U.S. for allegedly bombing Hanoi has received a very mixed reaction in free world countries. While most non-Communist media have been hesitant or unwilling to accept the Communist charges in full, they have generally emphasized three points: 1) regret that the U.S. bombing tactics should reach innocent civilians, 2) fear that these tactics at this time preclude an extended truce or peace talks, and 3) puzzlement at the lack of a clear explanation by the U.S. Free world comment, confined largely to Western Europe, has made little mention of the American suggestion that Communist defensive weapons around Hanoi may have caused the reported damage and casualties. (Worldwide Treatment of Current Issues, Interim Report, 19 December 1966: 4: Office of Research and Analysis)

This report noted that 'British papers were skeptical of U.S. explanations' and the reports quoted in it show that this press scepticism covered the spectrum of stances on Vietnam. Reactions ranged from the *Daily Telegraph* which usually supported the U.S. and so fairly mildly noted the unavoidability of '"incidental damage to civilian life and property"'; through the *Observer*'s complaints about the '"credibility gap"' reaching its 'peak'; to the much less surprising comments of the 'hypercritical' *Guardian,* which perceptively judged that the raids would '" . . . insure that the truces [holiday truces] do not blossom into any negotiations except on Washington's terms. Perhaps that is their purpose."' The fact that there was 'Sparse West German comment' must have provided a little relief to American propagandists, but what comment there was contained some harsh words:

> The independent *Stuttgarter Zeitung* said that President Johnson had 'made it clear that he is willing to negotiate only with Hanoi, but his increasing raids on North Vietnam makes it unlikely that Hanoi will react at all to a U.S. offer.' The paper said the 'militarily important targets' were so close to Hanoi's housing areas that Washington's intention was obviously to convince the enemy that it will continue its 'merciless crushing tactics. The women and children killed in

Hanoi will further blacken the image of the U.S. President, who must now decide whether to fight harshly or endlessly.' (Ibid.: 6)

Adverse French press comment was of course expected, but fortunately 'fell off after an early spate of skeptical or sarcastic comment on U.S statements'. But again the comment was perceptive, this time focusing on the contradictory explanations that could emanate from Washington and Saigon, thereby revealing more of the Administration's planning than it wanted to be made public:

Today's pro-Gaullist *Paris-Jour* said: 'In Europe, the "explanations" by the military command in Saigon – especially in regard to North Vietnamese rockets falling' on Hanoi, 'have convinced nobody' – all the more so since the U.S. military in Saigon had earlier said the bombardment of Hanoi 'was a decision which they had at last obtained from President Johnson.' (Ibid.: 7)

By the end of December, after Harrison Salisbury's articles had appeared in the *New York Times* detailing civilian damage and casualties, the Administration faced another barrage of criticism. A USIA media report for 30 December summarized the results of the mainly European press reports:

Commentators made these points: 1) further doubt has been cast on the veracity of official U.S. statements; 2) the deplorable loss of civilian life and property indicates that U.S. bombing is not as accurate as it claims to be; 3) there is now even more reason to stop the bombing of North Vietnam; 4) Salisbury should be believed and congratulated for his reporting work; and 5) Communist countries would never permit one of their editors to make such reports. (Worldwide Treatment of Current Issues, 30 December 1966: A-1)

While 'British, French . . . papers' 'praised the American system of democracy' due to press freedom to 'investigate and publish reports' which contradicted the Administration and 'allows officials to openly admit mistakes have been made', nevertheless these same reports 'urged an end to the bombing as '"the only answer to this dilemma" (pro-Labor *Sun*)'. The *Daily Mail* suggested that there was '"only one way to stop civilians from being killed in Vietnam. That is by ending the war"' Of the West German press quoted, the 'influential *Frankfurter Allgemeine*' reckoned that 'the U.S. Government had been "caught lying"' and though understanding '"the difficulties of warfare," the paper charged the U.S. with news management and said it hoped there would be a return to truthfulness'. Berlin's 'independent *Berliner Morgenpost'*, however, was more sympathetic to the Administration, pointing out that due to the '"close interlocking"' of military 'and other significant targets' with '"urban areas, the bombing of houses cannot always be avoided"' (Worldwide Treatment of Current Issues, 30 December 1966: A-1–A-4)

Although it subsequently became known that some of Salisbury's information about the damage and casualties had come from communist sources – which he had failed to disclose – the fact remained that the Administration handled the whole episode badly on a number of counts. Firstly, the impression had been given in official briefings that very little damage or civilian casualties occurred due to the precision bombing only of military targets, thus also endeavouring to give the impression of a clean, clinical war – something which official language also tried to reinforce. Secondly, the Administration then flatly denied the charges of U.S. involvement in any damage and casualties, and then tried to attribute this to the communists' own rockets. And thirdly, official spokesmen were then forced to admit that such damage had occurred as a result of U.S. bombing. So although Salisbury's reports contained some communist propaganda, the Administration was hardly in a position to complain about this, having itself disseminated an inaccurate picture, from the beginning, of the effects of U.S. bombing – in other words, presenting a biased view. For though the Administration was not deliberately targeting civilian areas and most newspapers recognized this, what mattered was the official denial of any such damage followed by the tardy admission that this sort of damage was in fact virtually inevitable, as Hammond notes in his study of military and media relations in Vietnam: 'While early in the controversy official spokesmen would concede only grudgingly that American bombing might have injured a relatively small number of civilians, by its end they were admitting, for example, that during one strike on the Yen Vien railroad yard three bombs had fallen on the target and forty outside' (Hammond, 1988: 279).

These are instances in which the Administration's general reputation for disseminating accurate accounts of events was publicly eroded, but there was also another way in which the Administration's credibility was slowly impaired and this concerned the progress – or lack of it – in the war. For the continuous escalation of the war in intensity and carnage cast doubt on the ability of the U.S. to do the job it had set out to do at a cost that was acceptable, not only in domestic political terms, but also in terms of world opinion. The difficulty that the U.S. administration faced was that these two sets of demands, internal public opinion and external opinion, were not easily reconcilable while the U.S. was trying to fight and win the war.

Obviously, U.S. public opinion was primarily concerned about U.S. war casualties and the financial strain of the war, and this resulted in pressure on the Administration to show some sort of 'progress' in order to justify these human and financial costs fighting a confusing war. Yet, as mentioned previously, this was a difficult task for U.S. propaganda in a war with no front lines and a frequently elusive enemy: thus the kill-ratio was the statistic used for the combatants, and then there were the statistics for the pacification effort, and aid generally to South Vietnam – all designed to measure the war and then publicized to show that the U.S. was making 'progress'.

This confusion over 'progress' was compounded by the Administration's multiple and frequently contradictory justifications for fighting the war, which required considerable modifications between 1965 and 1968. This was due partly to the behaviour of both the South Vietnamese Government and the South Vietnamese Army, and to the public exposure of the flaws in early U.S. propaganda on the war, such as the one-sided interpretation of the provisions and violations of the Geneva Agreements, and the gradual retreat from publicizing South Vietnam as 'democratic' and 'free'. And these factors, together with the rising casualties and looming elections, helped to impose a time-scale on the war, which meant that the Administration did not have unlimited time to fight a vicious war of attrition, as the President and his top advisers knew. Added to the pressure to demonstrate progress for domestic opinion was the pressure from the President's military advisers to continually escalate and intensify the war, both to try and break the stalemate and achieve victory, and to minimize U.S. casualties. And the President responded to this pressure because there was little alternative but withdrawal. Moreover the U.S. public responded favourably to the implementation of clear-cut Administration policies – whether these involved an escalation in bombing or the announcement of a peace move (see Mueller, 1985: 69–104: note that the U.S. public approved of the bombing while it was the official policy). And so the mainstream U.S. public continued to support the war (though this support was slowly eroding) until time ran out after the Tet Offensive in 1968 – it was the anti-war protesters who early on objected to the destruction and the war itself.

World opinion, however, was less concerned with the rise in U.S. casualties, or the need to minimize them by using air-strikes for instance, than with the cost of the war in terms of the carnage in South and North Vietnam, and the war's impact on international relations – particularly the possiblity of a wider conflagration. Therefore escalation was queried both on the grounds of the sheer scale of the destruction and that peace would be harder to achieve.

The Administration was thus in a cleft stick, needing to escalate to try and attain its objectives, and in order to retain domestic support (given that its brand of peace moves was unlikely to be successful), but in doing so progressively alienating foreign public opinion, including the media – which reported the carnage. For the European media would publish articles which the U.S. press were apparently chary of publishing as 'unsuitable for American readers' (Gellhorn, 1986: 254). Thus Martha Gellhorn's series of articles in September 1966 appeared in *The Guardian*. Focusing on the U.S. campaign to win 'Hearts and Minds' in South Vietnam, they carried descriptions of the effects of U.S. war methods on the population in South Vietnam – including the results of napalm and the refugee camps created – war methods which inherently defeated the drive to win over the people:

> We are not maniacs or monsters; but our planes range the sky all day and all night and our artillery is lavish and we have much more deadly stuff to kill with. The people are there on the ground, sometimes destroyed by accident, sometimes destroyed because the Vietcong are reported to be among them. This is indeed a new kind of war, as the [U.S.] indoctrination lecture stated, and we had better find a new way to fight it. Hearts and minds, after all, live in bodies. (*The Guardian*, 12 September 1966: 'A New Kind of War')

For all that the articles were too much for the U.S. market, and that *The Guardian*'s editor considered that Gellhorn's articles 'brought home, more effectively than anything I had read until then, the horror and the human cost of the war' (Hetherington, 1981: 228), in later years Gellhorn herself remarked that her articles on Vietnam 'are a model of self-censorship' but that 'to be heard at all, I had to suppress half of what I knew and gentle the rest' (Gellhorn, 1986: 254). It seems therefore, that even what was then taken to be (too) robust reporting of the war's carnage fell well short of depicting reality.

Nevertheless these articles, however 'gentle', came at a time when the Administration could ill-afford reports of the war's costs, for at the end of June 1966 the war had been escalated dramatically by the bombing of North Vietnam's petroleum, oil and lubricants (P.O.L.) depots near Hanoi and Haiphong, in an effort to cripple North Vietnam's continuing ability to wage war (Sheehan et al., 1971: 475–6). The raids were ultimately unsuccessful militarily, as the CIA had warned they would be, in that although 76 per cent of North Vietnam's bulk storage capacity was eliminated, sufficient supplies remained, supplemented by imports to meet North Vietnam's requirements, as had become apparent at the end of that summer; so infiltration continued and North Vietnam kept up the fight (Gravel, 1971, vol. IV: 29). Furthermore, the effect of the raids on America's allied government supporters was to increase the difficulties they already faced by mid-1966 in continuing to back U.S. involvement, due to a growing gap between governmental and general public sympathies.

Although a special effort had been made to enlist U.K. Prime Minister Wilson's support for the raids, this failed and Wilson felt obliged to publicly dissociate the British Government from these bombings; and despite having been informed beforehand (see below), this dissociation was a blow to the Administration (see Embtel 7103 [State Department] to London, 27 May 1966, United Kingdom Country File, Volume VIII, Cables 1/66–7/66; Classification Secret, NODIS; National Security File, Boxes 208–209, LBJ Library). For though the official British statement, reported by the media, expressed general support for U.S. assistance to South Vietnam and U.S. proposals for unconditional negotiations, and blamed North Vietnam for the continued fighting, the Administration's public reaction was one of 'deep chagrin', as *The Guardian* noted (30 June 1966: 'Attacks "Noted with Regret" – Premier'). And the natural corollary to this public disagreement was for the press to speculate on the effects that this would have on Anglo-American relations in the future, including a forthcoming visit by Wilson to Washington in mid-July (see *Financial Times*, 30 June 1966: 'McNamara Gives Reasons for Escalation').

The overall mood in Europe following the raids was noted in USIA's media round-up: 'Press reports of a widespread wave of indignation, dramatized by anti-US demonstrations in Europe, India, and Japan, were reprinted all over the world.' USIA then summed up the sources of the anxiety over this new escalatory step, and in doing so encapsulated most of the European fears about U.S. policy and the dangers associated with the war itself:

Adverse criticism was deeply rooted in fears of new escalation which might bring the Communist Chinese into the war. Many writers challenged the effectiveness of such raids or any comparable step-up in bringing Hanoi to agree to negotiations; they doubted whether civilian casualties could be avoided. Others pointed to "dissociation" statements to prove that the raids had sharpened differences among the allies. A severe setback to East–West "detente" hopes was seen by some. (Media Reaction Report, USIA/IOP/R, 8 July 1966: 1)

In addition, Administration optimism following the air raids was also discounted: French writers were reported to be sceptical about North Vietnam's supposed lack of expectation of a military victory combined with its 'war weariness', attributing this official optimism to 'upcoming Congressional elections'; and a West German newspaper noted that '"the President had failed to make the Vietnam situation plausible to many"' (USIA/IOP/R, 8 July 1966: 3).

Thus these raids, having firstly severely embarrassed European allied governments and sparked off demonstrations, finally resulted in a deleterious sharpening of the focus on U.S. war methods and aims.

The final blow as far as the Administration's credibility was concerned came in late 1967, when the Administration launched a campaign which had as one of its purposes the intention to demonstrate 'progress' in the war, for which General Westmoreland was required, as Hammond notes:

Although the purpose of the meeting was supposedly to discuss how the United States could achieve maximum progress during the next six months, there appears to have been little doubt in military circles that the general [Westmoreland] was participating in a major public relations initiative. His presence in Washington created opportunities not only to promote the theme of progress in the war but also to attack critics of the Administration's war policies and to bolster the president's sagging standing in the polls. (Hammond, 1988: 333)

Although this campaign to demonstrate progress was challenged by some sections of the U.S. press, nevertheless 'Westmoreland's remarks appeared prominently and in detail in the press' (Hammond, 1988: 335). And the same reaction was apparent in European newspapers, as a USIA Media Reaction report noted: 'Foreign editors reviewing last weeks's White House consultations on the Viet-Nam war concluded variously that 1) there was cause for some optimism in the progress of the ground war, 2) withdrawal possibilities should be considered, and 3) no significant change in U.S. Viet-Nam policy was in prospect' (Worldwide Treatment of Current Issues, 27 November 1967: 9). A West German newspaper was quoted as stating that Westmoreland's '"optimism came as a surprise to the public. It is partly due to election campaign considerations, but men as restrained as Westmoreland and Ambassador Bunker would not place themselves in an exposed position with such statements unless they had valid reasons for a more positive assessment of the situation."' This same paper then observed that Johnson '"had created the impression that the end of the tunnel is in sight . . . If he is able to maintain that impression, Johnson may win in the end, in the elections as well as in Viet-Nam, for Hanoi's perseverance is inspired by the idea that domestic considerations will compel the U.S. to give in sooner or later"' (ibid.: 10). Unfortunately for the Administration, rather than the end of the tunnel being in sight, what lay just round the corner was the Tet Offensive, which began just two months after this officially inaugurated bout of optimism. And interestingly, the other two West German newspapers that USIA quoted suggested that the U.S. should withdraw from Vietnam. Discounting Westmoreland's optimism about the situation in Vietnam on the grounds that '"the streets of Saigon are no longer safe in broad daylight, and that the primitively equipped Viet Cong . . . blew up the ammunition dumps in heavily fortified Dak To and disappeared unseen . . ."', the 'independent' *General-Anzeiger* of Bonn dismissed a major plank of the Administration's propaganda platform with the statement: '"Whether Washington's Asian goals are worth the sacrifice begs the question . . . All assurances to the contrary notwithstanding, most East and Southeast Asian nations desire no less than the withdrawal of American soldiers from Viet-Nam."' The pro-Social Democrat *Westfaelische Rundschau* based its case for a U.S. withdrawal on the grounds that the U.S. '"would not appear as a loser. Its prestige is too great to be seriously impaired by vacating a position to secure a better one. In holding on to Viet-Nam the U.S. serves Soviet and Chinese interests. A far-sighted Administration should concentrate on stabilizing positions from which it can protect its own security and that of its real friends. These positions do not include Viet-Nam"'. Again, several of the Administration's most important propaganda themes were discounted, along with a sharp reminder that U.S. involvement in Vietnam was a distraction from America's principal arena of interest – Europe (both papers cited in Worldwide Treatment of Current Issues, 27 November 1967: 10)

Nevertheless, despite such cautionary articles, with the *Financial Times* also pointing out that '"there is still no acceptable barometer for telling how the war is going. There is no indicator which says for example that one dead American for five dead North Vietnamese is a draw, and anything better than that is the beginning of a victory"' (Worldwide Treatment of Current Issues, 6 December 1967), the upbeat tone of Administration announcements helped to ensure that the scale and intensity of the Tet Offensive at the end of January 1968 came as a shock to the media – as indeed it did to the Administration itself.

From the beginning of the offensive correspondents' reports suggested that the communists' aims were to gain political and psychological ground, rather than a military victory, and they noted that the mere mounting of the offensive constituted a rebuttal of U.S. propaganda, as 'conservative' *Figaro* of Paris pointed out:

> "American positions are not endangered . . . This was not General Giap's aim. He aims at two objectives, both of an essentially political nature. On the domestic level, the Viet Cong has just won an enormous victory.
>
> "It has demonstrated to the Vietnamese population that it is capable of striking where and when it wants to. It ridicules the Saigon government and its army. It tightens its hold, at Saigon's expense, on a civilian population not necessarily friendly but filled with respect, fear and admiration . . .
>
> "Giap's second objective was evidently the American home front. His message is clear . . . 'We are stronger than ever.' The military authorities and President Johnson will find it rather difficult to demonstrate the contrary." (Worldwide Treatment of Current Issues, 31 January 1968: 4)

Hearteningly for the Administration at this stage, West German television 'characterized the Viet Cong attacks as a violation "of their own announced truce" and a demonstration that U.S. doubts about their "trustworthiness in negotiations" were justified' (Worldwide Treatment of Current Issues, 31 January 1968: 5). Thus initial coverage concentrated on the meaning of the offensive. However, as the fighting continued the focus shifted to include the carnage generated by these attacks. For instance on 2 February the reports that USIA included in its summary began: 'As correspondents' reports and shocking pictures brought home the "dreadful toll" of the street fighting in South Vietnamese cities, press commentators assessed the Viet Cong attacks as designed to win a political and psychological victory. Most thought they had succeeded, at least in part.' But this attention to the carnage could also constitute a bonus for the Administration, in that some newspapers placed much of the blame for the suffering of the South Vietnamese and the current horrors on the communists (see *Daily Telegraph* and *Daily Sketch*). As for assessments of success, *The Guardian* – invariably labelled by USIA as 'hypercritical' but dubbed 'liberal' in this report – pointed out:

"Hanoi implies that a final 'mighty push' is taking place and that the war will now be carried from the countryside into the towns of South Viet-nam. Yet its chances and the NLF's of holding any large towns for any length of time must be small. Even in the countryside the Viet cong seems to have been losing ground.

"Neither side can force the other to surrender; yet neither is winning, and both cause intolerable suffering. Negotiation is the only way to bring peace. But negotiation is impossible when only one side wants it." (Worldwide Treatment of Current Issues, 2 February 1968: 2)

French newspapers were reported to have given 'top placement to Viet-Nam developments' with 'headlines and pictures' conveying a 'sense of shock', with 'moderate-left' *France-Soir* stating that 'the attacks "are demonstrating in a bloody manner that no nation, however powerful, can win militarily in a revolutionary war"'. In West Germany 'pro-Christian Democratic *Frankfurter Neue Presse*' came to a similar conclusion: '"the Viet Cong must be seen as an important factor ... This has upset American calculations, even though certain people in Washington refuse to admit it. Efforts to represent the Communist offensive as mainly designed to improve Hanoi's position in future negotiations are interpretation acrobatics unrelated to the facts ... The White House will have to reappraise the Viet-Nam case. In so doing it cannot content itself with thinking in traditional military and political categories"' (both French and German comments from Worldwide Treatment of Current Issues, 2 February 1968: 2–3).

By 4 February USIA reported that 'British newspapers expressed a good deal of sympathy for the U.S., more support than criticism, and speculated on the future course of the war. Conservative papers condemned the Viet Cong's terrorism and murder of civilians, and declared that the U.S. is holding the line for civilization. Left-of-center papers, while not unsympathetic, urged the U.S. to find a way out of an impossible situation, even if it meant withdrawal' (Worldwide Treatment of Current Issues, 4 February 1968: 1).

The summing-up of the offensive, beginning on 5 February, carried a dual message for the Administration. On the one hand, as the USIA media summary noted: 'Influential British papers this morning emphasized that the people of South Viet-nam did not rise to support the Viet Cong as liberators, but frightened civilians might become more submissive to Communist pressures as a result of the audacious attacks.' And on the other hand, the same USIA report stated: 'Media in various countries saw the Viet Cong onslaught in the supposedly safe areas of South Viet-Nam as bringing into serious question the official U.S. position that the allied forces had been making "slow but steady progress." In fact, some papers stressed that Hanoi still had significant military strength in the south, and might make Khesanh "America's Dien Bien Phu"' (Worldwide Treatment of Current Issues, 5 February 1968: 1). This same line continued in the 7 February summary, with *The Guardian*'s Victor Zorza stating that: '"Something did go wrong with the plans for the South Viet-Nam uprising, on the Communists' own showing, although it is nothing like the failure that President Johnson claimed it was"', concluding optimistically that '"such evidence – admittedly incomplete – as is available suggests that the revolutionary storm is subsiding"' (Worldwide Treatment of Current Issues, 7 February 1968: 1–2). However, French and West German reports concentrated on the results for the U.S. and South Vietnamese:

> "For the first time since the beginning of the war in Viet-Nam, the ability of the American generals is being criticized in the U.S. Another consequence of the Viet Cong offensive is that the Saigon government is openly accused of indifference. And serious doubts are voiced regarding the possibility of pacifying South Viet-Nam, as much by the press as by Congressional circles and public opinion.
>
> "Discontent is shaping up, and even if it is not shared by the White House, some of Johnson's advisers are ready to admit that it is not without foundation . . . The reserved attitude he has been showing for some days toward his generals proves this." (*France-Soir* report cited in Worldwide Treatment of Current Issues, 7 February 1968: 3)

German reaction was summed-up by USIA under the heading 'German Disbelief'. In a report noting that 'West German news media rejected U.S. statements on the Viet Cong offensive', one paper was quoted as stating that: '"Now American credibility is probably completely destroyed"', and the specific foundations for German media scepticism were detailed:

German media contended that 1) contrary to U.S. claims, the South Vietnamese elections had not proved that the majority opted against the Viet Cong, 2) the South Vietnamese had shown no will to defend themselves and thus the U.S. contention that it is helping them to maintain freedom of choice is false, and 3) pacification has failed because even in secure areas the populations did not cooperate by reporting mass movements of Viet Cong through their areas. (Worldwide Treatment of Current Issues, 7 February 1968: 3–4).

Thus most of the Administration's propaganda arguments were dismissed in these media observations. And most importantly, USIA's summary of media reaction outside the U.S. shows that apart from some initial 'sensational newsplay' on the guerrilla attack on the U.S. embassy in Saigon (Worldwide Treatment of Current Issues, 31 January 1968: 1), much of the subsequent commentary focused on the significance of the offensive for both sides, with even the carnage being set in this broader context. Thus the allegations made against the U.S. press that it sensationalized the Tet Offensive, exaggerating the horror, disseminating the impression of a U.S. military defeat, and thereby creating a North Vietnamese/Viet Cong psychological and political victory, do not appear to apply to the European media. The latter quite rightly set the attacks within the context of U.S. Administration claims of progress in the war and pacification and saw the offensive as a rebuttal to these claims, and therefore a psychological and political setback; but equally the communists were seen to have suffered a setback in the lack of an uprising in the South. Thus the defeat for the U.S. focused on the hollowness of its claims, on virtually all aspects of its involvement in South Vietnam – demonstrated dramatically by the mere occurrence of the Tet Offensive – and exposed, but not created, by the media.

6

The balance sheet for LBJ (II): Government opinion by 1968

The Administration conducted its propaganda campaign on two levels, with each level serving a different, though linked, function. Firstly, there was the public campaign, with the dissemination of information, via the media, about Administration statements, press conferences, visits and appearances at various venues (even at debates overseas, such as in the Oxford Union in June 1965). Secondly, there was the background campaign conducted through confidential contact, primarily with friendly allied European governments, but also with élite figures in those countries.

By operating on these two levels the Administration hoped to keep its various audiences satisfied: European publics gleaned their information from the media; whilst their governments had additional knowledge vouchsafed them by Administration officials, intended not only to inform these governments in advance of sensitive developments, but also to reassure them about U.S. war policies, a need that often arose because of U.S. public statements on the war that conflicted with previous information. And the interrelationship between the two propaganda levels came with allied governments sometimes using this private information to help 'sell' support for the war to their own public – again often in the form of reassurance about U.S. aims – and on occasions to help deal with criticism of such support. For the minimum required by the U.S. Administration of its propaganda campaign in Europe was the continuing public support of the British and West German Governments (being the most important supportive allies in Europe), even while their publics turned against the war.

As the war lengthened and intensified, the problems that U.S. propaganda had to cope with, and by extension its allies' propaganda, changed and multiplied. As noted previously (Chapter 5), the initial task was to fix in the audiences' minds the justice of aiding South Vietnam militarily by blaming North Vietnam entirely for the turmoil in the South, with the concomitant need for the bombing campaign and the subsequent escalation of the war in the air and on the ground. This goal was mostly achieved (the main exception being French reaction), and was aided in the first few months of the war by press dissemination of the view that the Administration sincerely desired peace, and that therefore it was escalating reluctantly because of communist intransigence over negotiations. However, the accuracy of this picture was challenged and gradually modified during the years of public revelations about a number of important issues and events in the war, such as the nature of South Vietnamese 'democracy' and 'freedom'; the Administration's attitude to various peace moves during the war, and revelations about its past response, provoking doubts about the sincerity of 'peace' statements; and the confusion engendered by the nature of, and progress in, the war and the destruction caused by methods of fighting it.

The net result of the above factors was to slowly erode the Administration's credibility, resulting in even more debate on its statements on virtually all aspects of the war. And this diminution in Administration credibility and strength of its position, especially on issues such as peace offers and sincerity, was a bonus for the North Vietnamese and Vietcong, for though the latter's credibility and the strength of their case did not necessarily increase to the degree that the Administration's diminished, nevertheless it did become harder to dismiss the North Vietnamese/Vietcong case summarily, as had often happened earlier in the war. And the shifts that occurred in public perceptions of the Administration were accompanied by an erosion of support for the U.S. venture and a steady strengthening of the desire for a U.S. withdrawal. Thus the public climate in which U.S. propagandists and allied governments operated became increasingly more unfavourable to a venture which could only be of long duration (given the non-use of nuclear weapons, and the necessary political and geographical limits which forbade striking enemy sanctuaries outside Vietnam – although whether such strikes would have made any material difference to the U.S. war effort at the time is certainly debatable) and increasing destruction, if U.S. aims in Vietnam were to be achieved militarily and negotiations undertaken 'from strength'.

The impact of the U.S. information campaign and its consequences for its allies will now be assessed, focusing on the nature and timeliness (or otherwise) of information passed to other governments; the response of these governments; and lastly on public opinion, with the general public response manifested primarily through public opinion polls, and the attentive sections of the public making their opinion known through marches, demonstrations and other active measures.

United Kingdom government reaction and opinion

The problems facing the British Government in supporting U.S. actions in Vietnam can be categorized into those problems centring on the war itself, and independent of the Government's policy, and those concerning domestic politics and the position of the Labour government, some of which problems were often related to Government policy on the war. The first set of difficulties comprised the continuous escalation of the war and increasing carnage; and the perceived need for, but elusiveness of, negotiations to end the conflict – a need which Britain pursued primarily through diplomatic contacts with the U.S.S.R. (as the other Geneva Conference Co-Chairman) in an effort to recall the Geneva Conference and so mediate a settlement; and the Commonwealth. The second set of difficulties comprised the domestic setting of the Labour Government, its economic problems, its initial slender political majority (during the first Wilson government from 1964 to 1966), and the vociferous and active left-wing of the Labour Party, including some MPs in the Parliamentary Labour Party, which disagreed with the Government's policy on Vietnam.

The way in which the Government reconciled its desire to support the U.S. commitment in Vietnam with the often conflicting demands posed by these two sets of problems, was to support U.S. policy publicly, but to couple this role to a search for a peaceful solution to the conflict. As noted previously, the U.S. Administration was aware of the pressures on the British Government, was appreciative of its support for U.S. policy, and endeavoured to help the Government continue its assistance (see Chapter 4). However, the Administration's appreciation did not extend to British peace initiatives, which reduced the British Government to the role of passive supporter when these initiatives were dismissed by the Administration. And this was the attitude of the Administration from the earliest days of the conflict, as *The Pentagon Papers* make clear when discussing a British–Russian diplomatic initiative just prior to the Pleiku air-strikes, which, the study states, was regarded in Washington 'not as a potential negotiating opportunity, but as a convenient vehicle for the public expression of a tough U.S. position' (Gravel, 1971, vol. 3: 270). It can thus be seen that the British Government could expect to encounter difficulties from the very beginning concerning its support for U.S. policy in Vietnam, and its concurrent efforts to promote a peaceful settlement of the conflict. For the Government used suggestions of such peace moves to allay left-wing criticism of the Government's policy on Vietnam, and though these proposed peace initiatives yielded nothing in the way of a solution to the conflict, they did decrease domestic political pressure on the Government – pressure which was not only reflected in the media but which also eventually emanated from the media too. The Government's tactics were thus undermined when the U.S. Administration publicly discounted British suggestions of peace moves.

Furthermore, the Government's policy of strong public support for U.S. policy meant that its own image as an independent government and ally was tied to, and affected by, U.S. policy and actions in Vietnam. And as the war escalated so the role of supporting the U.S. became more difficult for the Government: domestic pressure in Britain increased over the war itself, over Government support for U.S. policy and over the Government's inability to exert any influence over U.S. policy, which was helping to create an image of passive acceptance of all U.S. actions on the part of the British Government. For increasingly, with escalation of the war, the Government's role and image of faithful ally was seen to be overshadowing and discrediting – in British critics' eyes – its image as an independent government, engendering domestic criticism on that aspect and thus increasing the Government's difficulties over supporting U.S. policy.

However, to some extent the converse was also true, in that when the U.S. desire for peace was emphasized in Presidential speeches, accompanied by offers to talk and develop Southeast Asia, domestic criticism in Britain of U.S. policy and of the British Government's support for the U.S. lessened – until the next escalatory step. In addition, any peace moves undertaken by the British Government were usually greeted enthusiastically by the domestic audience and therefore not only eased pressure on the Government, but, by dint of conforming to certain expectations about the Government's role, such moves improved the Government's image among critics – temporarily. The image improvement was never lasting because the peace moves always failed and the war continued to escalate, and thus the problems facing the British Government because of its policy remained.

On the U.S. side, the Administration was well briefed by its embassy in London on opinion on Vietnam and the problems encountered by the British Government, both inside Parliament and outside. For in addition to analysing pressures on Wilson from his own party, the embassy assiduously provided the Administration with information on the attitudes of various newspapers (see Country File United Kingdom [305], Volumes III–IV, Cables 2/65–4/65 to 7/65–9/65, National Security File, Boxes 207–208, LBJ Library). So the Administration was made aware of the effect of its policies and actions on the British Government's position as a supporter of U.S. policy, both through its embassy and through inter-governmental contacts (see for instance the Bruce telegram of 3 June 1965, mentioned in Chapter 4, or a memorandum of a telephone conversation between National Security Assistant McGeorge Bundy and Wilson's Private Secretary Oliver Wright: Office Files of the President, McGeorge Bundy, 31 March 1965, Memorandum for the Record [sanitized], LBJ Library, square brackets added). The fact that the Administration did keep the British Government reasonably well informed about the important features of U.S. policy gave the Government the advantage of the prior knowledge that it needed if it was to 'manage' (the Bruce telegram) party and public opinion. However, this prior knowledge did not in itself lessen the problems of continuing to support U.S. policy, for the foundation of domestic criticism against supporting the war rested on the war itself: its nature, its world impact and, increasingly, the way it was conducted by America.

In addition, where escalatory moves were concerned the British Government was placed in the awkward situation of being criticized whatever the state of its knowledge. For, on the one hand, if the public impression was gained that the Government had not known of such moves in advance, then this caused an outcry about the U.S. keeping its ally in the dark while merely requiring slavish support. On the other hand, if the Government was thought to have advance knowledge of escalatory moves, then it could be accused of the same sort of public relations practices as the Administration – charged by mid-1965 simply with not keeping its public informed, but with the obvious possibility ahead of being accused of lying to the public. Furthermore, the public criticism of U.S. escalation was also likely to rub off on the British Government, due to its support for the Administration.

Though there was agreement between the Administration and the British Government that the former would keep the latter informed of developments in U.S. policy on Vietnam, so that the British would be better able to support the U.S., that the Administration's war policy, coupled with its information policy, was likely to complicate the British Government's position was well illustrated early in the war by the furore over the State Department's 9 June 1965 announcement of the changed troop role. For given that this change had been kept secret from the U.S. public on the President's express orders, there was little the British Government could do to prepare or influence either its party or public opinion on this issue. The Government was thus forced to weather the storm, unexpectedly created by the Administration, as best it could.

Unfortunately for the British Government this was no isolated incident of poor coordination within the Administration; indeed, timely information and the appearance of a coherent information policy was the exception rather than the rule. And because of the Administration's initial secrecy concerning its war plans in Vietnam and its more usual adherence to this pattern, in phases of the war when the Administration was occasionally more publicly communicative, the increased flow of information was often the subject of debate in the media (U.S. and international) – because it was recognized to be a departure from the Administration's norm and therefore attracted the unwelcome (to the Administration and allied governments) suspicion that it was a public relations exercise and that the media were being manipulated in order to help 'manage' public opinion. The inevitable publication of this suspicion then helped to vitiate the utility of disseminating more information: the Administration was credited with being neither more 'open' as a government, nor more accurately communicative with its public; and such information tended to be dismissed as mere propaganda designed to create a favourable climate of opinion, regardless of reality (see for instance *The New York Times*, 23 April 1965: 'Truth or Propaganda'; or the *Sunday Times*, 29 August 1965: 'Rumours of Vietnam "Peace" Are Just Eye-Wash'; or the *Financial Times*, 7 July 1966:

'Administration Drive for more Support for Vietnam Policy'; or the handling of the December 1966 bombing of Hanoi, cited in Chapter 5).

In addition to these recurrent difficulties created by the Administration's information policies and performance, by the end of the first year of escalation the British Government discovered that it faced another major difficulty: by mid-December 1965 it had become apparent that the Government's policy was in fact vitiating its own ability to promote a settlement. For in supporting the U.S. so firmly, in the role of being a 'good ally' and in the hope of wielding some sort of influence on U.S. policy, the British Government had rendered itself unacceptable to North Vietnam.

To the North Vietnamese, by December 1965 the British Government was too closely aligned with the U.S. to be able to act as a mediator (see the series of articles by journalist James Cameron published in the *Evening Standard,* 7–13 December 1965; specifically the article on 13 December; 'North Vietnam's Premier Gives His War Aims: "U.S. Troops Must Go!"'). In diplomatic terms this meant that the British Government could act neither formally, in its role as Co-Chairman of the Geneva Conference, nor informally as one of the many nations which desired an end to hostilities, with any hope of success. Also, according to North Vietnamese Prime Minister Pham Van Dong, speaking in December 1965, any country desiring to mediate would first have to denounce U.S. aggression (*Evening Standard,* 13 December 1965). But the British Government's policy was based on the assumption that public criticism – let alone denunciation – of U.S. actions would immediately diminish any influence that it could exert on U.S. policy, an eventuality it desired to avoid. There seemed little chance therefore that the British Government would ever be in a position to satisfy the North Vietnamese requirement, and certainly no chance that it would do so simply in order to be able to act as a mediator.

The limitations that the Government's policy imposed on its mediation capacity had the propensity to create more problems for the Government. For one of the ways that the Government had previously combated domestic criticism of its policy – frequently from within the Labour Party's ranks – was to propose, and sometimes undertake, peace initiatives to try and achieve negotiations. If, therefore, the Government's capacity to credibly undertake such initiatives had been impaired because of its policy of support for the U.S., then not only did the Government lose a weapon to combat criticism, but those groups who opposed the Government actually acquired another weapon to use against it. For it could now be said that as long as the British Government supported the U.S., the Government would never be able to help negotiate the settlement that it publicly called for.

For much of the first year of the war, the saving grace for the British Government, as for the Administration, was that so often the North Vietnamese Government publicly rejected negotiation proposals. And until the revelations about the Rangoon peace intiative, followed soon after by the Fanfani débâcle (a peace feeler explored in November/December 1965 by Amintore Fanfani, President of the U.N. General Assembly, which ended in recriminations between the U.N. and the U.S.), the circumstances surrounding North Vietnam's rejections mattered little: it was the rejection that counted. So while the North Vietnamese and Vietcong (and Chinese) were perceived as opposed to negotiations, the fact that the British Government was in the process of rendering itself unable to mediate the conflict was obscured, and in these circumstances British support for U.S. policy had even been endorsed in a *Guardian* editorial in late September 1965 (see *The Guardian*, 30 September 1965: 'What Can Britain do for Vietnam?').

However, as doubts grew about the sincerity of the Administration's approach to peace moves, and as the war continued to escalate, the British Government's policy of refraining from criticizing the U.S., in order to try and exercise some influence over U.S. policy, was itself being criticized by June 1966 – even before the intensification presaged by the P.O.L. bombings. In a reversal of its September evaluation of the Government's performance, *The Guardian* stated that the Prime Minister should 'speak out' against U.S. policy, out of 'loyalty to the alliance, and his concern for the wellbeing of its leading member', and concluded: 'There is no virtue in cheering on a friend marching blindly into a swamp' (*The Guardian*, 1 June 1966: 'Plunging Ahead in Vietnam'). In fact, at that very moment President Johnson was privately endeavouring to persuade Wilson to support him in a giant step into the swamp – the P.O.L. bombings in Hanoi and Haiphong.

Having been persuaded by his military advisers that the P.O.L. bombings would bring great dividends, and despite having been previously informed by Prime Minister Wilson in December 1965 that he could not support this action, President Johnson still made considerable efforts in May 1966 to persuade Wilson to change his mind. Wilson again refused, in the strongest terms, and Defense Secretary McNamara then sent a special envoy to brief Wilson and Foreign

Secretary Michael Stewart on the proposed bombings in the hope of changing his mind. The day after this briefing, on 3 June, Wilson sent a letter to the President thanking him and explaining why he would still be forced to dissociate:

> However . . . I am bound to say that, as seen from here, the possible military benefits that may result from this bombing do not appear to outweigh the political disadvantages that would seem the inevitable consequence. If you and the South Vietnamese Government were conducting a declared war on the conventional pattern . . . this operation would clearly be necessary and right. But since you have made it abundantly clear – and you know how much we have welcomed and supported this – that your purpose is to achieve a negotiated settlement, and that you are not striving for total military victory in the field, I remain convinced that the bombing of these targets, without producing decisive military advantage, may only increase the difficulty of reaching an eventual settlement . . . (Gravel, 1971, vol. 4: 102)

Thus, the Administration's decision to fight an undeclared war had not only facilitated Senate criticism and opposition, but, in conjunction with its rhetoric stressing its desire for negotiations, formed the primary reason why its major non-combatant ally would now have to denounce U.S. military action and specify the terms of its continued public support. For while the U.S. military strove almost continuously to extend the scale and intensity of operations in Vietnam, with the result that there appeared to be few limits on the U.S. weapons and actions used to try and win the war (given that nuclear weapons could not be considered as a serious option, and that invasion of North Vietnam, and widening the war to neighbouring countries was far too risky politically), and had persuaded Johnson to agree to this, the British Prime Minister clearly perceived the disparity between the declared limited ends of U.S. policy – a negotiated settlement – and the almost unlimited means used to try and achieve this, when the U.S. and North Vietnam were not officially at war. Furthermore, as the Prime Minister also perceived, the means used by the U.S. would put the desired goal even further out of reach.

In his letter Wilson reiterated that despite 'our reservations about this operation', Britain would continue to support U.S. policy as defined in President Johnson's Baltimore speech, and he then predicted the consequences of the bombings for the British Government: 'But, while this will remain the Government's position, I know that the effect on public opinion in this country – and I believe throughout

Western Europe – is likely to be such as to reinforce the existing disquiet and criticism that we have to deal with' (Gravel, 1971, vol. 4: 102–3).

In his letter to Johnson, Wilson also noted that he would have to make it clear in his public dissociation that he had been given advance warning of the raids and that he in turn had 'made my position clear to you', thus publicly demonstrating the British Government's independence as a sovereign government and an ally, and showing that the U.S. Administration did recognize, and honour, the obligation to keep allies informed of future plans.

This episode was thus of use in correcting the public image that had hitherto been forming of the U.S.–U.K. relationship, in which the Administration planned its escalatory policies in Vietnam quite independently of its ally, and then informed the latter after implementation – an almost unavoidable situation publicly, given that the Administration obviously desired, and usually insisted on, strategic and tactical secrecy about future escalation and military targets, for to act otherwise would have apprised the communists of U.S. intentions. And this requirement of U.S. war policy – and thus information policy – was known to the British Government from the earliest stage of the war, as is made clear in a memorandum of a telephone conversation in March 1965, between the President's National Security Advisor McGeorge Bundy and the British Prime Minister's Private Secretary Oliver Wright:

> I also told Wright of the importance of not giving specific specific signals even inadvertently to the Communists with respect to our military intentions. I told him that the Prime Minister had handled matters very well in limiting himself to the statement that he knew we did not intend any war without limits. Such general statements were quite correct and understandably necessary in the light of the quotation attributed to General Taylor. What would give us more trouble would be statements indicating any specific American decision not to attack a specific area or target in North Vietnam. [Next section sanitized; 1.3 (a) (5)] I told Wright that we thought it was very important indeed not to give specific signals. In the first place, it was impossible for us to give specific assurances as to what we would or would not be doing in three or six or nine weeks from now. It might well be very embarrassing for the British if they should give assurances one week which they had to take back a week later. But still more important was the need to avoid giving unnecessary comfort to the Communists by sharply specifying the limits of our intention. I told Wright that we were carefully using such indefinite phrases as "measured, fitting and

adequate." I hoped the British could do the same. He told me that he understood the point clearly, and he seemed to accept it. (Memorandum For The Record, McGeorge Bundy, 31 March 1965, Classified 'Confidential', Document #3, Office Files of The President, LBJ Library)

As the above document shows, the Administration intended to keep all its military options open, using a policy of minimum 'hard' information to help retain this freedom of action, and even suggesting suitable wording for public announcements so that its main ally could help in these efforts. This close attention to the language of official statements assumed even more importance at particular junctures of the war, some of which were predictable – such as the resumption of bombing after a pause, or when actions were being undertaken that could be viewed as escalatory, or following a Presidential speech which could be perceived as more belligerent than conciliatory – and some of which were not – such as the gas warfare incident.

The P.O.L. bombings in the summer of 1966 were a prime example of one of these important junctures, with repercussions not only for the Administration's propaganda effort, but also for the U.S.–U.K. relationship. At first sight the clear, detailed, advance warning given by Prime Minister Wilson to the President meant that the Administration knew the British Government would dissociate from the P.O.L. bombings, and on what grounds. Thus the Administration's irritated reaction – noted publicly in the press – appears on the surface to be unwarranted, given that advance warning. However, there is a telegram from President Johnson to Prime Minister Wilson, classified 'Top Secret', which goes some way to explaining the President's and his top officials' 'deep chagrin' over the British dissociation, and the subsequent growth in Johnson's apparent distrust of Wilson – and which apparently did have some impact on the British–Soviet peace initiative undertaken in February 1967 (see Chapter 1 and below).

This telegram, dated 14 June 1966 and carrying the further handling instruction to the U.S. embassy of EXDIS (Exclusive Distribution), thus indicating the special sensitivity of the message, discussed both Vietnam and Wilson's upcoming visit to Washington. On the former, after explaining the reasons for the proposed bombing raids and noting Rusk's 'private talk' with Wilson about 'the problem of POL in Haiphong and Hanoi', President Johnson expressed the hope that Wilson would be able 'to maintain solidarity with us despite what you said in the House of Commons about Haiphong and Hanoi'. Stressing that the mooted P.O.L. attacks were not 'an air assault on civilian centers but a specific attack on POL installations with a direct relevance to the fighting in the South', Johnson then sharply attacked the British position of non-combat support for the U.S. from the angle of SEATO obligations:

I hope that you can give further thought to your own interests and commitments in Southeast Asia under the SEATO Treaty. Dean [Rusk, Secretary of State] tells me that, in his talk with you and your colleagues, several references were made to the "revival of SEATO." South Vietnam and five signatories of SEATO are not talking about a revival but are committing troops to repel an armed attack from the north. Nor do I believe that your role as co-chairman [of the 1954 Geneva Conference] means that Britain should stand aside; the other co-chairman [the Soviet Union] is furnishing large quantities of sophisticated arms and other assistance to North Viet Nam and is, therefore, an active partner in the effort to take over South Viet Nam by force. (Cable, President Johnson to Prime Minister Wilson, 14 June 1966, 'Wilson Visit', National Security Files of Walt W. Rostow, Boxes 7–18, LBJ Library; square brackets added)

After mentioning that he knew that they both had 'some problems over Viet Nam', Johnson then spelled out the grounds of their common approach to Vietnam, which he considered was soundly based on the 'simple principles of the Geneva Accords and the SEATO Treaty, and on the assumption that North Viet Nam will not be permitted to seize South Viet Nam'. Noting that they were both 'determined about the latter point', Johnson optimistically opined that 'much of the present criticism will come right at the end of the day'. Returning to the crucial issue of the P.O.L. raids and the British stance, he then recalled Rusk's talk with Wilson, in which the former had mentioned 'the possible combination of points which would put a different cast upon disassociation by you from a decision to strike the POL' and after 'frankly' and 'earnestly' hoping that Wilson would 'not find it necessary to speak in terms of disassociation', Johnson then listed the points that it was 'important' to the Administration for Wilson to include in such an eventuality:

1. You were informed of the possibility that such an action would, in our minds, become necessary.
2. You expressed your own views to us in accordance with statements which you have already made in the House of Commons.

3. The particular step taken by U.S. forces was directed specifically to POL storage and not against civilian centers or installations.
4. Since Britain does not have troops engaged in the fighting, it is not easy or appropriate for Britain to determine the particular military action which may be necessary under different circumstances.
5. It is a great pity that Hanoi and Peiping have been so unresponsive to unprecedented efforts by the U.S. and others to bring this problem from the battlefield to the conference table.
6. Britain is satisfied that U.S. forces have no designs against civilian populations and are taking every possible precaution to avoid civilian casualties.
7. Britain as a member of SEATO fully understands and supports the determination of its fellow SEATO members to insure the safety and the self-determination of South Viet Nam.

I would hope that you could in this context affirm your support for the effort in Viet Nam and your understanding that it is Hanoi which is blocking the path to peace. (Cables, President Johnson to Prime Minister Wilson, 14 June 1966, 'Wilson Visit', National Security Files of Walt W. Rostow, Boxes 7–18, LBJ Library)

Finally, Johnson ended his telegram with a reference to Wilson's forthcoming visit to Washington and the need for 'a good deal of blue sky between your visit and possible action in Viet Nam' – thereby indicating again the sensitivity of timing such visits, so that there would be less chance of concerted pressure on either party (from observers and critics) concerning Vietnam.

Taken as a whole, this telegram reveals the closeness of the relationship at this juncture between the U.S. Administration and the British Government over Vietnam, but also reinforces the status of the respective parties to this relationship, that is, America as the dominant partner. For though the British Government could not be prevented from dissociating, what the Administration desired from a British Government statement was not only an endorsement of the broad outlines of U.S. official propaganda but also a weakening of the latter's own argument on non-military intervention in the war (point 4), thus blunting the effect of such a dissociation and removing the impression of disapproval. Furthermore, even while requesting such verbal assistance, Johnson did not hesitate to criticize the official British standpoint on non-combat support for the U.S., whilst points 4 and 7, taken together and in the absence of any reference to Britain as Geneva Conference Co-Chairman, implied a deficiency on the part of the British Government in not joining its SEATO allies to safeguard South

Vietnam and also would have constituted prior approval of any future actions in Vietnam that the U.S. and its SEATO allies chose to undertake. And of course the Administration wanted particular emphasis on U.S. efforts to avoid civilian casualties.

Had Wilson issued a statement along all of these lines, he would have destroyed the delicate balance that he was striving to maintain in order to content his various domestic constituencies, and his main foreign ally, for the scales would have tilted more towards supporting the U.S. than pacifying the left-wing of the Parliamentary Labour Party and movement, and certain vocal sections of the public – although the Conservative Party and the Foreign Office would have approved of a more robust defence of U.S. actions.

When the P.O.L. storage depots were bombed Wilson reacted swiftly, issuing a statement which firmly dissociated the Government from these attacks, expressed general support for the U.S. assistance for South Vietnam and U.S. proposals for unconditional negotiations, and blamed North Vietnam for the lack of negotiations and the continued fighting (*The Guardian*, 30 June 1966: 'Attacks "Noted with Regret" – Premier'). Thus several of the elements requested by the Administration did appear in Wilson's statement, but, importantly, he also referred to the location of the targets and 'populated areas', so ignoring one of the guidelines issued by Johnson (points 3 and 6).

The effects of the dissociation, and this particular reference, on the Administration were summed up by Henry Brandon, Associate Editor of the *Sunday Times* and a Washington columnist noted for his sources in the Administration, which ensured a considerable degree of accuracy in his articles. Brandon's article tended to confirm the suspicion voiced in other press articles that relations between the two allies would be more difficult after the British dissociation. He noted the Administration's surprise at the speed of Wilson's dissociation, and concern over his mention of ""targets touching on the populated areas of Hanoi and Haiphong" when even the Russians, it is pointed out with slight irritation, referred only to targets on the "outskirts"'. Brandon also recorded the White House's dominant reaction to the dissociation, which ungraciously suggested that Wilson had given the President an inflated view of his own political abilities: 'Nevertheless, most of the comments made around the White House are more in sadness that Mr Wilson did feel strong enough to take a more muted line, that he does not seem to be as much in charge of his party as he privately likes to reassure the President he is.' Although Brandon observed that compared with the Senate opposition, which was truly 'damaging and annoying', Wilson's dissociation was 'viewed with a certain amount of charitable equanimity', he still judged that it was 'as well that Mr Wilson is not visiting Washington this week (as had been suggested earlier before the arrangements for late July were made) . . .' (*Sunday Times*, 3 July 1966: 'Johnson Puts a Bold Face on the Bombing').

The soundness of this, and other press judgements (see for instance, *The Guardian*, 1 July 1966: 'Cool U.S. Reception Now for Mr. Wilson'), on the effects of this dissociation were to surface later during the fiasco that was the British–Russian attempt at negotiation in early 1967. For although Wilson's visit to Washington on 29 July appeared to contradict predictions that the Prime Minister's reception would be less than warm – in fact the President toasted Wilson in hugely flattering terms despite having once more been refused the token British force that he had long desired – and though Wilson's memoirs record the visit as untroubled by any difficulties (Wilson, 1971: 262–5), given Lyndon Johnson's views on loyalty – that it should be absolute – the consequences of Wilson's dissociation were always likely to be considerable. Thus the public appearance of White House 'charitable equanimity' and the warm reception given to Wilson were ultimately misleading, and the dissociation could be expected not only to affect relations between the two leaders, but also to further affect the reception accorded by the Administration to British peace initiatives – a reception which had been erratic at the best of times, and was often unenthusiastic.

Wilson's problems over Vietnam were not, however, merely confined to managing his own party, as the White House suggested, for in addition to this undoubted problem Wilson also had to contend with the views of the bureaucracy. At this time, as a Labour Prime Minister, Wilson was attempting to balance the demands of the Labour left-wing against his own policy requirements and the needs of his U.S. ally, which was a difficult enough combination to juggle. However, the difficulties were increased by Whitehall's propensity to support U.S. policy more strongly than the Prime Minister and most of the Government. This phenomenon manifested itself publicly in the summaries of 'Whitehall's views' which appeared from time to time in the press, and in Foreign Office statements. In the case of the latter, this also tended to place the Foreign Secretary publicly on one side of a fence which the Prime Minister was clearly trying to straddle in the interests of domestic political harmony.

A clear example of this type of problem had occurred at the end of January 1966 when the U.S. resumed the bombing of North Vietnam after a 37-day pause and the Foreign Office put out a supportive and sympathetic statement, which was subsequently criticized by Labour MPs and led to the tabling of a Motion to censure the Government. As Wilson makes clear in his memoirs, and as press reports suggested at the time, he was consulted in advance neither about the intention to issue a statement, nor about the wording (Wilson, 1971: 204). Nevertheless, as Prime Minister it was Wilson who was the prime target for criticism over the Government's policy of support for the U.S. and who was called upon to defend this statement in concert with the Foreign Secretary. Probably any Government statement on the resumption of the bombing which did not deplore this action would have antagonized the Labour left-wing, but the wording of the Foreign Office statement was virtually certain to enrage it. Thus, this statement involved the Government in a quite unnecessary row with its back-benchers.

In the light of this earlier episode in January, it is noteworthy that when Wilson dissociated from the U.S. P.O.L. bombings, the statement was issued first from 10 Downing Street, and then repeated in Parliament. And as Wilson's memoirs make clear, the Foreign Office would have preferred a much 'softer' statement:

> The Foreign Office were warned that there should be no private enterprise comments – even on non-attributable terms – such as had occurred the previous January over the end of the bombing pause.
>
> The Foreign Office sought to water down my draft. At the very last they were hoping for a less forthright statement. Hopefully, they prepared a counter-draft of the controversial passages. Politely, but firmly, I indicated to them which part of their filing system they were free to put it. (Wilson, 1971: 247)

The Foreign Office's efforts to 'water down' Wilson's draft presumably indicated not only its desire to support U.S. policy through issuing a not-too-strenuous dissociation statement, but also some anxiety as to U.S. reaction to this statement. Although Wilson states in his memoirs that there was absolutely no indication during his visit to Washington, after the P.O.L. bombings and his dissociation, that relations between him and President Johnson – and thus to some extent between the Britain and America – had changed on the Vietnam Issue, U.S.

Assistant Secretary for Far Eastern Affairs William Bundy thought otherwise when considering the P.O.L. raids and the aftermath:

> ... of course, that was the break point in the President's relationship with Wilson too. And the files will show that we told Wilson well and truly what we were going to do and why we were going to do it, and he said, "well, I don't like it, I may have to dissociate myself from it," and in the event he did dissociate. And there's no doubt that in the President's mind this established Wilson, as far as I know unchangingly, as a man not to go to the well with. (William Bundy, Oral History Interview, Tape 3: 36)

Thus the Administration perceived Wilson's dissociation almost as a form of betrayal, despite receiving ample prior notice of his intention, and despite the fact that the U.S. embassy in London had kept the Administration fully informed of the political difficulties that the British Government faced on this issue (Embtel 229 (London), 12 July 1966, Volume VIII, Cables 1/66–7/66, UK Country File (305), Boxes 208–209, National Security File, LBJ Library). The embassy's analysis was reinforced in a U.S. Department of State Intelligence Note of 15 July, evaluating Wilson's forthcoming visit to Moscow, in which it was stated that:

> From the moment that the United States bombed POL facilities near Hanoi and Haiphong, Wilson faced a serious left-wing revolt within his own party. Many Laborite MPs were already disturbed by Mr. Wilson's incomes policy, his 'east of Suez' defense policy, and his slide toward favoring UK entry into the EEC. Although the Prime Minister immediately dissociated the UK from the US bombing action, the left-wingers called for a complete disavowal of the US policy in Vietnam – a step which Wilson resolutely refused to take. (U.S. Department of State, Director of Intelligence and Research to The Secretary, Intelligence Note – 448, 15 July 1966, 'Subject: Harold Wilson's Latest Journey to Moscow, July 16–18, 1966', Volume VIII, Memos 1/66–77/66, UK Country File (305), Boxes 208–209, National Security File, LBJ Library)

Nevertheless, even though Wilson's difficulties were acknowledged in Washington, Henry Brandon's comment in the *Sunday Times* after the dissociation seems an apt summary:

> The difficulty with President Johnson is that he is full of understanding of the domestic political problems of other statesmen as long as they do not conflict

with his own. The British Government's dissociation from this new stage in the war has given Mr Johnson's critics new ammunition and anything that tends to weaken the President's hand at this stage rankles. (*Sunday Times*, 3 July 1966: 'Johnson Puts a Bold Face on the Bombing')

Thus Wilson's dissociation marked a more important turning point for Johnson in some respects than it did for the British Government. For the Government still endeavoured to support U.S. policy in Vietnam, supposedly within the limits defined in the dissociation statement, whereas Johnson's distrust admitted of no ameliorating factors. However, no doubt due partly to his warm reception in Washington and the fact that Johnson's distrust was not on public display, Wilson continued to believe that it would be possible for him to broker a peace, and that the Administration would welcome such efforts. Unfortunately this was not the case, for though the British Government refrained from publicly dissociating again from U.S. policy, despite the almost constant escalation and intensification of the war, what little chance the Government had of mediating – and it was probably only ever a slender chance – vanished with the dissociation.

Given the often cool reception that the Administration had accorded to mediation attempts, and given also that this was a particularly difficult conflict to mediate – due to the stances of both sides, the fact that the war was publicly perceived and portrayed by the U.S. as a duel between competing ideologies for the continuing allegiance of regional and global allies and as a test of the superiority of democracy, and the fact that a superpower was pitted against a Third World country (even with Soviet and Chinese backing) – the question arises as to why the Prime Minister continued to believe that a peaceful solution could be negotiated by 'outsiders' despite the failure of previous efforts. His apparently perverse belief is partly explained by the fact that on occasions the Administration had used the British to undertake diplomatic probes, even though the Administration knew that its terms for negotiations were unacceptable to Hanoi, amounting to surrender.

An example of this occurred in February 1966, just after the resumption of the bombing following the 37-day pause. U.S. Secretary of State Rusk sent a message to British Foreign Secretary Michael Stewart about indications from the Russians 'within the last 24 hours' that Hanoi 'wishes to maintain contacts with us' and might be interested in a reconvened Geneva Conference. Rusk suggested that the British approach the Russians:

While we cannot yet gauge the validity of these indicators, we remain eager, as HMG [Her Majesty's Government] knows, to explore every opening and exhaust all possibilities of getting negotiations started. Therefore, it seems to us that another probe by UK of Soviet willingness to join them as co-chairman in convening a new Geneva Conference is worthwhile. Goldberg [U.S. Ambassador to the UN] took up this matter with Caradon this morning [Caradon was Minister of State for Foreign Affairs].

As UK knows, UN SC [United Nations Security Council] has adjourned subject to call of President while consultations are undertaken. We are quite content to let adjournment continue while private efforts to get talks going are in train and have no desire to let formal SC debate cut across such efforts. We would hope that soundings of this kind could be undertaken expeditiously so we can get clearer picture among other things, of how to play SC adjournment. (U.S. Department of State to U.S. Embassy, London, Outgoing Telegram 7103, 27 May 1966, Classification Secret, NODIS [No further Distribution], Volume VIII, Cables 1/66–7/66, UK Country File (305), Boxes 208–209, National Security File, LBJ Library; square brackets added).

This effort to reconvene the Geneva Conference sank without trace, as did all the others, although U.S. 'eagerness' to explore this particular diplomatic probe was understandable, both in light of the fact that it was a Russian move, and coming as it did after a number of other diplomatic moves (including efforts by the leaders of the UK and Ghana, the U.N.'s U Thant, and with de Gaulle having contacted North Vietnam's leader; see Sheehan et al., 1971: 477) and just prior to the planned P.O.L. strikes.

Where Britain was concerned, the unpromising record of past negotiation attempts included Washington's conduct during U.K. Foreign Secretary George Brown's foray into the negotiation labyrinth on a visit to the U.S.S.R. in November 1966, in which he put forward a U.S. negotiating formula, unaware both of other negotiating channels being used in conjunction with this formula (the Polish representative on the International Control Commission in an ultimately abortive peace manoeuvre code-named 'Marigold'), and thus of the likelihood that the Russians probably already knew of this 'new' Phase A–Phase B formula. With minimum effort, therefore, Washington eroded U.K. negotiating credibility, by neglecting to keep its ally informed on current diplomacy and by allowing this ignorance to become known to the opposing party (see Herring, 1983: 389; also Cooper, 1970: 342–5).

Nevertheless, despite this very recent débâcle, in February 1967 Prime Minister Wilson and Premier Kosygin joined the ranks of would-be negotiators. This attempt took place against the background of a recent exchange between the U.S. and North Vietnam following an interview with North Vietnamese Foreign Minister Trinh, the importance of which hinged on the language tense used to indicate the possibility of talks after the unconditional cessation of U.S. bombing. On the issue of talks and semantics, Chester Cooper, involved with the subsequent British attempt, remarks:

> Whether we would have stopped the bombing at this time if Trinh had used "would" [instead of 'could'] is a moot point. Most American policy-makers objected at that time to a trade-off between a bombing cessation and talks. In any case, for almost a year discussions of this issue took on a Talmudic quality, with great attention being paid to the slightest word or tense changes in statements emerging from Hanoi. When finally, in late December 1967, Hanoi changed its formulation from "could" to "will", there was a new flurry of diplomatic activity. (Cooper, 1970: 353)

The public impression given by 'most American policy-makers', however, was that it was just such a trade-off that they wanted. Undoubtedly the North Vietnamese were intransigent over their demand for a cessation of the bombing before considering the issue of talks and their position hardened as time passed, but their case had the merit of appearing relatively straightforward, whereas the official U.S. position seems, on occasions, to have borne little resemblance to more important private views that prevailed whenever there was a possibility of talks. Thus it was the Administration which gave the far stronger public impression of changing the rules whenever Hanoi appeared to be contemplating talking, unwilling to trade its 'blue chip' bombing programme for the mere possibility of talks, despite public statements. And it was this gap between rhetoric and reality – between official statements about a willingness to talk and actual difficulties about what conditions would be necessary to produce a cessation of bombing, and whether talks would then be probable or merely possible – that Wilson and Kosygin ran into, as well as Johnson's distrust of Wilson as prime peacemaker.

In brief, during Premier Kosygin's scheduled visit to the U.K. in early February 1967, Wilson and Kosygin discussed Vietnam and ways to begin negotiations, focusing on Trinh's statement and then the Phase A–Phase B formula. According to Chester Cooper, who was in London throughout this whole period at Wilson's request, Washington was not particularly in favour of Wilson undertaking this venture:

> There was a sense that the British Government was pushing hard, perhaps too hard, to undertake the role of mediator. To be sure the British could claim both a right and responsibility to assume such a role . . . But some of Wilson's American cousins felt his underlying motivation was to bolster his own and England's prestige . . . There was another, less articulated, but more deeply felt attitude about Wilson's imminent meeting that cooled Washington's interest and perhaps even contributed to the failure of the talks. After all the recent frustrations and disappointments of Warsaw and Moscow, the prospect that Wilson might be able to use American chips to pull off peace talks was hard for the President and some of his advisers to swallow. If the time was now ripe to get Hanoi to talk, Johnson, not Wilson, should get the credit. (Cooper, 1970: 355–6)

Thus, Wilson's belief in Washington's good faith concerning this round of the negotiating process was misplaced from the beginning. Even more crucially for this particular episode, Wilson was also unaware that in a hard-line letter to North Vietnam's President Ho Chi Minh, President Johnson had reversed the timetable for the Phase A–Phase B formula: previously, Phase A would be the cessation of U.S. bombing, followed by Phase B when North Vietnam would cease infiltration into South Vietnam, and then the U.S. would cease building up its own troop levels in South Vietnam. In his letter to Ho Chi Minh, Johnson now stated that only after Hanoi ceased infiltration would U.S. bombing and troop increases also cease – a proposal which Hanoi had already refused quite publicly. The result of these contradictory elements – the second of which, Johnson's more hard-line letter, was also unknown to Chester Cooper – was to place the British Government in an appallingly embarrassing position, as Wilson discussed with Kosygin, and asked him to transmit to Hanoi, a negotiating formula that was no longer current, and which Hanoi would know was now irrelevant, but which Wilson still believed was the official position (see Herring, 1983: 431–76; also Porter: 1979: 451–60).

In his memoirs Cooper describes the recriminations between Washington and London over this issue, when the difference was discovered, with Washington blaming London for advancing the original formula without specific prior approval (though having discussed it beforehand), and London blaming Washington for switching the formula in mid-negotiation (Cooper, 1970: 355–68). In addition, as was pointed out, this new formulation contradicted point 14 in Rusk's statement 'Fourteen Points for Peace in Southeast Asia', which had only just been publicly released. Even so, Washington contended that there was no change, as the new formulation was just that, new, and not simply the old one switched around; furthermore the Administration insisted that the change of tenses was basically irrelevant as Hanoi was uninterested in negotiations, having used this pause and previous ones to resupply and continue its build-up; and finally that as both Hanoi and the Soviet Union were aware of the 'change in tense in final draft' – the latter 'presumably through their Hanoi contacts' – this tense change 'did not repeat not come as surprise to Soviets or Hanoi and cannot have impaired British credibility' (Herring, 1983: 462, 459). None of these arguments, however, could obscure the fact that due to U.S. manoeuvres, for whatever reasons, Wilson had been made to look at best devious and at worst ill-informed to the parties to these attempted peace overtures – the only fortunate aspect to the affair was that subsequently the most important details remained secret from the public.

The fundamental reason given, both privately and publicly, for this change in stance was the continuing infiltration and resupply efforts of the North Vietnamese. And as Wilson attempted to delay resumption of the bombing, the old Administration argument about the bombing being a type of currency that could be traded surfaced yet again:

> 5. Wilson should be left in no doubt that we cannot prolong suspension of bombing in absence of firm word on infiltration. He should also know that when we say "stop infiltration" we mean "stop infiltration." We cannot trade a horse for a rabbit and will react to bad faith on this point. We are losing lives today because such commitments in Laos Accords of 1962 were treated with contempt by Hanoi and Co-Chairman and ICC could do nothing about it . . .
> 7. Wilson is of course already aware that the South Vietnamese and we are resuming bombing operations in the South tomorrow (112300 Zulu) and that we have been carrying on bombing operations in Laos thoughout. (Herring, 1983: 458)

In fact the bombing pause was extended, so that Wilson could have one last try at negotiations and endeavour to persuade Kosygin to contact Hanoi again and try to get an answer before what was a very tight deadline, even with a subsequent six-hour extension (Herring, 1983: 467–8, 469–70). The other motive for postponing the bombing was to allow Kosygin to at least leave London, and thereby minimize the embarrassment that would ensue for both the U.K. and U.S.S.R. were operations to be resumed while he was still there (bearing in mind that U.S. retaliatory attacks had been launched in 1965 while Kosygin was visiting Hanoi). However, so that Saigon was under no misconception as to why the bombing was not being immediately resumed, messages were sent explaining that 'this decision was dictated solely by extreme British concern and vital importance of British support,. . . .', and a later message for the ambassadors to Saigon and regional and military allies on the continuing pause emphasized the nature of the decision: 'This decision ... constitutes a one-shot exception to our standing policy, . . . Our policy on not repeat not stopping bombing in return for talks remains unchanged' (Herring, 1983: 459–60; original punctuation in both quotations).

The main arguments that the Administration advanced to justify publicly the resumption of the bombing were that Hanoi had used the Tet Truce and pause to continue infiltration and resupply, and that there had been no response from Hanoi to peace moves. Due to the secrecy surrounding the Wilson–Kosygin manoeuvres there appeared to be little likelihood that the short time allowed for Hanoi to respond to the switched formula would become public knowledge, or of course the fact that the negotiation formula had been changed.

There was, however, one major problem with the 'infiltration and resupply' argument: during the same period the U.S. itself had been resupplying and moving supplies forward on a far larger scale than the North Vietnamese. And despite the generally favourable press coverage, in which Hanoi was 'universally regarded as the villain in the piece' for failing to respond to peace efforts (Herring, 1983: 475), there were still some news reports which focused on the U.S. supply efforts. Furthermore, soon after the pause ended, the largest ground operation yet undertaken in the war – Operation Junction City – was launched on 22 February, and not surprisingly the press surmised that the U.S. had ferried in the requisite supplies during the pause (see Worldwide Treatment of Current Issues, Interim Report, 27 February 1967).

Even worse for the official propaganda line, the radical American journalist I.F. Stone also claimed, in a report carried in *The Guardian*, that the Pentagon had 'brainwashed correspondents into reporting massive movements by the North Vietnamese of men and military supplies southwards during the recent lunar new year truce' (see *The Guardian*, 25 February 1967, Richard Scott report, datelined Washington:

'Tet Truce: Pentagon Denial'; see also I.F. Stone, 1970: 63–5; Stone notes that the Saigon correspondents of *Le Monde* and *The Times* filed dispatches commenting respectively on the U.S. supply effort, and on the possibility that some of North Vietnam's supplies could be destined for North Vietnamese civilians in the southern part of North Vietnam). In his own *Weekly* report, Stone analysed the discrepancies in the official figures on the size of the North Vietnamese supply effort, which were revised downwards from the figure of 35,000 tons to 25,000 tons; on the numbers of trucks sighted; and on the numbers of ships. And as this *Guardian* report also noted, the Defense Department justification that Stone's allegation 'missed' the point because the U.S. had control of the air space and did not therefore require a ceasefire to resupply, simply meant that the Pentagon 'considers it legitimate for its own military supplies to be moved forward during a truce because it enjoys control of the air, but illegitimate for the other side to do so because it enjoys no such control' – a position that was as untenable as it was fatuous. Unfortunately for Wilson, following the official U.S. line, he too had used Hanoi's infiltration and supply moves to help justify the resumption of U.S. bombing, telling Parliament that these '"threatened to create a severe military imbalance"', which claim the *Guardian* also demolished, pointing out that 'since both sides appear to have raised to the maximum their supply efforts during the truce, what does seem certain is that there was no danger that "severe military imbalance" was being created'.

Thus, once again the Administration was embroiled in a row over the implications of its public statements compared with its actions, with the British Government sharing in some of the consequences of these contradictions – resulting in increased pressure from Labour Party protesters and observers, and for Wilson awkward questions in the Cabinet over the speed with which the bombing was resumed (see Howard (ed.), 1979: 282–4). Fortunately for the remnants of the Administration's credibility – and that of its U.K. ally – the continued bombing in Laos was not advertised, and the precise details of the attempted negotiations remained secret, although, to protect his own domestic and international political position and credibility (with the Soviet Union involved), Harold Wilson had alluded to this episode in the Commons – much to the Administration's intense irritation as only South Vietnam's Prime Minister Ky had been privy to the proposal: America's fighting allies had not been informed (see Herring, 1983: 476). Nevertheless, *The Guardian*'s Washington correspondent pieced together a version that was not too far from the bare record of the various moves, but was inaccurate in one crucial fact, which put a much better slant for the Administration on the whole episode: the *Guardian* article stated that the offer that Wilson relayed to Hanoi through Kosygin was a conditional one: 'The Soviet Premier insisted that the first step towards peace must be the unconditional ending of the bombing of North Vietnam. Mr Wilson indicated that Washington would not be budged from its basic demand that there must be some measure of reciprocity from the other side before it would stop the bombing; and he himself supported this position' (*The Guardian*, 3 March 1967: 'How the Vietnam hopes withered'). So, despite the Administration's irritation with Wilson for mentioning publicly the failed peace initiative, the more unsavoury aspects of the episode were blurred in subsequent press reportage, and criticism from Hanoi and the Soviet Union tended to be dismissed.

As to the chance that this peace initiative might have achieved either talks and/or a peace settlement, not surprisingly the verdict differs according to particular protagonists – Wilson was convinced that a major opportunity had been wrecked by the Administration (laying the blame principally on Rostow), while Johnson dismissed the episode as of little importance. Somewhat surprisingly Dean Rusk tended to agree with Wilson – that this had been an important move – but on the other hand Chester Cooper pointed out the obstacles that would still have bedevilled any talks – namely that the positions of the two protagonists were very far apart. (For Wilson's public revelation of his views on the incident in advance of the publication of his memoirs, see the *Sunday Times*, 16 May 1971: 'The night LBJ wrecked our secret manoeuvres for peace'; in his article Wilson also commented on the influence on LBJ of 'certain of the White House advisers' – undoubtedly a reference to Rostow, on whom he placed the principal blame for this débâcle; interview with author, 26 June 1981; see also Johnson, 1971: 252–6; Rusk, 1991: 408–10; and Cooper, 1970: 367–8.)

Once the bombing had resumed the Administration immediately examined the condition of its relations with the U.S.S.R. and Hanoi, and also probed the state of relations between the latter in the aftermath of the London peace attempt. Despite the denial of any double-dealing, in his conversation with Soviet Counsellor Alexandr Zinchuk of the U.S.S.R.'s Washington embassy, William Bundy asked whether 'the change of tenses . . . had in any way thrown the Soviets off'. And although Zinchuk replied that 'the change of tenses had not significantly disturbed the Soviets . . .', he had earlier made clear Hanoi's understanding that 'its Burchett interview position of willingness to talk if we stopped the bombing was in direct response to our own position'. Bundy's response was that U.S. statements on the bombing campaign 'had stressed its necessity to counter and impede infiltration above all, and had placed its relevance to negotiation in a much broader context than Zinchuk's summary of Hanoi's view would suggest' (Porter, 1979: 459–60). And, of course, by this broadening of the 'context', Bundy tried to fudge the entire issue of Hanoi's consistent demand for an unconditional bombing halt before considering the issue of talks, set against the Administration's more variable approach – caused partly by the tension between the Administration's private desire to achieve peace only on its own terms (effectively involving Hanoi's surrender), and its public protestations, engendering an image of more flexibility than was actually the case.

The Administration learned yet more about the ramifications of this affair in a conversation between U.S.S.R. Premier Kosygin and the U.S. Ambassador in Moscow, in which Kosygin stated that there was now considerable doubt on the part of the U.S.S.R. that the Administration's negotiation proposal had been serious, given the brevity of the response time that the U.S. had allowed for its final offer; the language of this message, 'couched in terms of an ultimatum'; and the exclusive focus on North Vietnamese infiltration, with the U.S. keeping silent on its own resupply efforts. Having already mentioned that the 'other side [North Vietnam] has no confidence in US intentions', Kosygin also reminded the ambassador pointedly – and ironically in view of the U.S. own lack of confidence in negotiations and North Vietnam – of the obvious: 'Confidence was most important in this situation' (Herring, 1983: 484–5).

Thus the end result, as far as negotiations were concerned, was entirely predictable: a hardening of attitude on both sides. And as for the 'far-reaching' political developments that the State Department speculated might result from the London débâcle – to whit that the U.S.S.R. might have compromised its relationship with North Vietnam merely by advancing the London proposals and thus appearing to the latter as 'a solid but compromise-minded friend', perhaps causing North Vietnam to turn more to the Chinese to 'give the kind of full support the Soviets are clearly not now inclined to give' (with doubtful results for the North Vietnamese cause) – Zinchuk assured Bundy that Hanoi depended on the U.S.S.R. to protect its interests and even that 'the Soviet standing had progressively increased in Hanoi over the past several months' (Herring, 1983: 483). Whatever the truth of this assertion, in practical terms the failure of the negotiation attempt and the subsequent U.S. escalation, rather than disrupting relations between the communist countries, resulted, according to the Soviet Ambassador, in pressure on them to increase arms to North Vietnam via China (Porter, 1979: 462). And certainly the war continued at a higher level of intensity, so though the aftermath of this episode could be termed 'far-reaching', it hardly conformed to Washington's desires.

The demise of its most serious attempt to arrange negotiations, and the subsequent strain on the Anglo-American relationship, meant that the Wilson government was thereafter unable to mute criticism of its policy of support for the U.S. by hinting at secret peace moves, or indeed by endeavouring to undertake them. And thus the continuing, and apparently inevitable (given the lengthy list of failed peace attempts) escalation of the war, accompanied by increased dissatisfaction with government policy and growing violence at demonstrations and marches, posed a problem that the government was now poorly placed to counteract while it continued to support U.S. policy in Vietnam. Though the criticism and violence in the U.K. did not pose a political danger to the government, it was an embarrassment which could only strengthen, for included in it was a factor over which the British Government had no control, that is, U.S. war policy (the riots and demonstrations in Europe at this time incorporated more than just anger over Vietnam, but the latter was undoubtedly a cause of unrest, as well as a symbol of dissatisfaction with other aspects of 'the system').

The government soon had a taste of what was to come in October 1967, when there was a weekend of riots in Europe, including a violent demonstration in London in which the U.S. embassy was attacked. These were quickly followed by the 1968 riots, in March and October in Britain, and in France the most famous of all the riots in May. Increasingly there appeared a gulf between government policy on Vietnam and public sentiment, expressed not only in these riots but also through opinion polls, in which the general, non-rioting public, while disliking the violent anti-war demonstrations and student riots, nevertheless still disagreed with the main thrust of official policy. Some relief was provided with Johnson's post-Tet announcement in March 1968 that he was henceforth seeking peace and not standing for re-election, but still the war ground on while the negotiators argued – and the demonstrations also continued with Vietnam as a theme (for further analysis of opposition, see Chapter 7, 'European public opinion by 1968').

So by 1968 the British Government had failed to achieve anything of note concerning Vietnam itself with its policy of support for the Administration, being neither able to influence U.S. policy nor mediate a settlement. However, though its policy was a failure on those terms the government had managed to retain U.S. support for its domestic policies and had avoided having to provide a more concrete manifestation of its support in the shape of troops, despite considerable U.S. pressure. The problem for the government was that whilst the riots in Britain expressed dissatisfaction with more than just the Vietnam War, there was still a considerable, vocal, and active opposition that was centred solely on the war, and the government's policy was clearly unable to damp down this sentiment, and was more likely to fuel it. But even if the government had dissociated completely from the Administration and condemned the latter's policies in Vietnam, it is highly unlikely that the demonstrations would have stopped as long as the war itself dragged on. For just as the war was only one factor in some of the riots, so British Government policy was only one element in these protests against Vietnam, in which the fact of the war itself played a larger part – both as a particularly devasting war and as a manifestation of a conflict between a small Third World nation and the technological (and to some, imperialist) giant of the West.

French Government reaction and opinion

Although de Gaulle's vocal, increasingly anti-American and pro-North Vietnam stance circumscribed the role that France played during the first three years of the war – in tune with his belief that until the U.S. realized it could not win the war militarily, and opted for a diplomatic solution, there was no role that France *could* usefully, or successfully undertake (see extract from de Gaulle's Phnom Penh speech in Lacouture, 1992: 404–5) – unlike the British Government such public diplomatic inaction (though it was accompanied by de Gaulle's denunciations) was no handicap to the French Government (see Chapter 4). For this policy also underlined France's independence from the U.S. (given added weight by France's withdrawal from NATO's military wing in July 1966), as well as insulating the former both from the consequences of yet another divisive war, and from the constant pressure exerted by the latter on other allies to extend at least diplomatic and material support, if troops were not to be forthcoming. And where America's other allies were cajoled or hectored into offering this support – and taken to task if they did not offer enough (see below) – de Gaulle early on dismissed the entire affray with the grand observation at a ministerial meeting: 'We are not disposed to accompany the Americans into every adventure that they think fit to throw themselves into' (cited in Lacouture, 1992: 403).

De Gaulle's policy also had the added benefit of keeping France clear of the repeated and fruitless mediation attempts which other countries undertook, and which usually ended in recriminations of varying degrees of bitterness. And even though U.S. policy generated disapproval across a wide political spectrum among politicians, the general public, and the media, there was no corresponding pressure on de Gaulle to try and produce a settlement, as there was in Britain. For de Gaulle's analysis of and approach to the problem was mostly accepted, and thus he had no need to discuss or undertake mediation attempts in order to fulfil diplomatic duties, give an impression of purposeful activity, or silence critics, as did the British Prime Minister.

Nevertheless, despite his condemnation of U.S. policies in Vietnam, when de Gaulle was approached for permission to allow one of the most spectacular events opposing American actions in Vietnam to be staged in France, namely the Russell Tribunal on U.S. 'war crimes' in Vietnam, he refused. And the grounds on which he refused show clearly the importance he assigned to the nation-state as an entity in global affairs, and the importance of upholding the rights of the nation-state – whatever policies a state chose to pursue, and however such policies were viewed by the French Government when headed by de Gaulle:

> The initiators of the 'Russell Tribunal' propose to criticize the Vietnam policy of the United States . . . Quite apart from the fact that the written and spoken word are free in our country, there would be no reason to turn down private individuals, particularly those whose theses on this subject are so close to the official position of the French Republic. But what is at stake here is neither the right to free assembly nor to free speech but the duty – all the more imperative for France as she has taken a position on the basic issue which is known to all – to see to it that no state with which she has relations and which in spite of all differences remains her traditional friend become, on her territory, the object of a procedure which runs counter to general law and international custom . . . (Grosser, 1980: 242)

Thus on this issue the Administration benefited from de Gaulle's belief in the nation-state (a belief that was also apparent in de Gaulle's vision of and attitude towards the European Economic Community) which influenced the expression of his opposition to U.S. policy in Vietnam and the U.S. position as leader of the Western bloc. For though the Russell Tribunal still took place, it was convened in Stockholm, and therefore denied the degree of credibility that being held in France – considering France's background of involvement in Indochina, current political stance and role as a medium power in the world – would have conferred on it. In addition, convening the tribunal in France would have granted it a higher profile and perhaps brought a greater amount of media coverage. So de Gaulle's rebuff prevented France from being embroiled in a profitless exercise that was viewed as an anti-American propaganda spectacle from the beginning, with the Tribunal having already reached its verdict before the proceedings started (for contemporary reportage of the Tribunal, see Worldwide Treatment of Current Issues, 1 May 1967: 3; for differing views of its activities see Caute, 1988: 7–8, 12–13; and Lewy, 1978: 311–13).

However, despite the fact that the French Government's disapproval of the U.S. involvement in Vietnam generated widespread approval in France, the latter did not escape the riots and demonstrations that erupted across Europe, with the Vietnam War as one theme among several others, such as student conditions (also a factor in Britain), the government and education authorities' attitude to students, and what Caute terms 'the wider grievance against technocratic authoritarianism' (Caute, 1988: 186; see also 68–71 and 183–209). Paradoxically the worst of the riots in France, in May 1968 and then again in October, took place after President Johnson's March announcement of a bombing cutback coupled with a readiness to negotiate. However, though the demonstrators were obviously unmoved by this development, de Gaulle welcomed it publicly as a genuine move in the direction of peace, even hailing Johnson's decision as 'an act of wisdom and political courage' (see Worldwide Treatment of Current Issues, 3 April 1968: 4).

Johnson's speech and de Gaulle's reaction initiated a better relationship between the two leaders concerning Vietnam, which was ultimately an important factor in beginning the peace process in Paris. For though France's friendly relations with Hanoi meant that the French Government was well-placed to help in any negotiation process (as Paris Radio was quick to point out; see Worldwide Treatment of

Current Issues, 1 April 1968: 5), the French Government's past opposition to the policies of the Johnson Administration and Saigon, coupled with its pro-Hanoi stance, had appeared to vitiate any chance that the French might have had to mediate in the conflict, by becoming unacceptable to the Americans and South Vietnamese – much as the British Government was now unacceptable to the North Vietnamese because of its pro-American stance. For American displeasure with the French Government's attitude had apparently reached further than just top Administration officials, as French officials themselves had been aware, and this discontent could have impacted on American public opinion concerning a site for peace talks:

1 When I called on Lucet [Charles Lucet, the new French Ambassador to the U.S.] at his request at Foreign Office this morning, I found him tired and discouraged . . . Lucet said he was forced to conclude that there existed very genuine resentment at French policies in US, and that there was a general distrust of France. He cited recent polls in this connection. He said US opinion did not seem to pinpoint its dissatisfaction with France but that there certainly was an increasingly unfortunate climate. I of course cited French policies on NATO and Vietnam as fundamental reasons for this unhappy attitude which he found in US. (Embtel 1393 [Paris] McBride to State Department, 28 July 1966, France, Memos, Volume IX, 1/66–9/66, France Country File, NSF, Box 172, LBJ Library; square brackets added)

Considering that Lucet had been 'given strict orders not to do or say anything that would antagonize the United States' when taking up his new post, de Gaulle's Phnom Penh speech, coming only two months later, must have seemed a particularly perverse gesture, virtually bound to exacerbate these already strained and delicate relations (CIA Intelligence Information Cable, 10 February 1966, France, Cables, Volume IX, 1/66–9/66, France Country File, NSF, Box 172, LBJ Library). And where Vietnam was concerned this distrust had been fully reciprocated by the French, right up to President Johnson's post-Tet speech:

There is in France and I believe throughout Western Europe a new and great wave of violent opposition to our Viet Nam policy . . .

We are seen as the greatest power in the world towering over little people in a little country. The enemy's casualty rate is proof of the cruel power we wield. The enemy's ability to continue to attack after suffering great losses is proof of the honesty and sincerity and the rightness of his desire to expel the alien invader . . .

Europeans are skeptics and cynics. They do not believe we are spending blood and treasure in Viet Nam for an altruistic even abstract reason such as preventing aggression. (Memo, Ernest Goldstein for the President, 23 February 1968, CO 81, France [1967–68], Confidential File, CO 52, Republic of Congo (1965), Box 8, LBJ Library)

In his memorandum Goldstein also pointed to a 'more fundamental and real pro-American current which is everywhere in Europe' and optimistically opined that a 'major address or an interview' (on the virtues of the U.S. involvement in Vietnam) combined with the establishment of 'a group equivalent to Peace with Freedom in Europe' would 'turn Europe around'. President Johnson did soon after make a major speech on 31 March, announcing the search for peace and bombing reduction – which helped to turn Europe around – but it was not along the lines envisioned by Goldstein, and it is hard to believe that such a speech at this juncture would have had a better or more lasting effect than any of Johnson's previous rallying calls.

In addition to its relationship with North Vietnam, the other point in France's favour was that however poor the public relations between the top echelons of the U.S. and French Governments, as mentioned previously contacts had always continued quietly at the lower governmental levels, and French Government officials, as well as private individuals, had been involved in peace probes between the two sides. With the change in approach by Johnson and de Gaulle it now became feasible for Paris to be chosen as an acceptable compromise site for peace talks after other possible locations had been discarded.

West German Government reaction and opinion

Although official West German support for U.S. policies in Vietnam was of necessity confined to verbal expressions of appreciation, more practical assistance was given to South Vietnam in the form of humanitarian and development aid – specifically non-military aid, for obvious reasons. This was West Germany's contribution to the anti-communist cause, and for the U.S. Administration it was part of an important demonstration of European commitment to the conflict in Vietnam. This practical assistance was required both as a signal that the Europeans appreciated the significance of the venture, and to help create an image of the U.S. acting in concert with its European allies – in addition to its more remote (from Europe) Antipodean and Asian comrades-in-arms – giving an impression of European involvement of some sort. Indeed, so important was this European involvement and impression of a concrete commitment, that – despite the known political sensitivity of this issue – U.S. Defense Secretary McNamara apparently broached the issue of sending FRG troops to South Vietnam. This emerged from a conversation that Henry Kissinger had with Chancellor Erhard in early 1966, which he later reported to the Administration:

American troops in Germany and Vietnam. Erhard asked about Vietnam and I gave him a brief description of the situation. He said he thought bombing of the North should be resumed lest America appear weak and indecisive. He expressed concern that the American involvement in Asia would reduce its interest in Europe. He asked whether we really wanted German combat troops in Vietnam. I said that I was unaware of any such request. Erhard said that Secretary McNamara had urged on Ambassador Knappstein that FRG send at least engineer batallions [*sic*] to Vietnam. He thought that sending uniformed personnel was out of the question. He was prepared, however, to make a real sacrifice in extending economic aid and encouraging German civilian construction firms to interest themselves in Vietnam. (Memo, from Secretary McNamara to the President, passed through Joe Califano; record of Henry Kissinger's conversations with De la Grandville and Erhard; document dated 23 March 1966; Confidential File CO 81, France 1966; filed in Confidential File CO 52, Republic of Congo, Box 8, LBJ Library)

Needless to say, McNamara's suggestion was not taken up, and West German support remained non-military in character. However, for most of this period the relationship between the successive governments in West Germany and Johnson's administration was close enough for the latter to obtain whatever official verbal and material support it calculated that the war increasingly demanded. For instance, during Johnson's peace spectacular in January 1966, when U.S. diplomats toured the world in search of peace, the U.S. Ambassador to the FRG requested some timely assistance:

> . . . I suggested to Chancellor Erhard in my meeting with him on Jan 5 that he might wish to make a public statement in support of the President's peace offensive in Viet-Nam. Press Sec Von Hase made a good brief statement in his press conference Jan 7 (Embtel 1983) which was followed a few hours later by the excellent official statement of the Chancellor's office. (reftel)
>
> The Chancellor's helpful attitude in this instance is, I believe, evidence of his sincere desire to do whatever he can, within the limits imposed by his own domestic situation, to be of assistance in Viet-Nam.

Ambassador McGhee then discussed Germany's current contribution to the conflict and the expected increase:

> . . . I believe we can look for further tangible evidence of German support in the near future, in addition to the increased funds already provided to Viet-Nam for refugees and increased aid authorization for 1966 (septels).
>
> In the light of those circumstances, I would recommend that the Dept suggest that the President send a personal, private letter to Erhard to let the Chancellor know that he is aware of, and appreciates, his statement. I feel that this would be most helpful, as we work with the FRG and with the Chancellor to bring about a greater German contribution to the struggle in Viet-Nam. (Embtel 1997 [Bonn] McGhee to State Department, 10 January 1966; Germany, Cables, Volume IX, 7/65–1/66, Germany Country File, NSF, Boxes 186–187, LBJ Library)

Even for the Europeans Vietnam was already beginning to resemble a bottomless pit, swallowing ever-greater amounts of aid, with Administration officials acting as a form of debt collector. When Vice-Chancellor Willy Brandt visited Washington in February 1967, West Germany's assistance to South Vietnam was carefully catalogued, including the numbers of German personnel helping in Vietnam and staffing the hospital ship; the numbers of South Vietnamese being trained in the FRG; and lastly a breakdown of the goods and materials that the FRG had provided, which to date had totalled credits of DM85.5 million, plus DM17.5 million worth of pharmaceuticals (and 30 ambulances and two mobile dental clinics), with a subsequent DM25 million voted for new aid (Background paper, H-German, WB/B-8, February 1967, Germany, Visit of Vice-Chancellor Brandt, Germany Country File, NSF, Box 193, LBJ Library). And as the new Federal Chancellor, Kiesinger, made clear at a press conference following a visit to Washington later that same year, the change of government would in no way affect the provision of aid to South Vietnam (Embtel 1969 [Bonn] to State Department, Part 2 of 2 Parts, 23 August

1967; Germany, Memos, Visit of Chancellor Kiesinger III, 8/67, Germany Country File, NSF, Box 193, LBJ Library).

The U.S. Administration utilized not only bilateral meetings to request assistance, but also the forum of NATO ministerial meetings to hammer home the message that Europe had a collective duty to help the U.S. and its allies in Vietnam. The language in which this recurrent theme was presented to European ministers contained a mixture of delicate arm-twisting and appeal to self-interest, illustrated in the following extract from an embassy post-mortem on the December 1965 meeting, transmitted to the State Department. The section on Vietnam begins with a reference to the current paucity of European aid and the grounds of their reluctant acceptance of the U.S. commitment:

> 2. There were of course two ghosts at the feast: France and Vietnam . . . Your [Secretary of State Dean Rusk] presentation on Vietnam was part of a fundamental shift in the terms of the Transatlantic dialogue on the non-NATO responsibilities of members . . .
>
> 4. Vietnam and China.
>
> Your stated concern about Vietnam, which was extended far into the future by Sec. McNamara's remarks on China, formalized and dramatized for our allies and the world the attitude at which we have been hinting for the past three months.
>
> (A) On Vietnam in the short run, there is grudging acquiescence that the United States has no honorable alternative to its present course, and we get increasing playback of the notion that US fidelity to its Far Eastern commitments is important to Europeans protected by the U.S. commitment here.
>
> (B) But apart from a verbal dividend here and there, such as Spaak's impressive statement on Belgian TV December 14, the sources of physical aid to South Vietnam do not leap to the eye. But continuing emphasis may produce a somewhat large non-military presence from Europe, which is something. (square brackets added)

The embassy's dissection then moved on to the warning underlying the U.S. request for European assistance and the related need for the U.S. to protect its own image as guarantor of peace in Europe, by ensuring that the Europeans were aware of the need for them to help assist in their own defence by helping the U.S. in Vietnam, and in the longer term elsewhere in the Far East. And in considering this issue in practical terms the embassy also spotlighted the unitary nature of the decision-making apparatus regarding bombing and peace negotiations, even though other nations were already involved in the conflict:

(C) Ministers can hardly have failed to get the point that increasing requirements for US effort in Vietnam are bound to have some impact on U.S. deployment of NATO support forces. As practical political leaders they can see that with growing U.S. casualties in Vietnam, American opinion will be increasingly impatient with a detached European attitude toward our commitment in Vietnam while they press us to honor every scruple of our pledge to them.
(D) When and if we have to move sizable units out of Europe, it will be important to have made, vigorously and continuously, the point that the only way Europeans can prevent our increasing Far Eastern efforts from degrading NATO is to join that effort themselves. This meeting was an excellent start in that direction.
(E) The expressed interest of European ministers in the conditions for peace has one meaning we should think about. Real military participation by Europeans in the Far East would I believe require a major change in the international framework of the defense of South Vietnam – at a minimum, a system of mutual international commitments that enable other substantial participants in the war to participate in decisions about bombing and peace negotiations as well.
(F) When it comes to the longer-run threat of a more powerful Communist China, the assembled ministers were certainly not stirred into eager acceptance of responsibilities beyond the NATO defense area, but the eloquent and serious expression of U.S. concern has been planted deep in some European political psyches.

The last two paragraphs of the embassy analysis suggested that the U.S. message about its far-flung commitments and the corresponding duties of its allies had not fallen on deaf ears, and also revealed a U.S. vision of its allies' future role, and current status, that most would have found disturbing – particularly given their relatively recent shedding of their former colonial commitments and ties – not to mention the worrying implications of U.S. policy towards China:

(G) From conversation around the edges of the meeting this week, I would judge that the most important thing that happened here was to bring home to governments a central fact about the next few years of international relations: That the United States would increasingly judge its bilateral relations with other nations by reference to the degree to which those nations feel responsible for joining us in building a dependable system of peaceful change in the more turbulent parts of the world. Most Europeans have in the first half of this decade started economic aid programs as partial recognition of this responsibility. I suppose it will take the second half of the 1960s to bring them fully into the peacekeeping business, and perhaps longer than that to find a formula for associating them with our determination to teach the Chinese Communists

that military militancy doesn't pay.
(H) To convert our continental allies from affluent protectorates to active participants in policing world order beyond Europe will be uphill missionary work for some time to come. But I suspect that more than one foreign minister will be ruminating on your throw-away comment on Thursday morning, that in a world where Chinese Communists have long-range missiles, NATO has to begin worrying about a QTE Western flank UNQTE in the Bering Sea. (Embtel 3491 [Paris] Cleveland to Rusk, 18 December 1965, Classification Secret; France, Cables [1 of 2], Volume VIII, 9/65–1/66, France Country File, NSF, Box 172, LBJ Library)

At subsequent NATO meetings the Administration kept up the pressure, linking its commitments to South Vietnam to its guarantees for Europe and reiterating the standard justifications for its involvement in the conflict :

US is committed by treaty in Southeast Asia to take action to meet common danger. US has special interest, moreover in view of other treaty agreements in area [*sic*]. US cannot be negligent about one treaty in area if it wishes to sustain others. If there are elements in European public opinion which request us to be unfaithful to treaty in Asia but faithful to Atlantic Treaty, they must be told to forget it. US is working in Vietnam to prevent World War III, rather than throwing ourselves down slippery slope towards World War III . . .

. . . (As for international aspect of conflict, Secretary [Rusk] expressed appreciation for assistance being provided in Viet Nam [*sic*] by 12 NATO countries.) . . .

Great deal of concern is being expressed that Vietnam gets in way of detente with USSR. Yet 30 years ago when Soviet troops entered into Azerbaidzhan, Western countries did not sit back and welcome them to it. Similarly threats to Berlin and agression [*sic*] in Korea were not regarded as gestures of friendship, nor were missiles in Cuba. We will not get detente by giving away little countries to a country with a big appetite . . .

We need a sence [*sic*] of solidarity of NATO countries with free countries in Asia, countries like Japan, which now live next door to great danger building up in Asia. US has placed more than 371,000 US troops in Vietnam without moving major units from the NATO area. US intends to maintain its commitment in NATO area as in Pacific. Problem in Vietnam remains manageable problem. Of corse [*sic*], there are dangers in it, but so is there lots of room for confidence. (Embtel 9244 Paris to State Department on Rusk remarks at 15 December NATO Ministerial meeting; 16 December 1966; France, Cables, Volume X, 10/66–1/67, France Country File, NSF, Box 173, LBJ Library)

These apparently relatively mild – though pointed – remarks on U.S. commitments and public expressions of appreciation for NATO assistance were not, however, the full story, as a separate telegram from Rusk to President Johnson makes clear:

The NATO meeting has gone well . . .

I gave the Council some QTE old-time religion UNQTE on Vietnam and believe that we can get some additional assistance from Germany, The Netherlands and some others but this must be developed bilaterally in capitals. I hit George Brown [UK Foreign Secretary] pretty hard on the point that they have the same treaty commitment that we have to QTE meet the common danger UNQTE in Vietnam. I intend to press them very hard for more participation [rest of paragraph sanitized]. (Embtel 9261 [Paris] Rusk to President Johnson, 'Personal for the President', 16 December 1966, Classification 'Secret NODIS'; France, Cables, Volume X, 10/66–1/67, France Country File, NSF, Box 173, LBJ Library; square brackets added)

Notwithstanding the persistent pressure from the U.S., the Europeans, although offering some assistance to American efforts in South Vietnam, remained cautious, participating with reluctance – and thereby fully justifying earlier U.S. fears that motivating these 'affluent protectorates' to help police 'world order beyond Europe' would indeed be 'uphill missionary work' (see above). For when the U.S. Administration considered requesting action from the United Nations on the Middle East (in the wake of the June 1967 war) and Vietnam in September 1967, while its fellow NATO members were receptive to U.N. action over the Middle East (particularly endeavouring to reopen the Suez Canal), their reaction concerning Vietnam was less than enthusiastic:

Vietnam

Regarding possible Security Council consideration, the reaction of others was characterized by "timidity and doubt."

[long paragraph sanitized]

In short, most members who spoke (seven out of fifteen members) expressed appreciation of our desire to try to involve the UN particularly in light of Charter responsibilities, doubted we could succeed, and thought the certain risks clearly outweighed the dubious benefits. Some concern was expressed that forcing the Soviets hand in the Security Council on Vietnam might jeopardize possible cooperation with them on the Middle East. [rest of paragraph and document sanitized] (Paris 3224, Cable From Ambassador Cleveland to State Department, Wednesday, 13 September 1967, Classification

Secret LIMDIS; France, Memos, Volume XII, 7/67–12/67, France Country File, NSF, Box 173, LBJ Library)

Whilst the 'timidity and doubt' that the U.S. ambassador chronicled could be put down to the natural apprehensiveness felt by NATO members when considering the vastly escalating war in Vietnam and the nature of North Vietnam's supporters, their divergent reactions to the Middle East and Vietnam also expressed the difference in degree of importance that the Europeans attached to the Middle East compared to Vietnam – both as an area of great importance to them economically and as a regional political problem with the capacity to generate a much larger conflict rapidly. Their differing responses also implied that two years of Administration explanation, justification, and exhortation about the vital importance of the Vietnam War had still not convinced European ministers.

The support that the West German Government afforded the U.S. Administration in Vietnam, whilst serving its domestic needs well as far as economics was concerned, acted as a further stimulus to the unrest that was sweeping Europe by the mid-1960s. As in Britain and France, though the war was a potent rallying issue, there were other causes which stoked the dissatisfaction of the demonstrators. And the Administration and its various embassies and agencies were quick to seize on any causes of unrest that were unrelated to the war. Following the October 1967 anti-war demonstrations in several European cities, USIA Director Leonard Marks produced a round-up for President Johnson:

Over the weekend demonstrations took place in a number of European cities protesting U.S. policy in Viet-Nam . . .

Berlin:

Initially, between 4,000 and 6,000 demonstrators marched peacefully along prescribed route, watched by 8,000–10,000 onlookers. Then most dispersed. Later, several thousand reassembled on Berlin's main thoroughfare (Kurfurstendamm) blocking traffic at major intersections and challenging police. Repeated police use of water cannon (and apparently some clubs) failed to disperse the crowd until after midnight.

Score: several reportedly injured, 23 demonstrators arrested, smoke bomb exploded without damage in America house.

NOTE: Post points out that confrontation with police had little to do with depth of feeling about Viet-Nam in Berlin. The disorder was a continuation of a test of strength between radical students and the Berlin city government that began early last June (ostensible issue at that time: alleged repression of liberties in Iran) and has continued sporadically ever since.

(Memo, Leonard H. Marks to the President, through Charles Maguire, 23 October 1967, National Security – Defense, Ex ND 19/CO 312; 10-21-67–10-27-67; Box 229, LBJ Library)

Whatever the 'real' issues underlying the demonstrations – as opposed to the 'ostensible' ones – the fact is that the Vietnam War featured in these violent protests. And though by now the war was a widely known fact of life, still these demonstrations were an unwelcome form of publicity – an embarrassment to the U.S. Administration and its allies alike. Marks' round-up noted of the London demonstration that it was 'described by local police as worst riot in memory'; but within six months this riot was to be eclipsed by an even more violent demonstration in March 1968, and seven months later there was yet another confrontation. Just as the war seemed endless – but less remote with such riots in European cities – so did the ensuing opposition.

7

The balance sheet for LBJ (III): European public opinion by 1968

The other target of the external U.S. propaganda campaign was public opinion in allied countries. Public opinion in these countries was important, forming, as it did, part of general international public opinion, but also more specifically because of its potential to exert pressure on America's allied governments: pressure that could either support allied government policy on the war (whether for or against), or militate against government policy.

As stated previously, U.S. propaganda could be disseminated via allied governments, in the form of government statements, briefings and actions; via the media, carrying both direct U.S. and allied government information; and via contact with private individuals from allied countries – often individuals or groups from key social strata, such as parliamentarians and press editors. Such contacts could be arranged through U.S. embassies in the respective countries. In addition, the embassies (and of course the Administration) could field representatives to put the U.S. case directly, at events such as debates or teach-ins, which often attracted considerable media coverage, particularly in the early years of the war.

That the Administration was aware of the continuing need to persuade its allies' populations of the justice of, and necessity for, the war is manifested in a memorandum from Assistant for National Security

Affairs Walt Rostow to President Johnson:

Pat Dean and Michael Stewart came in today with the following message from Prime Minister Wilson. They will be talking in the same vein to Secretary Rusk this afternoon.

1. It is clear that our planned increase in pressure on North Viet Nam will confront the Prime Minister with a problem of public opinion in the UK. Even the modest increased actions we have already taken have led to considerable increase in noise from the Labor opposition.
2. In general the U.S. is not getting through to British public opinion on the following points:
   – why we are in Viet Nam ;
   – why we believe our military and political policy will succeed;
   – why we believe the course of action we are pursuing will bring about peace. [next three paragraphs sanitized] (Memo, Rostow for the President, 6 March 1967, National Security File, Files of Walt W. Rostow; Folder, Pennsylvania etc.; Boxes 7–18, LBJ Library)

Rostow's concern about public opinion and his delineation of the specific points on which the British public remained either disbelieving, unenlightened, or confused (see below for analysis of public opinion) two years after the war had begun escalating, implied a belief that once the Administration succeeded in getting its message across to the public then public support would follow. (Rostow's views about public opinion were also echoed by other figures, for example Ernest Goldstein, quoted above; and General Maxwell Taylor, who expressed the view that U.S. opinion was not turning against President Johnson, the public was just confused, and all that was needed was to lay out the facts: interview with author, 6 October 1983.) This optimistic view overlooked, or disregarded, the possibility that yet more explanation and justification might have no further effect, and that the lack of public support might be based on disagreement with the war itself; distrust of the U.S. Administration's arguments, rather than ignorance of them or confusion; or of course a fundamental uninterest that no amount of information could reverse. Rostow's belief, that increasing and clearer exhortation would yield the required degree of public support, mirrored in the propaganda field the same beliefs held about the military effort: that piling on the pressure would eventually achieve victory – that it was simply necessary to hang on and then, despite all indicators to the contrary, the constantly escalating war would turn their way.

Mass public opinion, traditionally 'unconcerned' and 'inactive', especially on foreign policy issues, was 'measured' and monitored during these years mainly through opinion polls, whilst the much smaller section of 'active' and 'informed' opinion manifested itself in teach-ins, marches and demonstrations; through letter columns in the press and letters to political representatives; and through activities connected to organized bodies such as political parties and unions. As well as independent poll organizations such as Gallup Poll (international and national affiliates) and National Opinion Poll (U.K.), the results of which were often published in the press and were available to interested governments, the Administration could also monitor opinion through USIA polls, and of course through embassy round-ups of reaction to particular events/policies at various times of the war.

There was thus a considerable amount of feedback to the Administration and allied governments concerning public opinion – frequently involving a time-lag, but available to them nonetheless. And this information could be used to construct and subsequently modify propaganda policy, as the war continued and escalated: if the Administration's propaganda policy ultimately failed to achieve its objectives, it was not because the Administration was unaware of public reaction to the war or particular policies and events, and thus unable to tailor its information policies accordingly. Nor, obviously, was the Administration unaware of the need to 'sell' the war to the public, and whilst there was little coordination – according to both General Maxwell Taylor and State Department press spokesman Robert McCloskey – there was certainly a considerable effort to disseminate the Administration's version of the war to the public (General Taylor alone gave over 130 lectures on the war; while McCloskey stated that although answers to press questions were never consciously tailored as to how the public would perceive them, nevertheless as speeches were prepared the public was kept in mind; interviews with author, 6 October 1983; and 27 April 1983 respectively), and to impress upon the public certain aspects of Administration policy, particularly those concerning escalation, bombing, negotiations and peace.

Public opinion in the relevant allied countries will now be examined in turn, and some general conclusions then drawn. Unfortunately, due to the varying wording of questions used in opinion polls – wording which could differ, in what purported to be the same questions, from one month to the next, even when asked by the same polling organization – this survey of allied public opinion cannot comprise a strictly accurate comparison. For even what seemed to be only minor variations in phrasing may have stimulated different responses from poll respondents.

United Kingdom public opinion

January 1965–August 1966

British mass public opinion, as expressed in Gallup Polls, supported the U.S. involvement in Vietnam at the beginning of 1965. A poll published in December 1964 reported that 41 per cent of those polled approved of U.S. armed action, while 33 per cent disapproved, and 26 per cent didn't know. However, there was no inclination to help the U.S. if asked – 46 per cent of those polled in January 1965 opposed taking any part in the war; 10 per cent agreed to sending troops; 17 per cent agreed to sending war materials; while 29 per cent didn't know. But, in addition to supporting U.S. armed action, the majority of the public – 77 per cent – also favoured the notion of a Southeast Asia conference.

In March 1965, when the Administration began bombing North Vietnam, Gallup Poll again asked respondents what became a standard question – whether they approved or disapproved of 'recent American armed action in Vietnam' – and recorded a 40 per cent approval rating, with 31 per cent disapproving, and 29 per cent undecided ('don't know'). So the proportion of the public supporting armed action was much the same as in December 1964. At the same time the figures for another of their relatively long-lived questions (put to respondents fairly regularly, and in the same wording, up to September 1966) mirrored this response: when asked if the 'United States should continue its present efforts in South Vietnam, or should pull out its forces?', 40 per cent favoured continuation; 32 per cent wanted the U.S. to pull out; and there were 28 per cent 'don't knows'. But opposition to Britain taking any part at all was growing, now 50 per cent; although the proportion favouring sending war materials had also increased to 22 per cent; and the percentage favouring sending troops was 14 per cent; 15 per cent were undecided. National Opinion Polls (NOP) in March, however, put a different question to those polled on American involvement, asking whether U.S. handling of the situation had been 'too firm, not firm enough, or about right'. The poll recorded that 17 per cent thought U.S. handling was too firm; 17 per cent not firm enough; and 36 per cent thought U.S. efforts were about right. The poll thus registered criticism from both 'hawks' and 'doves' among the public.

In general it can be stated that in the period from January to March 1965, a plurality of the British public did approve of the U.S. involvement in Vietnam, although the public opposed any British involvement and favoured efforts to solve the conflict peacefully.

However, the 'active' section of British opinion was already beginning to make its views known on the Vietnam War. For instance, when the U.S. began its Rolling Thunder air-strikes on North Vietnam, 800 students protested outside the U.S. embassy, *The Guardian* reported. In addition, later in March there was the gas warfare episode, which prompted a march by Labour and Liberal MPs to the U.S. embassy, and the dispatch of a condemnatory telegram to the Foreign Secretary, who was then in Washington discussing Vietnam with the U.S. Administration. Thus the early stages of the escalation of the war provoked opposition from certain sections of British public opinion. As the war escalated more rapidly during April to July this opposition also grew, becoming more discernible and organized.

In April, Gallup again asked its standard question on 'recent American armed action in Vietnam', and this time the percentages were reversed, with 31 approving, 41 disapproving, with the undecided dropping only 1 per cent to 28 per cent. It is possible that this reversal reflected public disapproval of the gas warfare incident, because the figures recorded in March were based on fieldwork completed before this incident. For immediately after the gas episode, based on data gathered between 25 and 30 March, Gallup Poll recorded that 45 per cent of respondents disapproved of recent American armed action and thus the April figures, although still recording a reversal, in fact represented a slight drop from a higher level of disapproval. Furthermore, on the gas warfare incident both Gallup and National Opinion Polls (NOP) reported a majority disapproval of the use of gas. NOP put a straightforward question on the U.S. using 'non-killer gas' and recorded 58 per cent disapproval. Gallup asked if there was support for the protest by Labour and Liberal MPs against the use of gas and recorded that 55 per cent supported the protest. The supposition about the reasons for the drop in public support is strengthened by the fact that the April figures were recorded before President

Johnson's Baltimore speech while the figures in May, after that speech, showed a rise in public support for U.S. armed action and a corresponding drop in disapproval. It seems, therefore, that the methods by which the U.S. conducted the war appeared to be important to the public and could generate disapproval.

NOP also recorded a slight drop in April in support for the U.S., asking its standard question about U.S. handling of the situation in terms of firmness (see above). The percentages quoted by NOP, compared with the March figures, showed a 2 per cent increase over the previous 17 per cent in those thinking U.S. handling was too firm, and a 3 per cent drop from the previous 17 per cent in those thinking U.S. handling was not firm enough. NOP loosely attributed this 'small swing' in public opinion to 'recent events in Vietnam'. Presumably NOP was referring to the gas incident, for the other incident of note in early March was the dispatch of U.S. Marines to South Vietnam, and Gallup Poll, which kept a much closer watch on public opinion on Vietnam than NOP, had not recorded any fluctuation in public support at that time.

Gallup Poll's other findings in April showed a 6 per cent increase in those who did not want Britain to help the U.S. in Vietnam if asked, now totalling a clear majority of 56 per cent, while the numbers prepared to send either troops or war materials had dropped by 4 per cent and 3 per cent respectively from the March figures. This pacific trend was reinforced by the finding that an overwhelming majority of the public, 71 per cent, thought that Britain's task was to try to get peace talks started on Vietnam, whereas a mere 9 per cent judged it 'most important' for Britain to support the U.S. over Vietnam. On the subject of the likelihood of a world war, 62 per cent thought there was little danger, while 20 per cent thought there was much danger. However, the latter figure showed an 11 per cent increase over the September 1964 percentage, thus posing the question as to whether the escalation of the Vietnam conflict might have been one of the factors responsible for raising fears of another world war, especially as the Administration's rhetoric on the Vietnam War, officially echoed by the British Government, stressed the features of communist aggression and expansion. On the other hand the fact that 62 per cent of respondents took a more relaxed view of the possible dangers of a world war could suggest that either the Administration's propaganda campaign, with its direct connection of the Vietnam War to 'Munich' and the Second World War, was not having the desired effect, or that another strand of the Administration's campaign – that of fighting a smaller war to avoid a larger conflagration – was helping to calm public fears. In any case, the U.S. propaganda campaign was still in its infancy and more preoccupied at this time with justifying the bombing of North Vietnam and establishing the impression that escalation was an enemy-driven phenomenon.

As noted above, by May, in answer to Gallup Poll's standard question, the percentages of the general public approving or disapproving of U.S. armed action were now roughly even at 37 per cent and 36 per cent respectively. As the number of 'don't knows' was only 1 per cent different, it is apparent that there was a direct correlation between the drop in public disapproval and the rise in approval. In addition Gallup Poll also recorded that President Johnson was believed by 69 per cent of the public to be sincerely trying to end the war with his appeal for unconditional discussions and offer to develop Southeast Asia.

To judge from Gallup Poll's findings on opinion about relations with America, fluctuations in public opinion concerning the Vietnam War did not arise from anti-Americanism, for in May over half of the public, 54 per cent, considered the U.S. to be 'Britain's best friend', with the runner-up, Australia, coming a lot further down the list with 14 per cent. Also, the public was evenly balanced on the more sensitive issue of whether Britain should or should not work 'more closely with the U.S. in its political and military policies': 31 per cent thought Britain should work more closely, with the same percentage opting for less close cooperation; 20 per cent opted for no change; while 18 per cent were undecided. Thus on these figures over half of the public approved of cooperation with the U.S. in these spheres, with a preponderant percentage of this half preferring closer cooperation.

By contrast with previous months, July's Gallup Poll contained more information than usual on opinion about events concerning Vietnam. The standard question showed a slight increase of 2 per cent in disapproval of U.S. armed action, corresponding to a 2 per cent decrease in approval, giving figures of 42 per cent and 34 per cent respectively, with the number of don't knows remaining the same as in June, 24 per cent. However, public opinion now seemed to be split evenly three ways on the issue of whether the U.S. 'should continue its present efforts in South Vietnam' or withdraw its troops. This picture contrasted with the figures in March when 40 per cent had favoured a continuation of U.S. efforts. Now 33 per cent supported a continuation, the same percentage favoured withdrawal, while 34 per cent were undecided. That the decline in those favouring a continuation of U.S. efforts was matched by a rise in the number of 'don't knows' suggests that possibly the Vietnam conflict was beginning to be perceived as more complicated and difficult to solve than at an earlier stage; for it does not seem likely that a portion of the public which previously favoured continuing U.S. efforts would simply lose interest in the issue. The figures recorded when Gallup asked which side was thought to be winning in the war tend to confirm this hypothesis, with 39 per cent reckoning that neither side was winning; 33 per cent undecided; while of those who did pick one or the other side, 19 per cent thought the communists and Vietcong were winning, and only 9 per cent thought the South Vietnamese Government 'and supporters' were winning.

On the issue of the Prime Minister's peace proposals, however, there were more firm opinions expressed, with the proposals approved by a 65 per cent majority. On the other hand there was much less certainty about whether the peace mission would succeed, for 38 per cent thought that it would not, while 42 per cent were undecided on the matter. Possibly this low assessment of the peace mission's chances of success accounted for the figures when Gallup asked whether the Prime Minister's position had been 'improved or harmed' by this peace mission proposal, for though 38 per cent thought his position had improved, 46 per cent thought either that his position had been unaffected or did not know (16 per cent thought his position had been harmed). Finally, the Prime Minister's dispatch of Harold Davies to Hanoi was approved by 49 per cent of respondents, with 25 per cent disagreeing with the visit and 26 per cent undecided, thus confirming that almost half of the general public preferred to try and settle the conflict peacefully.

One of the most revealing factors in these general public opinion surveys (confirmed by relevant NOP surveys) was the fairly high percentage of respondents who were undecided or unconcerned about a variety of issues concerning the war. However, this was not the whole picture of British opinion on the war, for there were sections of the British public which were acutely concerned with, and often opposed to, the Vietnam conflict and the Labour Government's attitude to U.S. policy and the war. These sections comprised a mixture of elements, including groupings such as the high-profile, vociferous left-wing of the Labour Party (itself a group with diverse views), an *ad hoc* MPs' committee on Vietnam, CND, the Committee of 100, the Communist

Party of Great Britain (CPGB) and its youth wing the Young Communist League (YCL), individual unions, individual university committees, and an umbrella organization formed in April 1965 called the British Council for Peace in Vietnam. This organization was chaired by Labour Peer Lord Brockway and drew its support from a number of other organizations which included 29 political, religious, and labour groups (for press coverage of these groups, see *The Guardian*, *Daily Telegraph*, and *Daily Worker* in April, May and July 1965).

In these early days of the Vietnam War, the aims of these groupings concerning the conflict could be summarized broadly in terms of the aims of the British Council for Peace in Vietnam: to help achieve a cease-fire, a negotiated political settlement, and to stop the war spreading (see *The Guardian*, 20 May 1965). There were of course two constituent elements that these groups considered when pursuing these aims: firstly, U.S. policy and conduct of the war in Vietnam; and secondly, the British Government's public support for the U.S. over Vietnam. Concern about the Vietnam conflict was manifested when it began escalating after the Pleiku attacks. Then, following the subsequent escalatory moves, the protests against the conflict began. And whereas the general public's attitude to the war was not apparently based on anti-Americanism, some of these groupings were undoubtedly anti-American in character, such as the left-wing of the Labour Party.

The methods which these groups used to express views on the war included rallies, marches, demonstrations, public meetings and lobbying Parliament. Inside Parliament the methods used included letters to the Prime Minister, signed motions, and the use of Question Time to interrogate the Government on the Vietnam War and its policy. In addition the letter columns of the newspapers were a more amorphous channel through which to express views on the war, sometimes by well-known individuals. And sometimes protest took the form of full-page advertisements in a newspaper, often signed by prominent figures (see, for example, *The Times*, 23 December 1965; or *The Guardian*, 14 April 1967).

Not surprisingly, where press coverage of these rallies and protest meetings was concerned, it was the Communist Party organ, the *Daily Worker*, which carried the most information. The *Daily Worker* also played an active part in coordinating opposition to the war by publishing advance information on planned marches and protests, and urging attendance (for example, see the *Daily Worker* in April, May and

June 1965). However, other newspapers also covered such protests and meetings, particularly if these were large meetings in prominent public places such as Trafalgar Square and attended by Labour MPs, whose presence was likely to embarrass the Government (for example, see the press reports of early rallies on 5 April and 3 May 1965). In addition, the issue of Vietnam might be raised at other events – ostensibly unconnected with this subject – attended by Government figures and these too were covered by the press.

As to the importance of this opposition to the Vietnam conflict and British official policy, at this early stage the Labour Government had no real cause for concern. For although the public demonstrations were noisy and attracted press attention, they were still relatively small gatherings of that small section of the British public which was actually concerned about the war. Nevertheless there was the obvious danger for the British Government that this public opposition could grow and strengthen and become a real source of embarrassment, although not a serious political threat.

The source of opposition that could pose a political threat to the Government came from within the Labour Party, but the Labour Party opposition to the war worked within constraints which severely curbed its effectiveness. For the limit of the Parliamentary Labour Party protest was defined by the Labour Government's slim majority and there was no desire on the part of Labour MPs to bring down their own Government. In addition to this constraint, there was also the fact, noted in a *Financial Times* analysis, that the Parliamentary Labour MPs who opposed the Government's policy on Vietnam were not a particularly cohesive group and occupied a range of positions on the left-wing spectrum, which tended to dilute the effectiveness of their opposition (*Financial Times*, 18 June 1965: 'Labour's Left and Vietnam'). And as this *Financial Times* analysis also pointed out, the ability of the left-wing to influence Government policy depended on the amount of support that the left-wing could generate in the rest of the Labour Party, and the left-wing's 'tactician', John Mendelson, well understood what was required to achieve this support:

> For Mr. Mendelson is extremely careful not to let the 'Left' seem either sinister or wild. His tactics are clearly based on the principle that only by apparent moderation can the Left exploit the wider misgivings in the Party. (*Financial Times*, 18 June 1965: 'Labour's Left and Vietnam')

These constraints worked in the Government's favour, but nevertheless the Government was careful to emphasize its desire for, and efforts to achieve, a negotiated settlement – a goal which broadly coincided with that of the Labour Left and the 'concerned' section of public opinion.

However, although Labour MPs inside Parliament were under these constraints in opposing the Government's support for U.S. involvement in Vietnam, there were no such constraints on groups outside Parliament. Already in May, soon after its formation, the British Council for Peace in Vietnam had announced a mass lobby of Parliament, planned for 'Vietnam Day' on 30 June (see *The Guardian*, 20 May for advance details). The lobby and the accompanying teach-in in Central Hall in Westminster received varying degrees of press attention, with *The Guardian* and the *Daily Worker* concentrating on the lobby, while the *Daily Telegraph* reported on the teach-in.

The Guardian report on the lobby caught the atmosphere at the 'highly excited rally', stating that the audience of approximately 1500 'came with a lust for blood; chiefly Mr. Wilson's, with President Johnson as a close runner-up' (*The Guardian*, 1 July 1965: 'Vietnam Protest "Best Lobby Of Them All"').The *Daily Worker*, however, estimated the numbers at the rally to be approximately 10,000 and reported that the deputation had had a 'very frank discussion' with Lord Walston, Parliamentary Under Secretary of State in the Foreign Office (*Daily Worker*, 1 July 1965).

Despite two arrests during the mass lobby, this event appeared to be relatively well-ordered. However the teach-in was a different matter and the *Daily Telegraph* caption to its report reflected this: 'MP Shouted Down At Vietnam Teach-In; Gathering Loses Dignity' (1 July 1965). The report stated that Labour MP Dr Jeremy Bray was 'hissed and screamed at' and that the meeting quickly 'degenerated into an anti-American free for all'. This was not the form that the 'teach-in' currently took in America, where it was used to examine issues, rather than merely to provide a platform for the noisy expression of anti-American or anti-government views. This point was made by Professor Kenneth Boulding of Michigan University who had attended the Central Hall teach-in and was quoted in the *Daily Telegraph*; while Professor Hans Morgenthau from Chicago University, a well-known opponent of U.S. policy in Vietnam and participant in American teach-ins, labelled the teach-in a 'débâcle' with 'disgraceful scenes' (quoted in the *Observer*, 4 July 1965: 'The Quiet American Leftist').

Clearly the issue of Vietnam was capable of provoking strong reactions among some sections of the British public – even at this early stage of the war. Some of these reactions appeared to be based primarily on a dislike of U.S. involvement in the conflict, while others appeared to be based on a dislike of the conflict itself, in addition to dislike of the British Government's support for the Americans. Whatever the combination of dislikes, however, while there were sections of public opinion which disliked U.S. intervention in the conflict it was obvious that the protests would continue until the U.S. ceased to prosecute the war, regardless of British Government policy.

In the period from August to December 1965, as compared with February to July, neither of the two main polling organizations recorded much data on public opinion concerning the Vietnam War. Thus while a general trend can be observed, it is much more difficult in this period to assess whether public opinion was affected by specific U.S. actions, whether military or diplomatic.

In August Gallup Poll (see Gallup Polls for August, September and December 1965) asked its standard question about approval or disapproval of recent U.S. armed action in Vietnam and recorded 27 per cent approved; 38 per cent disapproved; and 35 per cent didn't know. Compared with July this was a 7 per cent drop in approval, a 4 per cent drop in disapproval, and an 11 per cent rise in the number of don't knows. This appeared to indicate that the public was either confused and/or indifferent to the war. If the public was confused then this might have been caused by the President's July speech, increasing the numbers of troops to be sent to Vietnam, but at the same time calling for negotiations. National Opinion Polls' only reference to Vietnam in its August poll was a passing remark that the economy was of 'more long-term concern' to the Government than a 'possible left-wing revolt over Vietnam or immigration policy' (see National Opinion Polls for August, September and December 1965).

In September Gallup Poll questioned its respondents on four issues, but omitted its standard question. Instead respondents were asked whether they would approve or disapprove if the British Government sent British troops to fight with the South Vietnamese. A large majority, 69 per cent, disapproved; 17 per cent approved; and 14 did not know. Obviously a large majority declined any share of active involvement in the conflict, but in some ways this was a curious question to ask. Given that many of Gallup Poll's questions focused on U.S. actions and involvement in Vietnam, it would have been more logical (and perhaps more pertinent) to ask whether British troops should fight alongside South Vietnamese and/or U.S. troops. For the fact that the U.S. was Britain's ally in two world wars and was still seen as a close ally might possibly have affected the poll results.

Gallup Poll also ascertained the public's views on who was to blame for the lack of negotiations: the Communists, 21 per cent; the Vietcong, 8 per cent; the Chinese, 8 per cent; the North Vietnamese, 7 per cent; the Americans, 13 per cent; the South Vietnamese, 1 per cent; others, 1 per cent; and 44 per cent did not know. Unfortunately this is not a particularly useful set of figures. Firstly, the category of 'Communists' was too amorphous – there was no indication of which countries or groups either Gallup Poll or its respondents considered to be 'communist'. Secondly, whichever countries or groups were judged to be communist, Gallup Poll implicitly excluded the Vietcong, Chinese and the North Vietnamese from this category by citing them separately, although they were most certainly communist. Had these countries been specifically identified as communist, or even had the 'Communists' category been differentiated, then the poll results might have been different, and they would in any case have had more meaning. The anomaly was pointed up by the fact that in another question Gallup Poll produced a category 'Communists (Viet-Cong)'. In addition the figures added up to 103 per cent instead of 100 per cent, which would make future comparisons with this set of figures even more difficult. With these limitations in mind, the poll indicated that the 'Communists' were judged to be the major culprits regarding the lack of negotiations, but that compared with the Vietcong, Chinese and North Vietnamese individually, the U.S. was clearly thought more culpable. The large percentage of don't knows could have indicated confusion, indifference, or ignorance, or a combination of all three.

On the issue of which side was winning the war, the South Vietnamese Government or the 'Communists (Viet-Cong)', 43 per cent judged that neither side was winning, which was a 4 per cent increase over the June percentage; 17 per cent thought that the 'Communists (Viet-Cong)' were winning, registering a 2 per cent drop compared with June; 11 per cent thought that the 'South Vietnamese Government and supporters' were winning, registering a 2 per cent increase from June; and 29 per cent didn't know, registering a 4 per cent drop from June. Thus the belief that neither side was winning was now held by a little under 50 per cent of respondents. However, of the 28 per cent of respondents who judged that one or the other side was winning, a greater proportion thought the communists were ahead. These two sets of figures seemed to indicate that U.S. military technology was not thought to render the U.S. invincible. And it seems that optimistic U.S. Administration statements, echoed in some British newspapers, that the tide was turning in the war in favour of the U.S. and South Vietnamese, had either not been digested yet by the public, or were discounted.

Gallup Poll's last question in September asked whether the Americans would or would not be justified in using nuclear weapons if they could not make any progress in the war without using them. A vast majority of respondents, 81 per cent, thought they would not be justified in using them; 7 per cent thought they would be justified; and 12 per cent didn't know. Perhaps the surprising figures are that 7 per cent of respondents either supported the Americans so strongly and/or opposed the other side so bitterly that nuclear weapons were perceived to be justifiable; and that 12 per cent of respondents either had no opinion or were indifferent.

In answer to a question about the British Government's policy in Vietnam, National Opinion Polls recorded in September that 49 per cent of respondents 'neither approve nor disapprove' of the Government's policy and NOP stated that this confirmed its earlier findings that 'a large section of the electorate is not much concerned about Vietnam'. Of those who did express an opinion, 33 per cent approved of the Government's policy, while 18 per cent disapproved. NOP further recorded that a majority of those who disapproved wanted the Government to 'play a more neutral role'. Because NOP's figures were then broken down on a party political basis, it was apparent that this was a majority across the Conservative, Labour, Liberal political spectrum, although Labour voters registered the highest percentage in favour of a more neutral role.

Gallup Poll returned to the issue of Vietnam in December with its standard question on recent U.S. armed action. Comparing the figures with August (August's figures were based on July fieldwork), this poll registered the same 27 per cent approval; a 1 per cent drop in disapproval, now registering 37 per cent; and a 1 per cent rise in don't knows to a figure of 36 per cent. There was thus virtually no change in opinion since August, with just over a third of respondents disapproving of U.S. armed action and much the same proportion having no opinion. It seems therefore that the U.S. build-up and escalation in fighting had not had much effect on public opinion since August. But on the other hand the fieldwork for this poll was completed between 25 and 30 November 1965, that is, before the U.S. bombed a power station close to Haiphong, which was a much more spectacular act of escalation than in the preceding months. However, on the question of which side was winning the war, there was a considerable change from the August period: 36 per cent thought neither side was winning, registering a 7 per cent drop; 10 per cent now thought the 'Communists (Viet-Cong)' were winning, which was a 7 per cent drop; 14 per cent thought the South Vietnamese Government and supporters were winning, registering a 3 per cent increase; but the number of don't knows had increased to 40 per cent from 29 per cent in August. The considerable fluctuation in the latter figure could well have been due to the confusing nature of the war. Also a steady trend seemed to be emerging indicating that of that small proportion of respondents who judged that one or the other side was winning, the South Vietnamese and supporters were believed to be slowly gaining ground – probably due to the huge U.S. build-up, while the drop in percentage of respondents believing that the communists were winning could well have been due to the same factor.

In December National Opinion Polls varied its September question 'fractionally' and apparently recorded an important change in opinion. Respondents were asked whether they approved or disapproved of the 'British Government's support for American policy in Vietnam', which was in fact a much more specific, even 'loaded' question than September's more general formulation. In answer, 36 per cent approved – a 3 per cent increase; 33 per cent disapproved – a 12 per cent increase; and 31 per cent didn't know – an 18 per cent decrease. As NOP noted, there was a striking decrease in the number of don't knows and a corresponding increase in the percentage of respondents disapproving. The breakdown in party affiliation revealed the same results. And when NOP polled disapprovers on its supplementary question on whether the Government should play a more neutral role or give the Americans more support, a decisive majority, 26 per cent (79 per cent of the original 33 per cent), wanted the Government to play a more neutral role and once again this figure held true for all three political parties. From these figures NOP concluded: 'There is no doubt that public hostility to the war in Vietnam has increased significantly during the last 3 months.' But the September and December questions were considerably different, not merely 'fractionally different', as NOP stated, and this could have affected the poll results.

NOP's more general question on the British Government's policy did not highlight any particular aspect of this policy, and therefore respondents could as easily recall the Government's commitment to a peaceful settlement and peace initiatives, as the other side of this policy – support for U.S. involvement in Vietnam. On the other hand December's question was directed specifically to the Government's support for U.S. policy. Therefore it could be possible that at this stage NOP's December poll may have tapped into an anti-America sentiment, as well as an anti-war sentiment. Because the same questions were not asked each time and because of the specific variation it is difficult to attribute the increase in disapproval to one factor alone.

During the period from August to December, the 'vociferous group of left-wingers and pacifists', as the U.S. embassy in London termed them, continued their activities. Lord Brockway, chairman of the British Council for Peace in Vietnam, visited Moscow in August and had talks with the North Vietnamese Ambassador there. The North Vietnamese objected to Brockway's publicized version of the talks and the peace initiative failed, as it was probably bound to, but the visit did underline the concern felt by some sections of the British public about Vietnam.

There were also two demonstrations against the war, the first in October and the second in November, which attracted considerable press attention. Both of these demonstrations were timed to coincide with U.S. 'parent' demonstrations (although the latter were much bigger). There were two days of non-stop protest organized over the weekend of 16–17 October, including a march to Grosvenor Square where a letter of protest signed by the British Council for Peace in Vietnam was handed over to the U.S. embassy; a protest rally at Trafalgar Square attended by American singer and activist Joan Baez; and also a protest concert at the Royal Festival Hall. The demonstrations were promptly covered by the press – the *Sunday Telegraph* on 17 October reported on them – which noted the 78 arrests and the organizing committees, the British Council for Peace in Vietnam, CND and the Committee of 100 (see the *Daily Worker*, 15 and 16 October 1965 for details of the planned marches; also *The Times, The Guardian* and the *Daily Telegraph* on 18 October).

The second of these large protests took place during a week that had been designated International Vietnam Week, which was to culminate in demonstrations in Britain and the U.S. on the weekend of 27–28 November. The marches and demonstrations were well covered in the

Sunday newspapers. The *Sunday Telegraph* reported the protest by several thousand young people in London and similar protests in Liverpool and Manchester, while the *Sunday Times* and the *Observer* covered the torchlight march in London (see these newspapers on 28 November). *The Times* report on 29 November focused on the eleven arrests that took place in Manchester.

In addition, when U.S. military escalation appeared imminent, Labour Party MPs still exerted pressure on the Government, this time on the occasion of the Prime Minister's visit to Washington.

During this period from August to December 1965 much of the Government, Parliament and press attention was focused on the crisis in Rhodesia. Even so the Vietnam conflict was still an important issue, hence once the immediate crisis over Rhodesia had passed it could be expected that Vietnam would again be a major focus of attention, involving the same close scrutiny of developments by all concerned.

In January 1966 Gallup Poll put its standard question to respondents on approval or disapproval of recent American armed action in Vietnam and compared the figures with the November 1965 poll. The January poll recorded a plurality of 45 per cent who disapproved – an 8 per cent increase; 31 per cent who approved – a 4 per cent increase; and 24 per cent who didn't know – a 12 per cent decrease. Thus the decrease in the number of don't knows indicated that the majority of the British public was now taking a stance on the war, and the balance was tilting against the U.S. This decline in either apathy or ignorance was reinforced in Gallup's next question on whether the U.S. should continue its present efforts in South Vietnam or pull out its forces, with 39 per cent in favour of the U.S. pulling out – a 6 per cent increase over the June 1965 figure; 35 per cent in favour of continuing present efforts – a 2 per cent increase over June; and 26 per cent who didn't know – an 8 per cent decrease from June. And again the percentage opposing U.S. efforts in Vietnam had grown.

In February Gallup posed the question of whether respondents would approve or disapprove if the British Government were to send troops to fight alongside the South Vietnamese in Vietnam, registering 78 per cent disapproval, compared with the figure of 69 per cent in August; only 10 per cent now approved, a drop of 7 per cent from August; and the don't knows had declined by 2 per cent to register 12 per cent. The desire to keep British troops out of the war was clearly strengthening. Gallup Poll also conducted a Top Gallup of '610 names . . . selected at random from the 1965 edition of Who's Who' and discovered that a large majority – 71 per cent – of these respondents, unlike the national poll cross section, favoured the U.S. continuing its present military efforts in Vietnam. However, in answer to a question about which side was winning, 64 per cent judged that neither side was winning, suggesting that the U.S. Administration's optimism and military build-up had been discounted. This view is further reinforced in the figures for those favouring one side or the other, for 14 per cent thought the communists were winning, while 10 per cent thought the South Vietnamese were winning – which was the exact inverse of the national poll's results in November 1965. A vast majority of Top Gallup respondents – 94 per cent – thought that the U.S. would not be justified in using nuclear weapons in the war. And on the lack of negotiations, 44 per cent reckoned that the Chinese were responsible; 31 per cent the North Vietnamese; 24 per cent the Vietcong; 13 per cent the Americans; 8 per cent the Russians; 3 per cent the South Vietnamese; and 18 per cent didn't know. Thus the Chinese were seen as the main culprits, followed by the other communist countries, with the U.S. being blamed by a relatively small percentage – but perceived as considerably more culpable than South Vietnam, which was the other major protagonist in the war when Gallup posed its question of sending British combat troops to Vietnam.

In May Gallup polled public opinion on the topic of British support for U.S. policy in Vietnam. The public was almost evenly split, with 34 per cent stating that Britain was right to continue its support; 32 per cent stating that Britain was wrong; and 34 per cent who didn't know. There were no previous figures for comparison, but considering that America was regarded as Britain's closest ally, these percentages suggested unease about British support for U.S. policy.

In June Gallup again asked whether the U.S. should continue its present efforts or pull out. The figures differed only marginally from the figures published in January. The same percentage – 39 per cent – still thought the U.S. should pull out; but those who favoured the U.S. continuing its present efforts had dropped 2 per cent to 33 per cent; while the don't knows had increased 2 per cent to 28 per cent. By contrast with this set of figures, 40 per cent now thought Britain was right to continue supporting U.S. policy in Vietnam – a 6 per cent increase over the previous month; the same total of 32 per cent reckoned Britain was wrong; and the percentage of don't knows had decreased proportionately, by 6 per cent to 28 per cent. This small fluctuation in favour of supporting the U.S., coexisting with the growing number who actually wanted the U.S. to pull out of Vietnam, could have been indicative of a type of 'rally-round-the-ally' syndrome, provided, of course, that supporting the ally did not involve sending British troops, a course which drew its customary large percentage – 75 per cent – of disapproval.

Gallup also produced a survey of company directors in June and recorded 70 per cent of respondents in favour of continued British support for U.S. policy in Vietnam. This result contrasted strongly with the general public's attitude in June, which only marginally favoured continued support over non-support, with a relatively high proportion of don't knows. It seems that it was the issue of Vietnam which attracted specific support from the company directors, for on the question of general foreign policy there was no strong demand to work more closely with the U.S. Possibly this was because Vietnam was a concrete problem involving an ally and was thus felt to demand a specific response, or possibly it was the anti-communist framework within which the U.S. set the conflict that drew this response. However, as the survey noted, this question was put to company directors before the U.S. bombing of North Vietnam's oil depots and the British Government's dissociation.

In June National Opinion Polls covered the topic of Vietnam (see National Opinion Polls for June – a reference only on the cover sheet – and July), but only in passing, as one of a number of 'issues on which Labour has been less than united'. Despite the problems that the Labour Government had had with its left-wing on the issue of Vietnam, it seems that NOP had not thought the issue even worth mentioning until June and still did not bother to conduct a poll.

July's Gallup Poll registered another fluctuation on the question of British support for U.S. policy in Vietnam, this time a 6 per cent swing towards disapproval, now totalling 38 per cent; with a 7 per cent drop in approval, to a level of 33 per cent; and a 1 per cent rise in the don't knows, standing at 29 per cent. As the fieldwork for this survey was completed before the U.S. P.O.L. bombings, this fluctuation could have been related to the political turmoil in South Vietnam, the latest, and most violent, phase of which had begun in mid-May and had just ended during the week that this report was compiled. However, when respondents were asked whether it was most important for Britain to support the U.S. in Vietnam or to attempt to get peace talks started, an overwhelming majority – 81 per cent – deemed the latter option the most important for Britain. The remainder were almost evenly split between support for the U.S. – 9 per cent – and don't knows – 10 per cent. Thus the vast majority of the general public thought it far more important to settle the conflict than to support Britain's ally.

On the issue of support for the U.S. continuing its efforts in Vietnam or pulling out, there was still a plurality in July favouring a U.S. withdrawal, up 1 per cent from June to 40 per cent; however the number of don't knows had declined by 5 per cent to 23 per cent; while the number of respondents who favoured the U.S. continuing its present efforts had risen to 37 per cent from 33 per cent in June. Again these figures were recorded before the P.O.L. bombings, but undoubtedly public opinion apppeared to be polarizing over Vietnam, with a lesser degree of apathy or ignorance.

Gallup Poll's next question was put during the week of the P.O.L. bombings (30 June–5 July), and registered a majority of respondents, 72 per cent, who thought that the U.S. should agree to peace talks even if there was a risk that South Vietnam would be taken over by the communists. Only 13 per cent thought that the U.S. should not agree to talks, while 15 per cent didn't know. This again demonstrated the public's overriding concern with ending the conflict, whatever the outcome in South Vietnam. And the public disapproval of sending British troops to South Vietnam had now increased by 6 per cent from June's published figure, to 81 per cent; with only 8 per cent in favour of sending troops, a decrease of 5 per cent; and 11 per cent don't knows, a decrease of 1 per cent.

In July National Opinion Polls did conduct a survey of public opinion on Vietnam, compiled after the Government's dissociation from the P.O.L. air-strikes. NOP compared its July figures on whether or not 'Britain should support the Americans in Vietnam' with those recorded in December 1965, in answer to a slightly different question on whether respondents approved of 'British support for American policy in Vietnam'. This comparison showed that disapproval had increased by 12 per cent to reach 45 per cent in July; approval had also increased, by 7 per cent, to total 43 per cent; and the number of don't knows had dropped by 19 per cent to a figure of 12 per cent. These figures, registering a sharper polarization on the issue of support for the U.S., led NOP to conclude: 'It seems that public opinion has moved against the United States.' However, these figures differed considerably from Gallup Poll's July and August findings on its own question of British support for *U.S. policy in Vietnam*, which still showed the public to be evenly divided three ways. This discrepancy poses the question as to whether NOP's surveys were polling more politically involved respondents, for their findings were always broken down on a party political basis, whereas Gallup Poll's surveys did not show any political party affiliation. Thus, it is theoretically possible that Gallup Poll's answers came from respondents with less interest in, or knowledge of, politics – although as Gallup Poll's respondents were quite clear on the issues of peace, the U.S. pulling out, and no British troops for Vietnam, this theory seems unlikely to account for this discrepancy. The other possibility is that the precise question asked had something to do with the answer, for NOP's question in December about support for *U.S. policy in Vietnam* had elicited a result that bore more resemblance to Gallup Poll's findings asking the same question in July and August – principally a three-way division with a slowly declining proportion of don't knows. In any case, NOP's July question on support for the U.S. did show a marginally greater percentage opposing British support for the effort in Vietnam.

On the issue of bombing military targets in North Vietnam, a majority thought that the Americans were right to do so – 58 per cent – as against 30 per cent who thought they were wrong, and 12 per cent who didn't know. However, NOP also polled respondents on whether the Americans would be justified in bombing civilian targets in North Vietnam, and recorded a huge majority opposed to this course: 87 per cent thought they would be wrong; 6 per cent thought they would be right; and 7 per cent were undecided. As NOP pertinently remarked: 'In the context of Vietnam the difference between a military and a civilian target may often be small, but it seems reasonable to infer that if the bombing causes heavy casualties Britain [*sic*] opinion will harden still further against the Americans.'

Asked whether Britain should send troops to Vietnam if the Americans requested them, 65 per cent thought troops should not be sent; 23 per cent thought they should be sent; and 12 per cent didn't know. Compared with Gallup Poll's findings for July, NOP's figures registered 16 per cent less disapproval of this proposal, and 15 per cent more approval, with roughly the same percentage of don't knows. The difference in the figures could once again be due to the difference in the questions asked, for while NOP asked its respondents to consider the dispatch of British troops at *American* request, Gallup Poll asked its respondents about the dispatch of troops to fight alongside the *South Vietnamese* – and whereas America was Britain's major ally, South Vietnam was not.

Gallup Poll's August survey incorporated more data recorded after the P.O.L. bombings. Asking its standard question on U.S. armed action in Vietnam, this poll registered a clear trend towards opposing U.S. action – 49 per cent now, which was a 4 per cent increase over the last time this was asked in December 1965 (appearing in the January 1966 survey). Approval had remained static at 31 per cent, so it was the don't knows which were decreasing, now totalling 20 per cent. Now, almost half of the British public disapproved of U.S. action in Vietnam.

The percentage of respondents favouring a U.S. withdrawal was also rising – 41 per cent in August, compared with 40 per cent in July's poll; those in favour of the U.S. continuing its present efforts had dropped 2 per cent to 35 per cent; while the don't knows increased by 1 per cent to 24 per cent.

Curiously, the percentage of respondents approving of British support for U.S. policy in Vietnam had risen 9 per cent since the figures published in July (based on June fieldwork) and now stood at 42 per cent; with a 1 per cent decline in those opposing British support, now 37 per cent; and an 8 per cent drop in the number of don't knows to 21 per cent. Thus, although the British public favoured a U.S. withdrawal and disapproved of armed action, there was still a tendency to want to support Britain's ally in general terms. Nevertheless, Prime Minister Wilson's public disapproval of the 'recent American bombing in North Vietnam' was approved of by 64 per cent of respondents; disapproved of by 23 per cent; while 13 per cent were undecided.

Public opinion had not greatly changed on the issue of British troops fighting with the South Vietnamese: 75 per cent still opposed the idea, a decrease of 6 per cent since the immediate impact of the P.O.L. bombings; 14 per cent approved, a 6 per cent increase; and the same 11 per cent didn't know.

The large majority who judged it more important for Britain to get peace talks started than to support the Americans had increased 6 per cent since the P.O.L. bombings to 87 per cent; with a 1 per cent decline to 8 per cent in those favouring support for the U.S. over peace talks; and a drop from 10 per cent to 5 per cent in the don't knows.

Posing a much simpler question than that published in the September 1965 poll, Gallup ascertained that the North Vietnamese and Vietcong were blamed by 31 per cent of respondents for the lack of negotiations; with 11 per cent blaming the South Vietnamese Government and Americans; 12 per cent blaming unnamed 'others'; and 46 per cent being unable to vouchsafe an opinion. Thus U.S.

Administration propaganda blaming the North Vietnamese and Vietcong exclusively for the lack of negotiations was believed by only a third of the public, disbelieved by a tenth, and a source of confusion or indifference to almost a half.

Finally, on the question of which side was winning the war, there was a clear trend towards believing that there was a military stalemate. Compared with the figures published in December 1965 (based on late November fieldwork), 56 per cent now judged that neither side was winning – a 20 per cent rise. Of those who opted for one or the other side, 16 per cent thought the South Vietnamese and Americans were winning – a 2 per cent increase; while only 4 per cent thought the North Vietnamese and Vietcong were winning – a 6 per cent decrease. The number of don't knows had declined by 16 per cent to 24 per cent. Thus, it seems that the U.S. military build-up and public optimism on the war had not persuaded the majority of the British public that the U.S. was winning – more of the public were venturing an opinion and this was increasing the overall percentage of the public perceiving a military stalemate. However, of the minority who did not believe there was a stalemate, the U.S. and South Vietnamese were believed to be gradually gaining ground and, as might have been the case in December, this could have been a reflection of the increased amounts of U.S. weaponry and troops and the perceived willingness to use this firepower ruthlessly as demonstrated in the P.O.L. attacks, all of which could perhaps be seen by this minority to validate the U.S. official optimism.

So, by July and August 1966 a majority of the general public no longer approved of U.S. armed action in Vietnam; thought that the U.S. should withdraw; believed that Britain's main task was to get negotiations started rather than to support an ally; preferred the U.S. to start peace talks on Vietnam even if a communist government were to be the outcome; and approved wholeheartedly of Britain staying out of the war. In fact, the general public was beginning to part company with the British Government over the issue of Vietnam.

That section of the British public which had manifested its concern and disapproval about the war more vociferously and tangibly grew more vigorous in its opposition. From the time that the Americans resumed the bombing of North Vietnam after the 37-day pause lasting from 25 December 1965 to 31 January 1966, the demonstrations outside and inside Parliament multiplied. There was a demonstration on 5 February, organized by the British Council for Peace in Vietnam, which drew hundreds to Trafalgar Square, after which there was a march to the U.S. embassy to hand in a petition, and then a rally in Hyde Park (*Sunday Telegraph*, 6 February 1966). Labour MPs censured the Government's Vietnam policy and Stewart and Wilson were heckled at a party meeting. On 12 February there was another protest against the war outside Parliament, during which 21 people were arrested (*Sunday Telegraph*, 13 February 1966).

When Wilson went to a private dinner party in Oxford on 22 March, he was heckled by a crowd complaining of his failure to keep his election promises and his support over Vietnam, and 150 policemen had to be sent to Oxford very early in the morning to control the crowd (*The Times* and *The Guardian*, 23 March 1966). And the next day Wilson was heckled about Vietnam at a Labour Party rally in Ayr (*Sunday Telegraph* and *Observer*, 24 March 1966).

On 17 April it was reported that the Stars and Stripes had been torn down from Westminster Abbey, where the Washington Cathedral Choir was due to sing during the 900th Abbey anniversary (*Sunday Telegraph*, 17 April 1966; *The Times*, 18 April 1966). On 18 April a BBC 'Panorama' programme was shown on television on the training of U.S. soldiers for Vietnam. The programme occasioned horrified letters to *The Times* and *The Guardian*, protesting that Americans were being trained to use torture in Vietnam (*The Guardian*, 22 April 1966: 'How Americans are Being Trained to Bong the Cong'; *The Times*, 23 April 1966: 'Training for Vietnam'). The U.S. Embassy then had to issue a denial, stating that the American troops were being trained to withstand torture, not inflict it (*The Guardian*, 28 April 1966: '"Torture" Film Misunderstood'). On 25 April a number of well-known figures – academics, arts personalities and trade unionists – published a full-page advertisement in *The Times* entitled 'Labour voters and Vietnam', which expressed opposition to U.S. policies in Vietnam and the British Government's 'endorsement of those policies' (*The Times*, 25 April 1966; also mentioned in *The Guardian*, 25 April 1966). On 26 April it was reported that Labour MPs had tabled a motion regretting the lack of reference to Vietnam in The Queen's Speech (*The Times*, *The Guardian*, *Daily Telegraph*, 26 April 1966).

In early May thirteen people were arrested at a ceremony at Leeds University, where the British Foreign Secretary received both an honorary degree and a rough reception over Vietnam.

On 6 June there were more reports of Labour left-wing unrest on Vietnam (*The Guardian*, *The Times*, *Daily Telegraph*, 6 June 1966). The

Communist Party announced a major campaign to stop 'U.S. aggression' in Vietnam, involving a series of meetings, with Communist Party activity in every major city in Britain from 12 June to 3 July, culminating in a rally on 3 July in Trafalgar Square. Thirty-five major meetings were planned and 400,000 leaflets were reported to have been produced for the campaign (*Morning Star*, 10 June 1966). *The Guardian* reported that 54 Labour MPs were going to sign a Vietnam Declaration which was to be sent to all constituency Labour Parties, which was intended to force the Government to end its support for the U.S. in Vietnam (*The Guardian*, 10 June 1966).

After the U.S. bombing of the P.O.L. depots near Hanoi and Haiphong, the pace and scale of protest quickened still further. On 30 June an advertisement appeared in *The Times* signed by 80 members of Southampton University deploring the Government's support for America (*The Times*, 30 June 1966). Also on the same day 250 supporters of the Committee of 100 gathered in Trafalgar Square and then marched to the U.S. embassy; there were some arrests (*The Times, The Guardian*, 30 June 1966). Senior members of Oxford University sent a telegram to Wilson urging the Government to prevent further escalation (*The Times*, 30 June 1966). Over 100 Labour MPs signed a motion denouncing the bombings and calling on the Government to dissociate completely from U.S. policy in Vietnam, and then pressured the Government to hold a debate on Vietnam. In the light of the uproar the Government conceded and the debate took place on 7 July. Though the Opposition amendment was defeated and the Government's motion passed, the abstentions of 32 Labour MPs indicated the depth of dissatisfaction among the Labour left-wing with the Government's Vietnam policy, and held the promise of more trouble in the future (see *The Times, The Guardian, Daily Telegraph*, 7–8 July 1966).

The Communist Party rally in London on 3 July took place as planned, attended by between 4000 and 5000 demonstrators. Violence erupted outside the U.S. embassy; five policemen were injured and 31 people were arrested (*The Guardian, The Times, Daily Telegraph*, 4 July 1966). *The Times* carried letters of protest on 4 and 5 July from academics at Cambridge University and Liverpool University. On 5 July *The Guardian* reported an anti-bombing march by 1000 demonstrators. Also on 5 July *The Times* and *The New York Times* reported that the American Independence Day celebrations in London were gatecrashed by two demonstrators, one of whom toasted the 'dead and dying in Vietnam' before being escorted out. The *Sunday Telegraph* reported that there were 50 or more organizations concerned with Vietnam, the majority of which the newspaper classed as 'pro-Hanoi and violently anti-American', and some of which supplied aid to the Vietcong (*Sunday Telegraph*, 10 July 1966: 'Britons Aid Vietcong').

On 17 July CND organized another protest rally in Trafalgar Square with 15,000 participants and a Labour MP as a speaker on the platform; letters were delivered to the three political parties' headquarters after the rally, calling for dissociation from U.S. policy in Vietnam (*The Guardian*, 18 July 1966). At the end of July, on the eve of the Prime Minister's visit to Washington, there was a lobby of MPs at Westminster, urging them to reverse the Government's policy of support for the U.S. over Vietnam (*Morning Star*, 28 July 1966).

Thus, by the end of July 1966, opposition to the war had grown both in scope and intensity. Many well-known and respected figures had articulated their anxiety and revulsion over U.S. policy in Vietnam, a principal focus of which was U.S. war methods, particularly the bombing. The size and frequency of demonstrations was increasing, as was the attendant rowdiness. U.S. escalation of the war could always be relied upon to provoke a series of demonstrations, but in the meantime the fact of the war itself, and the Government's support – even though 'qualified' – provided the reason for the demonstrations to continue and escalate.

September 1966–March 1968

The trends in public opinion on Vietnam that Gallup Poll was indicating by mid-1966 continued to strengthen, although from now on questions on Vietnam were posed considerably less frequently than previously. The next poll in December 1966 recorded that over half of respondents, 51 per cent, now disapproved of U.S. armed action in Vietnam, which was a 2 per cent increase over August's figure; 30 per cent still approved, a 1 per cent drop; and 19 per cent were undecided, again a 1 per cent decline. In answer to a new question, 75 per cent of respondents wanted the U.S. to halt armed action over the Christmas period; with 15 per cent disagreeing; and 10 per cent undecided. And this pacific sentiment was reinforced when Gallup asked whether the U.S. should, or should not, comply with the U.N. Secretary General's statement that the U.S. should agree to stop bombing North Vietnam 'without laying down conditions or a time limit': 49 per cent of respondents thought that the U.S. should agree to stop the bombing in these circumstances; 28 per cent thought the U.S. should not agree; while 23 per cent didn't know. Nevertheless, the public's feeling on Vietnam continued to be an expression of views on a specific issue rather than indicative of general anti-Americanism, for 54 per cent of respondents still reckoned that Britain and the U.S. did still have a 'special relationship'; with 32 per cent thinking that it was the same relationship as other 'leading European countries'; and 14 per cent undecided. And again a plurality, 37 per cent, disapproved of the suggestion that Britain should give up 'any claim to a "special relationship"' if it would help Britain enter the Common Market; 32 per cent were prepared to give up the 'special relationship'; and 31 per cent didn't know.

In January 1967 Gallup posed just one question on Vietnam, based on its previously standard formulation about the U.S. either continuing its present efforts in South Vietnam or withdrawing, but this question contained important alterations in wording, to read: 'Just from what you have heard or read, which of these statements comes closest to the way you yourself feel about the *US war in Vietnam*' (italics added). Obviously this question incorporated the potential for the war in Vietnam to be perceived differently from the view posed in previous questions, in which *U.S. efforts in South Vietnam* could be taken as supportive of the regime, rather than the conflict being straightforwardly America's war, as was now stated. In addition to this change, Gallup also added another category to its formulation, thus further refining the pattern of opinion, and the results now read: 42 per cent of respondents deeming that the U.S. should begin to withdraw its troops; 18 per cent believing that the U.S. should carry on its present level of fighting; then the new category, with 14 per cent thinking that the U.S. 'should increase the strength of its attacks against North Vietnam'; and 26 per cent who were undecided. From these results it appeared that this question tapped into a hawkish vein, in a section of the British public, that had not been expressed so clearly before.

Gallup next posed this question in March, registering a slight drop in respondents wanting a U.S. withdrawal – now 41 per cent; a 10 per cent increase in those wanting the U.S. to 'carry on its present level of fighting' – now 28 per cent; the same proportion wanting an increase in the strength of attacks against North Vietnam, that is, 14 per cent; and a 9 per cent decrease in those who were undecided. As the drop in the proportion of 'don't knows' coincided with an increase in those respondents wanting the U.S. to continue its present level of attacks, it is possible that the recent demise of the British–Russian peace initiative and resumption of U.S. bombing – publicly attributed to North Vietnamese intransigence and resupply efforts – contributed to this particular poll result (these figures were based on fieldwork carried out between five and ten days after the bombing resumption). This supposition seems reasonable in view of the response to a question on the U.S. resuming bombing, for although just under half of respondents – 49 per cent – thought America was wrong to resume bombing, over a third – 35 per cent – thought the U.S. was right, while 16 per cent didn't know. On the subject of Britain's role there was, as usual, no ambiguity, with only marginal fluctuations: 84 per cent thought Britain should try to get peace talks started – a 3 per cent decrease from the August 1966 poll; 10 per cent thought it more important to support the Americans – a 2 per cent increase; and 6 per cent didn't know – a 1 per cent increase.

In May 1967 Gallup again polled respondents on its question on troop withdrawal or continuing or strengthening attacks – but once more varied its wording, so that the question now asked respondents how they felt about the 'Americans and the war in Vietnam', thereby removing the more pointed reference to the 'U.S. war in Vietnam'. However, despite this 'looser' connection between the U.S. and the war, the percentage wanting a withdrawal continued to increase, now 47 per cent (6 per cent more than in March); 15 per cent wanted the fight to continue at present levels (a 13 per cent decrease); the hawks wanting an increase in the strength of attacks remained precisely the same at 14 per cent; and the don't knows had now risen by 7 per cent from March to total 24 per cent. Thus, though the public desire for a withdrawal was growing, so once more was the percentage of the public that was undecided – making March's picture of relative decisiveness the exception rather than the trend. When polled on whether Britain was right or wrong to continue supporting U.S. policy in Vietnam, the figures recorded were almost the inverse of those from August 1966: 42 per cent thought Britain was wrong (as opposed to 37 per cent in August); 38 per cent reckoned Britain was right (formerly 42 per cent); and 20 per cent didn't know (previously 21 per cent). These figures indicated that the gap was widening between the Government's policy of support for the U.S. on Vietnam and the public's view on this issue.

The shift in public opinion remained fairly static in July when Gallup posed its revised question on respondents' feelings about the

'Americans and the war in Vietnam': there was a 2 per cent decrease in those wanting a withdrawal – now 45 per cent; the same percentage wanted a continuation of the present level of fighting, 15 per cent; the hawks had increased by 1 per cent to 15 per cent; and the don't knows now numbered a quarter of respondents – 25 per cent – a 1 per cent increase. This poll also confirmed the validity of Rostow's assertion in March 1967 that the U.S. was not 'getting through to British public opinion' (see above, 'UK governmental reaction and opinion'), for only just over a third of the public – 35 per cent – had a 'clear idea of what the Vietnam war is all about, that is, what the Americans are fighting for'; while over half the public – 52 per cent – did not have a clear idea; and 13 per cent didn't know whether they had a clear idea or not! So, the previous two years of Administration propaganda on the war, disseminated through the media and aided by British Government statements, had apparently failed in the most basic objective of explaining what the war was about, leaving aside the more difficult task of justification.

The trend opposing British support for U.S. policy continued to strengthen, as October's poll showed (fieldwork for this poll was completed before October's anti-war demonstration), with 45 per cent now thinking Britain was wrong to continue this support (a 3 per cent increase on May's figures); 34 per cent wanting the support to continue (a 4 per cent decrease from May); and 21 per cent undecided (a 1 per cent increase). In addition, when offered the option of declaring neutrality in the conflict or supporting America (following a brief mention that the TUC was 'urging' the Government 'to withdraw support for America in the Vietnam fighting'), 61 per cent of respondents favoured neutrality, with 20 per cent favouring support, and 19 per cent undecided. These results did not, however, appear to indicate greater sympathy with the North Vietnamese case, for when Gallup asked respondents if they supported the U.S. position of being prepared to start negotiations and stop bombing simultaneously, or Hanoi's position of starting negotiations only if the U.S. agreed to 'take out all her forces', a plurality of respondents – 42 per cent – sided with the U.S.; with only 9 per cent favouring Hanoi's position; although 26 per cent supported neither side; and 23 per cent didn't know. (However, it must be borne in mind that these two formulations of U.S. and North Vietnamese negotiating positions were not similar in degree: Hanoi's position as stated demanded much more from the Americans before negotiations could start than the Americans required of the North

Vietnamese. Thus the poll results could reflect this dissimilarity.)

The final poll on Vietnam for 1967, in November, confirmed the British public's desire to keep well clear of involvement in Vietnam, for the percentage which now disapproved of the notion of British troops fighting alongside the South Vietnamese had risen by 7 per cent from July 1966 to 82 per cent; those approving had declined by 7 per cent to total 7 per cent; and the don't knows remained static at 11 per cent.

Concerning the British Government's policy towards the U.S. and the war, in January 1968 Gallup ascertained that over a third of the public, 34 per cent, was dissatisfied and thought British policy should be more critical of the Americans; 24 per cent thought present policy was right; 13 per cent wanted more support for the Americans; while a considerable proportion, 29 per cent, were undecided; thus the Government's policy on Vietnam, of offering verbal support to the U.S. but no troops, was not satisfying either its own public, or, of course, its major ally. On the question of which side was winning the war: 52 per cent thought neither side was winning, a 4 per cent decrease from August 1966 when this question was last posed; 15 per cent reckoned the South Vietnamese and supporters were winning, a 1 per cent decrease; 14 per cent deemed the North Vietnamese and Vietcong were winning, a 10 per cent increase; and 19 per cent didn't know. And these figures were a clear indication that despite the Administration's autumn 1967 propaganda campaign claiming that the tide was turning in their favour, the majority of the public still believed the war was a stalemate, while an increasing percentage thought that the North Vietnamese and Vietcong were now gaining ground and had as much chance as the South Vietnamese and 'supporters' – even after the relentless military build-up and bombing strikes of the past three years.

January's poll also reinforced the public interpretation of Britain's major role as being to get peace talks started rather than supporting the U.S., for 87 per cent now wanted this. Even in a stark reformulation of the 'help' question the public's uneasiness over the possibility of involvement in the war was manifest, for when respondents were asked what Britain should do if the Americans needed troops from 'Britain and other countries' in order not to have to withdraw from fighting in Vietnam (a dramatic option for the leading Western power), then 58 per cent of the British public preferred the Americans to withdraw, rather than send help; 22 per cent would send troops; and 20 per cent were undecided.

The same sentiment surfaced in February in response to a question based on the Opposition leader's (Edward Heath) request that the Government 'back United States Vietnam policy' – a curious request (and a vague question as it stood) as the Government was doing precisely that, but obviously not offering as much public support as the Opposition wanted, for 52 per cent of respondents disagreed with the Heath request, although 31 per cent did agree, and 17 per cent didn't know. A supplementary question on what type of support should be offered generated more insight into the public's dislike of becoming entangled in the war, for 39 per cent refused any support; 28 per cent favoured diplomatic support in the UN; 10 per cent wanted arms and supplies sent; only 5 per cent offered troop support; and 20 per cent were undecided. And by this time the public perception of the danger of a world war had almost doubled since April 1965, for 37 per cent now saw 'much danger' – as opposed to 20 per cent three years previously (and only 9 per cent in December 1964); 50 per cent perceived 'not much' danger – compared with 62 per cent in April 1965; while 13 per cent didn't know – a decline of 5 per cent. As to the source of such a war, although China topped the list being the choice of 20 per cent of respondents, the U.S. was placed *second* by 18 per cent, ahead of Russia which was chosen by 15 per cent; while both Russia and the U.S. accounted for a further 17 per cent, 16 per cent opted for some 'other way'; and 17 per cent didn't know. Thus, the U.S. was perceived as being only slightly less of a threat to world peace than China (which was busy tearing itself apart) and more of a threat than Russia!

The fieldwork for the March poll on Vietnam was conducted after most of the fighting during the Tet Offensive had taken place, and the U.S. and South Vietnamese were once more as much in control as they had been previously. Though the full impact of the Offensive had not been digested, nevertheless the poll reflected the current concerns of observers. Gallup asked respondents if they agreed with the proposition that a halt in the bombing 'will improve the chances for meaningful peace talks', or if, on the contrary, they thought that 'the Americans chances are better if bombing is continued': 54 per cent of respondents wanted a bombing halt; 24 per cent wanted the bombing to continue; and 22 per cent didn't know. On the issue of whether the war would end in 'all-out victory for the U.S. and the South Vietnamese, in a compromise peace settlement, or in a defeat for the U.S. and the South Vietnamese', a clear majority of the public – 60 per cent – reckoned that the result would be a compromise; only 10 per cent thought the U.S.

and South Vietnamese would gain a victory; even fewer though, 5 per cent, thought they would be defeated; and a quarter of respondents, 25 per cent, didn't know how the war would end. Gallup also probed the public response to President Johnson's standing in relation to peace negotiations with North Vietnam, and recorded that for a plurality, 44 per cent, Johnson's standing went up when he was trying to start negotiations; for 17 per cent his standing went down; for 21 per cent his standing was unaffected by the issue of negotiations; and 18 per cent were undecided. Finally a huge majority, 86 per cent, would disapprove if the U.S. were to use nuclear weapons in Vietnam.

The public desire for a peaceful settlement was again made clear in May's poll when a majority, 53 per cent, thought that the U.S. should accept North Vietnam's terms for negotiations – stated to be the unconditional cessation of 'all bombing and other attacks on North Vietnam' – while 27 per cent thought the U.S. should not accept this condition, and 20 per cent were undecided. Despite the Administration's long-running campaign (aided and abetted by the British Government) to convince public opinion that it had always worked hard to achieve peace talks – boosted by President Johnson's 31 March announcement of a bombing cut-back and search for peace – the public apparently had doubts, for when Gallup asked whether respondents thought the U.S. 'is or is not doing all it should to achieve peace talks with the North Vietnamese', 43 per cent thought the U.S. was doing all it should; but an almost equal proportion, 42 per cent, reckoned it wasn't; and a relatively low figure of 15 per cent didn't know. However, the suspicions about the U.S. were eclipsed by even greater doubts about North Vietnam, for a clear majority, 66 per cent, of respondents thought North Vietnam was not doing all it should to achieve peace talks with the U.S.; while only 12 per cent thought it was; and 22 per cent were undecided. So, though the Administration had managed to convince less than half of the public of its own case concerning negotiations, the North Vietnamese had failed on this issue to a greater degree – and possibly Administration propaganda consistently attributing the lack of talks to North Vietnamese intransigence, as well as the latter's own public pronouncements, may have contributed to the public's perceptions.

By the time of the June 1968 poll, President Johnson's March offer to the North Vietnamese had resulted in some progress towards talks, and Gallup asked respondents whether they were 'glad or sorry' about the 'U.S. and Hanoi (North Vietnam) meeting in Paris to have preliminary talks for a peace conference': a vast majority – 89 per cent – stated that they were glad; a mere 1 per cent said they were sorry; and only 10 per cent didn't know. Furthermore, on the issue of what the U.S. should do in peace negotiations, 69 per cent of respondents wanted the U.S. to 'do everything she can to keep the peace talks going'; only 13 per cent thought the U.S. should 'maintain a rigid stance in the peace talks with North Vietnam'; and 18 per cent didn't know. In order to 'get real peace talks going in Vietnam' 55 per cent of respondents were prepared for the U.S. to 'stop all aeroplane flights, including bombing flights, over North Vietnam', 20 per cent would not countenance this, and 25 per cent were undecided; and when considering political representation at the peace talks, 61 per cent of respondents were prepared to allow the 'National Liberation Front (political representatives of the Viet Cong)' to participate, while only 9 per cent were not prepared to allow this, and almost a third of respondents, 30 per cent, were undecided. Surprisingly, even though public opinion favoured what were considered concessions in order to get and keep peace talks going, when Gallup posed a question as to whether the U.S. 'should be willing to withdraw American troops from Vietnam, or should she insist on keeping some there if and when peace has been reached', less than half of the public, 43 per cent, favoured total withdrawal; and over a third of the public, 37 per cent wanted to keep some troops in Vietnam; and the usual fairly high proportion, 20 per cent, were undecided. The reasons why such a high proportion of the public wanted some U.S. troops to remain were not investigated by Gallup, but it is possible that such a miltary contingent could have been viewed as a deterrent against future trouble, whether originating from within the regime or outside it; as a measure of protection for the South Vietnamese Government from internal or 'external' threats. On the other hand Gallup addressed the possible position of the South Vietnamese regime after any peace agreement – and the result could hardly be interpreted as positively supportive of that regime: in the only question posed in its July poll, in which respondents were asked whether or not they would support the South Vietnamese Government if the latter stated that a North Vietnamese–U.S. agreement was a betrayal, 49 per cent said they would not support the South Vietnamese Government; only 10 per cent said they would; although a rather large proportion, 41 per cent, were undecided. Possibly the desire by 37 per cent of the public to retain some U.S. troops in South Vietnam could be seen as a face-saving result – for total withdrawal could be perceived as defeat, and there was no suggestion that mainstream British public opinion wanted the U.S. to be defeated in Vietnam, or wanted the North Vietnamese to win. What was very clear by now, however, was that the general public wanted the war to end and negotiations to begin.

The active anti-war elements in the public continued to demonstrate their dislike of the escalating war. The bombing near Hanoi in December 1966 occasioned angry protests from Labour and Liberal MPs, and a request that the Prime Minister '"reaffirm the Government's dissociation from the bombing of civilian targets"' (see the *Daily Telegraph*, 30 December 1966: 'Hanoi Reports "Noted"'). Such a request was unlikely to appeal to Wilson and his government, considering the U.S. Administration's response to the Government's dissociation in the summer, of which the press reminded him: '[President Johnson] . . . has forgiven, but has by no means forgotten Mr. Wilson's dissociation . . . It angered him that Mr. Wilson should solemnly dissociate himself from an action in a war for the conduct of which, in Mr. Johnson's view, Mr. Wilson bears no responsibility' (see the *Daily Telegraph*, 30 December: 'Johnson not Impressed by Protest'). And even before this particular débâcle, ending the war in Vietnam had been a major theme of world-wide Human Rights Day demonstrations in mid-December, including four around London alone, and elsewhere in the country (see *Morning Star*, 12 December 1966).

As the war continued the anger against U.S. involvement in the conflict was expressed ever more unpleasantly, even in purely verbal terms. For instance, during CND's annual two-day Easter demonstration in 1967, as the marchers passed the United States Airforce headquarters at Ruislip on their way to the final rally in Trafalgar Square, according to *The Times*, the 3000 demonstrators chanted not only 'Yankee murderers', but also the American anti-war chant, 'Say, say, L.B.J. – how many kids have you killed today?' (*The Times*, 27 March 1967). Despite the chants this rally passed off without much trouble, but in October 1967, during the weekend of demonstrations in Europe coordinated with those in the U.S., the violence escalated dramatically. USIA's Media Reaction Analysis devoted considerable space to the demonstrations in its issues from 18 October to 27 October. Initially foreign press coverage noted the planned local demonstrations, but concentrated mainly on those already taking place in the U.S., particularly that at Oakland which was generating headlines due to the violence of the official response, and the planned march in Washington (see Worldwide Treatment of Current Issues, respectively,

18 October 1967: 1 and 20 October 1967: 1–2). On 23 October USIA issued a Special Report dealing with the world-wide demonstrations, initially quoting the *Daily Express* in a comforting report on the London '"riot"' which was termed '"disgraceful"' and unrepresentative of the British people. In the sense that the public had little sympathy with demonstrations and their perpetrators this estimate was accurate (according to NOP in September 1968, before the October confrontation, 56 per cent of the public wanted political demonstrations banned), but it did not mean that the public approved of U.S. policy on Vietnam, for according to Gallup Poll a plurality of the British public (45 per cent in October) thought Britain was wrong to continue supporting the U.S. in the conflict by this time, and 61 per cent would have preferred to remain neutral (October), while National Opinion Poll stated flatly that since July 1966 'support for British policy in Vietnam has collapsed', with 66 per cent of the public disapproving of British support for the Americans. A later report on the same day highlighted the nature of the battle and police injuries: ' "400 Police Fight Riot Mob At U.S. Embassy" (Pro-Labor *Daily Mirror*)' and '"Thirty Police Hurt In Battle" (Conservative *Daily Mail*)'. The first post-mortem on the demonstrations noted that the foreign press was more concerned with the U.S. and Washington demonstrations – considering whether or not a broad-based opposition to the war was emerging, allied to the judgement that the demonstrations 'would not affect U.S. Viet-Nam policy at this time' – than with those in their own countries, and consequently, 'Few editorial judgements have been printed about the concurrent demonstrations overseas, whose largely leftist, anti-U.S. sponsorship was recognized' – a neat dismissal of what was, nevertheless, becoming a recurring problem, and which would not vanish through mere political labelling. And the final media verdict on the demonstrations in USIA's round-up on 27 October was even more dismissive of the demonstrations both in the U.S. and overseas:

New editorials reviewing last weekend's anti-war demonstrations in the U.S. and elsewhere indicate that the world press by and large considered the protests to have been ineffectual. Commentators taking a "second look" at the episodes made these points:

1) The demonstrators failed to offer useful alternatives to U.S. Viet-Nam policy.
2) Official restraint in dealing with the marchers had favorably impressed the world. (Worldwide Treatment of Current Issues, 27 October 1967: 4)

To some extent these judgements were accurate: the demonstrations did not win general public approval, and if U.S. policy on Vietnam was unlikely to be affected by riots in its own country then it was an even more remote possibility that it would be affected by riots overseas. However, the comment that the demonstrators 'failed to offer useful alternatives to U.S. Viet-Nam policy' missed the point: the demonstrations were not meant to be a device for debating and proffering to the U.S. policy alternatives, they had already decided on the sole option that was acceptable – a U.S. withdrawal (and on occasions a North Vietnamese victory), regardless of the consequences for U.S. policy either in Vietnam or elsewhere. And in any case, the judgement that the protests were 'ineffectual' was not precisely accurate, for the demonstrations did focus attention on the war, and though the demonstrators' methods of protest were generally disliked this was still not likely to effect a sea change in general opinion and render the war more acceptable to the public, while the protesters desire for an end to the war *was* in tune with general public sentiment. And the demonstrations were set to continue, thereby putting the authorities to the trouble of policing them.

The launching of the Tet Offensive at the end of January 1968 inevitably put the war centre-stage yet again, both in terms of the terrible carnage attendant on this conflict and the clash of policy, morality and basic human decency that the war had come to embody – and also to symbolize in a wider sense. For on 2 February the press published on their front pages what was probably the most notorious photograph of the war, the summary execution of a Vietcong prisoner in a Saigon street by the South Vietnamese Chief of Police, General Nguyen Ngoc Loan (see *The Times, The Guardian, Daily Telegraph*). This photograph immediately generated a horrified outburst from the public, which initially protested that the picture was too appalling to publish, thereby prompting *The Times* to defend its action (*The Times*, 7 February 1968: 'The Horrors of War'). Thereafter public reaction was manifested through voluminous letter columns on virtually a daily basis (see particularly *The Times* and the *Daily Telegraph*, 5 February–13 February 1968), all of which focused not only on the terrible photograph (ultimately the consensus of opinion was that the picture had to be published, showing the war as it truly was) and whether this constituted murder, but also on the nature of the war itself. And of course there were also editorials and articles dealing with the incident, usually from the standpoint that this was the 'Ugly Face of War' (*The*

Guardian, 7 February 1968), and 'The Dirty War' (*Sunday Times*, 4 February 1968), except for the *Daily Telegraph* which continued to support the U.S. in a war which it perceived as being in defence of the 'whole free world' (*Daily Telegraph*, 5 February 1968: 'The Stake in Vietnam'; and 10 February 1968: 'Vietnam – With Noises Off'). In addition to examining this particular incident, other articles widened the scope of the analysis and in so doing inevitably scrutinized the official explanations advanced to justify this savage war. And while partaking in this exercise, the *Observer* now joined *The Guardian* in perceiving the war as akin to the French experience in Algeria, reaching this verdict via the demolition of the Administration's historical propaganda parallels with Europe during the Second World War and subsequently Korea (*Observer*, 4 February 1968: 'The American Tragedy'). Thus official rhetoric on the war – encompassing both assessments of current events during the Tet Offensive and past justifications – was now under more pressure than ever before, and the Administration was not well-placed with regard to the credibility of its statements.

At the same time as the uproar over the Tet Offensive, it was reported that 'Demonstrators aim to step up anti-war protests', with the Committee of 100 promising the Prime Minister and Foreign Secretary that: 'Every move they make will catch the anger of the young for aiding and abetting Johnson' (*The Guardian*, 5 February 1968). And indeed February was a busy month (see *Daily Telegraph*, 23 February; *The Guardian*, 24 February; and *The Times*, 4 March 1968). But these activities were eclipsed by the 17 March demonstration against the war, which, after a 'relatively good humoured' rally attended by approximately 10,000 people in Trafalgar Square, erupted in violence outside the U.S. embassy, which was guarded by some 1300 police. According to *The Times* the embassy 'was virtually under siege for two hours' as 'thousands of people clashed with police'; 200 arrests were made (300 according to *The Guardian*); 86 people were treated for injuries on the spot and 50 were then taken to hospital, including, it was thought, 25 police officers (see *The Times* and *The Guardian*, 18 March 1968). These reports detailed the violence of the demonstrators and also that of the police in attempting to control the demonstration, noting, however, that: 'It was only after considerable provocation that police tempers began to fray and truncheons were used, and then only for a short time' (*The Guardian*, 18 March 1968: 'Police repel anti-war mob at US embassy'). But of course there were recriminations on both sides after these events, with the police stating that the violence had been premeditated rather than spontaneous and that the organizers had failed to control their marchers, and the demonstration organizers (the Vietnam Ad Hoc Committee) maintaining that the police had reneged on a promise to allow letters to be delivered to the embassy (see *The Times*, 19 and 20 March 1968).

Given the aims of the demonstrators – and the wider publicity afforded by media coverage, which was a welcome bonus for the activists (for the media could hardly ignore such events) – the end result of this episode was fairly predictable: the announcement by the demonstration's organizers of 'bigger and more militant demonstrations in future' (*The Times*, 20 March 1968: 'Bigger Vietnam Protests Plan').

Interestingly, though USIA had covered the October 1967 demonstration fairly extensively, its ordinary series of Media Reaction Reports for the month of March concentrated on the beginning of the Presidential election campaign, followed immediately by Lyndon Johnson's surprise announcement on 31 March of the bombing cutback and his decision not to seek a second term in office. Thus the March demonstration figured not all in USIA's coverage – perhaps due to its ineffectiveness – and nor, later in the year, did the October confrontation. As the latter demonstration came just prior to the U.S. Presidential election in November 1968, with the months between March and November constituting something of a hiatus for the Johnson administration, it will be considered in the chapter dealing with Richard Nixon's legacy from the former administration.

Public opinion in France and West Germany will now be examined, concentrating on general public opinion. A detailed analysis of demonstrations in these countries will not be undertaken, on the grounds that though public opinion in these countries *was* important to the Administration, British public reactions were more important, because neither the French Government's disapproval nor the West German Government's support was considered as vital as British Government support – which in turn endowed British public pressure with a particular degree of significance for its possible potential to modify British Government support for the Administration's Vietnam policies.

Public opinion in France

From the time that the conflict in Vietnam began to escalate in March 1965 the French public was polled fairly regularly on the topic of

Vietnam (surveys conducted by the Institut d'Opinion Publique), although not with the same frequency as the British public. And right from the start of the U.S. military campaign French public opinion displayed a considerable degree of disapproval, for when respondents were asked in March 1965 whether they approved or disapproved of American policy in Vietnam, only 10 per cent approved; 41 per cent disapproved; and 49 per cent had 'no opinion'. Thus French opinion was split between disapproval and no opinion – the percentage of 'approval' was so small as to be insignificant. Furthermore the conflict was thought to constitute a threat of a world war: 27 per cent perceived a 'great threat'; 32 per cent saw it as a 'small threat'; 16 per cent reckoned there was 'no threat'; and 25 per cent had 'no opinion'. So a majority of the public saw Vietnam as a destabilizing influence, even at this very early stage, before the U.S. had adopted bombing as a way of fighting the war and before the pattern of almost continuous escalation had been established.

In May de Gaulle's policy towards the U.S. was approved by 50 per cent of respondents, who reckoned that it was 'as it should be'; 16 per cent thought his policy was 'too harsh'; 6 per cent thought it 'too weak'; and 28 per cent had 'no opinion'. This degree of public confidence in de Gaulle's judgement on the U.S. was in inverse proportion to that concerning the ability of the U.S. 'to wisely conduct affairs in the Far East', on which issue 26 per cent of respondents confessed to a 'lack of confidence'; the same percentage registered 'a tremendous lack of confidence'; only 4 per cent said they had 'very great confidence'; 17 per cent – a 'fair amount of confidence'; and 27 per cent had 'no opinion'. Vietnam again figured as a topic in June, when respondents were asked their opinion on whether Vietnam would be reunited in five years. A third of the public, 33 per cent, answered affirmatively; 23 per cent said no; and a considerable percentage, 44 per cent, had no opinion. Of those who thought Vietnam would be reunited, three times as many respondents thought Vietnam would be under the influence of China – 35 per cent – rather than U.S. influence – 12 per cent; while a plurality reckoned it would be neutral; and 9 per cent had no opinion. In September after the summer escalation of the war, when respondents were again questioned on de Gaulle's policy towards the U.S., a high percentage still approved, 46 per cent; with 21 per cent disapproving; and 33 per cent returning 'no answer'.

Following this spate of questions Vietnam was next covered in the February 1966 poll, a time when the 37-day bombing pause and

Johnson's high-profile search for peace through the accompanying diplomatic 'offensive' would be fresh in the public's mind. Respondents were asked if they thought 'the Americans are really seeking a peaceful settlement in Vietnam?' The poll recorded a considerable degree of scepticism on this point: a plurality, 42 per cent, replied negatively; 35 per cent answered affirmatively; and 23 per cent didn't know. There was some small comfort for the U.S. Administration in the answers recorded to the same question about the Hanoi government's intentions, for exactly the same percentage – 42 per cent – reckoned Hanoi was not 'really seeking a peaceful settlement'; but a lower proportion thought they were – 22 per cent; and over a third of the public, 36 per cent, didn't know. Thus the U.S. was credited with better intentions by more of the population than Hanoi, and the figures suggested that the latter also provoked more confusion on this matter than did the Americans. For on the crucial question of sympathy for one or the other side, the French public was almost evenly split, with a very slightly lower total sympathizing with Ho Chi Minh, 26 per cent; as opposed to the Americans, 28 per cent; while almost half of the population, 46 per cent, stated that they didn't know with whom they sympathized! At face value, the latter figure appears to attest to a remarkable degree of confusion, or possibly apathy, concerning the conflict – particularly as the U.S. was officially France's ally. However, given the poor relationship between France and the U.S. at this stage (soon to worsen), the high percentage of don't knows could have been an indication of latent antipathy towards the latter in this war with a former colony of France, rather than confusion or apathy. There is also the possibility that this figure was an acknowledgement that the war was more complex than either the straightforward choice presented by the question, or the case disseminated through U.S. official propaganda. The case against public confusion or apathy is somewhat strengthened in the answers recorded to the last question put to respondents, asking whether they thought the 'present situation in Vietnam' presented a 'risk for a world war': in contrast with March 1965, 35 per cent now thought there was a 'great risk' – an increase of 8 per cent; 39 per cent said there was a 'small risk' – an increase of 7 per cent; 2 per cent more than in March 1965, 18 per cent, stated that there was 'no risk'; and only 8 per cent didn't know – a decrease of 17 per cent. So the majority of the French public undoubtedly took a stance on this question, perceiving the war as a potential catalyst for a world war.

Although the picture of French public opinion was not always clear-cut because of the sometimes high proportion of don't knows on particular questions, on the issue of the U.S. bombing raids in the summer of 1966 there was a much sharper response in the July 1966 poll: an overwhelming majority, 81 per cent, disapproved of the U.S. 'continuing to bomb Vietnam in the proximity of Hanoi and Haiphong'; only 8 per cent approved; and 11 per cent gave 'no answer'. The dislike of U.S. 'retribution' (of which the bombing was a form) extended to other events during the war, for even when there was a chance that North Vietnam might try and convict captured U.S. airmen as war criminals, a majority of respondents in August – 52 per cent – thought that it would be wrong for the U.S. 'to start military reprisals against North Vietnam'; although 26 per cent thought the U.S. would be right to do so; and 22 per cent gave no answer (although this is a curious question, as there was no mention of what type of 'reprisal' was contemplated to add to the bombing campaign already being conducted).

On the role that France could play in helping establish peace, the public was relatively evenly split three ways on the contribution that de Gaulle's forthcoming visit to Cambodia would make: 36 per cent reckoned his trip would contribute to bringing peace; 35 per cent said it would not; and 29 per cent had no answer. The French Institute pursued this particular visit the following month, at the end of de Gaulle's world trip in September. Interestingly, out of four speeches that he made – at Djibouti, Addis Ababa, Phnom Penh and Mururoa – which the Institute named for respondents, de Gaulle's Phnom Penh speech was rated the most useful (a difference of 5 per cent) and next to the least harmful (a difference of 1 per cent). Even though this speech blamed the U.S. for escalating the war, called for a unilateral American withdrawal, and was thought by French observers to be harsh and uncompromising in tone, 51 per cent of respondents deemed the speech 'useful'; 13 per cent said it would have 'no effect'; 7 per cent reckoned it was 'harmful'; and 29 per cent didn't know. Further confirmation of public support for de Gaulle's policy towards the U.S. was contained in answers to a question about the U.S. posture in Vietnam, in which 68 per cent of respondents thought that the U.S. 'should begin to withdraw their troops from Vietnam'; only 8 per cent thought they should 'maintain their military involvement as is'; 5 per cent thought the U.S. 'should increase the force of their attacks on North Vietnam'; and a relatively low figure of 19 per cent gave no answer. By now also the public perception of the danger of Vietnam had risen: now 60 per cent thought it could lead to a world war; 22 per cent thought there was a possibility; only 7 per cent thought it would not lead to a wider war; and 11 per cent returned no answer.

After 1966, the Vietnam war featured less often in this set of opinion polls, for by now the trend in public opinion on U.S. involvement in the war – disapproval – was fairly obvious, and sporadic later polls only served to confirm this view. Thus in May 1967, 71 per cent of respondents stated that they were 'against American policies', with a mere 8 per cent approving U.S. policies, and 21 per cent giving no answer. Also on the subject of which side was making the most effort to bring about peace, although a majority, 54 per cent, thought neither side was making an effort, of those respondents who took sides, 14 per cent thought the North Vietnamese were making the most effort as opposed to 11 per cent choosing the U.S. (5 per cent thought both sides were trying, and 16 per cent gave no answer).

Again public support for de Gaulle's approach to the war was confirmed in an August 1967 poll, with 56 per cent approval; 16 per cent disapproval; and 28 per cent giving no answer, while the trend favouring a U.S. withdrawal continued to strengthen: 72 per cent of the public now wanted the U.S. to start removing troops; 8 per cent wanted the maintenance of the present level of military engagement; 5 per cent desired increased forcefulness; and 15 per cent had no answer. And by the end of 1967, a plurality of the public – 49 per cent – held the opinion that Vietnam could start a third world war; as against only 20 per cent who thought it could prevent one; with 31 per cent returning no answer.

Finally in April 1968, against the background of the Tet Offensive and Johnson's peace move and cut-back in the bombing, when respondents were asked to judge for which side the war would have been a success or failure if it were to end at that point, the results show a clear belief that the U.S. – in the person of Johnson – had failed compared with Ho Chi Minh and the Vietcong: 39 per cent perceived failure for Johnson, with 27 per cent seeing success, and 34 per cent with no opinion. Whereas 40 per cent saw Ho Chi Minh as successsful, with only 10 per cent judging him to have failed, and 50 per cent with no opinion; and the Vietcong were seen as successful by 38 per cent of respondents, as a failure by 12 per cent, and again 50 per cent had no opinion. Johnson's peace move did not apparently dispel doubts about U.S. intentions on this score, for 43 per cent reckoned the Americans were not 'really looking for a peaceful solution', 32 per cent, though, did see genuine intent, and 25 per cent had no opinion. The North Vietnamese fared better, with 37 per cent of the public thinking they were looking for peace, 31 per cent doubting their intentions, and 32 per cent with no opinion.

So, throughout the whole of this period, from 1965 to 1968, in line with de Gaulle's approach the French public fairly consistently disapproved of U.S. actions in Vietnam, had little sympathy with the U.S. cause, and was sceptical of U.S. official protestations of its desire and search for peace. As far as the U.S. propaganda campaign on Vietnam was concerned, French public opinion was a lost cause from the very beginning.

Public opinion in West Germany

In order to assess West German public opinion the reports compiled by the Institut für Demoskopie Allensbach during the war have been used. The Institute began polling the public from the start of the escalation in February 1965. Having first established that 91 per cent of respondents knew of U.S. 'military aid in Viet Nam', the Institute then noted the recent heavy bombardment of targets in North Vietnam and asked those respondents who was to blame for the 'increase in tension, the Americans, or the communists'. The collective result showed that almost half, 49 per cent, of those respondents believed that the communists were to blame; only 9 per cent blamed the Americans; 20 per cent believed both sides were culpable; and 13 per cent were undecided (total percentage 91 per cent). However, even though almost half of those respondents blamed the communists for this escalation, on the question of whether the Americans were 'right to intervene in Viet Nam, or not' there was much less support for the U.S., and more uncertainty: 33 per cent approved of U.S. intervention; 27 per cent disagreed; 16 per cent were undecided; and 15 per cent had 'no opinion' (total 91 per cent).

In June and August 1965, pointing out that there were 'divergent views as to what policy the Americans should follow in Vietnam', respondents were then asked to choose from a list of five alternative policies: the first required that the U.S. withdraw its forces – 19 per cent favoured this in June, increasing to 21 per cent in August; the second alternative suggested that the U.S. 'stay in Vietnam but should stop bombing North Viet Nam and seek negotiations with the communists' – 30 per cent favoured this policy in June, decreasing to 29 per cent in

August; the third policy required the U.S. to 'maintain the present scale of bombing operations' but 'at the same time keep on offering to negotiate' – approved of by 13 per cent in June, increasing to 15 per cent in August; fourthly it was suggested that the U.S. should 'step up' attacks on the North and 'send more troops and weapons until the communists yield', a policy that garnered 10 per cent approval in both June and August; the fifth option was for the U.S. to 'wage all-out war on North Viet Nam, employ their entire military strength there and, if necessary, extend the war to China as well' – this drastic policy gained only 3 per cent support in June, but actually increased in attractiveness in August to total 5 per cent; finally a fairly high proportion, 25 per cent, had no opinion, decreasing to 20 per cent in August. Of the options presented to respondents the policy requiring the U.S. to stop the bombing and negotiate gained by far the greatest degree of support. But this was also accompanied by a desire not to see the U.S. withdraw from Vietnam, possibly because the war was now stated to be a contest between the values of Western democracy and communism (and was perhaps so perceived by some West Germans), and with communist East Germany as its neighbour West Germany did not want its major ally and military guarantor apparently ousted by a tiny communist regime (this could be one way of perceiving a U.S. withdrawal) with a possible deleterious effect on the U.S. image as world power and a reliable ally – a scenario to which the U.S. Administration always drew attention.

Apart from several questions aimed at eliciting the degree of public awareness and interest in the Vietnam War (approximately 70 per cent awareness and interest), the public was next polled on more substantive issues in January 1966, when respondents were asked whether they were 'for or against the Americans continuing the war in Viet Nam': a plurality, 45 per cent, were against; 26 per cent were in favour; 16 per cent were undecided; and 13 per cent had no opinion. In the light of recent government decisions the issue of aid was then tackled; after establishing that 84 per cent of the public were aware of the West German Government's decision to equip a hospital ship, respondents were asked if they agreed with the decision to send this ship 'to prove our friendship to America', or whether 'it would be better if we kept ourselves right out of Viet Nam': 48 per cent thought it was the right decision; 29 per cent thought it wrong; 13 per cent were undecided; and 10 per cent had no opinion. However, when questioned about whether they favoured the suggestion that 'German soldiers, volunteers, might be sent to aid the Americans, our allies' – and despite the pointed reference to helping the U.S. as an ally – an absolute majority, 81 per cent, rejected the suggestion (the same reaction as in Britain); with a mere 7 per cent in favour; 6 per cent undecided; and 6 per cent with no opinion. Thus, predictably, humanitarian aid was acceptable but not active involvement in the military arena.

In March 1966 the Institute questioned respondents on the justifications for the U.S. involvement in the war, effectively polling the public on one of the U.S. administration's key propaganda arguments – the close link between successfully fighting the war in Vietnam and both containing communism and maintaining freedom for other U.S. allies – but also introducing the counter-arguments of mere U.S. self-interest to account for their actions, and the ethics of U.S. involvement in this particular war. This basic theme was put to respondents in the form of two questions with subtle differences. The first question centred on two propositions; firstly, that some observers reckoned that the Americans in Vietnam 'are defending the Free World against communism and for this reason we should stand by America'; and secondly, that other observers thought that the Americans 'are only defending their own interests, and that they (these observers) can't understand why other countries let themselves get involved'. On the first proposition – that the U.S. was defending the Free World – 42 per cent of respondents agreed; 29 per cent agreed with the second proposition, that they were 'only defending their own interests'; and 29 per cent were 'undecided, no opinion'.

The second question focused on ethics versus ideology (and was used in successive years); the first proposition stated that some observers thought 'the Americans should get out of Viet Nam. It isn't their country and they have no right to fight a war there'; the second proposition stated that other observers reckoned that 'the Americans are fighting the communists in Viet Nam to maintain freedom. They must do this to prevent communism spreading and turning into a bigger danger.' The second proposition – maintaining freedom in Vietnam – was favoured by 44 per cent of respondents; 25 per cent agreed with the first – the U.S. had no right to fight a war there; and 31 per cent were 'undecided, no opinion'. Thus the idea that the U.S. was *maintaining* freedom in Vietnam and stopping the advance of communism in its tracks gained marginally more support than the more amorphous proposition that the U.S. was *defending* the Free World there. Of course the formulation of the question ignored the issue of whether there was any freedom in Vietnam to maintain: it was simply assumed that this was the case. Concerning the practical, or pragmatic, viewpoint that the U.S. was defending its own interests, again this gathered a little more support than the ethically based proposition that they had no right to fight there. Presumably the fairly high proportion of 'undecided, no opinion' were unconcerned or disbelieving either about the danger of possible communist expansion, or about the ethics of this war. On the likelihood of the Vietnam War leading to war with China, 30 per cent of the public saw this as possible – quite a high percentage; 39 per cent viewed it as 'very unlikely'; and 31 per cent had no opinion – reinforcing this image of a large sector of the public being uninterested in, or ignorant about, the publicized possible consequences of Vietnam. As to whether the U.S. could win this war, a plurality – 41 per cent – of respondents thought they could, 23 per cent reckoned that they hadn't 'a chance', and 36 per cent had no opinion: so in the military sphere the U.S. was trusted to achieve its aims.

The five policy alternatives that had been presented to respondents in June and August 1965 (see above) were put to them again in April, and a steadily growing trend in those wanting the U.S. to withdraw their forces was apparent – now 27 per cent (a 6 per cent increase); but the proportion wanting the U.S. to stay, stop bombing, and seek negotiations was also growing slowly – 32 per cent (a 3 per cent increase); there was a 5 per cent decrease in the percentage of respondents opting for the present scale of operations accompanied by negotiation offers – now 10 per cent; the hawks wanting more attacks, troops and weapons had grown by 1 per cent – now 11 per cent; those in favour of all-out war on North Vietnam and, if necessary, China decreased by 1 per cent to 4 per cent; and finally there was a 4 per cent drop in the percentage of respondents with 'no opinion' – now 16 per cent. Overall therefore, 57 per cent of respondents wanted the U.S. to remain in Vietnam, and of those 25 per cent wanted armed action to continue, either to achieve negotiations or to force a communist surrender.

Respondents were also asked in April whether they thought it was right or wrong for the U.S. to be fighting in Vietnam – similar enough to the question posed in February 1965 to allow a comparison (although February's question also built in a percentage of respondents who were not asked – see above). Now 41 per cent of respondents thought the U.S. was not right, a 14 per cent increase since 1965; 26 per cent favoured the intervention, a 7 per cent decrease; and 33 per cent were undecided, or had no opinion – a 2 per cent increase. Thus, even allowing for the differences in the numbers of category of respondents, public opinion was moving against U.S. intervention.

The U.S. escalation of the war in July 1966, when North Vietnam's P.O.L. installations were bombed, drew majority disapproval in West Germany: 51 per cent opposed the bombing escalation; 26 per cent favoured it; and a lesser proportion than usual were undecided, or had no opinion – 23 per cent. If this result is compared with figures from February 1965 when the bombing first began, a plurality of the public then blamed the communists for the 'increase in tension' leading to the escalation of the conflict in the form of bombing, whereas now a majority blamed the U.S. And although there were differences in the formulation of the questions – the February 1965 question focused generally on an *'increase in tension'* and then invited respondents to apportion blame, whereas the July 1966 question focused directly on American bombing escalation and prompted respondents to either agree or disagree with this *U.S.* escalation – presumably, if respondents had still thought that the communists were fundamentally to blame for the conflict and therefore provoked the U.S. into escalating (as the U.S. Administration always claimed), then they could have chosen to agree with this new escalation in July 1966 as a way of blaming North Vietnam, particularly as the targets were primarily military and not civilian and destroying the P.O.L. dumps could be perceived as a legitimate war objective.

The slowly emerging trends in public opinion on the war continued to strengthen in 1967. In answer to the Institute's alternative policy question, compared with April 1966, now 33 per cent of respondents wanted the U.S. to withdraw (a 6 per cent increase); 36 per cent wanted the U.S. to stay but stop bombing and negotiate (a 4 per cent increase); the same percentage – 10 per cent – favoured the present scale of operations accompanied by offers to negotiate; 7 per cent wanted stronger attacks (a 4 per cent decrease); 3 per cent favoured all-out war and with China too, if required (a 1 per cent decrease); and 11 per cent had no opinion (a 5 per cent decrease). Thus, though over two-thirds of the population had polarized between two options – either a complete U.S. withdrawal, or a continuing U.S. presence but with a cessation of bombing and negotiations – both these sections of opinion could be seen as wanting an end to the war.

In September 1967 respondents were questioned again on whether they thought the Americans had no right to fight a war in Vietnam, or whether they had to defend freedom in Vietnam and stop communism spreading. Compared with March 1966, when respondents were first polled on this, the figures showed a considerable change in sentiment, with the public split more evenly three ways, but with a growing plurality questioning the legitimacy of the venture: 37 per cent now thought the U.S. had no right to fight in Vietnam (a 12 per cent increase); 33 per cent saw a need to defend freedom in Vietnam (an 11 per cent decrease); and 30 per cent were undecided. As the 'undecided' had only changed by 1 per cent, obviously a quarter of respondents who previously favoured defending freedom had now changed position and questioned the war's legitimacy.

The last series of comparable polls during the Johnson administration occurred in February 1968, the time of the Tet Offensive. On the question of defending freedom, or having no right to fight, there was a brief upsurge in the percentage of the public supporting the U.S. need to defend freedom – 38 per cent (up 5 per cent from September 1967); there was a corresponding decline in the proportion of respondents believing the U.S. lacked the right to fight, now 31 per cent (down 6 per cent); and a 1 per cent rise in the undecided. As subsequent polls (see the chapters on Nixon) show that the previously prevailing trends in opinion resumed later, it appears likely that this set of figures resulted from the dramatic events of the Tet Offensive (the breach of the Tet truce, the degree of surprise, and the destruction), and on this issue specifically relating to 'freedom' public opinion rallied temporarily to the U.S. cause. For on other questions at this time the movement against U.S. involvement continued: by now a majority of 56 per cent was against the U.S. continuing to fight in Vietnam (a 12 per cent increase from January 1966); 19 per cent wanted the fight to continue (a 6 per cent decline); and 25 per cent were undecided (also down 6 per cent).

Finally, there was growing pessimism about the Americans' chances of winning the war: a third of the public, 33 per cent, thought they could – an 8 per cent decline from March 1966; 36 per cent thought the situation 'hopeless' – an increase of 13 per cent; and 31 per cent were undecided – a 5 per cent decline. So three years of escalation and an official U.S. propaganda campaign to 'sell' the idea of progress in the war had resulted in a growth in the proportion of the populace reckoning that the war was 'hopeless'; and the shock of the Tet Offensive, in the immediate wake of U.S. official optimism, must have contributed considerably to this sentiment. In general West German public opinion had changed considerably, from the days of support when the war first began to escalate in February 1965, to the desire to see the war end, and the belief that the Americans could not win.

8

Nixon's inheritance: war, peace and propaganda

Johnson's legacy to Richard Nixon, when the latter became President-elect in November 1968, was a complex mixture of internal and external problems, with the Vietnam War being the primary problem facing the Administration and, what was worse, one which by now incorporated both dimensions: threatening to split U.S. society, while at the same time undermining U.S. relations with both its ideological opponents (with whom the U.S. now wanted better relations) and its allies. Johnson's secrecy (and duplicity) over fashioning and implementing Vietnam policy, away from public scrutiny, followed by his attempt to wage war 'quietly' – in order to avoid both probable dissension over fighting a land war in Asia and the need to drum up public support with the attendant possibility of 'war hysteria' (either of which might result in public pressure on the Administration concerning its war policies), as well as to protect his 'Great Society' programme – had well and truly backfired. For the war had long since become the focus of intense public scrutiny – prompted in part by the Administration's attitude to disseminating 'information' on the war, and also due to the sheer size and intensity of the venture after three years of escalation – and had increasingly split the 'opinion leaders' in Congress, the media and top echelons of U.S. society into 'hawks' and 'doves', resulting in the very pressure Johnson had wished to prevent. And, of course, as the war's costs mounted, resulting in an ever-greater financial burden that could be met only with Congressional assistance, Johnson's hopes of establishing his 'Great Society' were endangered due to the lack of the necessary political and financial support that the programme would have required from Congress.

Fortunately for the incoming President his primary interest lay in foreign policy, and thus what was Johnson's greatest disappointment was of less significance to Nixon, as was the underlying malaise in American society – despite his election rhetoric: the importance of riots lay in their challenge to law and order, not their indictment of the social order – and they were treated accordingly. Nevertheless, even leaving aside that intractable problem, at first sight Nixon's inheritance still appeared to resemble a particularly arduous obstacle course, giving rise to considerable doubts over the prospects for successful completion.

Concerning Vietnam, Johnson's legacy will now be examined, focusing on the situation in the war when Nixon took over; the Paris peace talks; and the propaganda environment existing at that time. To complete the picture, a fourth factor relating to attitudes to Nixon and his principal advisers will then be considered briefly.

The Vietnam War by 1969

In April 1968, when President Johnson's surprise offer of peace talks was subsequently taken up by the North Vietnamese, observers worldwide expressed satisfaction and hoped that the conflict would soon be settled. Very quickly, however, it became apparent that the fundamental differences that had led to the war had merely been transported into another arena, as the main protagonists, the U.S. and North Vietnam, argued over the composition of the delegations, with each side denying the right of the other's client (South Vietnam and the Vietcong respectively) to a place at the conference table. Thus the early optimism about a settlement evaporated as the wrangling continued over these apparently irreconcilable demands, while on the battlefield the fight continued relentlessly, still escalating in size of operation, intensity, and in casualties: in the first half of 1968 more combat troops died than had throughout the whole of 1967 (see Millet, 1974, vol. 3: 138), whilst by the end of the year the number of combat deaths for 1968 almost equalled the total for the previous three years of war (14,998 deaths in

1968, as against 15,895 from 1965 to the end of 1967; see Gibson, 1986: 173).

Despite the losses inflicted on the Vietcong and North Vietnamese during the Tet Offensive, by mid-May there had been another coordinated series of attacks on Saigon and 118 other targets throughout South Vietnam, and at the end of May Saigon was again subjected to a heavy assault. August too was a month of activity, with U.S. and ARVN forces in a number of locations coming under simultaneous attack, followed only four days later on 22 August with the fourth attack on Saigon since the beginning of the year (including the Tet Offensive), and a day later by more nation-wide assaults on cities, towns and military bases (see Millet, 1974, vol. 3, respectively: 124–8, 131–4, 193–8).

Notwithstanding the efforts to begin talks, the U.S. too prosecuted the fight with increased vigour, continuing with search-and-destroy operations as part of '"an all-out" drive to defeat Communist forces in Vietnam' – although this effort was said not to be linked to the peace talks (Millet, 1974, vol. 3: 115). The biggest ground operation of the war so far, beginning in early April and lasting until the end of May, was designed to destroy opposition forces in the area around Saigon, but signally failed to achieve its objective, as shown by the subsequent attacks on Saigon. Other ground operations followed thoughout the spring and summer, necessitating a further injection of U.S. troops into Vietnam, raising the troop ceiling by another 24,500 men and bringing the total up to more than half a million troops. As for the bombing, until President Johnson's announcement on 31 October of a complete halt to the bombing of North Vietnam, areas in North Vietnam that were south of the 20th Parallel had been bombed, sometimes heavily; while air-strikes along the Ho Chi Minh Trail in Laos, and of course the bombing in South Vietnam, had continued unabated.

Due to the intensification of the fighting the destructiveness of the war also increased during this period, reflected not only in troop deaths but also in the numbers of South Vietnamese refugees generated and the numbers of civilian casualties in hospitals. Concerning refugees, the Tet Offensive alone had created 350,000 (to add to the 800,000 previously recorded), and the Saigon fighting in May added another 125,000 to the total; whilst from January through May 1968, the number of civilian casualties that required hospital treatment – 47,411 – was only marginally fewer than the total for the whole of 1967 – 49,037 (figures from Millet, 1974, vol. 3, respectively: 50, 133, 139).

Not until mid-October, when there were the glimmerings of a breakthrough on the impasse in the Paris negotiations, did the fighting begin to ease a little. Then on 31 October President Johnson announced a complete halt to the bombardment of North Vietnam in return for the resumption of the peace process with the participation of South Vietnam and the NLF. However, at the same time that it was announced that action against North Vietnam had been curtailed, the Administration stated that air-strikes along the Ho Chi Minh Trail were to be tripled and the bombing in South Vietnam itself would also be stepped up. Essentially, therefore, the war in South Vietnam continued, but against a background that was thought to improve the prospects for a peaceful settlement now that agreement had at last been reached – apparently – on the peace conference participants. The hopes raised by Johnson's announcement were immediately dashed by the South Vietnamese regime's refusal to take part in the talks, and it was not until 26 November – after Nixon's election to the Presidency – that they agreed to participate. There then followed another two months of diplomatic wrangling as Saigon stalled, so that the talks did not begin until 25 January 1969 – after Lyndon Johnson had left office.

Despite the expansion of the fighting involving U.S. troops throughout most of the year, the Administration had already begun to think in terms of strengthening the South Vietnamese Army to the point at which it could take responsibility for fighting the war – in other words, reversing the process begun in 1965 when the U.S. Army effectively took over the direction and prosecution of the conflict, leaving the ARVN to undertake the task of pacification. Unfortunately the results of the pacification programme had been less than satisfactory, due to a number of factors including corruption, brutality, the inability of the allied forces to maintain security in the villages – particularly during the night – and of course the devastation wrought by both the fighting and the bombing.

Thus, in the wake of what was basically the failure of pacification, ARVN was now also going to have to take on its former combat role. And due to the impact of the Tet Offensive on the Johnson Administration's perceptions of the conflict, and the shock administered to U.S. public opinion as the Offensive followed so closely on optimistic Administration war reports (meaning that the options and time available for dealing with the conflict were narrowing for this Administration), this whole process of equipping and training ARVN to take over from U.S. troops was given an added urgency (see Lewy,

1978: 162–4). This was well understood by McNamara's replacement, Defense Secretary Clark Clifford, who aimed to speed up the 'de-Americanization' programme and who also in August 1968 advocated a full bombing halt in order to revitalize the peace process (in opposition to Johnson), arguing his case on the basis of the implications of the time factor and its relationship to both the conflict and the prospects for peace:

> I argued that we had fulfilled our obligations to the South Vietnamese many times over. We had prevented their subjugation, prevented the enemy from taking over the cities, strengthened the South Vietnamese armed forces, and provided the South Vietnamese, to the extent we could, with the tools for self-determination. But we could neither outlast the North Vietnamese, nor bomb them into submission. *We could not hope for the creation of a viable, stable, effective, and honest South Vietnamese government in the time that the American people would allow*. Now was the last, best time for the Administration to seek a settlement in Paris. (Clifford, with Holbrooke, 1991: 568; italics added)

For its part, South Vietnam began to mobilize in earnest in 1968, beginning in February with a 10 per cent addition to troop strength – another 65,000 men to add to the current 700,000 – and culminating, via a series of incremental steps, in a general mobilization order that became law on 19 June 1968, despite opposition in the South Vietnamese National Assembly. The planned increases would bring the armed forces to a total of approximately 900,000 men (Millet, 1974, vol. 3: 295), and was hardly a signal that South Vietnam's current leaders were going to allow themselves to be negotiated out of power (and thus out of existence) because of U.S. political and domestic difficulties and North Vietnamese war strategy. And the U.S. strategy too, whilst aimed at scaling down the U.S. role in the fighting, did not necessarily represent a change in objective for the whole of what was by now a very divided Administration – Johnson, Rusk, and Rostow, for instance, still pursued the aim of an independent and non-communist South Vietnam and took a hard line on negotiations, as against Clifford and the Paris negotiators Harriman and Vance (see Clifford, with Holbrooke, 1991: 568) – and U.S. prestige was still bound up with its client state.

In addition to accelerating its training plans for the South Vietnamese Army, the Administration also turned its attention to the pacification programme. In spring 1967, in a bid to make this programme more effective, a new organization had been set up, combining both civilian and military personnel and under the command of the U.S.

military: Civil Operations and Revolutionary Development Support (CORDS). Although overall authority was held by the military, the head of CORDS was a civilian (Robert Komer, from March 1967 to November 1968), ranked as an Ambassador, and was officially a Deputy to the U.S. Commander in Vietnam – thus emphasizing the importance of the programme and its civilian head. Komer's aim was to revitalize pacification by improving the South Vietnamese forces involved in the pacification effort (incompetence and corruption were common); by intensifying the programme directed at securing enemy deserters and defectors (Chieu Hoi – 'Open Arms'); and lastly by re-invigorating the effort to penetrate and attack the Vietcong infrastructure through a new programme – 'Phoenix'.

Despite Komer's energy and the greater degree of integration achieved under these arrangements, judged as a whole this new drive to win 'hearts and minds' and provide more security in the countryside failed: the Tet Offensive alone constituted an immense psychological and physical blow to the entire programme. And whilst the Phoenix programme – which actually aimed at more than just killing suspected Vietcong cadres, but which came to be labelled as simply an assassination programme, thus causing an uproar when it came to light – was in fact more successful in damaging the enemy's infrastructure than was realized at the time (although the programme was particularly open to abuse, which was not helped by the imposition of a quota system), still the fundamental problems remained: a corrupt and incompetent central government unable and unwilling to win popular support and loyalty, and propped up by a foreign army; the same qualities duplicated in the network of officials in the countryside; and a method of waging war that devastated the very people it claimed to be protecting (see Lewy, 1978: 124–5, 279–84; also Kolko, 1986: 237–44, 397–8). And it was against this background that the South Vietnamese forces were now expected to assume greater responsibility for the war effort on all fronts.

The procedural obstacles that bedevilled implementation of the proposed Paris talks were eventually overcome by mid-January, with the first substantive session taking place on 25 January. However, the progress made on the diplomatic front (at least temporarily) was not accompanied by any significant reduction in the prosecution of the war: military operations continued on both sides. And it was the launching of another coordinated series of attacks by the communists in February 1969 that helped to propel Nixon towards his strategy of secretly bombing communist bases in Cambodia, both in retaliation for these attacks and as a warning to the communists – but also because resuming the bombing of North Vietnam was politically impossible at that juncture. For it was becoming increasingly obvious, even before Johnson handed over to Nixon, that the Administration was in the very position of both talking and fighting that it had previously wanted to avoid – with memories of the Korean War negotiations – unless it held some advantage over the communists, and formerly that advantage had been presumed to be the bombing. Now, though, due to the fact of the Paris talks (however frustrating and whatever the lack of substantial progress) and domestic and world opinion, bombing North Vietnam was not a tool or threat that the Administration could easily use at this time to try to produce results in any sphere of the war.

So the position in the first few months of Nixon's presidency was distinctly discouraging from the viewpoint of a possible peace settlement. For though the large-scale communist attacks in February may have violated an unwritten 'understanding' said to have been reached with the Johnson Administration before the announcement of the total bombing halt (although North Vietnam denied that it had ever agreed even implicitly to any 'conditions' proposed by the U.S. – one of which was that there should be no more concerted attacks on Saigon or South Vietnamese cities – and insisted that the bombing halt on 31 October 1968 had been 'unconditional'), nevertheless the U.S. too had continued its large-scale search-and-destroy operations along with its expanded bombing of the Ho Chi Minh Trail. There was thus every chance that the prevailing military hostilities would imperil the tenuous peace negotiations, as each side effectively sought to improve its battlefield position (particularly in the wake of the Tet Offensive), thereby also augmenting its bargaining strength.

The Paris peace talks

As noted previously, the Paris negotiations very quickly – and perhaps not unexpectedly, given the opposing objectives of the protagonists – became a diplomatic microcosm of the military and political aspirations and complexities that had led to the beginning and escalation of the war. For though each side had agreed to enter into discussions in April 1968, this was not necessarily indicative of any underlying broader basis for agreement on the solution of crucial differences blocking a settlement. But, due to the lengthy and tortuous past history of failed attempts to even agree to talk about discussions, the fact that this initial step had at last been been taken tended to endow it with the character of the beginnings of a process of negotiation. So the public impression generated, and welcomed almost universally, was that the warring parties were at last *en route* to settling the conflict, and for the Administration the eagerness with which the original announcement was greeted by the public afforded it a temporary respite from the relentless growth in criticism of its policies. But the expectations aroused by the prospect of an end to the war had the obvious potential to constrain the Administration's future actions in pursuit of its ultimate objectives: rather as previous bombing pauses had made it difficult for the Administration to resume bombing because of the public outcry, so the fact that some form of discussion had begun – a development that the Administration had always stated it desired – would tend to lock the Administration into this process, however slow and meagre the results and whatever the battlefield developments.

Six months after the initial moves, Ambassador Averell Harriman, who was leading the U.S. delegation to the Paris talks, admitted the lack of progress in an interview with Radio Luxembourg, complained about North Vietnamese escalation of the fighting, and also confirmed the main U.S. goal: 'Now we have made no progress, but I think the North Vietnamese realize better than they did before the simple objective of President Johnson – that the people of South Viet-Nam must be allowed to decide their own future, in fact, the same principle that we talked about in Yalta should apply to the people of South Viet-Nam' (Embtel 20642 [Paris] Jorden to Donnelly, 11 September 1968, p. 2 of 2, Text of Governor Harriman's interview with Radio Luxembourg on 10 September; France Memos, Volume XIV, 8/68–1/69, France Country File, National Security File, LBJ Library).

The problem with this formulation of U.S. aims was that it was incompatible with North Vietnamese and Vietcong objectives: it was, in fact, a restatement of the official U.S. justification for fighting the war. And as the 'people of South Viet-Nam' were represented by a government which had every intention of clinging to power as an independent government, this meant that for the South Vietnamese regime the end result of any 'negotiations' was already predetermined, for the regime had no desire at this time to reach a compromise settlement with its opponents (and of course the North Vietnamese would not accept a settlement that would safeguard the South Vietnamese regime indefinitely and keep the former from bidding for power in the South). Indeed, as the débâcle over Johnson's speech in October showed, the South Vietnamese Government was most reluctant even to attend the peace talks, considering the process to be a potential form of sell-out by the Administration. For as Ambrose notes, whilst the pre-election communications between Nixon's supporters and Thieu were undoubtedly intended to instil in the latter the idea of receiving a better deal on the war from a Nixon administration rather than one led by Humphrey, the Saigon regime already had other reasons to try and sink the Paris peace talks:

> In an unsigned, undated memorandum in the LBJ Library in Austin, with no salutation or other indication as to whom it was directed, Clark Clifford wrote by hand: "Reason why Saigon has not moved and does not want to move [on peace talks]. A.) Saigon does not want peace.
> 1. Make better political settlement later.
> 2. In no danger because of U.S. troops.
> 3. No compulsion to help ARVN.
> 4. Wealth in country.
> 5. Personal corruption."
> (Ambrose, 1989: 215, square brackets in Ambrose; citing papers of Clark Clifford, Box 6, Presentation on Paris Peace Talks, Nov. 11, [1], JL)

In addition, as previously mentioned, the Johnson Administration was by no means united on the value of the peace talks and the total bombing halt. There was still a tendency in some of the President's advisers to treat them more as utilitarian devices to demonstrate the Administration's good faith rather than as a necessity in order to disengage from an apparently unwinnable war: in fact there was still disagreement among these advisers as to whether the war *was* unwinnable, and whether the application of yet more military force might not just tilt the balance in America's favour, or at least buy sufficient time for the South Vietnamese to be able to fight well enough to secure their own future without the hitherto crucial determinant of U.S. military might. Johnson was in the middle of the battle between these two camps of advisers as they fought for his approval of their preferred option, but though temperamentally he still leaned more towards the hawks such as Rusk and Rostow and the Joint Chiefs of Staff who retained their doubts about a diplomatic solution, rather than Defense Secretary Clark Clifford who was solidly in favour of the peace talks – with or without Saigon's participation – and withdrawal from Vietnam, in the final days of his Presidency Johnson was naturally anxious for the diplomatic solution to succeed (see Clifford with Holbrooke, 1991: 600).

Nevertheless, Johnson's attitude to the peace talks had not always been so positive, as Clifford notes in his memoirs. In addition Johnson's chief negotatior to the Paris talks, Ambassador Averell Harriman, complained to a Nixon administration member in March 1969 that neither he 'nor Vance was allowed to do any real negotiating in Paris', a charge which he repeated a month later in the form of comments that he had 'wanted to quit Johnson's peace efforts numerous times, as he feltthey [*sic*] were a sham in large part', while also making plain his desire to continue working for peace in Vietnam (respectively, MEMO FOR THE RECORD, Daniel P. Moynihan, 6 March 1969; and Memo, Rita E. Hauser to the President, 29 April 1969; both documents in EX FO 6-1 Paris Peace (re: Vietnam) (1969–1970) Folder, EX FO 6 International Conferences (1969–1970), WHCF FO, Box 63, The Nixon Presidential Materials, NARA).

Thus various factors – Johnson's fluctuating attitude to the value of the peace talks and the bombing halts; the continuing communist and U.S. military activities, including Johnson's vigorous military reaction to communist shelling of South Vietnam's cities; and the public reluctance of the South Vietnamese regime to attend the peace talks – all combined to dissipate the early optimism about the peace talks and instead to substitute a considerable degree of confusion on what was actually happening, if anything, and of course some ridicule over the procedural arguments. Therefore by the time that Nixon assumed the Presidency, nothing of any substance had been achieved concerning a peace settlement – indeed, the 'real' talks did not begin until after his inauguration. And though agreement had been reached on which parties would attend the talks, which was in itself a subtle recognition of both the sources of the war and current political realities in South Vietnam, nevertheless this was still just a starting point.

The overall situation by the end of January 1969 was therefore obviously somewhat fluid, with nothing concrete achieved, but some officials of the previous administration certainly reckoned that *significant* peace talks would take place, with the military option having now apparently been set aside, as Clark Clifford noted to McGeorge Bundy: 'I am worn out with it now, but I am convinced that we have gone so far down the road that those who follow cannot turn back' (Clifford with Holbrooke, 1991: 605). And even though the atmosphere of diplomatic confusion and fluidity, marked by U.S. claims of the communists breaking a tacit 'understanding' and denials by the communists, meant that the future of the talks was by no means as assured as Clifford had assumed was the case – effectively giving Nixon a rather freer hand concerning the troubled peace talks – still one of the principal question marks over the Nixon Presidency concerns the lack of results at the Paris Peace Talks. For the specific charge against Nixon and his closest advisers is that, far from wishing to end the war through these negotiations, they intended to 'win' the war and ensure that South Vietnam remained an independent sovereign state – and if the Paris negotiations could not achieve this then military force would have to be employed again in one way or another.

The accusation that the Nixon administration squandered the opportunity to conclude a peace agreement through the Paris Peace Talks was taken sufficiently seriously by Nixon to warrant the dissemination of a public rebuttal, fundamentally dismissive of the entire episode but also alleging that if there had been any peace opportunity then it was the Johnson administration that had missed it (for further discussion of this, see below; Covering letter from Klein to newspaper editors with attachment, 16 August 1972, Vietnam Peace Opportunity Folder, WHSF Staff Member Ronald Zeigler, Box 16, The Nixon Presidential Materials, NARA).

Thus, far from 'locking' the Nixon Administration into the peace process the Paris Peace Talks – or rather the uncertainty and lack of progress – actually afforded Nixon the opportunity to continue the war if he so wished, with the crucial proviso that he nevertheless remained associated in public perceptions as committed to 'ending' the war (see below: 'The propaganda environment'). For the delays and contradictions could always be blamed on the communists (undoubtedly culpable on some counts, though Saigon was also at fault), and provided a U.S. negotiating team continued to toil in Paris there was the public illusion of an attempt to settle the war peacefully. Nixon and his advisers could then deal more freely with the problem of ending the war using such methods as they saw fit, to whit increased bombing, extending the war into Cambodia, and finally the parallel secret peace talks in Paris none of which could assist the progress of the official Paris Peace Talks.

The propaganda environment in 1969

If the pattern of the war was unpromising by the time of the 1968 elections, with the Tet Offensive in the very recent past, then on the surface Johnson's propaganda legacy to Nixon was even more inauspicious. For as Johnson's Administration had deepened the U.S. involvement in Vietnam; tied American prestige to a continuing commitment and a successful conclusion to the war via a military victory; escalated the war; and vastly expanded the forces and firepower needed to achieve these aims, so the gap had widened between the Administration's frequently uninformative – if not downright misleading – public statements and its actions in pursuit of its 'real' agenda. And one consequence of the repeated public exposure of these discrepancies was the inexorable growth of the 'credibility gap', with the result that Administration statements tended, at the very least, to be examined ever more rigorously by the media as the war lengthened, accompanied by an increasingly cynical attitude to the veracity of official statements. In effect there was a reversal of the media's former stance in the first two years of the war, whereby the Administration had been given the benefit of any doubt, but now it was perceived as more likely to 'lie' about its Vietnam policies on both war and peace than to give an accurate account of either.

However, the advent of the major effort to begin peace talks in Paris had gone some way to muting press criticism of the Johnson Administration, especially concerning its attitude to a peaceful settlement of the war. On this issue Johnson and his advisers were judged and portrayed, for the most part, as entirely serious about this offer, unlike past negotiation attempts which had eventually come to be viewed as either spectacles for public consumption or, if conducted more 'secretly' before they became public knowledge, still designed to placate public anxiety rather than being 'real' attempts to achieve a settlement. And, of course, one of the reasons for this former perception of Administration peace offers had been because the terms on offer effectively amounted to a North Vietnamese surrender, whereas Johnson's announcement of the March 1968 bombing halt and peace bid lacked the previous harsh rhetoric and conditions.

Thus the incipient peace process helped to engender a less unfavourable propaganda environment for Nixon than might have been expected after the first four years of the war – although the propaganda environment could not be termed precisely supportive because of the public hopes for the negotiations and thus an end to the war, which now constituted limiting factors even without the imposition of a strict time-scale. Still in these early days, the incoming Administration was able to reap the benefits of the peace process started by the Johnson Administration, particularly as the first substantive negotiations session started after Nixon assumed the Presidency. The overall effect was that Nixon was initially associated with 'peace' and an end to Vietnam conflict, as opposed to Johnson who, not surprisingly, was still primarily associated with 'war'. In addition, because this was a new Administration Nixon could also expect to benefit from the usual 'honeymoon' period granted to politicians when first elected, as observers waited to evaluate the new President and his officials and their policies. The U.S. electorate too, when polled by Gallup on the new President's handling of his job, traditionally registers a considerable proportion of 'no opinion', which serves as the equivalent of the honeymoon period (see Mueller, 1985: 201–4).

So at this stage in the Nixon administration the 'credibility gap' remained a label attached to the Johnson Administration and its particular officials and policies, rather than being transferred to *government per se*, and via that process to the incoming Administration. However, had the pre-election political machinations of Nixon's political entourage concerning the peace talks and Thieu's obduracy become public knowledge, then quite possibly the high expectations of the new Presidency might have been considerably dampened, and the 'credibility gap' might have remained an issue instead of fading into the background as it did, until Nixon's policies and actions brought it into focus again (see Mueller, 1985: 113).

Undoubtedly one of Nixon's strongest propaganda assets when he was elected was the publicly held belief in the U.S. and abroad that he intended to 'end' the war – for America at least. The headlines in Europe reflected this perception at his inauguration, with *The Times* stating 'Nixon Promises to Dedicate Himself to Peace' (Worldwide Treatment of Current Issues, 22 January 1969: 2); while *Paris-Jour* reproduced a strong official endorsement:

> "Elysee Palace circles are said to recognize that his broad appeal for peace justifies General de Gaulle's judgement of Nixon, 'He is a man of peace.' These same circles say the speech will certainly facilitate the task of the French people in their quest for a peaceful solution in the Near East, as in Viet-Nam.
>
> "The speech will have profound echoes in all nations because it is meant as

much for the strong nations as for the weak. It will restore to America a large part of the universal popularity that various conflicts and dramatic events have caused it to lose." (Ibid.: 6)

Figaro, however, was a little more cautious in its initial assessment, and after categorizing the inaugural speech as '"an invocation of universal peace rather than a traditional appeal to national unity"', the paper noted:

"He confined himself to generalities, without binding himself by any precise promise; that is to say, he limited himself to a declaration of good intentions... The new President nevertheless indicated clearly that he intends to keep for his country a role of arbiter and that the might of the U.S. remains in his eyes an indispensable element of peace . . ." (Ibid.: 5)

Most of the West German press too lauded Nixon's plainly peaceful intentions, with the added expectation that once Vietnam was resolved then the new Administration would take a greater interest in Europe than had Johnson (ibid.: 7–8).

Nixon *did* intend to bring the war to a close but, vitally, this did not necessarily mean that he was prepared to end the U.S. commitment – and thus 'end' the war and, almost certainly, the existence of South Vietnam – on just any terms. And this gulf between media and public perceptions of what ending the war meant and entailed, as against Nixon's interpretation, formed an accommodating background for Nixon to plan his policies on war and, eventually, peace. Ironically too, in view of both recent past and later events, at this time Nixon was judged to be more straightforward than Johnson in his dealings with the press. After his first press conference, *The Guardian*'s Washington correspondent offered the following assessment: '"He was more direct, less devious and discursive than his predecessor, and what is more he was more informative. Mr. Nixon surely must have gone some way towards melting the ice that has coated his relations with the press for the past several years"' (*The Guardian*, cited in Worldwide Treatment of Current Issues, 29 January 1969: 1). This perception, echoed in other press organs, was of course of considerable use in disseminating the illusion that 'peace' was being pursued in Vietnam, as opposed to war by less visible means. Unfortunately, even as the foreign press was applauding Nixon's performance and prophesying an extended honeymoon period (see Worldwide Treatment of Current

Issues, 7 February 1969: 1–2), Nixon was already issuing orders to General Wheeler 'to increase the military pressure in South Vietnam' (Memo, from The White House Staff Secretary for The President to H. Kissinger, 1 February 1969; EX FO 6-1 (re: Vietnam) Paris Peace (1969–1970); WHCF FO, EX FO 6 International Conferences (1969–1970), Box 63, The Nixon Presidential Materials, NARA).

Concerning the peace process, Nixon showed an early desire both to create room for manoeuvre and to forestall public pressure through using the media, as well as demonstrating an acute awareness of the importance of his domestic audience on the issue of peace in Vietnam. In a Memorandum to Kissinger, again on 1 February 1969, Nixon stated:

> In reading the news summaries, particularly the television coverage, the line is already developing that the negotiations in Paris are deadlocked. The next step we can anticipate is that the commentators will begin to demand that we change our position in order to make headway. I think it is important that you keep in close touch with Lodge – probably by telephone – so that (1) he does not become discouraged by this type of coverage, and (2) in his backgrounders and other press statements he can knock down the idea that we should expect any kind of progress at this early date. In fact, I think it would be helpful if he indicated that several months usually are required before parties on such basic substantive disagreements begin to make progress, but use your judgement as to how to handle it. (Memorandum, The President to Henry Kissinger, p.1, 1 February 1969; EX FO 6-1 (re: Vietnam) Paris Peace (1969–1970); WHCF FO, EX FO 6 International Conferences (1969–1970), Box 63, The Nixon Presidential Materials, NARA)

Following favourable comments on Lodge's (U.S. Ambassador Henry Cabot Lodge – Averell Harriman's successor to the Paris Peace Talks) appearance and performance on television, Nixon concluded with some propaganda instructions for his ambassador:

> You might read this to Lodge when you talk to him on the phone and indicate to him that he should find every opportunity to say something on TV which reaches the United States — forget what the Europeans, particularly the Parisians, may see or write. He should aim everything he says toward the United States indicating that the going is hard and that he does not hold out any false optimism, but that he is convinced that the negotiations will succeed, and that he is getting every possible encouragement from RN. (Memorandum, The President to Henry Kissinger, p.2, 1 February 1969; EX FO 6-1 (re: Vietnam) Paris Peace (1969–1970); WHCF FO, EX FO 6 International Conferences (1969–1970), Box 63, The Nixon Presidential Materials, NARA)

However, Nixon's policy of maintaining and publicizing an aura of official support for, and belief in, the ultimate success of the Paris negotiations was already operating alongside considerable contingency planning to expand the war into Cambodia. Even before his inauguration Nixon had requested information on the North Vietnamese forces in Cambodia and supported the U.S. military's desire to attack their bases, as Kissinger notes in his memoir of the period:

> These recommendations [from General Abrams in Saigon requesting permission on February 9, 1969 to bomb the bases in Cambodia, a request seconded by U.S. Ambassador Bunker in Saigon] fell on fertile ground. In the transition period on January 8, 1969, the President-elect had sent me a note: "In making your study of Vietnam I want a precise report on what the enemy is doing in Cambodia and what, if anything, we are doing to destroy the buildup there. I think a very definite change of policy toward Cambodia probably should be one of the first orders of business when we get in." (Kissinger, 1979: 241; square brackets added)

Thus, as Kissinger himself points out, Nixon was already predisposed to bomb Cambodia as a means of pressuring the communists, and as retaliation for communist attacks in South Vietnam which were becoming relatively costly in U.S. troop casualties. The picture was not one of unalleviated gloom for the U.S./South Vietnamese military forces, however, for they inflicted high casualties on the enemy in their own operations, as well as during enemy-initiated engagements. According to the U.S. and South Vietnamese military commands, during the period 26 January–1 February, the enemy death toll was the highest for five months, with 3190 killed compared with 3800 in September 1968; while in the same period the numbers of U.S. troops and South Vietnamese killed totalled 198 and 242 respectively (see Millet, 1974, vol. 4 – 1969: 12). Overall, from January 1961 to January 1969, U.S. combat deaths totalled 31,181, as against 438,937 communist deaths (Millet, 1974, vol. 4 – 1969: 13). The crucial difference, though, lay in the greater willingness of the North Vietnamese and Vietcong to suffer and absorb these high casualties, whereas Nixon's Administration could now ill-afford a casualty rate that would again focus attention on the continuation of the ground war.

Kissinger's justification for the bombing of Cambodia – an undoubted extension of the war, which had been previously vetoed by Johnson when the U.S. military proposed the idea in autumn 1967 and after the Tet Offensive (see Gravel, 1971, vol. 4: 210–16; and Clifford with Holbrooke, 1991: 457–8, 512–19) – was that the only alternative form of retaliation would have involved restarting the bombing of North Vietnam. And of course Kissinger, and other Nixon advisers, recognized that to start bombing the North again was politically impossible, unless the new administration wished to invite a barrage of public outrage only one month after assuming office. For as Laird apparently stressed during a meeting to discuss retaliation for communist attacks, 'the bombing halt [of November 1968] had encouraged public expectations that the war was being wound down' (Kissinger, 1979: 240). Kissinger himself states that in late January 1969 he was 'eager to give negotiations a chance', and therefore did not favour a resumption of the former bombing campaign. However, the other obvious strand to official policy, during this early period, lay in the desire to placate public opinion. At a meeting in mid-February to examine the option of bombing the communist bases in Cambodia, Kissinger, while not opposed to this course of action, nevertheless 'advised against the unprovoked bombing of the sanctuaries', and again wanted to 'give negotiations a chance . . . and seek to maintain public support for our policy' (Kissinger, 1979: 242).

Thus these war and propaganda policy requirements, of retaliation on the one hand but no more bombing of North Vietnam – just yet – and on the other hand the need for continued public support for a public policy based on negotiating an end to the war (with the added implication that the war was ending, if in a somewhat erratic and confusing manner), ensured that the bombing of Cambodia would be kept secret for as long as possible. And in both the increasing military pressure in South Vietnam and bombing Cambodia to try and destroy communist bases and signal his determination to North Vietnam's leaders, Nixon was not only reversing the thrust of the final stages of Johnson's Vietnam policy, but was also effectively reviving the previous Administration's fall-back position of wanting to negotiate from strength. And this was despite the fact that the previous four years of destruction and allied combat deaths had all demonstrated the inability of the U.S. military to achieve the necessary dominance to dictate peace on U.S. terms at an acceptable cost – if indeed the war could be won by primarily military means – a point that Johnson had eventually, grudgingly, accepted when he ordered the partial bombing halt in March 1968 and the total halt in November.

The other measure required to maintain public support for Nixon's Vietnam policy and sustain the belief that the war was beginning to end involved reducing the most visible element of the American commitment: U.S. ground troops. In terms of propaganda, one of the most difficult aspects of the war for Johnson's Administration to counter had been the picture of a constantly escalating and intensifying war with ever-greater numbers of troops being dispatched to Vietnam, accompanied by increasingly heavy casualties: these two features alone, over the previous four years, had constituted a formidable blow to the credibility of optimistic official announcements of 'progress' in the war, and militated against statements that the Administration wanted a negotiated settlement.

Covering this initial period in his memoirs (an announcement on troop withdrawals was made only six months after his inauguration), Nixon states that diplomatic considerations were foremost in the decision to withdraw some troops: 'Early in the administration we had decided that withdrawing a number of American combat troops from Vietnam would demonstrate to Hanoi that we were serious in seeking a diplomatic settlement; it might also calm domestic public opinion by graphically demonstrating that we were beginning to wind down the war' (Nixon, 1978: 392).

The subsequent statement at Nixon and Thieu's Midway meeting on 8 June 1969, about the withdrawal of 25,000 U.S. troops – or rather their 'redeployment' as Thieu preferred to term it (see Hung and Schecter, 1986: 33) – undoubtedly engendered a public impression, in Western Europe at least, that Nixon and his administration were serious about their desire to end the war, as USIA's media coverage 'graphically' demonstrated:

> Voluminous Western European and East Asian media coverage and comment on the Midway meeting of Presidents Nixon and Thieu indicate that it has generated a measure of hope for progress toward Viet-Nam peace.
>
> Even among commentators who think the 25,000-man troop withdrawal disappointingly small, there is a feeling that a significant step has been taken.
>
> West European comment includes these themes:
>
> – The troop reduction is a step towards American disengagement from the war.
> – The Midway communique offers room for maneuver and thus may open the way to a political solution.
> – President Nixon sincerely wants to end the war.
> – Initial negative Communist reactions indicate that Hanoi will not respond favorably to the U.S. move. (Worldwide Treatment of Current Issues; Special Report: Nixon–Thieu Midway Meeting; 10 June 1969: 1)

Given that the U.S. had been secretly bombing communist bases (even if with mixed results) in Cambodia since mid-March, beginning with a 'one-off' bombing raid which had since been followed by a number of other raids under the general code-name of 'Menu', the 'negative' communist response was hardly surprising – and as Nixon and Kissinger now knew, the North Vietnamese were not going to protest about this bombing because the latter's presence also violated Cambodian sovereignty and neutrality (see Kissinger, 1979: 247–54). But Nixon's dual policy of conciliating public opinion with statements about peace negotiations and even these token troop withdrawals, whilst trying to continue fighting the war if only to leave on U.S. terms, inevitably resulted in the same propaganda and war policy syndrome that had afflicted Johnson: having disseminated to the public the information that he knew they wanted to hear, Nixon was then, at some stage, required to satisy the hopes that had been raised. So, though initially pleasing the media and public, over time, far from staving off public pressure in order to give him the leeway he wanted for his war policy, this strategy provoked yet more generalized pressure.

Again the propensity obviously existed from the start for Nixon's public statements and policy actions to totally contradict one another; hence the desire for secrecy concerning the expansion and intensification of the war, to the extent that special handling procedures were instituted for the Cambodian bombing raids so that reports on them did not enter the normal communication channels (for the official reasoning on this episode, see Kissinger, 1979: 253; for the democratic implications and results, see Karnow, 1983/1991: 606–8; and Isaacson, 1992: 174–9). And despite Nixon's apparent public commitment to the peace process, even his early speeches muddied the waters, prompting observers to highlight what they thought was the main thrust of the speech – including analysis of the omissions – which frequently resulted in an optimistic slant, but not always. For there were some sceptical voices in the U.S., as I.F. Stone noted in his post-mortem on Nixon's major Vietnam address on 14 May, containing his eight points for negotiations:

> For those who wonder just what Nixon was up to in his May 14 peace proposals, the Nixon–Gorton (the Australian Prime Minister) visit offers another source of illumination. . .
>
> Those who are working themselves into euphoria by wishful exegesis of what Nixon did *not* say in his May 14 address would be wise to pause a

moment over what Nixon and Gorton did not say in their exchanges a week earlier. These, as expected, attracted little attention in this country, and did not have to take American peace sentiment into account. The Nixon farewell statement, which Gorton said was framed with his agreement and served as a final communique, spoke of their talks on "Vietnam and regional security." A continued U.S.–Australian protectorate over Southeast Asia was implied . . . But not a single word was said about the negotiations in Paris, or the hope of a turn toward peace.

Nixon, like Johnson, is playing for time. His May 14 address strongly recalls Johnson's at Johns Hopkins in April 1965. Johnson deluded many people into believing that he was moving toward peace at the very moment he was committing the first U.S. combat troops to the South. (Stone, 1970: 131–2; 'Same Old Formulas, Same Tired Rhetoric'; italics in original)

Stone also pointed to the unease in the Senate about the speech, which, despite Nixon's claims of differing from Johnson's negotiating position and method of delivery, revealed several striking similarities in both content and style:

For as Senator Gore showed in a devastating analysis on the Senate floor May 20, the speech was full of old formulas and tired rhetoric picked up almost verbatim from Johnson and Rusk. Even Nixon's titillating hints about free elections and a neutral South Vietnam were also uttered, as Gore found, in almost the same words by Rusk in 1966 . . .

The speech is so tricky it has everybody confused except Henry Kissinger. "Proponents leak stories that the President is sending subtle signals to the Reds that he'd let them share in a new Saigon government as part of a peace package," the *Wall St. Journal* said May 23. "Opponents warn this would bring about the 'disguised defeat' Nixon had vowed not to accept. White House aides insist no decision has been made." Never have there been so many hints with so little substance. (Ibid.: 132–3; italics in original)

Overall though, Nixon's speech was well received in the U.S., while in Europe USIA monitored a generally favourable reaction which appeared to negate the few doubts expressed on the issue of the 'originality' or otherwise of these proposals. In fact, of the European press it was the *Financial Times* again which was sceptical – as it had been so often during Johnson's administration – perceiving '"no particular grounds for optimism"', stating that the two sides were '"wide apart on fundamental matters"', and correctly summarizing the essentials of, and the limits to, Nixon's position thus: '"If U.S. public opinion is to give him the time he needs, he will have to go on demonstrating that the intransigence lies on the other side"' (Worldwide Treatment of Current Issues, 16 May 1969: President's Address on Viet-Nam – Second Report: 3–4). For the rest, USIA reported:

> Foreign media observers generally credit President Nixon with taking an important step toward a negotiated peace in Viet-Nam in his Wednesday night address.
>
> While pointing to wide differences which remain between the two sides in Viet-Nam, they praised him for making a sincere and realistic effort to bridge the gap.
>
> West European comment contains these emphases:
> - He set a "new tone" of candor and flexibility in U.S. statements on Viet-Nam. Opinion varied over whether new ground was broken.
> - His plan for mutual withdrawal of troops, "neither an ultimatum nor a disguised offer to surrender," opens the way to successful accommodation with Communist positions.
> - He will need the support of the American public if he is to realize his plan for Viet-Nam. (Ibid.: 1)

The optimism manifested by the European media after Nixon's speeches and the Midway summit was not shared by I.F. Stone, and in an article he wrote following Midway the view that the steps announced by Nixon constituted significant advances was contradicted by the simple expedient of quoting two important Senators, and by putting the speech in a broader context, using an address Nixon had made at the Air Force Academy four days before the Midway meeting:

> The Air Force speech [4 June 1969] is the best key to the charade on Midway Island. A President who believes that the U.S. must be the world's policeman is headed for more Vietnams, and is unlikely (as he said) to accept a "disguised defeat" in getting out of this one. The token withdrawal, which may prove to be largely support or kitchen troops, is aimed to appease and mislead opinion at home. The best guide to the realities lies in the astringent comments of the two Senators closest to the military. Russell said the withdrawal of 25,000 men "is of no great significance" and "will not substantially reduce American casualties." Stennis said he had no "high hopes" that the South Vietnamese army would soon be able to take over the war. If Nixon has his way we may keep troops in Vietnam indefinitely, as we have in Korea and Western Europe, to man "the frontiers of freedom."
>
> This is the meaning of Pax Americana, and if it leads to unrest at home, he is ready for it. "We have the power to strike back as need be," he said at Beadle

State. "The nation has suffered other attempts at insurrection." Though he proclaims an era of negotiation abroad, he is preparing for confrontation at home. (Stone, 1970: 136–7, 'Midway to a Nguyen Van Nixon Era')

Where specific pressure was concerned, of course, the U.S. anti-war movement was a particular thorn in the Administration's side – the Midway location for Nixon and Thieu's meeting had been chosen partly because of fears of disturbances if the meeting had taken place in America (see Kissinger, 1979: 272; and Hung and Schecter, 1986: 32). During Johnson's Administration the anti-war movement had grown and progressed, from a movement that was generally perceived (and of course portrayed by the Administration) at the beginning of the war as unpatriotic and 'wrong' in its attitude to the war, to one which, by the time Nixon was elected, was regarded as being more right than 'wrong' concerning the conflict. And even the violence surrounding the Democratic Convention in Chicago in August 1968, although disliked by the general public, had not stopped the movement gaining ever more broader-based sympathy for an end to the war, among both young and old alike (for an account of the U.S. anti-war movement, see Halstead, 1978: "Out Now!"; see also Caute, 1988: 9–16; for analysis of and opinion poll tables on U.S. public attitudes to Vietnam, see Mueller, 1985: 52–8 (the 'mistake' question on the war) and 275 (tables on age and support for the war)).

In addition, for all Nixon's dismissal of 'European' opinion in his instructions to Ambassador Lodge via Kissinger at the beginning of February (see above in this section), there was no desire on his part or his advisers to provoke or face the attention and embarrassment of anti-war movements in Europe, nor to create difficulties for the European governments which had supported U.S. policy in Vietnam. So to this extent the 'Europeans' did 'matter', and while not affecting the substance of U.S. policy now any more than they had done in the past, European opinion could still constitute a factor in the timing of official announcements on the war, as had occasionally happened during Johnson's administration. Kissinger highlights this point in his account of Nixon's visit to Europe in late February 1969, when, in retaliation for widespread North Vietnamese attacks in South Vietnam, Nixon 'suddenly ordered the the bombing of the Cambodian sanctuaries' while travelling to his first destination, Brussels. Despite favouring the bombing in principle, Kissinger demurred and advised against it:

I agreed with Laird's conclusions about the Cambodian bombing, if not with his reasoning [Laird wanted it delayed until "the provocation would be clearer" because of public opinion difficulties]. I thought that a failure to react to so cynical a move by Hanoi could doom our hopes for negotiations; it could only be read by Hanoi as a sign of Nixon's helplessness in the face of domestic pressures; it was likely to encourage further military challenges, as North Vietnam undertook to whipsaw Nixon as it had succeeded with Johnson. But the timing bothered me. I did not think it wise to launch a new military operation while the President was traveling in Europe, subject to possible hostile demonstrations and unable to meet with and rally his own government. I also did not relish the prospect of having Vietnam the subject of all our European briefings or of privately trying to offer explanations to allied governments not always eager to reconcile their private support of our Vietnam efforts with their public stance of dissociation. I said as much to the President. The following day, while we were in Bonn, Nixon canceled the plan. (Kissinger, 1979: 244; square brackets added)

In fact, despite Kissinger's reference to the 'public stance of dissociation' of European allied governments, those allied governments which supported the U.S. did so publicly as well as privately, that is the British and West German Governments. As for public dissociation, the British Government had taken this position only once, as against the more enduring policy of supporting U.S. goals in the war – an independent South Vietnam – coupled with efforts to try and settle the conflict peacefully. Furthermore it was this governmental backing of the U.S. that caused problems in Britain and West Germany; whereas private support but public dissociation would have saved these governments from the barrage of criticism – and sometimes more active opposition – that they faced. And where the anti-war movements were concerned there had been a steady increase in the level of violence attending demonstrations, with 1968 being a particularly troubled year. In most of the European capitals that Nixon was visiting there had been riots in March and May 1968; and though, for instance, the last demonstration in Britain in October 1968 had been remarkably peaceful – certainly by March's standards – this was no guarantee that future protests would not end in pitched battles between police and protesters; and 'Vietnam' was still a powerful symbol of oppression/destruction and a rallying cry.

The final element in the propaganda environment that Nixon inherited was the perception that the Vietnam War was a hindrance to better relations between East and West, which was still seen as a desirable goal despite the shock of the Soviet invasion of Czechoslovakia in the summer of 1968. Both the U.S. Administration and the Soviet leadership wanted an improvement in their relationship, but in addition Nixon and Kissinger also wanted an improvement in the previously hostile relationship with China. This in turn led to an important difference between the Nixon and Johnson Administrations concerning the war, for during the latter's tenure official rhetoric on the Vietnam War had often seemed to imply that the real enemy was China, rather than either the Vietcong or North Vietnam. Under Nixon this changed, with China being decoupled from responsibility for the war and its continuation, although this altered perception on Vietnam did not initially lessen Administration suspicions about China's wider purpose in international affairs; and nor did it alter China's general anti-U.S. stance and rhetoric. So, as Kissinger points out: 'The first few months were full of contradictory tendencies'; not the least of which was Nixon's attitude, ranging from 'veiled references to the new Administration's willingness to talk to China', in his Inauguration speech, to press conferences which 'poured more cold water on the prospects of a Sino-Soviet rapprochement' (see Kissinger, 1979: 168–9). Nevertheless, the basic desire was there, even if the route was still unclear (Kissinger, 1979: 171; see also Isaacson, 1992: 334–6).

By June 1969 the worsening relations between the Soviet Union and China gave the Administration the opportunity to begin the attempt at a better understanding with, and a new policy towards, China (see Kissinger, 1979: 171–82). With this prospect ahead, the Administration now had even more reason to end the war in Vietnam. However, the relationship between the Administration's most important foreign policy goals appeared to be one of conflict (as with Johnson's), for Nixon wanted to retain South Vietnam's independence as a 'sovereign' non-communist state – which would be a U.S. victory; he also wanted to end the war without the U.S. 'losing face' and thus prestige and credibility in both military and political terms – which would be difficult to achieve without 'winning' the war; and he wanted to improve relations with the Soviet Union and begin a new relationship with China – the two countries which supplied military aid and diplomatic support to the North Vietnamese.

Up to now, the increasing friction between North Vietnam's backers had not impeded the flow of aid, but could be said to have stimulated it, as China challenged the Soviet Union's communist credentials and forced the latter to compete in supporting North Vietnam's fight against the U.S. and South Vietnam. This point had been cogently argued by General de Gaulle in a conversation with Nixon during the latter's foreign policy fact-finding trip to Europe and other areas in the summer of 1967 (see Embtel 20998 (Paris) Cleveland to State Department; 'Nixon–de Gaulle Conversation, June 8, 1967'; 29 June 1967; France, Memos, Volume XI, 1/67–7/67, France Country File, NSF, Box 173, LBJ Library). And if, by early 1969, the North Vietnamese were apparently apprehensive that this situation might change, it had not done so yet (see Kissinger, 1979: 173). But with regard to the war, what Nixon and Kissinger hoped was that the lure of better relations with the U.S. – including trade, of course – alongside the political leverage that the U.S. would possess if it could maintain a relationship with both of the communist powers, in the light of their own clashes, might be of use in settling the war, providing the U.S. with the 'maneuvering room' that Kissinger refers to regarding the 1972 peace agreement (Kissinger, 1979: 194).

Attitudes towards Nixon

Although the margin by which Nixon won the Presidential election was very narrow (Nixon garnered 43.4 per cent of the popular vote against Humphrey's 43 per cent), this result did not appear to reflect an opinion on Nixon's capabilities. For in the same report in which Gallup International analysed the result, it also reported that 6 per cent of Americans thought he would be a 'great' President; 51 per cent thought he would be 'good'; and 34 per cent reckoned he would make a 'fair' President. Only 6 per cent of those polled expressed the view that he would be a 'poor' President, while the remaining 3 per cent held no opinion. So, despite Nixon's past political demeanour, expectations were high in the U.S. concerning the new incumbent in the Presidency.

European public opinion also approved of the choice of Nixon as President when their reactions were polled in May 1969. According to Gallup International Special Report Number 109, the directors of 26 Gallup-affiliated organizations (including the British, French and West German) found that 'President Richard Nixon appears to have won many new friends abroad'. Interestingly, though, the report then continued: 'The typical reaction of people in many nations to President Nixon's performance after nearly three months in office is one of pleasant surprise.' The unflattering suggestion that his performance was better than might have been expected could have been due to either Nixon's past political performance being viewed as inadequate, or to a European preference for a different Presidential candidate: for instance in Britain in May 1968 Gallup Poll recorded a 59 per cent preference for Robert Kennedy as President as opposed to only 21 per cent for Nixon; although with a changed Democratic candidate French Gallup Poll in September 1968 recorded equal percentages – 20 per cent – favouring Nixon and Humphrey, with a majority 60 per cent holding no opinion. Despite this unpromising start, however, by February 1969 French Gallup Poll recorded 61 per cent of those polled holding a 'rather favorable' opinion of Nixon concerning American foreign policy; while the Allensbach Institut für Demoskopie noted in its own poll that although in January 1969 39 per cent of the public held a 'good opinion' of Nixon (with 8 per cent holding 'no good opinion'; 43 per cent holding neither good nor bad; and 10 per cent don't knows), by April 1969 66 per cent of those polled held a 'good opinion' (those holding 'no good opinion' had halved to 4 per cent; the percentage of neither good nor bad had diminished to 25 per cent and the don't knows had also halved to 5 per cent). Thus Nixon's popularity had increased considerably between January and April.

Undoubtedly one of the most important factors in Nixon's growth in popularity in European eyes was his eight-day visit to Europe in February/March 1969 right at the beginning of his Presidency, thereby seeming to endow Europe with an importance that, to European leaders, appeared to have all but vanished during Johnson's Presidency. And the fact that in the end his visit was a huge success was all the more noteworthy given the dismal start, with a diplomatic row breaking out between Britain and France (over de Gaulle's proposal that a free-trade area be created) and communist attacks on South Vietnam's cities.

The European media covered the visit, which included a speech to the NATO Council, in great detail, and overall the assessment of Nixon was highly favourable, as West German television reported from London: '"Rarely has a politician's public image changed so fast as has Richard Nixon's, who until recently was considered a dangerous outsider and extremist. Now the British want to see him as a sober, wise and well-advised statesman"' (Worldwide Treatment of Current Issues; Foreign Media Reaction to President's European Tour, Report No. 5, 26 February 1969). Supporting West German television's thesis, the 'conservative' *Evening Standard* wrote: '"After a faultless month in office and with all the eyes of Europe upon him, one thing is clear about the President. . . He has lost the label 'unmitigated disaster' . . . He could well be the right man in the right place at the right time"' (Foreign Media Reaction to President's European Tour, Report No .5, 26 February 1969: 3). And not even the storm caused by the BBC commentator David Dimbleby's remarks about both President Nixon and Prime Minister Wilson, variously described as 'joking references', 'extremely uncharitable', or an 'acid attack', could dampen the official and media enthusiasm for Nixon. The media also admired Nixon's handling of the British–French dispute, in which he reaffirmed the 'special relationship' with the UK but also '"superbly ignored the obstacles placed in the way of Franco-American rapprochement which remains the essential purpose of his visit . . ."' ('Pro-Gaullist' *Parisien-Libéré* cited in Foreign Media Reaction to President's European Tour, Report No. 5, 26 February 1969: 5).

Thus, Nixon's European visit both added to his public exposure and probably aided his popularity, and also gave Europeans the feeling that relations with the U.S. under this President would be better than under Johnson. And as far as the Vietnam War was concerned, the good news for Nixon was that Gallup International in its May report, based on field work in April, noted that: 'Altough [*sic*] the people in other nations of the world are deeply troubled by the U.S. involvement in Vietnam, the chief worries in most nations are economic ones that are close to home – the high cost of living and unemployment' (Gallup International: Special Report; May 1969, No. 109: 90). And Europe was no exception to this trend. Henceforth, although Vietnam was still an issue and of interest to the media and public, coverage of Vietnam was not on the scale that the Johnson era had witnessed, and thus the Nixon Administration had a somewhat 'easier' time than had Johnson and his officials. Also the war was supposed to be ending according to official rhetoric.

9

The balance sheet for Nixon

Nixon's goals and propaganda themes

In his memoirs, Nixon stated that he came to office with 'three fundamental premises' concerning Vietnam:

> First, I would have to prepare public opinion for the fact that total military victory was no longer possible. Second, I would have to act on what my conscience, my experience, and my analysis told me was true about the need to keep our commitment. To abandon South Vietnam to the Communists now would cost us inestimably in our search for a stable, structured, and lasting peace. Third, I would have to end the war as quickly as was honorably possible. (Nixon, 1978: 349)

Of these three premises however, laudable though they appear, only the third accorded with the overall tenor of his election rhetoric and contemporary public expectations, whilst a closer inspection of the three reveals a considerable degree of incompatibility. Regarding the first premise, there was no need to prepare public opinion for a lack of total military victory, for the Johnson Administration had been particularly careful to give the impression that it was not aiming for total military victory, so the public had long been accustomed to official statements that U.S. aims were limited to repelling North

Vietnamese/Vietcong aggression, not destroying them – it could even be said that the military methods used were far more effective in destroying South Vietnam. And the second premise effectively cancelled out the third premise: keeping the U.S. commitment to South Vietnam inevitably meant continuing the war while the South Vietnamese Government was unable to support itself. On this latter point Nixon was quite frank about the reasons for supporting Thieu, illuminating once again the crippling weaknesses of the South Vietnamese political system and also exposing the mockery of U.S. official propaganda on the reasons for intervention:

> I was aware that many Americans considered Thieu a petty and corrupt dictator unworthy of our support. I was not personally attached to Thieu, but I looked at the situation in practical terms. As I saw it, the alternative to Thieu was not someone more enlightened or tolerant or democratic but someone weaker who would not be able to hold together the contentious factions in South Vietnam. The South Vietnamese needed a strong and stable government to carry on the fight against the efforts of the Vietcong terrorists, who were supported by the North Vietnamese Army in their efforts to impose a Communist dictatorship on the 17 million people of South Vietnam. (Ibid.: 348)

Needless to say, this damning, if accurate, view of Thieu was not publicly aired: official statements naturally stressed the loyalty of the U.S. Government to Thieu, and of course thereby undermined any incentive Thieu might have had to broaden his political and popular appeal, as had previously happened with Diem (comparison is made with Diem as being the longest serving leader before Thieu came to power). As for the stability Nixon so prized, it was bought at the expense of any effort to secure political freedom and diversity. Nixon's chosen approach to the problem, for all the vaunted publicity during his election campaign about ending the war – leaving aside the accidental fortuitousness of the 'secret plan' episode – differed little from the previous Administration's perceptions of the war and public formulations of a solution:

> Since I had ruled out a quick military victory, the only possible course was to try for a fair negotiated settlement that would preserve the independence of South Vietnam. Ideally the war could be over in a matter of months if the North Vietnamese truly wanted peace. Realistically, however, I was prepared to take most of my first year in office to arrive at a negotiated agreement. (Ibid.: 349)

Of course, by the time that Lyndon Johnson offered a partial bombing halt and attempted to start negotiations (31 March 1968), he and his advisers had also ruled out a 'quick' military victory; moreover Johnson's speech was carefully crafted to exclude prescribing the end result of negotiations, that is, South Vietnam's independence as a sovereign nation – unlike earlier peace offers (see complete text of speech in the *International Herald Tribune,* 2 April 1968: 'President Johnson's Address') – although obviously the goal of South Vietnamese self-determination did not exclude the option of independence. Nixon's goal of a 'fair negotiated settlement' preserving South Vietnam's independence was thus a retrograde negotiating step, for North Vietnam's leaders had already made it perfectly plain that their goal was a unified Vietnam – and indeed South Vietnam's leaders had also claimed this aim on occasions, though the two sides naturally differed on the nature of the dominant unifying political system and leaders.

So despite inheriting an apparent commitment to ending the war in Vietnam – and having stressed this very point in his 1968 election rhetoric – Nixon continued to fight for four more years for the same goals in Vietnam that Lyndon Johnson had originally espoused, including the all-important goal of maintaining U.S. credibility, whilst at the same time endeavouring to foster the public illusion that he *was* still committed to his electoral stance. For it was obvious by 1969 that the propaganda battle to justify U.S. troops fighting and continuing the war had been lost – Nixon's own election had been a rejection of the war policy of 'more of the same'. One of Nixon's primary propaganda goals, therefore, was to maintain this public image of an Administration seeking peace in Vietnam, and thereby retain the approval and support of his domestic and allied publics.

The peace image

This propaganda theme and public image had also been disseminated by the Johnson Administration, but with the crucial difference that the desire for 'peace' then had been used as a public justification to escalate and intensify the war and by so doing achieve 'peaceful' negotiations, because communist intransigence and desire for conquest were alleged to be the driving forces behind the origins and continuation of the war and their continual spurning of U.S. offers of negotiations. In Nixon's Administration, however, the search for 'peace' could not openly be used to justify fighting the war, for the public climate had changed too much in favour of ending the war. Thus the goal of 'peace' (however defined) had to appear to be pursued more rigorously in the early stages of Nixon's reign, utilizing means that appeared to be inherently more peaceful – or at least less aggressive – than Johnson's bombing and troop augmentation programmes.

Achieving this goal was vital for two reasons: firstly, in order for Nixon to be able to continue to prosecute the war with as little public pressure as possible, for the secret bombing of Cambodia (some press reports of the initial air raids in March and April 1969 had appeared in the U.S. press) and the subsequent ground incursion in 1970 cannot be regarded as signals of peaceful intent by any criteria. But secondly, Nixon needed the image of a quiescent domestic public for any negotiations with the North Vietnamese and Vietcong, for as he knew well the North Vietnamese leadership had in the past expected domestic discontent over a high-cost, confusing and seemingly interminable war to eventually exert pressure on the Johnson Administration, especially in a Presidential election year (see Nixon, 1978: 398–9). And the knowledge that his Administration was losing public support over its handling of the war – not that this indicated general public disapproval of the war itself – *had* put pressure on Johnson and his advisers in their post-Tet policy deliberations, forcing an assessment of the costs of continuing the war against what could be achieved, with the conclusion that the war could not be won – or possibly even continued – at an acceptable price in casualties, finance and social rifts. So, Nixon wanted to avoid having his options for dealing with the war, and peace, narrowed by such presssure. Furthermore he also believed in the same precepts for negotiations that Lyndon Johnson had once embraced – from a position of strength:

> Between the hammer of antiwar pressure and the anvil of Hanoi, it was not surprising that there were important differences in the attitudes and expectations of the various leaders of the new Administration. It was the better part of a year before we had a settled strategy for negotiations. The President was the most skeptical. He did not believe that negotiations would amount to anything until the military situation changed fundamentally. He thought Hanoi would accept a compromise only if it had no other choice. On the whole, he favored a policy of maximum pressure; he was not too eager for negotiations until some military progress had beeen made. (Kissinger, 1979: 263)

Fortunately for Nixon, the domestic and international pressure experienced by Johnson and his team had eased with the change in Administration, the Paris Peace negotiations, and the honeymoon period: the initial atmosphere was therefore one of a fairly high degree of approval for the new Administration, combined with a willingness to 'wait and see'.

From the start of his Presidency Nixon thus developed a two-track policy: one track was concerned with secret military pressure on North Vietnam (later this became overt), coupled with regular public threats (sixteen between March 1969 and January 1972) of taking 'strong and effective measures' if North Vietnam jeopardized the safety of the remaining U.S. forces (see the list compiled for Press Secretary Ron Zeigler during the North Vietnamese Spring Offensive across the Demilitarized Zone launched in March 1972: Memorandum from National Security Council, Sven Kraemer to Ron Zeigler, 4 April 1972; Paris Talks, File #3 RN 8-point peace plan II (2–18); WHSF, Staff Member Ron Zeigler, Box 24; The Nixon Presidential Materials, NARA).

The other policy track was concerned with publicly strengthening the 'peace' image of the Administration and at the same time shoring up U.S. credibility, both locally and globally as the guarantor of world 'stability'. The main strands used to boost the 'public' peace image were the policy of the announced – even if erratically implemented – withdrawal of U.S. troops linked to the policy of Vietnamization; the continuation of the Paris Peace Talks combined with other Presidential and diplomatic overtures; the reform of the draft; and the absence of any return to direct bombing of North Vietnam until May 1970.

The uses of Vietnamization

The main plank in the efforts to maintain America's global position was 'Vietnamization', a policy which was more valuable as propaganda than as a military programme, for the time and conditions needed to accomplish the task thoroughly were not available. In terms of propaganda, 'Vietnamization' worked on several levels: firstly, the U.S. could not be said to have abandoned its ally when it was engaged in strengthening and training the South Vietnamese Army to perform better than in the past, and by shifting the primary responsibility for the fighting from the U.S. to the South Vietnamese this process could be expected to help insulate U.S. credibility from the eventual outcome of the war, if it was less than favourable; secondly, coupled with U.S. troop withdrawals, it emphasized the Nixon Administration's tangible commitment to withdrawing from South Vietnam, but it also theoretically permitted control to be exercised over the rate of U.S. withdrawal according to both the pace and success of Vietnamization, and enemy offensives; thirdly, the policy was a practical embodiment of the Nixon Doctrine, now emphasizing the supporting role of the U.S. in helping other nations to help themselves; fourthly, the U.S.–South Vietnamese role reversal and the initial, measured U.S. troop withdrawals not only reassured the domestic public that the U.S. was disengaging, but also disseminated an impression of an Administration that was more in control of events than the previous Administration, which was reassuring both domestically and internationally; fifthly, for the Administration Vietnamization offered, in theory, an 'honourable' way for the U.S. to remain in South Vietnam and help 'win' the war (by keeping South Vietnam independent), while still appearing to disengage – in this way it would therefore buy time for the Americans as much as for the South Vietnamese leadership and military; and lastly, though the Administration still intended to 'win' the war, on the surface Vietnamization did not appear to undermine the Paris Peace Talks, and could thus be promoted without fear of a public backlash that official policy was jeopardizing attempts to settle the war.

The problems of peace talks

As if two levels of policy were not enough to juggle with their overlapping problems, from August 1969 the secret military pressures and public peace overtures/official negotiations/overt war policy were joined by secret negotiations between the U.S. and North Vietnam, leaving out the other parties to the conflict, and thus adding a third complicating level to U.S. policy (see Nixon, 1978: 394–7; and Kissinger, 1979: 278–82). Once these talks began between Nixon's National Security Adviser Henry Kissinger and North Vietnam's negotiators Xuan Thuy and Le Duc Tho, the combination of Nixon and Kissinger's commitment to them and preference for secrecy, coupled with the possibility over time that they might yield a settlement, rendered the official Paris Peace Talks little more than a public charade. And accordingly the Administration's attitude to them changed completely: from being publicly extolled as an opportunity to arrive at a peaceful settlement, they were dismissed as a non-opportunity.

In fact, given Nixon's desire to preserve South Vietnam's independence thereby gaining a U.S. victory, his private doubts about the negotiations (see Nixon, 1978: 341) and the communist demands, the chances of the official Talks being successful were certainly slim, but this is a different argument to that used by the Administration to discredit the Paris Talks. For just as Johnson had attempted to discredit domestic opposition to U.S. military involvement and previous peace initiatives such as Rangoon in 1964, so Nixon used the same technique, countering claims of squandering the 1968 peace initiative by denigrating those peace efforts. The problem, of course, was the lack of any visible progress in ending the war – a variant of the problem that had faced Johnson. So, as the war continued, with spreading repercussions from the U.S.–South Vietnamese incursion into Cambodia in March/April 1970, followed by another invasion in February 1971 by the ARVN – a discouraging performance by the ARVN – and despite continuing U.S. troop withdrawals, élite and general opposition in America to the Administration's Vietnam policies had gathered pace again.

In the election year of 1972, Nixon's political opponent (Democrat Sargent Shriver, Presidential candidate McGovern's running-mate) and Johnson's original envoys to the Paris Peace Talks (Averell Harriman and Cyrus Vance) joined forces and publicly questioned the reasons for the lack of results at the official Paris negotiations, alleging that Nixon '"missed" an opportunity to end the war' (see Worldwide Treatment of Current Issues, No. 98, 14 August 1972; Vietnam: U.S. Debate). To make matters worse, at this juncture the Administration was also under fire for its air-strikes in response to the latest North Vietnam offensive, with Hanoi charging that the U.S. had been deliberately targeting its dyke system; and ten days earlier the U.S. Senate had voted an amendment to force withdrawal of all U.S. troops within four months if Hanoi released its POWs.

Although Hanoi's allegations were almost certainly without substance – dykes may have been hit, but not deliberately – and the Senate amendment would not necessarily become law, these events were indicative of the pressures that were progressively narrowing Nixon's options. As for the Shriver allegations, Nixon came off relatively lightly in the foreign press which preferred to focus on the 'secret' talks – deliberately publicized by Nixon in January 1972 – noting Kissinger and Le Duc Tho's visits to Paris and speculating both on the chances of a breakthrough and, by August 1972, on the likelihood of Thieu accepting the terms (see Worldwide Treatment of Current Issues, Nos. 11–16, 1/26/72–2/4/72; and No. 101, 21 August 1972). But the U.S. media were treated to an official thirteen-page rebuttal of the Shriver, Vance and Harriman allegations that instead of pursuing peace negotiations Nixon had continued to fight the war through Vietnamization and bombing.

The dominant theme of Director of Communications Herbert Klein's rejoinder to these claims was that in 1969 there was 'no peace opportunity, real or possible, during the period in question' (Covering letter from Director of Communications for the Executive Branch, Herbert G. Klein, to newspaper editors with attachment, 16 August 1972: 5; Vietnam Peace Opportunity Folder, WHSF Staff Member Ronald Zeigler, Box 16, The Nixon Presidential Materials, NARA). However, to cast the issue in terms of whether or not it would have been possible to conclude a peace agreement based on the public Paris Peace Talks was a form of obfuscation; the crux of the matter was whether the Nixon Administration had truly tried to use the Paris Talks as a negotiating forum and what its then public stance on the Talks was. Concerning the latter, the fact is that in 1969 Nixon publicly supported the official Paris Peace Talks, and issued orders to his Ambassador to the Talks to state that he was convinced that the negotiations would succeed and that Nixon was right behind him (see Memorandum, The President to Henry Kissinger, 1 February 1969; EX FO 6-1 (re: Vietnam) Paris Peace (1969–1970); WHCF FO, EX FO 6 International Conferences (1969–1970), Box 63, The Nixon Presidential Materials, NARA). So in the light of the 1972 judgement that there was 'no peace opportunity, real or possible', Nixon's public attitude and private instructions to his ambassador appear to be manifestations of either extreme cynicism, or appalling judgement about the chances for success. More simply, Nixon's stance on the official peace talks could be perceived as part of a propaganda campaign waged to contain general public pressure and the then quiescent U.S. peace movement. For by lauding the peace talks and appearing convinced of eventual success Nixon could buy more time for his war policies – having ordered more military pressure to be exerted in the war at precisely the same time that he was ordering his peace ambassador to appear positive, followed very soon after by the first bombing raids on Cambodia. And it is Nixon's early military actions that contradict his professed desire for, and belief in, the future success of the official Paris negotiations, along with the fact that from August 1969 Kissinger's secret talks became the preferred channel for eventually ending the war, not the public Paris 'negotiations'.

For a short time Nixon's public stance on the war engendered the desired result, muting the criticism that had plagued Johnson's handling of the war and 'peace'. However, despite Nixon's emphasis on ending the war, in a May 1969 Gallup International poll 40 per cent of the U.S. public discerned no difference between Johnson's Vietnam policy and Nixon's, while 40 per cent thought he was following a 'different policy', and 20 per cent didn't know. Considering the percentage of the public reckoning that Johnson's policy was Nixon's, and given the decline in confidence in Johnson's handling of the war, this poll could be viewed as an early warning of future public discontent with Nixon's policy. Despite this public perception though, Nixon was not yet in trouble, for 44 per cent of the U.S. public still approved of his 'handling of the Vietnam situation' (with 24 per cent disapproving and 32 per cent not knowing).

European perceptions of Nixon and the war

In Europe, the often sporadic and somewhat erratic nature of polling on Vietnam and the Presidential incumbent became even more marked after Nixon assumed the Presidency. This may have been due to a belief that the war *was* ending now that Nixon was in office, and it may have owed something to the fact that the number of journalists covering the war from Vietnam dropped dramatically after the exposure of the My Lai massacre. For though the massacre took place in March 1968 it was not until November/December 1969 that it received extensive press coverage, generating world-wide revulsion. As Knightley points out, My Lai was not an isolated incident, so more atrocity stories could have been published before that particular massacre – despite the difficulties placed in the way of publicizing My Lai by media figures hostile to the expected damage to the U.S. image – which suggested that the U.S. military had come off relatively lightly with regard to widespread publication of combat atrocities by U.S. troops or even the South Vietnamese (Knightley, 1975: 390–6). But though the massacre engendered some further reminiscences of atrocities, it also had the unfortunate appearance of a type of climax to the war, resulting in a loss of interest on the part of the media which in turn led to far fewer correspondents in Vietnam and far less coverage of the war, even though the war was *not* winding down in the way that Nixon claimed. And the difficulties in publicizing the war could, of course, only be of assistance to the Administration as it continued to fight.

In addition, Nixon's standing as a political leader remained fairly high in Europe, even after the Cambodian débâcle and even though the latter itself was not a popular venture. In Britain, 43 per cent disapproved of the U.S. sending troops into Cambodia, as against 29 per cent who approved (The Gallup Poll, June–July 1970: 1099); 54 per cent of respondents disapproved in West Germany, although 38 per cent approved (Research Memorandum, U.S. Information Agency, M-15-70; 18 May 1970); while the 'adverse French reaction to Cambodia' may well have contributed to an improvement in the peace image of the U.S.S.R., and the inevitable corollary that 'the view that the U.S. today is a greater peril to peace than the USSR predominates in French public opinion', marking a change from the view held six months previously when the U.S. was rated 'slightly more favourably than the Soviet Union on the peace issue' (Research Memorandum, U.S. Information Agency, M-16-70; 10 June 1970). Despite this disapproval, three months later when Gallup assessed Nixon's standing in Britain in October 1970, 46 per cent of respondents held a 'good opinion' of Nixon, only 12 per cent had a 'bad opinion' of him, while 32 per cent had neither a good or bad opinion, and 10 per cent didn't know. In France, Gallup Poll asked respondents to name which living man they admired the most in the world and Nixon came eighth out of a list of the ten who were most frequently mentioned. Unfortunately, although Allensbach's (Institut für Demoskopie) respondents in West Germany were polled on their opinion of Nixon in both January and April 1969 and elicited an increasingly favourable response (39 per cent rising to 66 per cent who held a 'good opinion'), the question was not then put to respondents again until autumn 1973, so it is not possible to compare his popularity with events during the remainder of the war, or with public perceptions of him in Britain and France at that time. However, Allensbach's figures do show that by September 1973 Nixon's standing in West Germany had plummeted, with only 19 per cent holding a good opinion and 51 per cent a poor opinion.

The U.S. peace movement

But the general, and apparently steady, level of approval in Europe was not a mirror image of U.S. public reactions. For by autumn 1969, with little tangible progress to show either in the war, troop withdrawals, or on the peace front, Nixon's popularity was slipping in the U.S. polls, with both a steady increase in the percentage of respondents disapproving of the way he was 'handling his job as President' and a decrease in those approving. In late July 65 per cent approved of Nixon – this figure was itself a 7 per cent increase on early July, attributed by Gallup International to 'the successful Moon mission' – but by October, before the Vietnam Moratorium, this had declined to 57 per cent; while the 17 per cent disapproval of late July had grown to 24 per cent. In addition, Gallup found that a majority of the U.S. public approved (53 per cent as against 34 per cent disapproval) both of the standstill ceasefire in the war proposed by Cyrus Vance in July 1969, and subsequently in October Senator Goodell's proposed Congressional Bill stating that all U.S. troops be withdrawn by the end of 1970, the fighting turned over to the South Vietnamese, with the U.S. providing only military supplies and financial help: 57 per cent hoped Congress would pass the Bill, 31 per cent wanted it to be defeated, and 12 per cent didn't know. This poll also recorded that by now 58 per cent of Americans believed that it was a 'mistake' to have sent troops to Vietnam, but still the general public had 'at no time favoured an abrupt and total withdrawal'.

As could be expected from this lack of progress on ending the war in Vietnam, the peace movement in America was now on the march again. And both the perceived expectations of the general public about ending the war, and the more obviously expressed discontent of the various factions of the peace movement, were factors that could impact on the way in which Nixon presented and implemented his war and peace policies. However, although both the peace movement and the traditionally passive general public wanted an end to the war, they differed on methods to attain this end, and Nixon was an astute enough politician to be able to exploit this division. The chief disagreement between the passive public and even a now more broadly-based peace movement was clearly manifested in a poll taken after the Vietnam Moratorium on 15 October 1969, at which the perceived goal was the unilateral, immediate and total withdrawal of all U.S. troops from Vietnam. There were huge rallies in many U.S. cities – 250,000 in

Washington, DC, 100,000 in New York and Boston – and many of those marching were 'ordinary' Americans rather than just the committed activists, underlining the undoubted fact that the appeal of the peace movement was spreading fairly dramatically. Ironically, when discussing the forthcoming Moratorium the London *Economist*, anti-communist and also a staunch supporter of the U.S. venture in South Vietnam and of Nixon, dissected the latter's 'technique' in Vietnam, revealing the crucial gulf between rhetoric and actions and thus incidentally illuminating the Administration's duplicity and undermining its 'peace' image, as the hawkish Joseph Alsop had once done to Johnson's Johns Hopkins speech in spring 1965:

"Mr. Nixon is talking as if he had reversed the policies that took the U.S. into Viet-Nam while in fact doing things which show that he remains essentially loyal to them . . .

"The weakness is that . . . he has confined himself to an essentially passive role. He seems to have decided that the only means open to him to preserve the necessary margin of public support for the war – and therefore, perhaps, for his whole management of the Presidency – is the periodic withdrawal of another batch of American troops. He has largely left the intellectual argument about the rights and wrongs of the war to the opposition . . .

"He may not be unwise to play it this way: Quite possibly, most Americans are less concerned about the moral issues than about the number of American soldiers who get killed. But it is difficult not to come to the conclusion that at some point or another Mr. Nixon will have to make a more positive appeal to his countrymen than this." (Worldwide Treatment of Current Issues, 10 October 1969, No. 56: 3–4)

Le Monde, however, while understanding Nixon's irritation with U.S. domestic opposition to the war, still queried Nixon's dismissal beforehand of the protests, and then focused on yet another aspect of growing dissatisfaction with the Administration:

"According to Mr. Nixon, there is no 'American combat force' in Laos, and the American pilots who bomb the famous Ho Chi Minh trail every day are merely conducting 'reconnaissance missions.' On this point Mr. Nixon is reviving an old, bad habit of the previous Administration: The American press long ago revealed what those 'reconnaissance missions' consisted of . . . Fleeced by five years of camouflaged truth, many Congressmen are becoming increasingly worried by the discrepancies between reality and official statements." (Ibid.: 4)

Given that the U.S. bombing of Cambodia was still a closely held secret, *Le Monde* and Congress' concern about U.S. official veracity was based on what were far more minor infractions!

On 15 October, media coverage of the Moratorium was voluminous, stressing that time had run out for Nixon and that he was being pressured by the '"broadest anti-war coalition ever"'; that the demonstrations were peaceful, but clearly wanted more political action than just troop withdrawals; and suggesting that the consequences of a decision by Nixon either to '"stand firm" in Vietnam', or to end the war immediately – for the Moratorium was held to have vitiated the purpose of the official Paris negotiations by exposing the weak position of the Administration (the secret negotiations were still a secret at this time) – would mean respectively either the "almost complete evaporation of his power at home", or a "disastrous" defeat (see Worldwide Treatment of Current Issues, 16 October 1969; No. 59: 1–6). But it was not all gloomy news for Nixon, for by 20 October, though the special summary of reaction to the Moratorium noted a 'widespread expectation' that there would be 'new U.S. initiatives to end the Viet-Nam war', the round-up also pointed to media reports noting 'insistent evidence of much public support and sympathy for the President and his war aims', and also that there was media disagreement on whether the Moratorium was or was not a success, with the criteria being the numbers demonstrating and the degree of general hostility displayed by the rest of the U.S. public (Worldwide Treatment of Current Issues, 20 October 1969; No. 62: 1–2).

The media disagreement about the size of the demonstrations notwithstanding, the fact remained that the Moratorium was a success both from the point of view of drawing world-wide media attention to the broad nature of opposition to the war, and also keeping up the pressure on the Administration: Halstead points out that despite its public dismissal of dissent, the Administration was forced to take account of the anti-war movement, tailoring public speeches in order to defuse the movement's momentum (see Halstead, 1978: 491–2). And certainly Nixon's 3 November speech to the 'Silent Majority' was aimed not only at rallying public support and thereby generating a national image of unity rather than disunity – and perhaps discouraging the North Vietnamese, so Nixon hoped – but also at undercutting the next scheduled Vietnam Moratorium on 15 November, as noted in a White House staffer's Memorandum on the subject: '"For example, if the President should determine the war has to be escalated and it is announced November 3, unless the stage is properly set, the action will only fuel the November 15 movement. (If the President de-escalates the war on November 3, then the action can be built upon in order to head off November 15)"' (White House aide Dwight Chapin, Memorandum to chief White House staff member H.R. Haldeman, 16 October 1969; cited in Halstead, 1978: 492). The remainder of that Memorandum set out a detailed eighteen-day programme of actions – using Congressmen and Senators; the media; Cabinet and agency heads and other officials; and Justice Department and FBI spokesmen – designed to '"isolate the leaders of the "Moratorium" event and the leaders of the "Mobilization" committee"' (Halstead, 1978: 493).

Whatever the success of the Administration's anti-Moratorium measures, Nixon's speech on 3 November was undoubtedly effective in rallying the general public. For even if it is accepted that a proportion of the messages of support recorded in the White House were prompted by White House staff themselves (see Kissinger, 1979: 307), opinion poll results showed not only that the Moratoriums had provoked general public hostility but that Nixon's popularity had increased again. Thus the point in USIA's media round-up on the 15 October Moratorium proved accurate: a Gallup International poll ascertained that 'unfavourable comments' on the Moratorium 'outweighed favourable ones 3 to 1', and also that public reaction to a current suggestion by some U.S. Senators that an immediate withdrawal of all U.S. troops in Vietnam be effected was overwhelmingly rejected by 74 per cent of respondents, approved by only 21 per cent, with a mere 5 per cent not knowing. Based on these results Gallup stated that 'one important reason' for the lack of general public support for the Moratorium was this demand for 'immediate and total' troop withdrawal. Nixon's approval rating for handling the situation in Vietnam rose 6 per cent from October's figure of 58 per cent, with disapproval declining 7 per cent to 25 per cent; and his overall approval rating as President also increased by 12 per cent from October to its highest total yet of 68 per cent, with disapproval lessening by 10 per cent to 19 per cent. Gallup attributed the rise in public approval of Nixon's handling of the war to the 'unfavourable reaction to the "moratorium" and a favourable reaction' to his 'recent speech on Viet-Nam' and this 'gain on the war issue' was in turn reflected in the improvement in his overall popularity (Gallup International: USA; December 1969; No. 116: 260).

One of the reasons why Nixon was so anxious to stifle the anti-war movement at this particular stage of the war lay in an ultimatum that he had issued in July 1969 to the North Vietnamese leadership as part of 'an elaborate orchestration of diplomatic, military, and publicity pressures' designed to force Hanoi to agree by 1 November (the anniversary of Johnson's total cessation of bombing over North Vietnam) to settle the war by negotiations or face a renewed U.S. military offensive to achieve a settlement by force (Nixon, 1978: 393–402). In reply Hanoi had merely lauded the U.S. anti-war movement and its forthcoming 'fall offensive', leaving Nixon with the unpalatable option of either carrying out his threat – which would undoubtedly enrage the anti-war movement and alarm the general public if such military action was overt and so appeared to be reversing the current trend of withdrawing troops gradually – or if he did nothing, of having his bluff called, which would further underline for Hanoi the current overt restrictions on the Administration's freedom of military action in Vietnam.

Having thus manoeuvred himself into a cleft stick Nixon needed the breathing space afforded by his successful appeal to the nation, for though he reassured the general public that he was still concerned to end the war (pointing to the 60,000 troops who would be withdrawn by the end of December) and had initiated several strategies to achieve this – unlike the previous Administration which, according to Nixon, lacked plans either to deal with the war, or to end it – nevertheless he purposely refrained from detailing a timetable for withdrawal, stating that Hanoi would then lack any incentive to negotiate.

That the speech achieved its objective points to the fact that it was another triumph of rhetoric over reality: Nixon's plans consisted, as had Johnson's prior to and after the Tet Offensive, in line with de-Americanization, of 'buying time' for the South Vietnamese, and his unannounced alternative was to apply more military pressure in the hope that the communists would desist – and the latter hope was as unlikely during Nixon's Presidency as it had been during Johnson's. For the mere lack of a withdrawal schedule could not conceal the need for further troop withdrawals to fuel the general belief that the U.S. was withdrawing, and this, combined with the secret negotiations that the U.S. had initiated, could hardly have suggested to Hanoi that Nixon was working from a position of strength: there was, in fact, nothing to dissuade them from believing that, in the long run, time was still on their side. In the short term, however, Nixon had managed to create more of an impression of unity, though the primary point of agreement between President and people, according to Gallup Poll, was the rejection of a unilateral withdrawal from Vietnam, which was scarcely a mandate for continuing the war. Nevertheless, according to his memoirs, this was precisely what Nixon chose to assume from the reaction to his speech, although he also acknowledged the essentially ephemeral nature of this burst of public and Congressional support:

> I had the public support I needed to continue a policy of waging war in Vietnam and negotiating for peace in Paris until we could bring the war to an honorable and successful conclusion . . .
>
> At the same time I was under no illusions that this wave of Silent Majority support could be maintained for very long. My speech had not proposed any new initiatives; its purpose had been to gain support for the course we were already following. I knew that under the constant pounding from the media and our critics in Congress, people would soon be demanding that new actions be taken to produce progress and end the war. (Nixon, 1978: 410–11)

Nixon's speech had juxtaposed the two options which he said were available: either 'an immediate, precipitate withdrawal of all Americans from Vietnam without regard to the effects of such action', or persistence 'in our search for a just peace through a negotiated settlement if possible, or through continued implementation of our plan for Vietnamization if necessary – a plan in which we will withdraw all of our forces from Vietnam on a schedule in accordance with our program, as the South Vietnamese become strong enough to defend their own freedom' (Remarks of the President on Vietnam, Delivered to National Television and Radio Audiences from The White House; Office of The White House Press Secretary, 3 November 1969; Vietnam, Paris Talks 02-18 (2 of 2); White House Staff Member and Office Files Ronald Ziegler, Box 23; The Nixon Presidential Materials, NARA). In effect the first formulation presented a worst-case scenario, suggesting both dire consequences if the U.S. pulled out and, contrasted with the second option, conveying an image of the U.S. running out on the defenceless South Vietnamese. Nixon's preferred options, on the other hand, still centred on disengagement but focused too on a 'just peace' in Vietnam, which would also benefit the rest of the world, and of course would preserve U.S. prestige and credibility. And despite the threat to take 'strong and effective measures' if Hanoi jeopardized the remaining U.S. troops, the primary emphasis was on Nixon's plan to end the war, underlined by the stated decrease in both enemy infiltration and U.S. casualties. So it was hardly surprising that the general public supported Nixon's choice, the 'right course' as he termed it, although to I.F. Stone, one of the most discerning of journalists, this speech actually signalled Nixon's determination to 'seek a political victory' and his willingness to 're-escalate if necessary to get it' (Stone, 1970: 379).

To state, as Nixon does though, that this public support, combined with an 'optimistic estimate' by the British counter-insurgency expert Sir Robert Thompson that 'within two years we would be able to achieve victory' (which he defined as an 'acceptable negotiated settlement' or successful Vietnamization), were the factors which led to him deciding to continue the war, is misleading (Nixon, 1978: 413). For Nixon's July ultimatum to Hanoi gave November as a deadline, which, if not met, would lead to stronger measures being taken: there was no suggestion in that message that the Administration would contemplate withdrawal from the war until it had achieved a peace of its own definition (ibid.: 393–4). In the event the threatened military measures were never implemented, although Kissinger and his staff undertook the planning for an operation code-named Duck Hook and 'designed for maximum impact on the enemy's military capabilities' (Kissinger, 1979: 284). However, Kissinger subsequently decided that 'no quick and "decisive" military action seemed attainable', that the Administration lacked the necessary unity 'to pursue so daring and risky a course', and advised Nixon against it, linking this deferment to an assessment of enemy infiltration (ibid.: 285). Kissinger later acknowledged in his memoirs that linking military action to infiltration actually evaded tying it to the real issue, which was 'the progress of negotiations', or more correctly, the lack of progress (ibid.: 285, footnote). Clearly re-escalation was still too sensitive an issue to contemplate at this stage, and thus Nixon's July ultimatum was revealed to the North Vietnamese as hollow rhetoric rather than the credible threat which Nixon had desired as part of his war tactics.

More importantly, Kissinger also questioned again the basis of the Administration's key policy of Vietnamization, the very policy which was supposedly building a foundation from which the Administration could withdraw its troops and also negotiate from strength; for it was South Vietnam's weakness that had not only made U.S. intervention necessary in the first place but which continued to require the presence of U.S. forces if a comprehensive defeat was to be avoided. Kissinger pointed out that viewing Vietnamization as 'viable' required 'favorable assumptions about a number of factors' and also required that 'Hanoi as well will come to accept them'. These vital factors included U.S. and North Vietnamese 'calculations' of :

> – the pace of public opposition in the US to our continuing the fight in any form. (Past experience indicates that Vietnamization will not significantly slow it down.)
> – the ability of the US Government to maintain its own discipline in carrying out this policy. [Kissinger expected 'increasing governmental disarray' as public pressure increased]
> – the actual ability of the South Vietnamese Government and armed forces to replace American withdrawals – both physically and psychologically. (Conclusive evidence is lacking here; this fact in itself, and past experience, argue against optimism.)
> – the degree to which Hanoi's current losses affect its ability to fight later – i.e., losses of military cadre, political infra-structure, etc. (Again, the evidence is not definitive. Most reports of progress have concerned security gains by US forces – not a lasting erosion of enemy political strength.)
> – the ability of the GVN to gain solid political benefit from its current pacification progress. (Again, reports of progress have been largely about security gains behind the US shield.) (Kissinger, 1979: 285–6; square brackets added)

Kissinger concluded that Vietnamization rested 'on a series of favorable assumptions which may not be accurate – though no one can be certain on the basis of current analyses' (ibid.: 286). Nevertheless, there was no alternative to Vietnamization that could be 'sold' publicly in the contemporary domestic climate – particularly if immediate withdrawal was ruled out and a decisive military blow was not achievable – so despite the wide-ranging reservations expressed by Nixon's major foreign policy adviser, Vietnamization was pressed publicly as the 'right' policy to attain an honourable end to the war and to maintain U.S. standing in the world.

The Cambodian incursion

The breathing space afforded Nixon was of a relatively short duration, for the horrors of the My Lai massacre surfaced mid-November and the second Vietnam Moratorium took place on 15 November. However, both of these events paled beside the impact, five months later, of the U.S.–South Vietnamese invasion of Cambodia in April 1970 in order to strike at North Vietnamese communist bases there, and the subsequent deaths on 4 May of four students at Kent State University following an anti-war demonstration. That the Cambodian incursion was a political and public relations disaster quickly became apparent, for not only did it revitalize the anti-war movement which had been undercut by Nixon's troop withdrawals, but it also led to Congressional unrest, with an amendment proposed to cut off funds for all U.S. military activity in Southeast Asia (later rejected by the House), followed by a proposal by Republican Senator Dole to repeal the Tonkin Gulf Resolution. Nixon dealt with Congress by pledging on 5 May that U.S. troops would not remain in Cambodia longer than three to seven weeks, and he reinforced this publicly on 3 June by announcing that U.S. troop involvement in Cambodia would end by 30 June, as would air support for allied troops, although interdiction air-strikes on the enemy would continue. As for the repeal of the Tonkin Gulf Resolution (passed in the Senate by 81 votes to 10), Nixon and his officials simply denied that it was this Resolution that permitted U.S. military action in Vietnam and Cambodia, preferring instead to rely on the President's Constitutional power to deploy U.S. troops to safeguard U.S. lives abroad – a position which bypassed Congress' Constitutional right to declare war, apparently signifying that the Vietnam War and the Cambodian venture were Executive wars that did not require the approval or consent of Congress and thus 'the people'.

Quite apart from the Constitutional dangers of this Presidential stance as it applied to Vietnam, the implications for future U.S. foreign policy and military ventures were frightening, and again could only detract from the desired image of a 'responsible and responsive' Administration – for even Johnson had endeavoured to base his intervention in Vietnam on more solid legal and Consitutional ground than Presidential fiat. Nevertheless, despite Nixon and his Administration's apparent disregard for the U.S. Constitution, the fact was that in conducting the Vietnam War and associated ventures they recognized the almost overriding need for some degree of public support and a minimum of anti-war violence, and were thereby forced to wage war within some publicly imposed limitations, even if Congress itself did appear incapable of exerting any limiting influence on the Administration at this juncture.

Although this series of pledges by Nixon contained Congressional – and general public – mutiny within acceptable bounds while the operation was continuing, the credit and support that had accrued to Nixon from his 'Silent Majority' speech, and from his most recent announcement (20 April 1970) of the withdrawal of another 150,000 troops by spring 1971, was effectively squandered in this military venture. Ultimately the Cambodian operations (the South Vietnamese Army moving into the Parrot's Beak area and a combined U.S.–South Vietnamese move deeper into the Fishhook area of Cambodia) proved difficult to defend, even militarily, because they neither solved the Cambodian military and political crisis nor improved the military position in Vietnam – instead they merely widened the field of operations – while politically they muddied the waters still further in Cambodia itself and provided a further stimulus to U.S. domestic opposition to the war (see Halstead, 1978: 536–62; and Stone, 1970: 407–8).

There were also widely publicized reports of dissent within the Administration itself, including the resignations of two of Nixon's aides, the later sacking of his Secretary of the Interior, and persistent reports of disagreements between the White House and the State Department and Pentagon Secretaries over the Cambodian operation with contradictory statements emanating from all three, adding to the picture of disarray. For the European media, on balance by the time that President Nixon delivered his judgement on 30 June that the operation had been successful they had concluded that the incursion had achieved little of significance concerning the war or the long-term prospects for peace, judging the situation to be 'confusing' after two months of fighting and bombing (Worldwide Treatment of Current Issues, Nos. 163, 184, and 9, respectively 13 May, 1 July, and 17 July 1970 – numbering as per the issues). European public opinion did not favour the intervention in Cambodia, with 43 per cent of British respondents disapproving, 29 per cent approving, and 28 per cent undecided (The Gallup Poll, June–July 1970). French reaction was noted by USIA to be adverse, while an early poll in West Germany recorded 54 per cent of respondents stating that the incursion was 'not justified', 38 per cent perceiving it as 'justified', and 8 per cent with no opinion (Research Memorandum M-15-70, 18 May 1970; USIA Historical Archives).

Furthermore, not content with these moves, Nixon also ordered bombing raids on military targets in North Vietnam, which, despite his desire for, and attainment of, secrecy over their execution, were still bound to become public knowledge when Hanoi duly denounced them. In doing this Nixon was compounding the dangers attached to the Cambodian incursions, for his original reason for the secret bombing of Cambodia in 1969 had been that bombing North Vietnam was too politically sensitive, and yet now he had reverted to the very tactic which in Johnson's Administration had obstructed any possibility of peace negotiations and had thus ensured that the war would not wind down.

In addition, the way in which Nixon had originally announced the initial incursion on 30 April, in a bombastic and belligerent television announcement, was hardly likely to add to official efforts to project an image of an Administration seeking peace and negotiations. Nor could it be perceived as helping towards ending the Vietnam War when he mentioned his disinclination to see the U.S. 'accept the first defeat in its proud 190-year history', and set this judgement within a wide-ranging framework that could be perceived as pointing towards even more U.S. intervention in foreign conflicts instead of less involvement. This framework was reinforced in a press conference statement a week later that withdrawal from Vietnam would mean the end of the U.S. peacekeeping role in the region (see Stone, 1970: 'Only the Bums Can Save the Country Now': 408). However, while many observers in the U.S. saw these moves as a widening of the war (see Karnow, 1983/1991: 625), those in Europe mainly perceived the incursions as the one-off military operations that the Administration stated they would be, and thus the wider implications of Nixon's statements tended to be lost amid speculation over the details of the operations and the anti-war violence that had been sparked off. And of course, the secret bombing of Cambodia was still a secret, so Nixon's statements that Cambodian neutrality had hitherto been respected and that there had been no previous actions against communist bases in Cambodia were taken at face value, adding credence to the Administration's arguments and concealing the true extent of the Administration's deception (see Worldwide Treatment of Current Issues, 29 April–1 July 1970; Nos. 155–184).

Again, one of the motivations for Nixon's actions in Cambodia was to demonstrate to the North Vietnamese his commitment to South Vietnam, presumably in the hope that a decisive display of U.S. will and capability might drive the North Vietnamese to the negotiating table on terms more favourable to the U.S. than previously seemed attainable (see Nixon, 1978: 445). But he also adduced another reason for launching the Cambodian operation – South Vietnamese morale: 'Giving the South Vietnamese an operation of their own would be a major boost to their morale as well as provide a practical demonstration of the success of Vietnamization. It would also be good diversionary cover for the more important and more difficult Fishhook operation' (Nixon, 1978: 449). This need for a morale-booster for the South Vietnamese suggested that U.S. official optimism about the situation in South Vietnam – both in terms of progress in the war and in Vietnamization – was not a judgement shared by the South Vietnamese themselves, and this was reinforced in a later interview with Thieu by *Le Monde* (Paris) under the encouraging headline: 'War Will Go on for Years, President Thieu Tells U.S' (Worldwide Treatment of Current Issues, No. 176, 15 June 1970: 4).

The Kent State University deaths and the subsequent abysmal handling of public relations by the President and his top officials (particularly Nixon's remarks following a Pentagon briefing about 'bums' blowing up campuses; see Nixon, 1978: 454–5) highlighted another feature of this Administration and its President – the vigorous efforts to discredit opposition to the war, a propaganda technique that had been favoured in Johnson's Administration. Nixon's Administration, however, used this technique even more extensively than had happened in the past, reflecting, in part, Nixon's belief about the importance of 'image' and the media's role in sustaining or destroying an 'image', allied to his low expectations of relations with the press – which he assumed would 'be at best an uneasy truce' – and also the Administration's aggressive response to criticism (Nixon, 1978: 354–5). And although Nixon was naturally far more concerned about domestic reaction to the course of the war and particular events, foreign media reaction was also followed by the Administration through the use of USIA's media round-ups, especially when certain actions seemed likely to create controversy such as the allied interventions in Cambodia and Laos in 1970 and 1971 respectively, thereby refocusing European media attention on Vietnam – attention which had lessened somewhat after the Nixon Administration had assumed office stating that it would be ending the war. It appears too that USIA's efforts to monitor, and on occasions to analyse, foreign media reports were more appreciated in the Nixon Administration than during Johnson's era, with the increasingly voluminous reports being directed to National Security Adviser Henry Kissinger (see for instance the series of reports 9–11 February 1971 from the Acting Director Research and Assessment, USIA to Henry Kissinger, in folder EX FO 5-3, 1/1/71–2/28/71, Publicity International, WHCF FO, EX FO 5-3, 1/1/71–2/28/71,

Box 60, The Nixon Presidential Materials, NARA).

Thus, from the beginning of Nixon's Presidency, committees were created to attack various anti-war organizations, whether composed of students or Senators, and at particular stages of the war – especially critical stages such as the Cambodia incursions – these attacks were often accompanied by the time-honoured technique of providing specific material for the media in order to disseminate the official viewpoint (see White House Memorandum from Herbert Klein for The President, Action Memorandum No. 740 on the committee to attack the student mobilization committee, 18 August 1969, (CF) ND 18/CO 165 (Vietnam) 1 Aug 1969–28 Feb 1970 (1969–1970), White House Special Files (CF) ND 18/CO 165 Wars/Vietnam, Box 42, The Nixon Presidential Materials, NARA; also in Box 42 as above see Memorandum from Al Haig to H.R. Haldeman on material provided by Dr Kissinger to various press organs concerning the President's decision on Cambodia, 18 July 1970, (CF) ND 18/CO 165 (Vietnam) 3/1/70–7/31/70 (1969–1970)).

But in addition, the Administration 'generated' letters from the public on specific issues or events, both to demonstrate support for the Administration and in order to put pressure on a particular media organ and/or journalist because their coverage was judged to be biased in some way, or simply not supportive enough according to the Administration's standards. For instance in July 1970, as part of a House fact-finding visit to South Vietnam two Congressmen (Harkins and Anderson) visited the South Vietnamese Tiger Cages of Con Son Island, established by the French but now used to imprison Vietcong and convicted criminals. Photographs of the cages taken during the visit were later published in *Life* magazine in the U.S., generating not only domestic criticism of the South Vietnamese regime but also of course in Europe (including television coverage in Britain), with a London *Times* editorial succinctly stating the problem that had always plagued the U.S. intervention in Vietnam: '"the tiger cages speak for themselves all too clearly. What sort of government is being defended at great cost in American lives?"' A BBC journalist added helpfully that 'the South Vietnamese people are "naturally tough" and capable of great cruelty', while its Washington correspondent suggested that this story constituted a threat to the Nixon Administration, and that there were worries that as a result of the treatment of the Vietcong in Con Son American POWs in North Vietnam might suffer.

However, it was not all bad news for the Administration, for the other side to the story that was publicized focused on the fact that conditions in Con Son had been revealed, thus proving that American democracy was still working: '"America's prestige was impaired by Con Son . . . but this much-berated America can muster the courage and the moral strength to reveal ills without tactical consideration, and see to it that evils are redressed"' (Worldwide Treatment of Current Issues, Nos. 6, 7 and 8, 10 July, 13 July and 15 July 1970; see also Hung and Schecter, 1986: 166–7).

Despite the positive angle to the story, the Administration was prompted to take counteraction domestically, and Nixon therefore requested that his aides 'generate some "silent majority" demands that CBS grant equal TV time to members of the House fact-finding group other than Congressmen Hawkins and Anderson', subsequently receiving an encouraging reply from Herbert Klein:

> Letters are being sent to CBS urging equal time for a report on the findings of the other ten members of the House fact-finding group.
>
> However, we believe it would be a mistake to place those members in a position where they will be asked what they know about Con Son. They did not visit it; hence, they cannot refute it.
>
> We came out of the fact finding committee story amazingly well in the first instance. The prison story has become a legitimate news story.
>
> Our approach should be not to attack this head-on, but to get our people to charge that the peaceniks seize on any excuse to try to force the President out of South Vietnam, that they have not shown similar concern for those mistreated by the North Vietnamese, or for our men who are POW's. In other words, we need to turn this into a political issue instead of a moral one.
>
> We will, of course, continue the attacks on CBS. (Covering Memorandum from Alexander P. Butterfield for The President, 18 July 1970, and Memorandum from Herbert Klein for John R. Brown III, Re: Action Memorandum P-483, 14 July 1970, (CF) ND 18/CO 165 (Vietnam) 3/1/70–7/31/70 (1969–1970), White House Special Files (CF) ND 18/CO 165 Wars/Vietnam, Box 42, The Nixon Presidential Materials, NARA)

So, even though the Administration was not itself the prime target of attack, criticism of the regime it was supporting triggered a vigorous effort to fudge the original issue and turn it to a political purpose, using the manufactured support of the 'Silent Majority' with the Administration carefully disguising the fact that it had prompted these public complaints.

In the wake of the Cambodia incursion, and during this same

fraught period, CBS' distinguished journalist Eric Sevareid became the target of an Administration campaign due to his coverage of the casualty figures and his reporting of the 'war in general'. Using the same technique, the campaign aimed at suggesting not only that Sevareid's reporting was 'unfair' to the Administration, but also that September's lower casualty figures was proof that the Cambodian operation had achieved one of its main aims. Naturally the source of the letters was camouflaged: 'Five letters with variations of wording and type have been sent to our mailing contacts to be directed to Sevareid' (Memorandum from Jeb Magruder for L. Higby, 11 September 1970, and Memorandum from the Staff Secretary John R. Brown III for J. Magruder, 8 September 1970, (CF) ND 18/CO 165 (Vietnam) 8/1/70–12/29/70 (1969–1970), White House Special Files (CF) ND 18/CO 165 (Vietnam), Box 42, The Nixon Presidential Materials, NARA). The 'Silent Majority' was thus a useful propaganda device, allowing the Administration to orchestrate apparently spontaneous general public dissatisfaction against a specific target on either a particular or a more general issue.

The end of the U.S. commitment and 'peace'

Despite the troop withdrawals and the promise of more, the Cambodian intervention firmly united Nixon to the *war* in Vietnam as against his initial identification with some sort of peace – or the end of the war – when he took office. Vietnam now became Nixon's war just as earlier it had been Johnson's war, and the same disadvantages to this association surfaced, with his handling of the war increasingly questioned and his popularity slipping. Thus, as the war continued with no prospect of peace in sight, so Nixon's options concerning how to end it on his terms progressively narrowed, for with fewer and fewer ground troops to carry on fighting there was even less chance that Kissinger could negotiate from strength. And the need for an end to the U.S. commitment was becoming ever more imperative: in order to be able to quell the growing tide of domestic opposition, which was more difficult if Nixon's commitment to peace was being questioned; in order to eliminate the international embarrassment that the war had become; and to facilitate not only relations with the Soviet Union through détente, but also the new link with China that Nixon and Kissinger envisaged.

In addition, by 1971 Nixon was looking ahead to the 1972 elections

– a very important reason to want progress of some description in the war for domestic consumption, and to try and forestall any advantage that might accrue to the North Vietnamese in an election year – bearing in mind the pressure that Johnson came under in just such circumstances (see Karnow, 1983/1991: 644). These were considerations that were taken into account when the decision was taken to intervene in Laos in February 1971.

The operation, with the aim of cutting North Vietnamese supply lines along the Ho Chi Minh Trail so as to disrupt the possibility of a major North Vietnamese offensive in 1972, was undertaken by South Vietnamese troops with U.S. air cover (U.S. ground troops having now been forbidden to operate in Cambodia or Laos by Congress). However, unlike Cambodia, which, though not as successful militarily as Nixon claimed, was not precisely a reverse (discounting the revitalized domestic anti-war movement), the Laotian incursion could be, and was, perceived as precisely that, for it focused attention on aspects of the war and South Vietnamese performance which were inimical to the U.S. Administration's effort to end the war on its terms.

In this process of media analysis Vietnamization was a prime casualty and a 'credibility gap' was reported to be opening up, due to the confusing justifications for the incursion advanced by Administration spokesmen (see Worldwide Treatment of Current Issues, Nos. 15–47, 3 February–29 March 1971; see also Kissinger, 1979: 984–1012). For the flaws in the ARVN's performance, and the subsequent disorderly withdrawal, demonstrated once more how vulnerable the South Vietnamese regime would be after the U.S. withdrew its forces and thus exposed its ally to the inevitable communist assault, and presumed take-over, that it had spent seven years endeavouring to repel and had repeatedly stated would constitute a danger to the rest of the world (not just Southeast Asia), and therefore could not be allowed to happen.

On the other hand, as Nixon knew, if the U.S. did not withdraw it would be locked into an endless war – to its detriment both domestically and internationally. And by now the ranks of the anti-war movement included numbers of Vietnam veterans, some of whom were filmed throwing away their medals on the steps of the Capitol during a march by 200,000 in Washington in April 1971 – just one rally in a weekend of anti-war riots (see Worldwide Treatment of Current Issues, Nos. 59–61, 23–28 April 1971). The presence of these veterans made the anti-war movement far harder to dismiss on the grounds of ignorance of the war and unpatriotism, justifications which had been useful propaganda stand-bys for both the Johnson and Nixon Administrations. However, despite the presence of the veterans, Nixon reverted to his earlier stance, retiring to the country for the weekend and disdaining to acknowledge the uproar in his capital. A USIA round-up of European coverage of the demonstrations noted a pertinent question posed by the 'conservative' London *Daily Mail*: '"What will happen now that Nixon's majority are [*sic*] turning sour?"' So, far from expanding Nixon's options through a decisive strike against North Vietnamese supply lines, the incursion was another step in narrowing them.

Obviously by this stage the advantages in propaganda terms that Nixon had possessed when assuming the Presidency had vanished, and he faced mounting pressures from several sources, with time becoming an increasingly important factor, not only because of the looming Presidential election but also because of the sheer length now of the war. Like Johnson before him he was trapped by his own rhetoric, for having emphasized ending the war but having instead widened it to no avail, he was now perceived to have little room for manoeuvre, and fluctuations in his popularity too were becoming dependent on public perceptions of him taking some action in the war – the rally-round-the-flag-and-President syndrome – although the subsequent failure of any action to bring the war closer to ending then resulted in a further loss of popularity. In fact the 'downward spiral' that the North Vietnamese leadership had earlier observed would trap Johnson had also trapped Nixon.

Committed to a phased withdrawal of U.S. troops to appease domestic opinion – whether or not Vietnamization was succeeding – Nixon had less leverage in either public or secret negotiations with the North Vietnamese. And his increasing need to extricate the U.S. through a negotiated settlement would not meet with the South Vietnamese regime's approval unless it guaranteed the latter's survival – as he and Kissinger were already aware. Again this was a situation that Johnson had faced in 1968 when the proposed peace conference (with 500,000 U.S. troops still in South Vietnam) had provoked a public South Vietnamese refusal to tow the line. However, Thieu's reaction then had benefited Nixon, whereas such a public disagreement now, if followed by a settlement that was disadvantageous in some way to the South Vietnamese but which facilitated the end of the U.S. commitment, would be disastrous for the maintenance of the

U.S. image as a faithful and reliable ally. And the South Vietnamese still did not appear capable of defending themselves, as *Figaro* (Paris) pointed out while summing up the cleft stick in which Nixon now found himself after Laos: '"It seems inconceivable that in the political situation in which he finds himself Mr. Nixon can afford not to continue the withdrawal of American troops. But the unfortunate operation in Laos has torn to shreds the fiction that such withdrawal would be possible without endangering Saigon"' (see Worldwide Treatment of Current Issues, No. 47, 29 March 1971: 3).

Along with the travails of Laos, 1971 was also the year in which the My Lai trial ended and Lieutenant William Calley was sentenced to life imprisonment. As usual press reaction paid tribute to the U.S. political system in holding the trial at all, observing the '"feeling of historic guilt" for most Americans', although some commentators questioned 'whether the burden of guilt should be placed on a single individual', noting that Calley was 'widely seen to be a "scapegoat" and a "sacrifice for the national conscience" (BBC-TV)'. Yet other observers focused on the relationship of the massacre to the whole war, stating that My Lai was 'an indictment of guerilla warfare as fought in Vietnam (*Le Monde* of Paris) and of modern war itself (London *Daily Mail*, *Salzburger Nachrichten*)' (see Worldwide Treatment of Current Issues, Nos. 48 and 49, respectively 31 March and 2 April 1971).

Nixon had barely ridden out the pressure caused by My Lai and the subsequent disappointment caused by his failure to announce accelerated troop withdrawals and an end to the war – expectations that were originally predicated, thought the *Daily Mail*, on the fact that Nixon was '"deeply impressed by the slump in public support for his Vietnam policy"' – when *The Pentagon Papers* was published by *The New York Times*. This history of decision-making on Vietnam during Johnson's Administration, commissioned by the then Defense Secretary Robert McNamara, gave the media another startling event to analyse and kept Vietnam in the forefront of international consciousness. For international coverage tended now to focus on sensational events and operations, as against the much greater routine coverage in the early days of the war, and even during the sensational events the period of coverage was shorter with the volume of comment lessening much more quickly. In this sense Nixon and his officials came off more lightly in international press comment than had Johnson, but part of this changed media environment was due to the expectation, prevalent from the date of Nixon's inauguration, that the war was ending, whereas Johnson had been fighting the war and endeavouring to win it. Thus Johnson had been judged both in terms of his success in achieving not only his two sets of stated objectives, progress in fighting the war itself and making 'progress' and in achieving negotiations, but also in terms of the war methods employed and their consequences. After Nixon's election however, media attention centred on how close – or otherwise – the war was to ending, meaning that less attention was paid to other aspects such as the continuing fighting, refugees, and the general performance of the South Vietnamese Government – all of which had provided a regular diet of stories during Johnson's era.

As with some other incidents during the Vietnam War, press coverage of the publication of *The Pentagon Papers* began with relatively moderate amounts of attention and then increased, as the Administration waged a legal battle – all the way to the Supreme Court – to stifle further publication of the remaining documents, and as the furore mounted in America. The case was important to the Administration for several reasons, including potential problems for Nixon's current Vietnam policy that might be caused through exposure of the Johnson Administration's economy with the truth; there was the issue of press freedom, something Nixon would have liked to curb given his dislike of the media; and there was the more general issue of a possible undermining of faith in the U.S. Government. Interestingly, the main argument that Nixon used to justify the attempt at censorship, that of the danger to U.S. national security, was brushed aside by the public, and subsequently by the Supreme Court, as irrelevant. However, the arguments over *The Pentagon Papers* concerned more than just the U.S. Administration's interests and embarrassment, as the London *Times* pointed out, in an article urging full publication on the grounds that it would do less damage than '"partial truth"':

> "The revelations about the conduct of the war in Vietnam . . . concern America's allies almost as much as they concern the American press, Congress and public opinion. Incomplete though they are, they contain enough to show that public policy statements on matters of international importance were further from the truth than could be reasonably expected, even by people hardened to the realities of international diplomacy.
>
> "A full verdict is impossible without the publication of the documents on the diplomatic aspects of the war. But even on present evidence it is reasonable to assume that debates in the British House of Commons would have taken a

different course if members had known then what they know now." (Worldwide Treatment of Current Issues, No. 84, 21 June 1971)

The British Government's concern about possible dissemination of confidential and sensitive material was made known via the British Ambassador in Washington. And though the embarrassment suffered by the publication of these particular documents would be felt only by the British Government – for *The Pentagon Papers* contained no revelations that could embarrass the Nixon Administration concerning its Vietnam policies – Kissinger had urged censorship on Nixon primarily for that reason: that foreign governments would be wary of dealing with the U.S. if their communications were leaked and became public property at some stage in the future. And if America's allies were concerned about leaks, then how much more concerned might be America's opponents, such as the People's Republic of China, relations with which were at a delicate but promising stage (see Kissinger, 1979: 729–30; and Isaacson, 1992: 328–31)? Nixon's desire to stop the leaks, and the methods chosen by his staff members Erlichman and Haldeman, were to lead eventually to Watergate, the destruction of his Administration, and the Congressional veto on assistance to South Vietnam which resulted in Nixon's complete inability to honour the secret commitment to the South Vietnamese regime that he later undertook in order to help extricate the U.S. from its involvement in the war.

Apart from signalling a legal defeat for the Nixon Administration in its battle to prevent publication of *The Pentagon Papers*, the episode had little impact on contemporary events relating to the war. The negotiations with China continued and were ultimately successful in paving the way for Nixon and Kissinger's visit to Beijing in February 1972. However, the pressure that Kissinger had hoped the Chinese leadership would exert on North Vietnam's leaders, in order to end the war, was still difficult to accomplish, even with the now antagonistic relations between China and the Soviet Union. For though the Sino-Soviet split propelled China (and accelerated the same process with the Soviet Union) towards better relations with the U.S. and thus, in theory, opened up the possibility of Chinese pressure, in practice there was still the fact that the Soviet Union was supporting North Vietnam and China had no desire to provide the Soviet Union with ideological ammunition in their rivalry.

There was also the problem of the Geneva Accords in 1954, which both China and the Soviet Union had urged on North Vietnam; for it was a settlement that had been far more favourable to the French and South Vietnam than the battlefield dispositions had warranted, but which North Vietnam's leaders had finally signed in the expectation that unifying elections – stipulated in the Accords – would be held two years later. When South Vietnam subsequently refused to hold elections and was supported by the U.S., with the International Control Commission sitting impotently on the sidelines, not surprisingly North Vietnam regarded the Geneva Accords as a sell-out. Thus any pressure from either China or the Soviet Union was unlikely to be regarded favourably by the North Vietnamese. So, even if China and the Soviet Union could be prompted into persuading North Vietnam of the benefits of a settlement, the chances of their success was related to Hanoi's perception of its own prospects for success in achieving its clear-cut objectives of unifying Vietnam and replacing the South Vietnamese regime.

Any hope that Nixon and Kissinger had at this stage that China – or the Soviet Union – could pressure the North Vietnamese into a settlement seemed to be dashed when the communists launched their nationwide Spring Offensive in March 1972, only a month after Nixon and Kissinger's visit to China. This offensive was as shocking in its way as the Tet Offensive in 1968, with the same ferocity and duration of fighting, and though the North Vietnamese were eventually repulsed, once again it had been made obvious that South Vietnam's existence as a sovereign state depended on U.S. military assistance – in this instance on massive air-strikes on both North Vietnamese positions in South Vietnam and again on North Vietnam itself, including Hanoi's environs, and the mining of Haiphong harbour. In effect the Spring Offensive reinforced the truth of Thieu's untimely statement a year earlier, during the Cambodian incursion, that the 'war would go on for years'. Certainly this offensive disproved the official U.S. claims that Vietnamization was working, and the U.S. troop withdrawals were seen to be quite obviously a unilateral measure independent of South Vietnam's general security, or ability to repel the North Vietnamese advance. And of course the offensive added to the pressures on Nixon in the Presidential election year, just as the Tet Offensive had increased the difficulties that Johnson had been experiencing.

However, the saving grace for Nixon lay in the secret negotiations between the U.S. and North Vietnam which, as noted earlier, were now no longer secret, due to his need to make them public in January 1972 in order to stave off yet more domestic criticism of official policy and the lack of a date to end U.S. involvement. By mid-summer 1972, with the Presidential election only three months away, Nixon again needed to be able to point to progress towards a peace settlement, although there were disagreements among his advisers as to whether it was preferable to settle before or after the election, with Nixon favouring a post-election settlement, thus negotiating from political, if not military, strength (see Isaacson, 1992: 441–3). And now the North Vietnamese too were prepared to negotiate, partly because of the rapprochement between the U.S. and both the Soviet Union and China – so this diplomatic gambit was finally beginning to pay dividends for the U.S., if only because North Vietnam was starting to feel of less importance to its communist allies – and again, with U.S. forces being withdrawn anyhow, time was still on North Vietnam's side in the long term.

The differences between the U.S. and North Vietnamese negotiating positions had been progressively whittled down in the secret meetings until they hinged on a basic disagreement over the fate of the Thieu regime, which North Vietnam wanted ousted before a settlement could be agreed – for by May 1971 the U.S. had dropped its demand for a withdrawal of North Vietnamese forces in return for a U.S. withdrawal (see Kissinger, 1979: 1016–31; also Isaacson, 1992: 331–2).

As events turned out, Nixon was not to be denied the pleasure of fighting the election without a peace agreement, for though Kissinger and Le Duc Tho agreed terms, they had neither been agreed or discussed with South Vietnamese President Thieu. Furthermore, the terms themselves, which included a cease-fire in place – leaving North Vietnamese troops in the South, although infiltration was to cease – were not acceptable to Thieu, because without U.S. military troops it would only be a matter of time before his regime was overrun if the North Vietnamese were not behind their own border. And the concession by North Vietnam to gain agreement – leaving Thieu's regime in place as well as the Vietcong's Provisional Revolutionary Government but with a National Council of National Reconciliation that would organize national elections and perhaps undertake other functions – was also unacceptable to Saigon.

Thieu's disagreement over the terms, and the secrecy of the process, naturally torpedoed the possiblity of a pre-election settlement, especially as the South Vietnamese leadership then put forward amendments to the agreement, which in turn led the North Vietnamese to accuse the U.S. of bad faith. The upshot was that further talks on these amendments between Kissinger and Le Duc Tho broke down, with the North Vietnamese declining to agree to the amendments, and the U.S. then unleashed over North Vietnam the Christmas bombing campaign of 1972, which occasioned a world-wide storm of protest.

The real problem for the U.S., however, was not North Vietnamese demands, but South Vietnamese intransigence, and the latter was only relieved both by the secret agreements that Nixon signed stating that the U.S. would enforce the provisions of the agreement on Saigon's behalf using military force, and ultimately by Nixon's threat to conclude a peace treaty without Saigon's concurrence if need be (see Kissinger, 1979: 1469). Following the Christmas bombing 'negotiations' resumed and a peace treaty was formally signed on 27 January 1973. U.S. involvement in the Vietnam War had finally come to an end, and would not be permitted by Congress to resume even when Saigon fell to the communists in 1975.

As for America's European allies, by the time that the peace treaty was signed British public opinion was unimpressed with U.S. handling of the situation; did not think that Nixon had achieved peace with honour; and was evenly split as to whether North Vietnam or both sides had achieved a better peace deal, but did not reckon that the U.S. and South Vietnam had achieved the better outcome (see Gallup Poll, January and February 1973). As for the fate of South Vietnam, over a third of West German public opinion in 1973 reckoned that South Vietnam would become communist after the U.S. withdrawal (Allensbach figures, February 1973). And after the fall of Saigon in 1975, a USIA research memorandum summarized European attitudes:

> Surveys taken in Great Britain, France, West Germany ... in late May and early June – some weeks after the fall of Vietnam – indicate major declines in U.S. standing.
>
> Measured in the aftermath of recent Indochina developments (including the Mayaguez incident), both trust in the credibility of U.S. defense commitments and confidence in U.S. wisdom in world affairs have declined to record lows in some of the countries surveyed . . .
>
> Asked specifically if the U.S. did or did not do all it should to meet its commitments to South Vietnam, the predominant answer in five of the six countries surveyed was in the negative. The sixth country, Australia, was no better than close to evenly divided on the issue.
>
> Also, much larger proportions in all six countries believe that U.S. influence in world affairs, in the aftermath of recent events in Vietnam, will in the long run decrease rather than increase, though many believe – the majority in Great

> Britain – that U.S. influence will remain about the same.
>
> Earlier surveys indicate that despite the widespread adverse reaction to recent Indochina developments a Communist takeover was widely anticipated, and in fact widely preferred to a protracted American participation in the Vietnam War. One is thus left to surmise that the suddenness of the South Vietnamese collapse had a large hand in producing the extent of negative response – this along with the fact that anticipated and even accepted developments can be a shock when they occur since their implications must then be faced. ('U.S. Standing in Foreign Public Opinion Following Recent Indochina Developments', 2 July 1975, USIA/IOR/R; USIA Historical Archives)

USIA's assessment was that 'these reactions to recent Indochina developments, while not immediate, are relatively short term', and that it was possible that 'adverse sentiments will diminish in the longer perspective'. The legacy of Vietnam, however, was only just beginning to take hold and the reverberations, for both the U.S. and its allies, were to continue for a very long time, as both the Johnson and Nixon Administrations had feared, and as they had helped, effectively, to ensure.

Conclusion

The United States Administration faced two sets of interlinked propaganda problems when it began its involvement in Vietnam; firstly there were problems centred on international and regional politics, and on the strategic political and military assumptions underpinning U.S. intervention, that is, the wider context in which the U.S. was fighting the war and the reasons for the war; and secondly there were problems specific to the war itself, such as interpretation of the Geneva Accords, methods of fighting and the destruction entailed, the measurement of progress and the time factor, and the issue of credibility.

Concerning the wider context, United States involvement in the Vietnam War began at the tail end of the Cold War and ended eight years later in an era that ushered in détente, and in this changing international political environment lay one of the problems that helped to vitiate the official U.S. propaganda campaign. In fact, when President Lyndon Johnson first escalated the war overtly in February 1965, on the grounds that 'free and democratic' South Vietnam could not be allowed to fall prey to Sino-Soviet international communist expansionism exercised through North Vietnam's 'aggression', the relationship between America's (and by definition the rest of the West's) two major political and ideological opponents had already been changing from friendship to distrust and rivalry for some time.

From the beginning of escalation there was thus a dichotomy between the international political environment as perceived and portrayed in U.S. official propaganda, which laid the blame for the origins of political unrest and the war in South Vietnam wholly on China and the Soviet Union (principally China in the early war years), and the actual international political environment, in which these two powers were reluctant to become involved in the conflict but were compelled to do so from reasons of rivalry, both between themselves and between them and the United States.

This U.S. official perceptual framework to the conflict, focusing on international ideology and power politics, therefore simply ignored, or on later occasions downgraded, the local political, social, and economic factors that were operating quite independently to produce political unrest and dissatisfaction in South Vietnam. Most importantly though, North Vietnam was pictured as a 'tool' of international communism, and its commitment to the goal of unification and willingess to make the huge sacrifices necessary to achieve its aim were both understated and completely underestimated. However, whereas the U.S. Administration's perceptions of the Sino-Soviet relationship did eventually come to accord with the reality (hence Nixon's visit to China in 1972), its perceptions of the relationship between North Vietnam and its communist supporters – and by definition North Vietnamese will and determination to prevail in the conflict – remained 'unrealistic' for far longer.

In terms of propaganda, these perceptions of the conflict resulted in an official portrayal of the war that was, at best, a simplistic and inaccurate reflection of 'reality', and at worst a complete distortion, and in either case was a propaganda reverse waiting to happen. For so long as the Administration was trusted by media and public as both a source of information on the war and the sole guardian of the 'wider picture', particularly in the confusion of the early days of the war, the disjuncture between official information and reality, when noticed, could be glossed over by officialdom and was excused by the media and the public. But the differences between official perceptions and reality – especially regarding the nature of the South Vietnamese regime and by extension the sources of political unrest and conflict – were too great to remain submerged, and once exposed constituted a considerable and continuing weakness in the Administration's propaganda campaign.

Not surprisingly, those propaganda problems relating specifically to the war tended to intensify and increase as the war itself escalated and lengthened. The difficulty concerning the Geneva Accords was a propaganda problem similar to the contextual problems of the war, that is, it had its origins in the U.S. official interpretation and subsequent dissemination of this one-sided viewpoint, and was virtually bound to cause trouble when the U.S. version was placed alongside the text of the Accords – which was freely available to any observer who cared to read it. However, other propaganda problems relating to the war were created as it was fought, became even more of a problem as it continued, and quite early on could only be tackled on the basis that it was communist intransigence that was prolonging the fighting and that U.S. war methods were aimed at producing a settlement. The prime examples of these problems were the bombing of North Vietnam, the level of human and material destruction caused by U.S. war methods in South Vietnam and the concomitant numbers of refugees generated because of the war. The credibility of President Johnson's Administration eventually became a propaganda disaster, and that too was created and intensified as the war dragged on, as officially trumpeted 'progress' in the conflict was time and again contradicted by both events and constant escalation, and as the Administration was shown to have lied on occasions, particularly about possible negotiating opportunities.

These then were the propaganda issues that needed to be tackled to generate and maintain allied governmental and public support for the war. Given that the U.S. official propaganda campaign under President Johnson was frequently inept and failed in its objective of maintaining allied governmental and public support – although initially support was forthcoming – the question arises as to whether his Administration devoted much attention to the issue. However, *The Pentagon Papers* show clearly that any failure of the U.S. official propaganda campaign at this stage was not due to a lack of effort or awareness on the Administration's part, for the Administration actually assigned an important place to propaganda in its war policy, was aware of the difficulties faced by those European allies which supported U.S. policy, and made considerable efforts to keep those allies 'on board'. President Johnson's Administration was initially aided in this task by the press in allied supportive nations, which performed a dual role in transmitting Administration statements to their respective publics, but also formed part of the audience for U.S. propaganda, analysing official U.S. statements and then drawing and presenting their conclusions to their publics. The press also constituted a valuable source of feedback for the Administration on other governments' and publics' reactions (including U.S. domestic reaction) to U.S. official announcements and actions during the conflict. And of course the press performed the same functions of transmitter, audience and potential critics for their own governments.

Despite the inherent weaknesses in the Johnson Administration's main propaganda justifications, when the conflict began to escalate the main sections of the press in allied nations supporting America were not unsympathetic to U.S. policy in Vietnam. In fact some newspapers such as the *Daily Telegraph* and *Daily Express* in Britain, America's staunchest supporter, were strong sympathizers and accepted the use of military might as legitimate in pursuit of the Administration's goals of a South Vietnam free of its neighbour's 'aggression', which would then result in 'peace'. Thus much of the British and West German press began by relaying the Administration's interpretation of events in South Vietnam, blaming the North Vietnamese and Vietcong for the conflict and unrest in South Vietnam, and accepting thereby the U.S. interpretation of the 1954 Geneva Agreeements. In addition the effects of this sympathy, combined with an assumption that the Administration possessed integrity and credibility, also showed in press reports that for some considerable length of time gave the Administration the benefit of any doubt on the many occasions when its public rhetoric was directly contradicted by its actions – for instance, on escalation of the war – or was contradicted by later revelations – for example, its public attitude to negotiations compared with the Rangoon revelations. Other early propaganda errors, such as, for instance, the gas warfare episode and the secrecy over the U.S. Marines' role from March to June 1965, generated much agitated press comment but sympathy for the U.S. cause still survived, despite the uncoordinated, contradictory, and at best, confused reactions that the Administration invariably displayed in response to press and public questioning and criticism. Indeed most press criticism of Administration actions or statements during this early period was offered in a spirit of sorrow or exasperation, not anger or rejection, although there were exceptions, even in Britain, such as *The Guardian*, whose editorials not only disseminated a different and more accurate interpretation of the Geneva Agreements, but also disagreed with the Administration's presentation of the war as a case of North Vietnamese aggression and invasion, stating instead that it was a civil war and likening it to the

Algerian war. These editorials therefore constituted an alternative viewpoint to set against the Administration's views of the conflict.

However, the devastation caused by U.S. methods of fighting the war was an aspect of the conflict which disturbed most of the press in allied nations – including even outright supporters of the U.S. war effort – from the beginning of escalation, a feeling that grew into horror as time passed and the war expanded, bringing with it mounting pressure for negotiations. As the pressure grew for negotiations, so did the strain on the Administration's negotiating posture: the Administration's propaganda demanded that the blame for the lack of negotiations should rest on the North Vietnamese and 'communists' – mainly China. The issue of negotiations was also particularly important for the British Government as a supporter of U.S. policy and as Co-Chairman of the 1954 Geneva Conference, for it was expected by press and public to actively seek a peaceful settlement of the conflict. As the war continued, and expanded, press opinion divided over what the British Government's primary role should be: whether its primary duty was to support the U.S in its fight against communist aggression, with the lack of negotiations blamed on the communists; or whether the Government's main duty was to strive to get the warring parties to the conference table. However, as the war continued and intensified, accompanied by reports about the occasional clash of uninvited British Government peace initiatives, or talk of them, with the Administration's policy – all this helped to erode the early faint hope, held by both the Government (principally the Prime Minister and his Foreign Secretary) and the press, that by not criticizing the Administration openly the British Government could influence and moderate U.S. policy. When this hope had been extinguished by spring 1966, coupled with ever more war devastation, these newspapers were more interested then in urging the British Government to openly voice its concern over the conflict. This, of course, rendered more difficult the British Government's task of reconciling its need to maintain good relations with the Administration by supporting U.S. policy, with its concomitant need to contain the domestic political unrest that was fuelled by Government support for U.S. involvement. And this parting of the ways between much of the British press and the Government was not to the U.S. Administration's advantage either, although it had originally helped to engender the problem with its frequently cavalier attitude to, and casual dismissal of, possible peace proposals. Her Majesty's Government could, however, console itself with the fact that the Administration's attitude to peace proposals was not confined solely to British Government peace initiatives, but encompassed proposals from divers sources. Again there was a contradiction between the stress in official U.S. propaganda on the desire for peace accompanied by the official 'open invitation' to others to help achieve this goal of 'unconditional' negotiations, and the fact that in reality any such peace initiatives were accorded a very cool reception and foundered at an early stage.

The passage of time also worked against the Johnson Administration in more direct ways, because many of its propaganda techniques and propaganda lines, such as silence, secrecy, a one-sided interpretation of the Geneva Agreements, and its insistence that it sought no wider war, were suitable only for the short term. Some of these techniques were exposed and contradicted by events, such as the admission about the changed Marine role in the summer of 1965 and the general expansion and intensification of the war, including of course the P.O.L. bombings in the summer of 1966 and the steady increase in U.S. troop deployments. Other propaganda lines were contradicted by press analysis, such as the interpretation of the 1954 Geneva Agreements (known to the French and British press), the Administration's historical analogies with Munich before the Second World War, the long line of attempted communist take-overs after that war, and the Korean War – for as the Vietnam War lengthened it inevitably generated more press comment and analysis. And as the press in European nations that supported America untangled the web of emotive analogies, with most newspapers deciding that the roots of the Vietnam conflict lay in a civil war (a position long held in France, of course), the Administration's argument that the Vietnam War was part of the communist bloc's expansionist conspiracy began to unravel. This resulted in even more attention being concentrated on the regime in South Vietnam, on which so much U.S. money was being expended and to whose aid so many troops and weapons had been dispatched. Naturally U.S. propaganda on South Vietnam then also came under closer scrutiny, and was again contradicted by events. U.S. official propaganda claims for South Vietnamese democracy and its people's freedom to choose their own way of life, free from the coercion that was practised in North Vietnam, were all nullified both by the political turmoil in South Vietnam, with a series of short-lived governments – until Thieu and Ky wrested power from the previous government – and by the repression practised by the South Vietnamese military junta. This was a problem for both the Johnson and Nixon Administrations and continued until the end of U.S. involvement.

Paradoxically, however, while the Johnson Administration's claim that the conflict was inspired by communist expansionism was disbelieved by much of the press, there was nevertheless considerable anxiety about the conflict's effect on international relations in general, because of the involvement of the U.S., and the Soviet Union and China, in backing their respective client states. The worst fears focused on the possibility of the Vietnam war igniting a third world war, but instead of producing solid support for U.S. policy in Vietnam – as both U.S. Administrations had hoped when harping on the importance of the war for the rest of the world – these fears led to increased pressure on both Administrations to begin, and then to continue, negotiations and so lower the level of tension and ward off a potential flashpoint. British fears on this score were sharpened by the occasional rumours in 1965 and 1966 that British troops might be dispatched to Vietnam, giving the British press even more reason to be concerned about the outcome of U.S. policy in Vietnam.

Concern about U.S. policy on Vietnam also focused on the manner in which the Johnson Administration executed this policy – and other policies – for as early as the end of 1965 the Administration, particularly the President, was being criticized for being too secretive in general. This charge was levied not only by critics, but also by supporters of U.S. involvement in Vietnam, who time and again complained that America's allies needed more information, and in better time, to support the Administration effectively.

The Administration's secrecy about its policy-making, long-term planning and ultimate goals in Vietnam was one of the biggest obstacles to an effective, long-term propaganda campaign, but this secrecy was a deliberate choice from the beginning and became a virtual necessity for Johnson. For the Administration neither declared war openly on North Vietnam – preferring to rely on the 1964 Tonkin Gulf Resolution as authority for its policy – nor publicly admitted the extent of its involvement and contingency planning when the war escalated in 1965. Thus, while the Administration had retained a free hand in constructing and implementing its Vietnam policy away from any possible public pressures and criticism, it had placed itself in the awkward position of having to enlist the support of its own public, and other allied governments and publics, for what it privately estimated would be a long and hard war which was already escalating, but which it had not publicly acknowledged. Even when the war had expanded far beyond the March 1965 bombing and troop levels, the Johnson Administration still tended to obscure these aspects of the war, mentioning them only occasionally in 1966. And there were other reasons for this early intention to divulge as little real information as possible, such as Johnson's desire to protect his Great Society legislation from possible pressures – an attempt which ultimately failed – and, it seems, Johnson's personal preference for secrecy. Moreover, the intention to present the Johnson Administration's policies as a continuation of past Administrations' policies reinforced the desire to minimize information on the escalation of the conflict, and thus also information about this Administration's entire war planning. This last injunction naturally covered such aspects as the gloomy evaluations of the bombing programme, and the equally gloomy estimations of the ground war which involved voracious demands for more U.S. troops, simply in order to maintain the status quo at an ever-higher level of troops and intensity of combat.

Nevertheless, even under these conditions, initially the Johnson Administration still managed to enlist the support of its own public and, publicly, of its main allies in Europe, Britain and West Germany. But there was no firm foundation for this support, for, as President Johnson had been warned in July 1965, the U.S. public supported him on Vietnam because he was the President, not because South Vietnam was of great interest or concern; and in effect the 'rally-round-the-President' syndrome was being expected to generate sufficient support to fight a major, vicious war with rapidly increasing casualties. And the British and West German Governments supported the Administration because a good relationship with the U.S. was perceived as a necessity by both governments in order to carry out their own policies – with some ideological sympathy on the part of West Germany due to its own location as the border between East and West. However, where Britain was concerned, not even the desire for good relations with the U.S. could persuade Prime Minister Wilson to dispatch British troops to Vietnam and thereby incur the wrath of his own party and public. And eventually Wilson decided that U.S. war methods were overstepping the bounds of what was permissible in an undeclared war, leading to a public dissociation. Ironically, though this gesture was not repeated, any faint hope that the British Government might be able to influence U.S. policy, or act as mediator, disappeared with this public disavowal.

Although some of Johnson's advisers wished to warn the U.S. public about the length and expected difficulties of this war, this recommendation was ignored and the U.S. public was not informed that America was entering a major land war in Asia. The U.S. public gleaned its information on the war from what the press could prise out of the Administration. So the Administration made and implemented its crucial decisions in secret, invariably suppressed as much information on these decisions as it could, and on occasions deliberately misled the press and public in its vague statements or its abrupt denials of rumoured actions. Thus, when subsequent events invariably contradicted U.S. official 'information' – particularly on negotiations and the steady escalation of the war – the Administration was open to a wide range of press and public criticism: a pitfall that the Administration had dug for itself! And despite the early media assessment that he was more open than his predecessor, Nixon too created the same trap for himself. Effectively both Administrations helped to erode their own credibility.

Just as important for the Johnson administration's propaganda effort was the fact that because its mode of handling 'information' became the recognized norm – that is, vagueness and denials followed by factual contradictions – when the Administration wished to depart from this pattern in order to emphasize publicly some current aspect of its policy or actions, the media focused upon the very fact that this was a departure from the norm, highlighting this and scrupulously dissecting the reasons for the Administration's unusual bursts of public eloquence. It was only a short step to labelling these particular Administration statements as propaganda, thereby immediately diminishing their effectiveness. Thus, on the one hand the Administration stood accused of being too secretive, and on the other hand it was accused of providing information purely for public effect in order to calm public fears or to disarm public criticism.

Finally, the Johnson Administration's propaganda campaign had an additional burden to cope with during the Vietnam War, for there was rarely a time when the war went well for the Americans, notwithstanding Administration statements to the contrary. Both the U.S. and European press were aware that the constant escalation of the war, in numbers of troops and the tonnage of bombs dropped on North and South Vietnam, was designed to stave off defeat. And as the war lengthened and this cycle continued, it became ever more apparent that the Vietcong and North Vietnam were not going to give up the struggle, despite the terrible devastation in both halves of the country. Yet it was equally plain that the Administration intended to continue the policy which entailed such destruction. When the Administration's more 'concrete' reasons for fighting the conflict, such as South Vietnamese democracy and freedom, were undermined by events, this left only the more intangible reasons for the U.S. commitment: the fear of communist expansion, that is the domino theory, and the Administration's rhetoric about the need to protect its reputation as a guarantor, effectively, of world peace. The Administration had no intention of testing the accuracy of its predictions, and thus engaged in destroying another country. The paradox was that while observers did not initially subscribe to the Administration's dire predictions of the consequences of 'losing' South Vietnam, they subsequently recognized that U.S. intervention had so raised the stakes in the battle that the Administration's statements were likely to become a self-fulfilling prophecy – hence the fears that the U.S. might be risking a general conflagration with its commitment to the war in Vietnam. And by overstating the importance of the loss of South Vietnam, both Administrations paved the way to damaging America's reputation as a 'guarantor' of peace when it finally pulled out – having also in the meantime severely shaken its allies' confidence in its political judgement by investing such resources in this particular war. In many ways, therefore, U.S. official propaganda, even before the end of Johnson's Administration, was being called upon to justify what to many observers was already inherently unjustifiable.

Bibliography

Unpublished material

Lyndon Baines Johnson Library, Austin, Texas

National Security Files, Country Files: United Kingdom; France; West Germany; Vietnam.
White House Central File, Country United Kingdom.
White House Central File, Confidential File, Country United Kingdom.
White House Central File, Meetings Notes File.
Office Files of The President; McGeorge Bundy.
National Security File; Files of Walt W. Rostow.
National Security – Defense; EX ND 19/CO 312; Box 229.

Oral History Collection

Bundy, William P. (Assistant Secretary of State for Far Eastern Affairs); Interview May–June 1969, Tapes 1–5.

National Archives and Records Administration, Washington, DC
The Nixon Presidential Materials

White House Special Files; Confidential Files, Country Vietnam.
White House Special Files; Confidential Files, ND (National Defense), Wars/Vietnam.

White House Central Files, FO (Foreign Affairs); GEN and EX FO.

White House Special Files, Central Files; Publicity.

White House Special Files; Confidential Files, Staff Member and Office Files, Ronald Ziegler (Press Secretary).

White House Special Files, Staff Member and Office Files, John Scali (Special Assistant to The President).

United States Information Agency (USIA), Historical Collection, Washington, DC

USIA Media Reaction Analysis, Office of Policy and Research Service: World Media Treatment of Major Issues, later Worldwide Treatment of Current Issues, 1966–1973.

USIA Research Surveys:

European Public Opinion on the American Role in Vietnam; 14 April 1965.

The Standing of the U.S. in West European Opinion – 1965; R-145-65; October 1965.

Worldwide, December 1965; R-176-65.

Western Europe, December 1965; R-201-65.

Reaction to Current U.S. Peace Efforts; R-6-66; 7 January 1966.

Current Comment on Vietnam Peace Moves; R-20-66; 20 January 1966.

Reactions in Eight Countries to President Nixon's Viet-Nam Policy Address; R-14-69; 8 December 1969.

West German Reaction to Cambodian Situation; M-15-70; 18 May 1970.

The U.S. Peace Image in France; M-16-70; 10 June 1970.

West European Public Opinion on Issues of Relevance to U.S. Interests; R-33-71; 28 December 1971.

U.S. Standing in Foreign Public Opinion Following Recent Indochina Developments; 2 July 1975; USIA/IOR/R.

Theses, unpublished manuscripts

Black, John Buchanan, 'The Coordination and Control of Propaganda Used as an Instrument of Foreign Policy: a Comparative Study of Present-day Governmental Practice in the United States and the United Kingdom' (Ph.D. thesis, University of London, 1969).

Page, Caroline, 'The Strategic Manipulation of American Official

Propaganda During the Vietnam War, 1965–1966, and British Opinion on the War' (Ph.D. thesis, University of Reading, 1989).

Author: interviews

McCloskey, Robert (U.S. State Department Press Spokesman), 27 April 1983.

Taylor, General Maxwell D. (U.S. Ambassador to South Vietnam, 1964–65), 1983.

Wilson, Sir Harold (British Prime Minister), 26 June 1981.

Published material

Documents, polls and newspapers

Herring, George C., ed., *The Secret Diplomacy of the Vietnam War: The Negotiating Volumes of the Pentagon Papers* (University of Texas Press, Austin, 1983).

Kearns Goodwin, Doris, *The Johnson Presidential Press Conferences*, Vols. 1 and 2 (Heyden & Son, London, 1978).

Porter, Gareth, *Vietnam: The Definitive Documentation of Human Decisions*, Vol. 2 (Heyden, London/Philadelphia/Rhine, 1979).

The Senator Gravel Edition, *The Pentagon Papers, The Department of Defense History of United States Decisionmaking on Vietnam*, Vols. 1–4 (Beacon Press, Boston, 1971).

Sheehan, Neil, Smith, Hedrick, Kenworthy, E.W. and Butterfield, Fox, *The Pentagon Papers as Published by the New York Times* (Bantam Books, New York, 1971).

South Vietnam: U.S.–Communist Confrontation in Southeast Asia, Vols. 2–7, *1966–1973* (Facts on File, Inc., New York, 1973/1974) (various editors).

State Department, Office of Media Affairs, *Aggression from the North* (Washington, DC, February 1965).

Stebbins, Richard P. and Adams, Elaine P., *Documents on American Foreign Relations 1965* (Harper & Row, London, 1966).

U.S. Department of Defense, *United States–Vietnam Relations, 1945–1967*, Books 1–12 (Washington, DC, 1971).

U.S. Government Printing Office, *Why Vietnam?* (Washington, DC, 23 August 1965).

United States Information Service (USIS), Press Releases 1965–66, U.S. Embassy, London.

Gallup, George H., *Gallup International*, Public Opinion Polls, 1966–69.

Gallup, George H., *The Gallup International Public Opinion Polls, France 1939, 1944–1975* (2 Vols.) (Random House, New York, 1976).

Gallup Poll, The, United Kingdom, 1965–73.

National Opinion Polls, United Kingdom, 1965–69.

Noelle, Elisabeth and Neumann, Erich Peter (Institut für Demoskopie Allensbach), *Jahrbuch: Der Offentlichen Meinung 1965–1967* (Verlag für Demoskopie, Allensbach und Bonn, Germany).

Noelle-Neumann, Elisabeth (Institut für Demoskopie Allensbach), *The Germans, Public Opinion Polls, 1967–1980* (Greenwood Press, USA, 1981).

British newspapers

The Times
The Guardian
Daily Telegraph
Financial Times
Daily Express
Daily Worker
Morning Star
Evening Standard
Sunday Times
Sunday Telegraph
Observer

U.S. newspapers

Christian Science Monitor (London edition)
The New York Times
New York Herald Tribune (European edition)
New York Herald Tribune/Washington Post (International edition)
International Herald Tribune

Books

Ambrose, Stephen E., *Nixon: The Triumph of a Politician 1962–1972* (Simon & Schuster, New York/London, 1989).

Balfour, Michael, *Propaganda in War 1939–1945* (Routledge & Kegan Paul, London, 1979).

Berman, Larry, *Planning a Tragedy* (W.W. Norton Company, New York/London, 1982).

Berman, Larry, *Lyndon Johnson's War* (W. W. Norton & Company, New York/London, 1989).

Bogart, Leo, *Premises for Propaganda* (The Free Press, New York, 1976).

Braestrup, Peter, *Big Story* (abridged edition) (Yale University Press, New Haven/London, 1978/1983).

Brandt, Willy, *My Life in Politics* (Penguin, London, 1992/1993).

Cameron, James, *Witness: The Complete Story of James Cameron's Journey to North Vietnam with Epilogues in China Russia America* (Victor Gollancz Ltd, London, 1965/1966).

Castle, Barbara, *The Castle Diaries, 1964–1976* (Papermac, London/ Basingstoke, 1990).

Caute, David, *Sixty-Eight: The Year of the Barricades* (Hamish Hamilton Ltd, London, 1988).

Clifford, Clark, with Holbrooke, Richard, *Counsel to the President: A Memoir* (Random House, Inc., New York, 1991).

Cooper, Chester, *The Lost Crusade: America in Vietnam* (Dodd, Mead & Co, New York, 1970).

Elder, Robert E., *The Information Machine, The United States Information Agency and American Foreign Policy* (Syracuse University Press, New York, 1968).

Ellul, Jacques, *Propaganda: The Formation of Men's Attitudes* (Vintage Books, New York, 1965/1973; Vintage Books edition February 1973).

Falk, Richard A., ed., *The Vietnam War and International Law* (Princeton University Press, Princeton, 1969).

Fall, Bernard B., *Vietnam Witness 1965–1966* (Frederick A. Praeger/Pall Mall Press, New York/London, 1966).

Foot, Paul, *The Politics of Harold Wilson* (Penguin, Harmondsworth, 1968).

Gelb, Leslie H. and Betts, Richard K., *The Irony of Vietnam: The System Worked* (The Brookings Institution, Washington, DC, 1979).

Gellhorn, Martha, *The Face of War* (Virago Press, London, 1986).

Gibson, James William, *The Perfect War: Technowar in Vietnam* (The

Atlantic Monthly Press, Boston/New York, 1986).

Grosser, Alfred, *The Western Alliance: European–American Relations Since 1945* (The Macmillan Press, London/Basingstoke, 1980).

Halstead, Fred, *Out Now! A Participant's Account of the American Movement Against the Vietnam War* (Monad, New York, 1978).

Hammond, William M., *The Military and the Media, 1962–1968* (Center of Military History, United States Army, U.S. Government Printing Office, Washington, DC, 1988).

Hetherington, Alastair, *Guardian Years* (Chatto & Windus, London, 1981).

Howard, Anthony, ed., *The Crossman Diaries, Selections from the Diaries of a Cabinet Minister, 1964–1970* (Book Club Associates, London, 1979).

Hung, Nguyen Tien and Schecter, Jerrold L., *The Palace File* (Harper & Row, New York, 1986).

Isaacson, Walter, *Kissinger: A Biography* (Faber & Faber, London, 1992).

Jervis, Robert, *Perception and Misperception in International Relations* (Princeton University Press, Princeton, 1970).

Jervis, Robert, *The Logic of Images in International Relations* (Princeton University Press, Princeton, 1976).

Johnson, Lyndon B., *The Vantage Point: Perspectives of the Presidency 1963–1969* (Weidenfeld & Nicolson, London, 1971).

Jowett, Garth S. and O'Donnell, Victoria, *Propaganda and Persuasion* (2nd edition) (Sage Publications Inc., Newbury Park, CA/London, 1992).

Kahin, George McT., *Intervention: How America Became Involved in Vietnam* (Anchor Press/Doubleday, Garden City, NY, 1987).

Kahin, George McTurnan and Lewis, John W., *The United States in Vietnam* (Delta, 1967).

Karnow, Stanley, *Vietnam: A History* (Pimlico Edition, London, 1983/1991).

Kearns Goodwin, Doris, *Lyndon Johnson and the American Dream* (St Martin's Press, New York, 1976/1991).

Kegley Jr, Charles W. and Wittkopf, Eugene R., *American Foreign Policy: Pattern and Process* (third edition) (Macmillan Education Ltd., Basingstoke/London, 1987).

Kissinger, Henry A., *The White House Years* (Weidenfeld & Nicolson, and Michael Joseph, London, 1979).

Knightley, Phillip, *The First Casualty* (Quartet Books Ltd, London, 1975).

Kolko, Gabriel, *Vietnam: Anatomy of a War 1940–1975* (Random House

Inc., New York/Allen & Unwin, London, 1986).

Lacorne, Denis, Rupnik, Jacques and Toinet, Marie-France, *The Rise and Fall of Anti-Americanism: A Century of French Perception* (The Macmillan Press Ltd, Basingstoke/London, 1990).

Lacouture, Jean, *De Gaulle, The Ruler: 1945–1970* (Harvill, imprint of HarperCollins, London, 1992).

Lewy, Guenter, *America in Vietnam* (Oxford University Press, New York, 1978).

Lorell, Mark and Kelley Jr, Charles, with the assistance of Hensler, Deborah, *Casualties, Public Opinion and Presidential Policy During the Vietnam War* (R-3060-AF, Project Air Force, Rand Corporation, Santa Monica, CA, March 1985).

McLaine, Ian, *Ministry of Moral*e (George Allen & Unwin, London, 1979).

May, Ernest, R., *'Lessons' of the Past* (Oxford University Press, London/Oxford/New York, 1973).

Millet, Stanley, ed., refer to section above: 'Published Material: Documents, Polls and Newspapers': *South Vietnam: U.S.–Communist Confrontation in Southeast Asia,* Vols. 3 and 4 (Facts on File, Inc., New York, NY, 1974).

Mueller, John E., *War, Presidents and Public Opinion* (University Press of America, Lanham, MD/London, 1985)

Nixon, Richard, *The Memoirs of Richard Nixon* (Sidgwick & Jackson, London, 1978).

Qualter, T.H., *Propaganda and Psychological Warfare* (Random House, New York, 1962).

Rosenbaum, Naomi, ed., *Readings on the International Political System* (Prentice-Hall, Englewood Cliffs, NJ, 1970).

Rowan, Carl T., *Breaking Barriers: A Memoir* (HarperCollins Publishers, New York, 1991).

Rupen, Robert A. and Farrell, Robert, *Vietnam and the Sino-Soviet Dispute* (Frederick A. Praeger, New York/London, 1967).

Rusk, Dean, *As I Saw It: A Secretary of State's Memoirs* (I.B. Tauris & Co Ltd, London/New York, 1991).

Schlesinger, Arthur M. Jr, *The Bitter Heritage* (Fawcett Crest, New York, 1966).

Short, Anthony, *The Origins of the Vietnam War* (Longman Group UK Ltd, Harlow, 1989).

Smith, Alfred G., *Communication and Culture, Readings in the Codes of Human Interaction* (Holt, Rinehart & Winston, New York, 1966).

Smith, R.B., *An International History of the Vietnam War,* Vol. 2: *The Struggle for South-East Asia 1961–1965* (Macmillan Press Ltd, Basingstoke/London, 1985).

Sorensen, Thomas C., *The Word War: The Story of American Propaganda* (Harper & Row, New York/London, 1968).

Steel, Ronald, *Walter Lippman and the American Century* (Little, Brown & Company, Boston, 1980).

Stone, I.F., *Polemics and Prophecies 1967–1970* (Little, Brown & Company, Boston/Toronto/London, 1970).

Sullivan, Marianna P., *France's Vietnam Policy: A Study in French–American Relations* (Greenwood Press, Westport, CT, 1978).

Tanham, George K., *War Without Guns: American Civilians in Rural Vietnam* (Frederick A. Praeger, New York/London, 1966).

U Thant, *View from the UN* (David & Charles, Newton Abbot, 1978).

Walzer, Michael, *Just and Unjust Wars: A Moral Argument with Historical Illustrations* (Penguin, Harmondsworth, 1980).

Williams, William Appleman, McCormick, Thomas, Gardner, Lloyd and LaFeber, Walter, *America in Vietnam: A Documentary History* (W.W. Norton, New York/London, 1989).

Wilson, Sir Harold, *The Labour Government 1964–1970: A Personal Record* (Weidenfeld & Nicolson, and Michael Joseph, London, 1971).

Index